Introduction to International Relations

Introduction to

International Relations

Theories and Approaches

Sixth Edition

Robert Jackson

Georg Sørensen

OXFORD
UNIVERSITY PRESS

OXFORD

UNIVERSITY PRESS

Great Clarendon Street, Oxford, OX2 6DP,
United Kingdom

Oxford University Press is a department of the University of Oxford.
It furthers the University's objective of excellence in research, scholarship,
and education by publishing worldwide. Oxford is a registered trade mark of
Oxford University Press in the UK and in certain other countries

Published in the United States of America by Oxford University Press
198 Madison Avenue, New York, NY 10016, United States of America

British Library Cataloguing in Publication Data

Data available

Library of Congress Control Number: 2015941387

ISBN 978–0–19–870755–4

Printed in Italy by L.E.G.O. S.p.A.

To our students

■ ACKNOWLEDGEMENTS

This sixth edition has benefitted from helpful comments made by the readers of the first five editions. We were encouraged to stay with the basic aim and format of the book: a succinct and readable introduction to the major IR theories and approaches. We also followed suggestions for a sharper focus on 'why study IR' in Chapter 1, a significant update of Chapter 7 to include more contemporary topics and theories, and an expansion of the coverage of 'key issues' in Chapter 11. All chapters are brought up to date in the light of current international events and ongoing debates in the discipline. The book now has clearer structure, with chapters organized in four parts: (1) Studying IR; (2) Classical Theories; (3) Contemporary Approaches and Debates; and (4) Policy and Issues. Questions linking theory to practice have been added at the end of each chapter. The supporting website has been revised and expanded; web links now include a section with 'links to current affairs' in order to sharpen the connection between theory and practice. A revised glossary with key terms is included at the end of the book.

We are grateful for support and encouragement from a large number of people. Tim Barton of Oxford University Press warmly supported this project from the very start. Several anonymous readers made constructive suggestions for revisions and clarifications. Many colleagues provided advice or encouragement: Will Bain, Derek Beach, Michael Corgan, Kenneth Glarbo, Hans Henrik Holm, Kal Holsti, Peter Viggo Jakobsen, Brian Job, Knud Erik Jørgensen, Anne Mette Kjær, Tonny Brems Knudsen, Mehdi Mozaffari, Liselotte Odgaard, Elias Götz, Jørgen Dige Pedersen, Nikolaj Petersen, Thomas Pedersen, Jennifer Jackson Preece, Mette Skak, Sasson Sofer, Morten Valbjørn, and Mark Zacher.

Sarah Iles was a great help as commissioning editor for this sixth edition. Annette Andersen again handled the paperwork with her usual efficiency and punctuality. Lotte Dalgaard Christensen and Maiken Gelardi Madsen proofread text, suggested references, revised tables, and helped revise the various elements at the book's Online Resource Centre with Oxford University Press (case-studies, review questions, web links, and flashcard glossary). In all this, they did a superb job of coming up with ideas, adding material, and making corrections, making very sure that everything was put in its proper place. We owe special thanks to those readers who provided us with useful comments on the fifth edition, including nine anonymous referees. We have tried to deal with their many excellent suggestions for improvement without sacrificing the aims and qualities of previous editions on which most of them commented very favourably. We are confident that both instructors and students will find that this sixth edition has managed to achieve that goal.

Finally, we are grateful once again to our wives and children for their support in our continuing endeavour to produce an IR textbook that can communicate to readers not only in North America and Europe but also everywhere that international relations is taught and studied as an academic discipline.

Aarhus and Redbourn
November 2015

▌ NEW TO THIS EDITION

- Increased coverage of contemporary issues in global politics including terrorism, war and peace, religion, and the environment.
- New end-of-chapter questions challenge you to analyse how the presented theories organise and shape global viewpoints.
- A substantially updated chapter on contemporary debates in international political economy includes material on capitalist diversity, models of development, and inequality.
- Expanded coverage of 'key issues' in Chapter 11.
- A clearer link between theory and practice in web resources and study questions.

∎ OUTLINE CONTENTS

DETAILED CONTENTS

Part 2 Classical Theories

Part 4 Policy and Issues

ABOUT THIS BOOK

Today, virtually the entire population of the world lives within the borders of those separate territorial communities we call states—about seven billion people are citizens or subjects of one state or another. For more than half a billion people living in the developed countries of Western Europe, North America, Australia, New Zealand, and Japan, basic security and welfare are often taken more or less for granted, because it is guaranteed and sometimes directly provided by the state. But for several billions of people who live in the developing countries of Asia, Africa, and the former Soviet Union, basic security and welfare is not something that can be taken for granted. Protection, policing, law enforcement, and other civil conditions of minimal safety for all cannot be guaranteed. For many people, it is a daily challenge to provide adequate food, clean water, housing, and similar socio-economic necessities. The academic subject of international relations (IR) seeks to understand how people are provided, or not provided, with the basic values of security, freedom, order, justice, and welfare.

What is in the Book?

First and foremost, this book is an introduction to the academic discipline of IR. What is a 'discipline'? It is a branch of knowledge, aimed at the systematic understanding of a subject. As is often the case in the social sciences, in IR there is no one best way to master the subject. Instead, what we have are several significant theories and theoretical traditions: Realism, Liberalism, International Society, Social Constructivism, and International Political Economy. They interact and overlap in interesting and important ways that we investigate in the chapters that follow. However, each one explores the subject of IR in its own distinctive way. Realism, for example, is focused on the basic value of security, because according to realists war is always a possibility in a system of sovereign states. Liberals, on the other hand, argue that international relations can be cooperative and not merely conflictive. That belief is based on the idea that the modern, liberal state can bring progress and opportunities to the greatest number of people around the world.

All the most important theories and theoretical traditions of IR are presented in the chapters that follow. There is no need to give a detailed account of each chapter here. But a brief consumer guide may be helpful. What is it that this book has to offer? The main elements can be summarized as follows:

- This sixth edition provides an introduction to the analytical tools that the discipline has on its shelves: IR theories and approaches. Some theories have proved to be of more enduring importance than others. In the central chapters, we focus on those theories, which we call 'established' or 'main theoretical' traditions. They are Realism, Liberalism,

International Society, and important theories of International Political Economy (IPE). There is also a chapter on a major new approach, Social Constructivism, as well as a chapter on theories involved in foreign policy analysis. Finally, we review 'post-positivist' theories that have gained prominence in recent years.

- Theories are presented faithfully, by focusing on both their strengths and their weaknesses. The main points of contention between theories are thoroughly discussed. The book makes clear how major theoretical debates link up with each other and structure the discipline of IR.

- The book places emphasis on the relationship between 'IR theory' (academic knowledge of international relations) and 'IR practice' (real-world events and activities of world politics). Theories matter for their own sake, and theories also matter as a guide to practice. The book carefully explains how particular theories organize and sharpen our view of the world. We often assume that the sword is mightier than the pen, but it is the pen, our guiding ideas, and assumptions which usually shape the ways that swords are put to use.

Learning Aids

To facilitate a rapid entry into the discipline of IR, the chapters have the following features:

- Summary: each chapter begins with a brief summary of the main points.
- Key Points: each chapter ends with a list of the key points brought forward in the chapter.
- Questions: each chapter provides a number of study questions that can be used for discussions or as topics for essays.
- Guide to Further Reading: each chapter provides a brief guide to further reading on the subject of the chapter.
- Web links: each chapter provides specific references to relevant web links. Web links mentioned in the chapter plus additional links can be found on the book's companion website at: **www.oxfordtextbooks.co.uk/orc/jackson_sorensen6e/**
- Glossary: key terms are highlighted in bold throughout the text and then presented in the Glossary at the end of the book.
- The companion website contains case-studies organized by chapters, additional study questions, and web links that include links to specific countries/regions and to essential international organizations.

Every chapter is guided by our aim to enable students to acquire knowledge of IR as an evolving academic discipline. Although we have written the book with introductory-level courses foremost in mind, it also contains much information and analysis that will prove valuable in higher-level courses, making it possible for students to advance more swiftly in their study of IR.

▌ GUIDE TO LEARNING FEATURES

This book is enriched with a range of learning tools to help you navigate the text and reinforce your knowledge of International Relations. This guided tour shows you how to get the most out of your textbook package.

▌ Summary

This chapter answers the question 'why study IR?' It begins by introducing basis of international relations, or IR. The aim of the chapter is to emphasi international relations in our everyday lives and to connect that practical r study of international relations. The chapter makes that connection by foc ical subject matter of IR: modern sovereign states and the international relat Why do states and the state system exist? Three main topics are discus international relations in everyday life and the main values that states exis evolution of the state system and world economy in brief outline; and the world of states.

Chapter Summaries

Brief summaries at the beginning of every chapter set the scene for upcoming themes and issues to be discussed, and indicate the scope of coverage within each chapter.

BOX 2.1   Leadership misperceptions and war

It is my conviction that during the descent into the abyss, the perceptions of states als were absolutely crucial. All the participants suffered from greater or lesser dis images of themselves. They tended to see themselves as honorable, virtuous, an adversary as diabolical. All the nations on the brink of the disaster expected the potential adversaries. They saw their own options as limited by necessity or 'fate', of the adversary were characterized by many choices. Everywhere, there was a empathy; no one could see the situation from another point of view. The characte leaders was badly flawed by arrogance, stupidity, carelessness, or weakness.

Stoessinger (2010: 21–3)

Boxes

Throughout the book, boxes provide you with extra information on particular topics that complement your understanding of the main chapter text.

▌ GLOSSARY

anarchical society A term used by Hedley Bull to describe the worldwide order of independent states who share common interests and values, and subject themselves to a common set of rules and institutions in dealing with each other. The concept of 'anarchical society' combines the realist claim that no world 'government' rules over sovereign states, with idealism's emphasis on the common concerns, values, rules, institutions,

and Thomas Hobbes. the means, and the us occupations of interna arena of continuous ri conflict between states goals of security and neorealism, which larg considerations in IR, c

Glossary Terms

Key terms appear in bold in the text and are defined in a glossary at the end of the book to aid you in exam revision.

Key Points

Each chapter ends with a set of key points that summarize the most important arguments developed within the chapter.

Questions

A set of carefully devised questions has been provided to help you assess your understanding of core themes, and may also be used as the basis of seminar discussion or coursework.

Further Reading

Reading lists have been provided as a guide to finding out more about the issues raised within each chapter and to help you locate the key academic literature in the field.

Online Resource Centre

Each chapter provides references to relevant annotated web links which can be found on the Online Resource Centre that accompanies this book.

■ GUIDE TO THE ONLINE RESOURCE CENTRE

The Online Resource Centre that accompanies this book provides students and instructors with ready-to-use teaching and learning materials. These resources are free of charge and designed to maximize the learning experience.

www.oxfordtextbooks.co.uk/orc/jackson_sorensen6e/

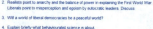

FOR STUDENTS:

Case studies

Each chapter is supplemented with a short case study, which is accompanied by assignments, designed to reinforce your understanding of the chapter themes.

Review Questions

Additional questions allow you to test yourself and provide valuable exam practice.

7.01. Click here for the homepage of the "Berkeley Roundtable on the International Economy" (BRIE). The site contains several working papers as well as links to related sites.
http://brie.berkeley.edu/

7.02. Drake University hosts a site with several links to websites on international political economy.
http://www.drake.edu/artsci/PolSci/ev/IPEx/links.html

7.03. Another comprehensive collection of links to websites on international political economy is hosted by Middlebury College.
http://community.middlebury.edu/~scanner/IPE/personal-homepage/ipexlinks.html

7.04. The International Economics Network provides several links to research papers on international political economy.

Web Links

A series of annotated web links, organized by chapter, points you in the direction of different theoretical debates, as well as information on International Relations situations in different locations across the world.

There are web links to important treaties, working papers, and articles, as well as maps, information on international organizations, and a collection of the most important documents on the Iraq War.

FLASHCARDS   EXIT

Use 'Flip Card' to see the second side of the card
Use 'Next' and 'Previous' to move between cards

‹ PREVIOUS   FLIP CARD   NEXT ›

Globalization

Flashcard Glossary

A series of interactive flashcards containing key terms and concepts has been provided to test your understanding of IR terminology.

BOX 3.8   Schelling on the diplomacy of violence

The power to hurt is nothing new in warfare, but . . . modern technolog tance of war and threats of war as techniques of influence, not of de deterrence, not of conquest and defense; of bargaining and intimidatic like just a contest of strength. War and the brink of war are more a conte of pain and endurance . . . The threat of war has always been somew tional diplomacy . . . Military strategy can no longer be thought of . . . victory. It is now equally, if not more, the art of coercion, of intimidation strategy . . . has become the diplomacy of violence.

Schelling (1996: 168, 182)

FOR INSTRUCTORS:
Boxes from the Text

All boxes from the text have been provided in high-resolution format for downloading into presentation software or for use in assignments and exam material.

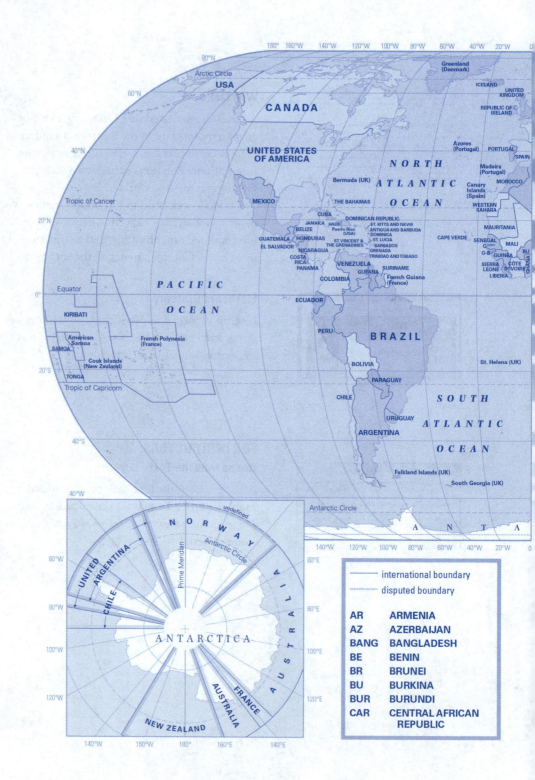

180° 160°W 140°W 120°W 100°W 80°W 60°W 40°W 20°W 0

80°N
Arctic Circle
60°N   Greenland
USA   (Denmark)
                                                                    ICELAND   UNITED
CANADA   KINGDOM
                                                                    REPUBLIC OF
                                                                    IRELAND
40°N
UNITED STATES   N O R T H   Azores   PORTUGAL
OF AMERICA   (Portugal)   SPAIN
                                 A T L A N T I C   Madeira
                                                    (Portugal)
                    Bermuda (UK)   MOROCCO
                                 O C E A N   Canary
Tropic of Cancer   Islands
MEXICO   (Spain)
                    THE BAHAMAS   WESTERN
20°N   SAHARA
                    CUBA   DOMINICAN REPUBLIC
                    JAMAICA HAITI   ST. KITTS AND NEVIS
                BELIZE   Puerto Rico   ANTIGUA AND BARBUDA   MAURITANIA
        GUATEMALA HONDURAS (USA)   DOMINICA   CAPE VERDE
        EL SALVADOR   ST. LUCIA   SENEGAL
                    NICARAGUA   BARBADOS   G-B   MALI   BU
                COSTA   GRENADA   SIERRA   CÔTE
                RICA PANAMA TRINIDAD AND TOBAGO   LEONE   D'IVOIRE
                    VENEZUELA SURINAME   LIBERIA
0°   COLOMBIA GUYANA
Equator   French Guiana
        P A C I F I C   ECUADOR (France)

KIRIBATI   O C E A N   PERU   B R A Z I L

        American   St. Helena (UK)
        Samoa   French Polynesia
SAMOA   (France)   BOLIVIA
        Cook Islands
        (New Zealand)   PARAGUAY
TONGA   S O U T H
20°S
Tropic of Capricorn   CHILE   A T L A N T I C
                                              URUGUAY
                                                         O C E A N
40°S   ARGENTINA

                                     Falkland Islands (UK)

                                     South Georgia (UK)

Antarctic Circle
                                              A N T A   T A   A

140°W 120°W 100°W 80°W 60°W 40°W 20°W 0

40°W
                    undefined
        N O R W A Y
                                 Antarctic Circle
60°W
UNITED ARGENTINA
                                              60°E
80°W   CHILE
                                              80°E
        A N T A R C T I C A
100°W   100°E
                                     FRANCE
120°W   AUSTRALIA   120°E
        NEW ZEALAND
140°W 160°W 180° 160°E 140°E

        Prime Meridian
        ———————— international boundary
        ------------ disputed boundary

AR   ARMENIA
AZ   AZERBAIJAN
BANG   BANGLADESH
BE   BENIN
BR   BRUNEI
BU   BURKINA
BUR   BURUNDI
CAR   CENTRAL AFRICAN
        REPUBLIC

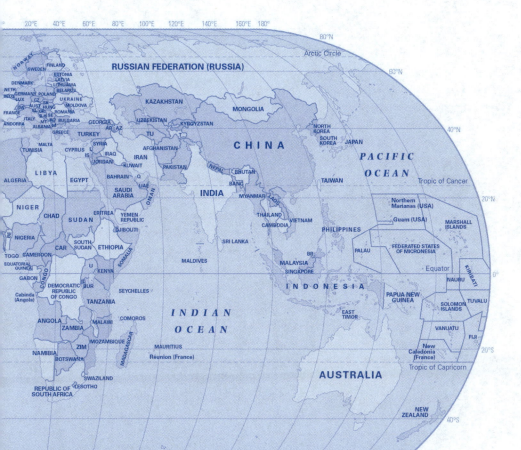

PART 1

Studying IR

Why Study IR?

▌ Summary

This chapter answers the question 'why study IR?' It begins by introducing the historical and social basis of international relations, or IR. The aim of the chapter is to emphasize the practical reality of international relations in our everyday lives and to connect that practical reality with the academic study of international relations. The chapter makes that connection by focusing on the core historical subject matter of IR: modern sovereign states and the international relations of the **state system**. Why do states and the state system exist? Three main topics are discussed: the significance of international relations in everyday life and the main values that states exist to foster; the historical evolution of the state system and world economy in brief outline; and the changing contemporary world of states.

International Relations in Everyday Life

IR is the shorthand name for the academic subject of international relations. It can be defined as the study of relationships and interactions between countries, including the activities and policies of national governments, international organizations (IGOs), non-governmental organizations (NGOs), and multinational corporations (MNCs). It can be both a theoretical subject and a practical or policy subject, and academic approaches to it can be either empirical or normative or both. It is often considered a branch of political science, but it is also a subject studied by historians (international or diplomatic history), and economists (international economics). It is also a field of legal studies (public international law) and an area of philosophy (international ethics). From that broader perspective, IR clearly is an interdisciplinary inquiry. Aspects of international relations, and in particular war and diplomacy, have been scrutinized and remarked upon at least since the time of the ancient Greek historian Thucydides, but IR only became a proper academic discipline in the early twentieth century.

The main reason why we should study IR is the fact that the entire population of the world is divided into separate political communities or independent countries, nation-states, which profoundly affect the way people think and live. Nation-states are involved with us, and we are involved with them. In highly successful nation-states most of the population identify, often quite strongly, with the country of which they are citizens. They are proud of their country's flag. They sing the national anthem. They do not sing the anthems of other countries. They see the world's population as divided and organized in terms of separate nation-states. 'I'm American, you're French, he's German, she's Japanese, the man over there is from Brazil, the woman is from South Africa, the other fellow is Russian . . .' And so it goes right around the world.

As a practical matter it is difficult and probably impossible for most people to escape from the various effects of nation-states on their daily lives, even if they wanted to. The state is involved in protecting them and providing for their security, both personal and national, in promoting their economic prosperity and social welfare, in taxing them, in educating them, in licensing and regulating them, in keeping them healthy, in building and maintaining public infrastructure (roads, bridges, harbours, airports, etc.), and much else besides. That involvement of people and states is often taken entirely for granted. But the relationship is profound. People's lives are shaped, very significantly, by that reality.

IR focuses on the various activities of nation-states in their external relations. To begin to do that some basic concepts are required. An independent nation or **state** may be defined as an unambiguous and bordered territory, with a permanent population, under the jurisdiction of supreme government that is constitutionally separate—i.e., independent—from all foreign governments: a **sovereign state**. Together, those states form an international state system that is global in extent. At the present time, there are almost 200 independent states. With very few isolated exceptions, everybody on earth not only lives in one of those countries but is also a citizen of one of them and very rarely of more than one, although that possibility is increasing as the world becomes ever more interdependent. So virtually every man, woman, and child on earth is connected to a particular state, and via that state to the state system which affects their lives in important and even profound ways, including some of which they may not be fully aware.

States are independent of each other, at least legally: they have sovereignty. But that does not mean they are isolated or insulated from each other. On the contrary, they adjoin each other and affect each other and must therefore somehow find ways to coexist and to deal with each other. In other words, they form an international state system, which is a core subject of IR. Furthermore, states are almost always involved with international markets that affect the economic policies of governments and the wealth and welfare of citizens. That requires that states enter into relations with each other. Complete isolation is usually not an option. When states are isolated and cut off from the state system, either by their own government or by foreign powers, the people usually suffer as a result. That has been the situation at various times recently with regard to Burma (officially, the Union of Myanmar), Libya, North Korea, Iraq, Iran, and Syria. Like most other social systems, the state system can have both advantages and disadvantages for the states involved and their people. IR is the study of the nature and consequences of these international relations.

The state system is a distinctive way of organizing political life on earth and has deep historical roots. There have been state systems at different times and places in different parts of the world, in, for example, ancient India, ancient Greece, and Renaissance Italy (Watson 1992). However, the subject of IR conventionally dates back to the early modern era (sixteenth and seventeenth centuries) in Europe, when sovereign states based on adjacent territories were initially established. Ever since the eighteenth century, relations between such independent states have been labelled 'international relations'. Initially, the state system was European. With the emergence of the United States in the late eighteenth century it became Western. In the nineteenth and twentieth centuries, however, the state system expanded to encompass the entire territory of the earth—east and west, north and south. Today, IR is the study of the global state system from various scholarly perspectives, the most important of which will be discussed in this book.

The world of states is basically a territorial world. People must live somewhere on the planet, and those places must relate to each other in some way or other. The state system is a way of politically organizing populated territory, a distinctive kind of territorial political organization, based on numerous national governments that are legally independent of each other. The only large territory that is not a state and cannot be a state because it lacks a population is Antarctica. But it is administered by a consortium of states that have an interest in its environment and its potential for scientific research and economic development. To understand the significance of IR, it is necessary to grasp what living in states basically involves. What does it imply? How important is it? How should we think about it? This book is centrally concerned with these questions and especially with the last one. The chapters that follow deal with various answers to that fundamental question. This chapter examines the core historical subject matter of IR: the evolution of the state system and the changing contemporary world of states. History is important because states and the states system had to come into existence, had to be a practical reality, before they could be studied theoretically.

Why study IR? To begin to respond to that question, it may be helpful to examine our everyday life as citizens of particular states to see what we generally expect from a state. There are at least five basic social values that states are usually expected to uphold: security, freedom, order, justice, and welfare. These are social values that are so fundamental to human well-being that they must be protected or ensured in some way. That could be by social organizations other than the state, e.g., by families, clans, ethnic or religious organizations, villages, or cities. In the modern era, however, the state has usually been involved as the leading institution in that regard: it is expected to ensure these basic values. For example, people generally assume the state should underwrite the value of security, which involves the protection of individual citizens and the people as a whole from internal and external threats. That is a fundamental concern or interest of states. However, the very existence of independent states affects the value of security; we live in a world of many states, almost all of which are armed at least to some degree and some of which are major military powers. Thus, states can both defend and threaten people's security. That paradox of the state system is usually referred to as the '**security dilemma**'. In other words, just like any other human organization, states present problems as well as provide solutions.

Most states are likely to be cooperative, non-threatening, and peace-loving most of the time. But some states may be hostile and aggressive at times and there is no world government to constrain them. That poses a basic and age-old problem of state systems: **national security**. To respond to that problem, most states possess armed forces. Military power is usually considered a necessity so that states can coexist and deal with each other without being intimidated or subjugated. Unarmed states are extremely rare in the history of the state system. That is a basic fact of the state system of which we should never lose sight. Many states also enter into alliances or defence organizations with other states to increase their national security. NATO (the North Atlantic Treaty Organization) is by far the most important example of a military alliance in recent history.

To ensure that no great power succeeds in achieving a hegemonic position of overall domination, based on intimidation, coercion, or the outright use of force, history indicates it may be necessary to construct and maintain a balance of military power. This approach to the study of world politics is typical of realist theories of IR (Morgenthau 1960). It operates on the assumption that relations of states can best be characterized as a world in which armed states are competing rivals and periodically go to war with each other.

The second basic value that states are usually expected to uphold is freedom, both personal freedom and national freedom or independence. A fundamental reason for having states and putting up with the burdens that governments place on citizens, such as taxes or obligations of military service, is the condition of national freedom or independence that states exist to foster. We cannot be free unless our country is free too: that was made very clear to millions of Czech, Polish, Danish, Norwegian, Belgian, Dutch, and French citizens, as well as citizens of other countries which were invaded and occupied by Nazi Germany during the Second World War. Even if our country is free, we may still not be free personally, but at least then the problem of our freedom is in our own hands. War threatens and sometimes destroys freedom. Peace fosters freedom. Peace also makes progressive international change possible; that is, the creation of a better world. Peace and progressive change are obviously among the most fundamental values of international relations. That approach to the study of world politics is typical of liberal theories of IR (Claude 1971). It operates on the assumption that international relations can be best characterized as a world in which states cooperate with each other to maintain peace and freedom and to pursue progressive change.

The third and fourth basic values that states are usually expected to uphold are order and justice. States have a common interest in establishing and maintaining international order so that they can coexist and interact on a basis of stability, certainty, and predictability. To that end, states are expected to uphold international law: to keep their treaty commitments and to observe the rules, conventions, and customs of the international legal order. They are also expected to follow accepted practices of diplomacy and to support international organizations. International law, diplomatic relations, and international organizations can only exist and operate successfully if these expectations are generally met by most states most of the time. States are also expected to uphold human rights. Today, there is an elaborate international legal framework of human rights—civil, political, social, and economic—which has been developed since the end of the Second World War. Order and justice are obviously among the most fundamental values of international relations. That approach to the study of world politics is typical of International Society theories of IR (Bull 1995). It operates on the assumption that international relations can best be characterized as a world in which states are socially responsible actors and have a common interest in preserving international order and promoting international justice.

The final basic value that states are usually expected to uphold is the population's socio-economic wealth and welfare. People expect their government to adopt appropriate policies to encourage high employment, low inflation, steady investment, the uninterrupted flow of trade and commerce, and so forth. Because national economies are rarely isolated from each other, most people also expect that the state will respond to the international economic system in such a way as to enhance or at least defend and maintain the national standard of living.

Most states nowadays try to frame and implement economic policies that can maintain the stability of the international economy upon which they are all increasingly dependent. This usually involves economic policies that can deal adequately with international markets, with the economic policies of other states, with foreign investment, with foreign exchange rates, with solvent banks, with international trade, with international transportation and communications, and with other international economic relations and conditions that affect national wealth and welfare.

Economic interdependence, meaning a high degree of mutual economic dependence among countries, is a striking feature of the contemporary state system. Some people consider this to be a good thing because it may increase overall freedom and wealth by expanding the global marketplace, thereby increasing participation, specialization, efficiency, and productivity. Other people consider it to be a bad thing because it may promote overall inequality by allowing rich and powerful countries, or countries with financial or technological advantages, to dominate poor and weak countries which lack those advantages. Still others consider national protectionism as preferable to economic interdependence as the best way to respond to financial and economic crises which periodically disrupt the world economy. But either way, wealth and welfare obviously are among the most fundamental values of international relations. That approach to the study of world politics is typical of IPE (International Political Economy) theories of IR (Gilpin 1987). It operates on the assumption that international relations can best be characterized as a fundamentally socio-economic world and not merely a political and military world.

Most people usually take these basic values (security, freedom, order and justice, and welfare) for granted. They only become aware of them when something goes wrong—for example, during a war or a depression, when things begin to get beyond the control of individual states. On those acute learning occasions, people wake up to the larger circumstances of their lives which in normal times are a silent or invisible background. They become conscious of what they take for granted, and of how important these values really are in their everyday lives. We become aware of national security when a foreign power becomes belligerent, or when international terrorists engage in hostile actions against our country or one of our allies. We become aware of national independence and our freedom as citizens when peace is no longer guaranteed. We become aware of international order and justice when some states, especially major powers, threaten or attack others with armed force, or when they abuse, exploit, denounce, or disregard international law, or trample on human rights. We become aware of national welfare and our own personal socioeconomic well-being when foreign countries or international investors use their economic clout to jeopardize our standard of living.

There were significant moments of heightened awareness of these major values during the twentieth century. The First World War made it dreadfully clear to most people just how devastatingly destructive of lives and living conditions modern mechanized warfare between major powers can be, and just how important it is to reduce the risk of war between great powers (see web link 1.09). Such recognition led to the first major developments of IR thought which tried to find effective legal institutions—e.g., the Covenant of the League of Nations—to prevent great-power war (see web link 1.10). Those efforts were not as successful as was hoped. But IR remains important because it seeks to understand as fully as possible the different ways that international relations can enhance but also undermine the quality of life of so many people that live in different countries around the world.

The Second World War not only underlined the reality of the dangers of great-power war, but also revealed how important it is to prevent any great power from getting out of control and how unwise it is to pursue a policy of appeasement—which was adopted by Britain and France with regard to Nazi Germany just prior to the war, with disastrous consequences for everybody, including the German people.

There were also moments of heightened awareness of the fundamental importance of these values after the Second World War. The military occupation of Eastern Europe by Stalinist Russia alarmed leaders of Western nations and led to the Cold War. The Cuban missile crisis of 1962 brought home to many people the dangers of nuclear war and the shocking fact that it could destroy human civilization. The anti-colonial movements of the 1950s and 1960s in Asia and Africa, and the secessionist movements in the former Soviet Union and former Yugoslavia at the end of the Cold War, made it clear how important self-determination and political independence continue to be. The Gulf War of 1990–1 and the conflicts in the Balkans, particularly in Bosnia (1992–5) and Kosovo (1999), were a reminder of the importance of international order and respect for human rights. The attacks on New York and Washington (2001) awakened many people in the United States and elsewhere to the dangers of international terrorism (see web link 1.16). More recently, the popular uprisings ('Arab Spring') in North Africa and the Middle East (2010–13), the Syrian Civil War (2011– ongoing at the time of writing), the conflict between Israel and the Palestinians in Gaza, the war of secession in Ukraine and the threatening posture of Vladimir Putin's Russia in Eastern Europe (2014– ongoing), and the rise of the radical terrorist organization Islamic State of Iraq and the Levant (ISIL) (2014– ongoing) demonstrate, yet again, the vital importance of the same values.

The Great Depression (1929–33) brought home to many people around the world how their economic livelihood could be adversely affected, in some cases destroyed, by collapsing market conditions, not only at home but also in foreign countries (see web link 1.11). The global inflation of the 1970s and early 1980s, caused by a sudden dramatic increase in oil prices by the OPEC cartel of oil-exporting countries, was a reminder of how the interconnectedness of the global economy can be a threat to national and personal welfare anywhere in the world. For example, the oil shock of the 1970s made it abundantly clear to countless American, European, and Japanese motorists—among others—that the economic policies of the Middle East and other major oil-producing countries could suddenly raise the price of gas or petrol at the pump and lower their standard of living. The global financial crisis of 2008–9 recalled the lessons of the Great Depression and underlined the extent to which it was a global episode and not merely a Western crisis. Both crises were addressed and overcome by massive state intervention in the economic system, particularly the financial and banking sectors. The military intervention of Putin's Russia in Ukraine, together with the dependency of Germany on Russian gas supplies, revealed both the power and the vulnerability of major countries.

For a long time, there has been a basic assumption that life inside properly organized and well-managed states is better than life outside states or without states at all. History reminds us of that fact. For example, the Jewish people spent well over half a century trying to get a state of their own, Israel, in which they could be secure. They finally succeeded in 1948. As long as states and the state system manage to maintain the foregoing core values, that assumption holds. That has generally been the case for developed countries, especially the states of Western Europe, North America, Japan, Australia, New Zealand, Singapore, and some others. That gives rise to more conventional IR theories which regard the state system as a valuable core institution of modern life. The traditional IR theories discussed in this book tend to adopt that positive view (Table 1.1).

But if states are not successful in that regard, the state system can be easily understood in the opposite light: not as upholding basic social conditions and values, but rather as undermining them. More than a few states fail to ensure any of them. That is the case with regard to many states in the non-Western world, especially sub-Saharan Africa and the Middle East. The conditions inside some of these countries are so bad, so adverse to human well-being, that people are driven to flee to neighbouring countries to find safety. They are forced to become refugees. The plight of such people, whose numbers now run into the millions,

TABLE 1.1   IR (theories and focus)

THEORIES	FOCUS
• Realism	• Security power politics, conflict, and war
• Liberalism	• Freedom cooperation, peace, and progress
• International Society	• Order and justice shared interests, rules, and institutions
• IPE theories	• Welfare wealth, poverty, and equality

TABLE 1.2   Views of the state

TRADITIONAL VIEW	ALTERNATIVE OR *REVISIONIST* VIEW
States are valuable and necessary institutions: they provide security, freedom, order, justice, and welfare	States and the state system are social choices that create more problems than they solve
People benefit from the state system	The majority of the world's people suffer more than they benefit from the state system

puts into question the credibility and perhaps even the legitimacy of the state system. It promotes a contrary assumption that the international system fosters or at least tolerates human suffering, and that the system should be changed so that people everywhere can flourish, and not just those in the developed or advanced countries of the world. That gives rise to more critical IR theories which regard the state and the state system as a less beneficial and more problematic institution. The alternative IR theories discussed later in this book tend to adopt that critical stance (Table 1.2).

To sum up thus far: states and the system of states are territory-based social organizations which exist primarily to establish, maintain, and defend basic social conditions and values, particularly, security, freedom, order, justice, and welfare. These are the main reasons for having states. Many states, and certainly all developed countries, uphold these conditions and values at least to minimal standards and often at a much higher level. Indeed, those countries have been so successful in promoting those values over the past several centuries that standards of living have steadily increased and are now higher than ever. These countries set the international standard for the entire world. But many states and most underdeveloped countries often fail to meet even minimal standards, and as a consequence their presence in the contemporary state system raises serious questions, not only about those states, but also about the state system of which they are an important part. The state system may be criticized, at a minimum, for tolerating adverse and harmful socioeconomic conditions in some countries. At a maximum, it has been condemned for producing those conditions. That has provoked a debate in IR between traditional theorists who by and large view the existing state system in positive terms, and radical theorists who by and large view it in negative terms.

Brief Historical Sketch of the State System

States and the state system are such basic features of modern political life that it is easy to assume that they are permanent features: that they have always been and always will be present. That assumption is false. It is important to emphasize that the state system is a historical institution. It is not ordained by God or determined by Nature. It has been fashioned by certain people at a certain time: it is a social organization. Like all social organizations, the state system has advantages and disadvantages which change over time. There is nothing about the state system that is necessary to human existence, even though there may be many things about it that are advantageous for better living conditions. The following sketch of international history underlines that fact.

People have not always lived in sovereign states. For most of human history, they have organized their political lives in different ways, the most common being that of clans or tribes on a smaller scale and that of political empire on a larger scale, such as the Roman Empire or the Ottoman (Turkish) Empire (Box 1.1). In the future, the world may not be organized into a state system either. People may eventually give up on sovereign statehood. People throughout history have abandoned many other ways of organizing their political lives, including city-states, feudalism, and colonialism, to mention a few. It is not unreasonable to suppose that a form of global political organization which is better or more advanced than states and the state system will eventually be adopted. Some IR scholars discussed in later chapters believe that such an international transformation, connected with growing interdependence among states (i.e., globalization), is already well under way. But the state system has been a central institution of world politics for a very long time, and still remains so. Even though world politics is always in flux, states and the state system have managed to adapt to significant historical change. But nobody can be sure that that will continue to be the case in the future. This issue of present and future international change is discussed later in the chapter.

There were no clearly recognizable sovereign states before the sixteenth century, when they first began to be instituted in Western Europe. But for the past three or four centuries, states and the system of states have structured the political lives of an ever-increasing number of people around the world. They have become universally popular. Today, the

---

BOX 1.1   The Roman Empire

Rome began as a city state in central Italy . . . Over several centuries the city expanded its authority and adapted its methods of government to bring first Italy, then the western Mediterranean and finally almost the whole of the Hellenistic world into an empire larger than any which had existed in that area before . . . This unique and astonishing achievement, and the cultural transformation which it brought about, laid the foundations of European civilization . . . Rome helped to shape European and contemporary practice and opinion about the state, about international law and especially about empire and the nature of imperial authority.

Watson (1992: 94)

system is global in extent. During that same period, many alternative ways of organizing political life have been driven to the margins or become obsolete. Others linger on or occasionally reappear. That has happened in the Middle East recently where violent attempts have been made to revive Islamic Caliphates. But even when that happens, the state and state system are the main points of reference in people's lives.

The era of the sovereign state coincides with the modern age of expanding power, prosperity, knowledge, science, technology, literacy, urbanization, citizenship, freedom, equality, rights, and so on. This could be a coincidence, but that is not very likely when we remember how important states and the state system have been in shaping the five fundamental human values discussed above. Of course, it is difficult to say whether states were the effect or the cause of modern life, and whether they will have any place in a postmodern age. Those questions must be set aside for later.

However, we do know that the state system and modernity are closely related historically. In fact, they are completely coexistent; the system of adjoining territorial states arose in Europe at the start of the modern era. And the state system has been a central if not defining feature of modernity ever since. Although the sovereign state emerged in Europe, it extended to North America in the late eighteenth century and to South America in the early nineteenth century. As modernity spread around the world the state system spread with it. The reverse was also the case: the state system spread modernity because it was itself modern. Only slowly did it expand to cover the entire globe. Sub-Saharan Africa, for example, remained isolated from the expanding Western state system until the late nineteenth century, and it only became a regional state system after the middle of the twentieth century. Whether the end of modernity will also bring the end of the state system is an important question that must be left for later in this book.

Of course, there is evidence of political systems that resembled sovereign states long before the modern age. They obviously had relations of some sort with each other. The historical origin of international relations in that more general sense lies deep in history and can only be a matter of speculation. But, speaking conceptually, it was a time when people began to settle down on the land and form themselves into separate territory-based political communities. The first examples of that occurred in the Middle East and date back more than 5,000 years (Table 1.3).

The relations between independent political groups make up the core problem of international relations. They are built on a fundamental distinction between our collective selves and other collective selves in a finite territorial world of many such separate collective selves in contact with each other. Here we arrive at a preliminary definition of a state system: it stands for relations between separate human groupings which occupy distinctive territories, are not under any higher authority or power, and enjoy and exercise a measure of independence from each other. International relations are primarily relations between such independent groups.

The first relatively clear historical manifestation of a state system is that of ancient Greece (500–100 BCE), then known as 'Hellas' (see web link 1.01). Ancient Greece was not a nation-state the way it is today. Rather, it was a system of many city-states (Wight 1977; Watson 1992). Athens was the largest and most famous, but there were also many other

TABLE 1.3   City-states and empires

500 BCE–100 BCE	Greek city-states system (Hellas)
200 BCE–AD 500	Roman Empire
306–1453	Orthodox Christianity: Byzantine Empire, Constantinople
500–1500	Catholic Christendom: The Pope in Rome
1299–1923	Ottoman (Turkish) Empire, Istanbul (Constantinople)
Other historical empires	Persia, India (Mogul), China

city-states, such as Sparta and Corinth. Together they formed the first state system in Western history. There were extensive and elaborate relations between the city-states of Hellas. But the ancient Greek city-states were not modern sovereign states with extensive territories. They were far smaller in population and territory than most modern states. Greek intercity relations involved distinctive traditions and practices, but they lacked the institution of diplomacy, and there was nothing comparable to international law and international organization. The state system of Hellas was based on a shared language and a common religion— Greek culture—more than anything else. The ancient Greek state system was eventually destroyed by more powerful neighbouring empires, and in due course the Greeks became subjects of the Roman Empire, which occupied most of Europe and a large part of the Middle East and North Africa. Empire was the prevalent pattern of political organization that gradually emerged in Christian Europe over several centuries after the fall of the Roman Empire (Figure 1.1). Rome's two main successors in Europe were also empires: in Western Europe, the medieval (Catholic) empire based at Rome (Christendom); in Eastern Europe and the near east, the Byzantine (Orthodox) empire centred on Constantinople or what is today Istanbul (Byzantium). Byzantium claimed to be the continuation of the Christianized Roman Empire. The European medieval Christian world (500–1500) was thus divided geographically most of the time into two, oftentimes rival, politico-religious empires. There were other political systems and empires further afield. North Africa and the Middle East

FIGURE 1.1   The Christian commonwealth of medieval Europe

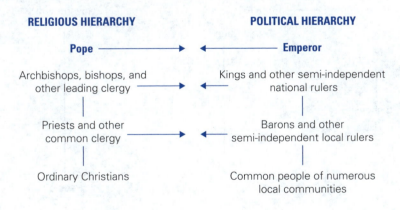

formed a world of Islamic civilization which originated in the Arabian peninsula in the early years of the seventh century (see web link 1.18). There were empires in what are today Iran and India. The oldest empire was the Chinese, which under different dynasties survived for about 4,000 years until the early twentieth century. Perhaps it still exists in the form of the Chinese Communist state, which resembles an empire in its hierarchical political and ideological structure and in the necessity to impose its will on some of its outlying territories from time to time. The Middle Ages were thus an era of empire and the relations and conflicts of different empires (see web links 1.03, 1.04, and 1.05). But contact between empires was intermittent at best; communications were slow and transportation was difficult. Consequently, most empires at that time were a world unto themselves.

Can we speak of 'international relations' in Western Europe during the medieval era? Only with difficulty. States existed, often in the form of kingdoms, but they were not independent or sovereign in the modern meaning of these words. There were no clearly defined territories with delineated borders. The medieval world was not a geographical patchwork of sharply differentiated colours representing different independent countries. Instead, it was a complicated and confusing intermingling of overlapping territories of varying shades and hues. Power and authority were organized on both a religious and political basis: in Latin Christendom, a Pope and an emperor were the heads of two parallel and connected hierarchies, one religious and the other political. Kings and other rulers were subjects of those higher authorities and their separate set of laws. Kings were not fully independent. And much of the time, local rulers were more or less free from the rule of kings: they were semi-autonomous but they were not fully independent either. The fact is that territorial political independence as we know it today was not present in medieval Europe (Figure 1.2).

The medieval era was also one of considerable disarray, disorder, conflict, and violence which stemmed from this lack of clearly delineated territorial political organization and

FIGURE 1.2   Medieval and modern authority

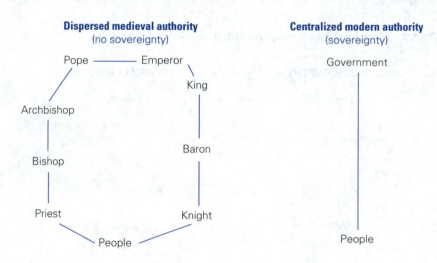

control. There was no clear distinction between civil war and international war. Medieval wars were more likely to be fought over issues of rights and wrongs: wars to defend the faith, wars to resolve conflicts over dynastic inheritance, wars to punish outlaws, wars to collect debts, and so on (Howard 1976: ch. 1). Wars were less likely to be fought over the exclusive control of territory or over state or national interests. In medieval Europe, there was no exclusively controlled territory, and no clear conception of the nation or the national interest.

The values connected with sovereign statehood were arranged differently in medieval times. The key to that difference is the fact that no one political organization, such as the sovereign state, catered for all these values. That high degree of political and legal integration of territorial societies had yet to occur.

Instead, those values were looked after by different organizations which operated at different levels of social life. Security was provided by local rulers and their knights who operated from fortified castles and towns. Freedom was not freedom for the individual or the nation. Rather, it was freedom for feudal rulers and their followers and clients, or it was freedom for fortified cities or towns. Order was the responsibility of the emperor, but his capacity to enforce order was very limited, and medieval Europe was punctuated by turbulence and discord at all levels of society. The provision of justice was the responsibility of both political and religious rulers, but it was separate and unequal justice. Those higher up the political and religious hierarchies had easier access to justice than those at the bottom. There were different laws and courts, different rights and duties, for different classes of people. There was no police force, and often justice was meted out by the people themselves in the form of revenge or reprisal.

What did the political change from medieval to modern basically involve? The short answer is: it eventually consolidated the provision of these values within the single framework of one unified and independent social organization: the sovereign state. In the early modern era, European rulers liberated themselves from the overarching religious–political authority of Christendom. They also freed themselves from their dependence on the military power of barons and other local feudal leaders. The kings subordinated the barons and defied the pope and the emperor. They became defenders of their own sovereignty against internal disorder and external threat. Their sovereignty later evolved into state sovereignty. Peasants began their long journey to escape from their dependence on local feudal rulers to become the direct subjects of the king: they eventually became 'the people' upon whom sovereignty came to rest: popular sovereignty.

In short, power and authority were concentrated at one point: the king and his government. The king now ruled a territory with borders which were defended against outside interference. The king became the supreme authority over all the people in the country, and no longer had to operate via intermediate authorities and rulers. That fundamental political transformation marks the advent of the modern era.

One of the major effects of the rise of the modern state was its monopoly of the means of warfare within its area of control (Box 1.2). The king first created order at home and became the sole centre of power within the country. Knights and barons who had formerly controlled their own armies now took orders from the king. Many kings then looked outward with an ambition to expand their territories or out of fear that a neighbouring ruler would invade and conquer them. As a result, international rivalries developed which often resulted in wars and the enlargement of some countries at the expense of others. Spain, France, Austria, England, Denmark, Sweden, Holland, Prussia, Poland, Russia, and other states of the new European state system were frequently at war. War became a key institution for resolving conflicts between sovereign states and enforcing international law (Box 1.3).

In the traditional view of the episode, the political change from medieval to modern thus basically involved the construction of independent territorial states across Europe. The state captured its territory and turned it into state property, and it captured the population of that territory and turned them into subjects and later citizens. In the modern international system, territory is consolidated, unified, and centralized under a sovereign government. The population of the territory owe allegiance to that government and have a duty to obey its laws. All institutions are now subordinate to state authority and public law. The familiar territorial patchwork map is in place, in which each patch is under the exclusive jurisdiction of a particular state. All of the territory of Europe and eventually that of the entire planet became partitioned by independent governments. The historical end point of the medieval era and the starting point of the modern international system, speaking very generally, is usually identified with the Thirty Years War (1618–48, see Box 1.2) and the Peace of Westphalia which brought it to an end (see Box 1.3 and web link 1.06).

From the middle of the seventeenth century, states were seen as the only legitimate political systems of Europe, based on their own separate territories, their own independent

---

BOX 1.2   The Thirty Years War (1618–48)

Starting initially in Bohemia as an uprising of the Protestant aristocracy against Spanish authority, the war escalated rapidly, eventually incorporating all sorts of issues . . . Questions of religious toleration were at the root of the conflict . . . But by the 1630s, the war involved a jumble of conflicting states, with all sorts of cross-cutting dynastic, religious, and state interests involved . . . Europe was fighting its first continental war.

Holsti (1991: 26–8)

BOX 1.3   The Peace of Westphalia (1648)

The Westphalian settlement legitimized a commonwealth of sovereign states. It marked the triumph of the *stato* [the state], in control of its internal affairs and independent externally. This was the aspiration of princes [rulers] in general—and especially of the German princes, both Protestant and Catholic, in relation to the [Holy Roman or Habsburg] empire. The Westphalian treaties stated many of the rules and political principles of the new society of states . . . The settlement was held to provide a fundamental and comprehensive charter for all Europe.

Watson (1992: 186)

governments, and their own political subjects. The emergent state system had several prominent characteristics, which can be summarized. First, it consisted of adjoining states whose legitimacy and independence was mutually recognized. Second, that recognition of states did not extend outside of the European state system. Non-European political systems were not members of the state system. They were usually regarded as alien and politically inferior and most of them were eventually subordinated to European imperial rule. Third, the relations of European states were subject to international law and diplomatic practices. In other words, they were expected to observe the rules of the international game. Fourth, there was a balance of power between member states which was intended to prevent any one state from getting out of control and making a successful bid for **hegemony**, which would in effect re-establish an empire over the continent.

There were several major attempts by different powers to impose their political hegemony on the continent. The Habsburg Empire (Austria) made the attempt during the Thirty Years War (1618–48), and was blocked by a coalition led by France and Sweden. France made the attempt under King Louis XIV (1661–1714), and was eventually blocked by an English–Dutch–Austrian alliance. Napoleon (1795–1815) made the attempt and was blocked by Britain, Russia, Prussia, and Austria. A post-Napoleonic balance of power among the great powers (the Concert of Europe) held for most of the period between 1815 and 1914. Germany made the attempt under Hitler (1939–45), and was blocked by the United States, the Soviet Union, and Britain. For the past 350 years, the European state system has managed to resist the main political tendency of world history, which is the attempt by strong powers to bend weaker powers to their political will and thereby establish an empire. At the end of the Cold War it was debated whether the sole remaining superpower, the United States, had become a global hegemon in this meaning of the term. The rise of China and the reassertion of Russian military power cast serious doubt on that assertion. Instead, it suggested that the international system was again establishing a bipolar or multipolar world of great powers.

This traditional or classical view has been questioned. In Carvalho et al.'s (2011) revisionist interpretation, the story of Westphalia is a historical myth invented by IR scholars who wanted to create a foundational basis in history for their realist or international society theories. The revisionists argue that there is no solid basis in the historical evidence for the traditional claim that the modern, post-medieval system or society of states emerged out of the Peace of Westphalia and successive episodes, such as the Congress of Vienna (1815) or the Peace of Paris (1919). They argue that historical scholarship has 'demolished these myths', but they note that traditional or classical IR scholarship nevertheless persists in reiterating them. The revisionists argue that realist or international society scholars do not wish to lose their predominant position in the discipline and so they perpetuate the Westphalian myth in their textbooks used in teaching future IR scholars.

These conflicting interpretations are not merely different points of view or selections of evidence. Rather, they are different methodological assumptions and approaches. The traditionalists are historicists and empiricists, in the sense that they see existential evidence of the birth of modern statehood in the Westphalian episode. For them, it is the historical occasion when the sovereign state and the anarchic state system came into existence as the dominant political feature of the European world: state sovereignty, state-controlled military power, diplomatic interaction and negotiation, peace settlement, treaties, etc. (see Part 2). The revisionists, on the other hand, are constructivists and critical theorists (see Part 3). They view Westphalia as a conception or construction of IR scholars that promotes their theoretical biases. For them, the historical reality, the actual Westphalia, was an ambiguous world of contradictory and confusing ideas and beliefs, and was far from a sharp and defining historical break with the past. Methodological issues such as these are examined in Part 3.

Globalization and the State System

While Europeans created a state system in Europe, at the very same time they also constructed vast overseas empires and a world economy by which they controlled most non-European political communities in the rest of the world. The Western states that could not dominate each other succeeded in dominating much of the rest of the world both politically and economically (Box 1.4). That outward control of the non-European world by Europeans began at the start of the early modern era in the sixteenth century, at the same time that the European state system was coming into existence. It lasted until the middle of the twentieth century, when the remaining few non-Western peoples finally broke free of Western colonialism and acquired political independence. The fact that no Western state was able to completely dominate the European state system but many Western states were capable of imposing European sovereignty and control on almost everybody elsewhere has been crucially important in shaping the modern international system. The global ascendancy and supremacy of the West is vital for understanding IR even today. Whether that may now be changing with the rise of China, the resurgence of Russia, and—to a lesser extent—the emergence of India and Brazil is a question that can be asked and is being asked both inside and outside the West.

The first stage of the globalization of the state system was via the incorporation of non-Western states that could not be colonized by the West (Box 1.5). Not every non-Western country fell under the political control of a Western imperial state; but countries that

BOX 1.4	President McKinley on American imperialism in the Philippines (1899)

When I realized that the Philippines [a Spanish colony] had dropped into our laps [as a result of America's military defeat of Spain] . . . I did not know what to do . . . one night late it came to me this way . . . (1) that we could not give them back to Spain—that would be cowardly and dishonourable; (2) that we could not turn them over to France or Germany—our commercial rivals in the Orient—that would be bad business and discreditable; (3) that we could not leave them to themselves—they were unfit for self-government—and they would soon have anarchy and misrule over there worse than Spain's was; and (4) that there was nothing left for us to do but take them . . . [and] put the Philippines on the map of the United States.

Bridges et al. (1969: 184)

BOX 1.5	President Ho Chi Minh's 1945 declaration of independence of the Republic of Vietnam

All men are created equal. They are endowed by their Creator with certain inalienable rights, among these are life, liberty and the pursuit of happiness . . . All the peoples on the earth are equal from birth, all the peoples have a right to live, be happy and free . . . We members of the provisional Government, representing the whole population of Vietnam, have declared and renew here our declaration that we break off all relations with the French people and abolish all the special rights the French have unlawfully acquired in our Fatherland . . . We are convinced that the Allied nations which have acknowledged at Teheran and San Francisco the principles of self-determination and equality of status will not refuse to acknowledge the independence of Vietnam . . . For these reasons we . . . declare to the world that Vietnam has the right to be free and independent.

Bridges et al. (1969: 311–12)

escaped colonization were still obliged to accept the rules of the Western state system. The Ottoman Empire (Turkey) is one example: it was forced to accept those rules by the Treaty of Paris in 1854. Japan is another example: it acquiesced to them later in the nineteenth century. Japan rapidly acquired the organizational substance and constitutional shape of a modern state. By the early twentieth century, that country had become a great power—as demonstrated by its military defeat of an existing great power, Russia, on the battlefield: the Russo–Japanese war of 1904–5. China was obliged to accept the rules of the Western state system during the nineteenth and early twentieth century. China was not acknowledged and fully recognized as a great power until 1945.

The second stage of the globalization of the state system was brought about via anti-colonialism by the colonial subjects of Western empires. In that struggle, indigenous political leaders made claims for decolonization and independence based on European and American ideas of self-determination (see web link 1.16). That 'revolt against the West', as Hedley Bull put it, was the main vehicle by which the state system expanded dramatically after the Second World War (Bull and Watson 1984). In a short period of some twenty years, beginning with the independence of India and Pakistan in 1947, most colonies in Asia and Africa became independent states and members of the United Nations (UN) (Box 1.6).

European decolonization in the Third World (now developing countries) more than tripled the membership of the UN from about fifty states in 1945 to more than 160 states by 1970. About 70 per cent of the world's population were citizens or subjects of independent states in 1945 and were thus represented in the state system; by 1995, that figure had increased to virtually 100 per cent. The spread of European political and economic control beyond Europe thus eventually proved to be an expansion of the state system which became completely global in the second half of the twentieth century. The final stage of the globalization of the state system was the dissolution of the Soviet Union, together with the simultaneous break-up of Yugoslavia and Czechoslovakia at the end of the Cold War. Expanded UN membership reached almost 200 states by the end of the twentieth century.

BOX 1.6	Global expansion of the state system

1600s Europe (European system)

1700s + North America (Western system)

1800s + South America, Ottoman Empire, Japan (globalizing system)

1900s + Asia, Africa, Caribbean, Pacific (global system)

Today, the state system is a global institution that affects the lives of virtually everybody on earth, whether they realize it or not. That means that IR is now more than ever a universal academic subject. That also means that world politics at the start of the twenty-first century must accommodate a range and variety of states that are far more diverse—in terms of their cultures, religions, languages, ideologies, forms of government, military capacity, technological sophistication, levels of economic development, etc.—than ever before. That is a fundamental change in the state system and a fundamental challenge for IR scholars to theorize.

IR and the Changing Contemporary World of States

Many important questions in the study of IR are connected with the theory and practice of sovereign statehood, which, as indicated, is the central historical institution of world politics. But there are other important issues as well. That has led to ongoing debates about the proper scope of IR. At one extreme, the scholarly focus is exclusively on states and interstate relations; but at another extreme, IR includes almost everything that has to do with human relations across the world. It is important to study these different perspectives if we hope to have a balanced and rounded knowledge of IR.

Our reason for linking the various IR theories to states and the state system is to acknowledge the historical centrality of that subject. Even theorists who seek to get beyond the state usually take it as a starting point: the state system is the main point of reference for both traditional and new approaches. Later chapters will explore how IR scholarship has attempted to come to grips with the sovereign state. There are debates about how we should conceptualize the state, and different IR theories take somewhat different approaches. In later chapters, we shall present contemporary debates on the future of the state. Whether its central importance in world politics may now be changing is a very important question in contemporary IR scholarship. But the fact is that states and the state system remain at the centre of academic analysis and discussion in IR.

We must, of course, be alert to the fact that the sovereign state is a contested theoretical concept. When we ask the questions 'What is the state?' and 'What is the state system?' there will be different answers, depending on the theoretical approach adopted; the realist answer will be different from the liberal answer, and those answers will be different from the International Society answer and from the answer given by IPE theories. None of these answers is strictly speaking either correct or incorrect because the truth is that the state is a multifaceted and somewhat confusing entity. It is not a thing in itself. It is a historical idea and institution that is open to a variety of interpretations and understandings. There are different concepts of the state. There is disagreement about the scope and purpose of the state. The state system consequently is not an easy subject to grasp theoretically, and it can be understood in various ways and with contrasting points of emphasis.

There are, however, ways of simplifying it. It is helpful to think of the state as having two dimensions, each divided into two broad categories. The first dimension is the state as a government versus the state as a country. Viewed from within, the state is the national government: it is the highest governing authority in a country, and possesses domestic sovereignty. That is the *internal* aspect of the state. The main questions in regard to the internal aspect concern *state–society* relations: how the government rules the domestic society, the means of its power and the sources of its legitimacy, how it deals with the demands and concerns of individuals and groups that compose that domestic society, how it manages the national economy, what its domestic policies are, and so forth.

Viewed internationally, however, the state is not merely a government; it is a populated territory with a national government and a domestic society. In other words, it is a country. From that angle, both the government and the domestic society make up the state. If a country is a sovereign state, it will be generally recognized as such. That is the *external* aspect of the state in which the main questions concern *interstate* relations: how the governments and societies of states relate to each other and deal with each other, what the basis of those interstate relations are, what the foreign policies of particular states are, what the international organizations of the states are, how people from different states interact with each other and engage in transactions with each other, and so forth.

That brings us to the second dimension of the state, which divides the external aspect of sovereign statehood into two broad categories. The first category is the state viewed as a *formal* or legal institution in its relations with other states. That is the state as an entity that is constitutionally independent of all foreign states, is recognized as sovereign or independent by most of those states, enjoys membership in international organizations, and possesses various rights and obligations under international law. We shall refer to that first category as **'juridical' statehood**. Constitutional independence and recognition are essential elements of juridical statehood. Constitutional independence indicates that no foreign state claims or has any legal authority over a state. The constitution of an independent country belongs exclusively to that country. Recognition acknowledges that fact of independence, and paves the way for membership of International Society, including membership of the UN. The absence of constitutional independence and recognition denies it. Not every country is independent and recognized as such; an example is Quebec, which is a province of Canada. To become independent it must be separate from Canada and be recognized as such by existing sovereign states, by far the most important of which for Quebec are first Canada and second the United States (Table 1.4) (see web links 1.31 and 1.32).

There are fewer independent countries than there might be. Quebec, Scotland (part of Great Britain), and Catalonia (part of Spain) could each be independent. A referendum in

TABLE 1.4   External dimension of statehood

The state as a country:	Territory, government, society
Legal, juridical statehood:	Recognition by other states
Actual, empirical statehood:	Political institutions, economic basis, national unity

Quebec (1995) and another in Scotland (2014) each failed to secure enough votes for independence. Catalonia has thus far not succeeded in getting the Spanish government to hold an independence referendum for that part of the country. Most countries refuse to allow secession. In many it would be unthinkable. The international state system is generally unsympathetic to the idea of dividing the territory of countries. Existing countries would lose not only territory but also population, resources, power, status, and so on. Partition would also set a precedent that could destabilize the state system if a growing number of currently subordinated but potentially independent countries lined up to demand sovereign statehood or union with a foreign country. That latter demand is widely seen as particularly dangerous. That is strikingly evident in the widespread international concern, particularly of the European Union (EU) and the United States, in response to Russia's annexation of Crimea and intervention in the civil war in eastern Ukraine. The international state system reveals a major predilection, or bias, in favour of the preservation of existing borders between countries. That is widely understood as an essential element of international order. The second category is the state viewed as a substantial political–economic organization (Figure 1.3). That category has to do with the extent to which states have developed efficient political institutions, a solid economic basis, and a substantial degree of national unity; that is, of popular unity and support for the state. We shall refer to that second category as **'empirical' statehood**. Some states are very strong in the sense that they have a high level of empirical statehood. Most states in the West are like that. Many of those states are small, for example Sweden, Holland, and Luxembourg. A strong state in the sense of a high level of empirical statehood should be held separate from the notion of a strong power in the military sense. Some strong states are not militarily powerful; Denmark is an example. Some strong powers in the military sense, such as Russia, are not particularly strong states. On the other hand, the United States is both a strong state and a strong power (see Table 1.5).

This distinction between empirical statehood and juridical statehood is of fundamental importance because it helps to capture the very significant differences that exist between the almost 200 currently independent and formally equal states of the world. States differ enormously in the legitimacy of their political institutions, the effectiveness of their governmental organizations, their economic wealth and productivity, their political influence and status, and their national unity. Not all states possess effective national governments. Some states, including both large and small, are solid and capable organizations: they are strong states. Most states in the West are more or less like that. Some tiny island microstates in the Pacific Ocean are so small that they can hardly afford to have a government at all. Other states may be fairly large in terms of territory or

FIGURE 1.3   State types in the global state system

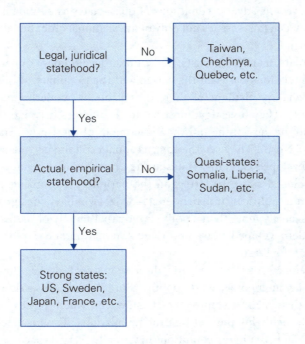

population or both—e.g., Sudan or the Congo (formerly Zaïre)—but they are so poor, so inefficient, and so corrupt that they are barely able to carry on as an effective government. A large number of states, especially in the non-Western world, have a low degree of empirical statehood. Their institutions are weak, the economic basis is frail and underdeveloped, and there is little or no national unity. We can refer to these states as **quasi-states**: they possess juridical statehood but they are severely deficient in empirical statehood (Jackson 1990).

Different conclusions can be drawn from the fact that empirical statehood varies so widely in the contemporary state system, from economically and technologically advanced and mostly Western states at one extreme, to economically and technologically backward and mostly non-Western states at the other. Realist IR scholars focus mainly on the states at the centre of the system: the major powers, and especially the great powers. They see underdeveloped countries as marginal players in a system of power politics that has always rested on 'the inequality of nations' (Tucker 1977). Such marginal or peripheral states do not affect the

TABLE 1.5   Examples of strong/weak states—strong/weak powers

	STRONG POWER	WEAK POWER
Strong state	USA, China, France,	Denmark, New Zealand, Singapore
Weak state	Pakistan, North Korea, Nigeria	Somalia, Libya, Liberia,

system in any very significant way. Other IR scholars, usually liberals and International Society theorists, see the adverse conditions of quasi-states as a fundamental question for the state system, which raises issues not only of international order but also of international freedom and justice.

Some IPE scholars, usually Marxists, make underdevelopment of peripheral countries and the unequal relations between the centre and the periphery of the global economy the crucial explanatory element of their theory of the modern international system (Wallerstein 1974). They investigate international linkages between the poverty of the developing world, or the South, and the enrichment of the United States, Europe, and other parts of the North. They see the international economy as one overall 'world system', with the developed capitalist states at the centre flourishing at the expense of the weak, underdeveloped states suffering on the periphery. According to these scholars, legal equality and political independence—what we have designated as juridical statehood—are scarcely more than a polite facade that merely obscures the extreme vulnerability of underdeveloped states and their domination and exploitation by the rich capitalist states of the West.

The underdeveloped countries certainly disclose in a striking way the profound empirical inequalities of contemporary world politics. But it is their possession of juridical statehood, reflecting their membership of the state system, which places that issue in sharp perspective, for it highlights the fact that the populations of some states—the developed countries—enjoy far better living conditions in virtually every respect than the populations of other states; that is, the underdeveloped countries. The fact that underdeveloped countries belong to the same global state system as developed countries raises different questions from those that would arise if they belonged to entirely separate systems; that is, the situation that existed before the global state system came into existence. We can see the issues of security, freedom and progress, order and justice, and wealth and poverty far more clearly when they involve members of the same international system. For *inside* a system the same general standards and expectations apply. So if some states cannot meet common standards or expectations because of their underdevelopment, it becomes an international problem and not only a domestic problem or somebody else's problem. This is a major change from the past when most non-Western political systems either were outside the state system and operated according to different standards, or were colonies of Western imperial powers that were responsible for them as a matter of domestic policy rather than foreign policy (Table 1.6).

These developments are a reminder that the world of states is a dynamic, changing world and not a static, unchanging one. The world is always in flux. In international relations, as in other spheres of human relations, nothing stands still for very long. International relations change along with everything else: politics, economics, science, technology, education, culture, and the rest. An obvious case in point is technological innovation, which has profoundly shaped international relations from the beginning and continues to shape it in significant ways that are never entirely predictable. Over the centuries new or improved military technology has had an impact on the balance of power, arms races, imperialism and colonialism, military alliances, the nature of war, and much else. Economic growth has

TABLE 1.6   Insiders and outsiders in the state system

PREVIOUS STATE SYSTEM	PRESENT STATE SYSTEM
Small core of insiders, all strong states	Virtually all states are recognized insiders, possessing formal or juridical statehood
Many outsiders: colonies	Big differences between insiders: dependencies; some strong states, some weak quasi-states

permitted greater wealth to be devoted to military budgets, and has thus provided a foundation for the development of larger, better-equipped, and more effective military forces. Scientific discoveries have made possible new technologies, such as transportation or information technologies, which have had the effect of knitting the world more closely together. Literacy, mass education, and expanded higher education have enabled governments to increase their capacity and expand their activities into more and more specialized spheres of society and economy.

It cuts both ways, of course, because highly educated people do not like being told what to think or what to do. Changing cultural values and ideas have affected not only the foreign policy of particular states but also the shape and direction of international relations. For example, the ideologies of anti-racism and anti-imperialism that were first articulated by outspoken intellectuals in Western countries eventually undermined Western overseas empires in Asia and Africa, and helped bring about the decolonization process by making the moral justification for colonialism increasingly difficult and eventually impossible.

Examples of the impact of social change on international relations are almost endless in their number and variety. The relationship is undoubtedly reversible: the state system also has an impact on society, economy, science, technology, education, culture, and the rest. For example, it has been compellingly argued that it was the development of a state system in Europe that was decisive in propelling that continent ahead of all other continents during the modern era. The competition of the independent European states within their state system—their military competition, their economic competition, their scientific and technological competition—catapulted those states ahead of non-European political systems which were not spurred by the same degree of competition. One scholar has made the point as follows: 'The states of Europe . . . were surrounded by actual or potential competitors. If the government of one were lax, it impaired its own prestige and military security . . . The state system was an insurance against economic and technological stagnation' (Jones 1981: 104–26). We should not conclude, therefore, that the state system merely reacts to change; it is also a cause of change.

The fact of social change raises a more fundamental question. At some point, should we expect states to change so much that they are no longer states in the sense discussed here (see web links 1.21, 1.25, 1.26, and 1.27)? For example, if the process of economic globalization continues and makes the world one single marketplace and one single production site, will the state system then be obsolete? We have in mind the following activities which might bypass states: ever-increasing international trade and investment; expanding multinational business activity; enlarged NGO activities; increasing regional and global communications; the growth of the Internet; expanding and ever-extending transportation networks; exploding travel and tourism; massive human migration; cumulative environmental pollution; expanded regional integration; the global expansion of science and technology; continuous downsizing of government; multiplying privatization; and other activities that have the effect of increasing interdependence across borders.

Or will sovereign states and the state system find ways of adapting to those social changes, just as they have adapted time and again to other major changes during the past 350 years? Some of those changes were just as fundamental: the scientific revolution of the seventeenth century; the Enlightenment of the eighteenth century; the encounter of Western and non-Western civilizations over the course of several centuries; the growth of Western imperialism and colonialism; the Industrial Revolution of the eighteenth and nineteenth centuries; the rise and spread of nationalism in the nineteenth and twentieth centuries (see web link 1.30); the revolution of anti-colonialism and decolonization in the twentieth century; the spread of mass public education; the growth of the welfare state; the control of disease, the spread of public health, the increase in life expectancy; and much else. These are some of the most fundamental questions of contemporary IR scholarship, and we should keep them in mind when we speculate about the future of the state system.

Conclusion

The state system was European in the first instance. During the era of Western imperialism, the rest of the world came to be dominated by Europeans and Americans, either politically or economically or both. Only with Asian and African decolonization, after the Second World War, did the state system become a global institution. The globalization of the state system vastly increased the variety of its member states and consequently its diversity. The most important difference is between strong states with a high level of empirical statehood and weak quasi-states, which have formal sovereignty but very little substantial statehood. In other words, decolonization contributed to a huge and deep internal division in the state system between the rich North and the poor South; i.e., between developed countries at the centre, which dominate the system politically and economically, and underdeveloped countries at the peripheries, which have limited political and economic influence.

Recently, this divergence between developed and underdeveloped countries has taken a more complex and worrying turn. Failed states have emerged, particularly in the Middle East and Africa, which have had the unintended effect of setting the foreign policy and military policy agendas of advanced countries. The erosion and sometimes collapse of government power and authority in these areas has created vacuums of power and authority. That has set the stage for the emergence of armed terrorist organizations that are particularly hostile not only to their own governments, or Western governments, but also to the very notion of modern, enlightened, and humane government itself. That was first evident in the so-called war on terror waged by the United States and its allies in Iraq and Afghanistan. An unintended effect of those wars—and others in the Horn of Africa, North Africa, and West Africa—has been the emergence of more extreme forms of terrorism.

The most extreme by far has been the rise of ISIL, the Islamic State of Iraq and the Levant (Syria). This is an acutely violent and barbaric form of terrorism, but also a more capable and determined form that has targeted the very foundations of modern statehood and civil society by employing the most shocking methods and tactics imaginable. Their murderous rampages against innocent populations, including children, their cruel public beheadings of civilian captives, their apparent callous indifference to the suffering they cause, all that and much more has shocked the conscience of people all over the world. More than that, it has also provoked some very dissimilar governments to collaborate and take concerted political, diplomatic, and military action against them. At the time of writing, we are witnessing what may truly become an anti-terrorist war by both Western and non-Western states against ISIL. This new form of barbarism reminds us of the basic values that states and the state system exist to defend. International relations is, of course, about power. But terrorism reveals that there is more to it than that. People expect states to uphold certain key values: security, freedom, order, justice, and welfare. States do not always defend them. Some states assault those values at certain times or in certain places. Hitler, the Japanese military dictatorship, and Stalin massively assaulted them during the Second World War. But the values remain. IR scholarship must therefore focus on them. It is, therefore, ironic that ISIL calls itself a 'state', while it is in fact not only a non-state actor of a particularly violent and malevolent kind, but also an actor that is waging its terrorist war against the modern state system itself. That is indicated not least by the alarmed reaction to it of a great many states, both Western and non-Western, and by their determination to do whatever may be necessary to defeat it. This recent episode reveals, as clearly as any episode could, the values that are associated with the modern state and the state system and which they are prepared to defend, if they have to, by means of armed force.

This leads to the larger issue of whether the state system is worth upholding and defending or whether it ought to be replaced by another system. IR theories are not in agreement on this issue; but the discipline of IR is based on the conviction that sovereign states and their development are of crucial importance for understanding how basic values of human life are being, or not being, provided to people around the world.

The following chapters will introduce the theoretical traditions of IR in further detail. Whereas this chapter has concerned the actual development of states and the state system, the next chapter will focus on how IR as an academic discipline has evolved over time.

KEY POINTS

- The main reason why we should study IR is the fact that the entire population of the world is living in independent states. Together, those states form a global state system.

- The core values that states are expected to uphold are security, freedom, order, justice, and welfare. Many states promote such values; some do not.

- Traditional or classical IR scholars generally hold a positive view of states as necessary and desirable. Revisionist scholars view them more negatively as problematical, even harmful.

- The system of sovereign states emerged in Europe at the start of the modern era, in the sixteenth century. Medieval political authority was dispersed; modern political authority is centralized, residing in the government and the head of state.

- The state system was first European; now it is global. The global state system contains states of very different types: great powers and small states; strong, substantial states and weak quasi-states.

- There is a link between the expansion of the state system and the establishment of a world market and a global economy. Some developing countries have benefitted from integration into the global economy; others remain poor and underdeveloped.

- Economic globalization and other developments challenge the sovereign state. We cannot know for certain whether the state system is now becoming obsolete, or whether states will find ways of adapting to new challenges.

- States and the state system not only uphold certain values, they also embody them.

QUESTIONS

- What is a state? Why do we have them? What is a state system?

- When did independent states and the modern system of states emerge? What is the difference between a medieval and a modern system of political authority?

- What are two different interpretations of Westphalia?

- Why did the modern state and state system emerge in Europe and not somewhere else?

- We expect states to sustain a number of core values: security, freedom, order, justice, and welfare. Do states meet our expectations?

- Should we strive to preserve the system of sovereign states? Why or why not?

- Explain the main differences between strong, substantial states and weak quasi-states; great powers and small powers. Why is there such diversity in the state system?

- Does it make sense to view modern terrorism as an attack on the state system itself?

- What are some practical ways that states sustain the core value of security?

→ GUIDE TO FURTHER READING

Bull, H. and Watson, A. (eds) (1984). *The Expansion of International Society*. Oxford: Clarendon Press.

Darwin, J. (2007). *After Tamerlane: The Global History of Empire*. London: Allen Lane.

Fukuyama, F. (2014). *Political Order and Political Decay. From the Industrial Revolution to the Globalization of Democracy*. London: Profile Books.

Osiander, A. (1994). *The States System of Europe, 1640–1990*. Oxford: Clarendon Press.

Wallerstein, I. (1974). *The Modern World System*. New York: Academic Press.

Watson, A. (1992). *The Evolution of International Society*. London: Routledge.

⊕ WEB LINKS

Web links mentioned in the chapter, together with additional material including a case-study on the relationship between history and theory, can be found on the Online Resource Centre that accompanies this book.

www.oxfordtextbooks.co.uk/orc/jackson_sorensen6e/

CHAPTER 2

IR as an Academic Subject

▌ Summary

This chapter shows how thinking about **international relations (IR)** has evolved since IR became an academic subject around the time of the First World War. Theoretical approaches are a product of their time: they address those problems of international relations that are seen as the most important ones in their day. The established traditions deal, nonetheless, with international problems that are of lasting significance: war and peace, conflict and cooperation, wealth and poverty, and development and underdevelopment. In this chapter, we shall focus on four established IR traditions. They are **realism**, **liberalism**, **International Society**, and **International Political Economy (IPE)**. We shall also introduce some recent, alternative approaches that challenge the established traditions.

Introduction

The traditional core of IR has to do with issues concerning the development and change of sovereign statehood in the context of the larger system or society of states. This focus on states and the relations of states helps explain why war and peace is a central problem of traditional IR theory. However, contemporary IR is concerned not only with political relations between states but also with a host of other subjects: economic interdependence, human rights, transnational corporations, international organizations, the environment, gender inequalities, economic development, terrorism, and so forth. For this reason, some scholars prefer the label 'International Studies' or 'World Politics'. We shall stay with the label 'International Relations' but we shall interpret it to cover the broad range of issues.

There are four major classical theoretical traditions in IR: realism, liberalism, International Society, and IPE. In addition, there is a more diverse group of alternative approaches which have gained prominence in recent years. The most important of these are **social constructivism** and **post-positivist approaches**. The main task of this book is to present and discuss all these theories. In this chapter, we shall examine IR as an evolving academic subject. IR thinking has developed through distinct phases, characterized by specific debates between groups of scholars. At most times during the twentieth century, there has been a dominant way of thinking about IR and a major challenge to that way of thinking. Those debates and dialogues are the main subject of this chapter.

There are a great many different theories in IR. They can be classified in a number of ways; what we call a 'main theoretical tradition' is not an objective entity. If you put four IR theorists in a room you will easily get ten different ways of organizing theory, and there will also be disagreement about which theories are relevant in the first place! At the same time, we have to group theories into main categories. Without drawing together main paths in the development of IR thinking, we are stuck with a large number of individual contributions, pointing in different and sometimes rather confusing directions. But the reader should always be wary of selections and classifications, including the ones offered in this book. They are analytical tools created to achieve overview and clarity; they are not objective truths that can be taken for granted.

Of course, IR thinking is influenced by other academic subjects, such as philosophy, history, law, sociology, and economics. IR thinking also responds to historical and contemporary developments in the real world. The two world wars, the Cold War between East and West, the emergence of close economic cooperation between Western states, and the persistent development gap between North and South are examples of real-world events and problems that stimulated IR scholarship in the twentieth century. And we can be certain that future events and episodes will provoke new IR thinking in the years to come: that is already evident with regard to the end of the Cold War, which is stimulating a variety of innovative IR thought at the present time. The terrorist attacks that began on 11 September 2001 are another major challenge to IR thinking; the financial crisis that broke in 2008 and the current conflicts in the Middle East are other examples (see Figure 2.1).

There have been three major debates since IR became an academic subject at the end of the First World War, and we are now in the early stages of a fourth. The first major debate was between utopian liberalism and realism; the second between traditional approaches and

FIGURE 2.1   The development of IR thinking

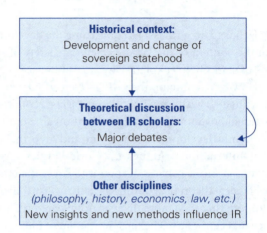

Historical context:
Development and change of
sovereign statehood

Theoretical discussion
between IR scholars:
Major debates

Other disciplines
(philosophy, history, economics, law, etc.)
New insights and new methods influence IR

behaviouralism; the third between neorealism/neoliberalism and neo-**Marxism**. The emerging fourth debate is between established traditions and **post-positivist** alternatives. We shall review these major debates in this chapter because they provide us with a map of the way the academic subject of IR has developed over the past century. We need to become familiar with that map in order to comprehend IR as a dynamic academic subject that continues to evolve, and to see the directions of that continuing evolution of IR thought.

Utopian Liberalism: The Early Study of IR

The decisive push to set up a separate academic subject of IR was occasioned by the First World War (1914–18), which produced millions of casualties; it was driven by a widely felt determination never to allow human suffering on such a scale to happen again. That desire not to repeat the same catastrophic mistake required coming to grips with the problem of total warfare between the mechanized armies of modern industrial states which were capable of inflicting mass destruction. The war was a devastating experience for millions of people, and particularly for young soldiers who were conscripted into the armies and were slaughtered by the million, especially in the trench warfare on the Western Front. Some battles resulted in tens of thousands and sometimes a hundred thousand casualties or even more. The famous Battle of the Somme (France) in July–August 1916 inflicted casualties on that scale. It was referred to as a 'bloody holocaust' (Gilbert 1995: 258). The justification for all that death and destruction became less and less clear as the war years went by, as the number of casualties kept on increasing to historically unprecedented levels, and as the war failed to disclose any rational purpose. On first learning of the war's devastation, one man who had been isolated was quoted as follows: 'Millions are being killed. Europe is mad. The world is mad' (Gilbert 1995: 257). That has come to be our historical image of the First World War (see web link 2.01).

Why was it that the war began in the first place? And why did Britain, France, Russia, Germany, Austria, Turkey, and other powers persist in waging war in the face of such slaughter and with diminishing chances of gaining anything of real value from the conflict? These questions and others like them are not easy to answer. But the first dominant academic theory of IR was shaped by the search for answers to them. The answers that the new discipline of IR came up with were profoundly influenced by liberal ideas. For liberal thinkers, the First World War was in no small measure attributable to the egoistic and short-sighted calculations and miscalculations of autocratic leaders in the heavily militarized countries involved, especially Germany and Austria.

Unrestrained by democratic institutions and under pressure from their generals, these leaders were inclined to take the fatal decisions that led their countries into war (see Box 2.1). And the democratic leaders of France and Britain, in turn, allowed themselves to be drawn into the conflict by an interlocking system of military alliances. The alliances were intended to keep the peace, but they propelled *all* the European powers into war once *any* major power or alliance embarked on war. When Austria and Germany confronted Serbia with armed force, Russia was duty-bound to come to the aid of Serbia, and Britain and France were treaty-bound to support Russia. For the liberal thinkers of that time the 'obsolete' theory of the balance of power and the alliance system had to be fundamentally reformed so that such a calamity would never happen again (see Box 2.2).

BOX 2.1   Leadership misperceptions and war

It is my conviction that during the descent into the abyss, the perceptions of statesmen and generals were absolutely crucial. All the participants suffered from greater or lesser distortions in their images of themselves. They tended to see themselves as honorable, virtuous, and pure, and the adversary as diabolical. All the nations on the brink of the disaster expected the worst from their potential adversaries. They saw their own options as limited by necessity or 'fate', whereas those of the adversary were characterized by many choices. Everywhere, there was a total absence of empathy; no one could see the situation from another point of view. The character of each of the leaders was badly flawed by arrogance, stupidity, carelessness, or weakness.

Stoessinger (2010: 21–3)

BOX 2.2   Making the world safe for democracy

We are glad now that we see the facts with no veil of false pretense about them, to fight thus for the ultimate peace of the world and for the liberation of its peoples, the German peoples included: for the rights of nations great and small and the privilege of men everywhere to choose their way of life and of obedience. The world must be made safe for democracy. We have no selfish ends to serve. We desire no conquest, no dominion. We seek no indemnities for ourselves, no material compensation for the sacrifices we shall freely make. We are but one of the champions of the right of mankind. We shall be satisfied when those rights have been made as secure as the faith and the freedom of nations can make them.

Woodrow Wilson, from 'Address to Congress Asking for Declaration of War', 1917, quoted from Vasquez (1996: 35–40)

Why was early academic IR influenced by liberalism? That is a big question, but there are a few important points that we should keep in mind in seeking an answer. The United States was eventually drawn into the war in 1917. Its military intervention decisively determined the outcome of the war: it guaranteed victory for the democratic allies (US, Britain, France) and defeat for the autocratic central powers (Germany, Austria, Turkey). At that time, the United States had a president, Woodrow Wilson, who had been a university professor of political science and who saw it as his main mission to bring liberal democratic values to Europe and to the rest of the world. Only in that way, he believed, could another great war be prevented. In short, the liberal way of thinking had a solid political backing from the most powerful state in the international system at the time. Academic IR developed first and most strongly in the two leading liberal-democratic states: the United States and Great Britain. Liberal thinkers had some clear ideas and strong beliefs about how to avoid major disasters in the future; e.g., by reforming the international system, and also by reforming the domestic structures of autocratic countries.

President Wilson had a vision of making the world 'safe for democracy' that had wide appeal for ordinary people. It was formulated in a fourteen-point programme delivered in an address to Congress in January 1918 (see web link 2.02). He was awarded the Nobel Peace Prize in 1919. His ideas influenced the Paris Peace Conference which followed the end of hostilities and tried to institute a new international order based on liberal ideas. Wilson's peace programme calls for an end to secret diplomacy: agreements must be open to public scrutiny. There must be freedom of navigation on the seas and barriers to free trade should be removed. Armaments should be reduced to 'the lowest point consistent with domestic safety'. Colonial and territorial claims should be settled with regard to the principle of self-determination of peoples. Finally, 'a general association of nations must be formed under specific covenants for the purpose of affording mutual guarantees of political independence and territorial integrity of great and small nations alike' (Vasquez 1996: 40). This latter point is Wilson's call to establish a League of Nations (see web link 2.05), which was instituted by the Paris Peace Conference in 1919.

Two major points in Wilson's ideas for a more peaceful world deserve special emphasis (Brown and Ainley 2009). The first concerns his promotion of democracy and self-determination. Behind this point is the liberal conviction that democratic governments do not and will not go to war against each other. It was Wilson's hope that the growth of liberal democracy in Europe would put an end to autocratic and warlike leaders and put peaceful governments in their place. Liberal democracy should therefore be strongly encouraged. The second major point in Wilson's programme concerned the creation of an international organization that would put relations between states on a firmer institutional foundation than the realist notions of the Concert of Europe and the balance of power had provided in the past. Instead, international relations would be regulated by a set of common rules of international law. In essence, that was Wilson's concept of the League of Nations. The idea that international institutions can promote peaceful cooperation among states is a basic element of liberal thinking; so is the notion about a relationship between liberal democracy and peace. We shall return to both ideas in Chapter 4.

Wilsonian idealism can be summarized as follows. It is the conviction that, through a rational and intelligently designed international organization, it should be possible to put an end to war and to achieve more or less permanent peace. The claim is not that it will be possible to do away with states and statespeople, foreign ministries, armed forces, and other agents and instruments of international conflict. Rather, the claim is that it is possible to tame states and statespeople by subjecting them to the appropriate international organizations, institutions, and laws. The argument liberal idealists make is that traditional power politics—so-called 'Realpolitik'—is a 'jungle', so to speak, where dangerous beasts roam and the strong and cunning rule; whereas under the League of Nations the beasts are put into cages reinforced by the restraints of international organization; i.e., into a kind of 'zoo'. Wilson's liberal faith that an international organization could be created that could guarantee permanent peace is clearly reminiscent of the thought of the most famous classical liberal IR theorist: Immanuel Kant in his pamphlet *Perpetual Peace* (1795).

Norman Angell (see web link 2.06) is another prominent liberal idealist of the same era. In 1909, Angell published a book entitled *The Great Illusion*. The illusion is that many statespeople still believe that war serves profitable purposes; that success in war is beneficial for the winner. Angell argues that exactly the opposite is the case: in modern times territorial conquest is extremely expensive and politically divisive because it severely disrupts international commerce. The general argument set forth by Angell is a forerunner of later liberal thinking about modernization and economic interdependence. Modernization demands that states have a growing need of things 'from "outside"—credit, or inventions, or markets or materials not contained in sufficient quantity in the country itself' (Navari 1989: 345). Rising interdependence, in turn, effects a change in relations between states. War and the use of force become of decreasing importance, and international law develops in response to the need for a framework to regulate high levels of interdependence. In sum, modernization and interdependence involve a process of change and progress which renders war and the use of force increasingly obsolete.

The thinking of Wilson and Angell is based on a liberal view of human beings and human society: human beings are rational, and when they apply reason to international relations they can set up organizations for the benefit of all. Public opinion is a constructive force; removing secret diplomacy in dealings between states and, instead, opening diplomacy to public scrutiny assures that agreements will be sensible and fair. These ideas had some success in the 1920s; the League of Nations was indeed established and the great powers took some further steps to assure each other of their peaceful intentions. The high point of these efforts came with the Kellogg–Briand pact of 1928, which practically all countries signed. The pact was an international agreement to abolish war; only in extreme cases of self-defence could war be justified. In short, liberal ideas dominated in the first phase of academic IR. In the international relations of the 1920s, these ideas could claim some success.

Why is it, then, that we tend to refer to such ideas by the somewhat pejorative term of 'utopian liberalism', indicating that these liberal arguments were little more than the projection of wishful thinking? One plausible answer is to be found in the political and economic developments of the 1920s and 1930s. Liberal democracy suffered hard blows with the growth of fascist dictatorship in Italy and Spain, and Nazism in Germany. Authoritarianism also increased in many of the new states of Central and Eastern Europe—for example, Poland, Hungary, Romania, and Yugoslavia—that were brought into existence as a result of the First World War and the Paris Peace Conference and were supposed to become democracies. Thus, contrary to Wilson's hopes for the spread of democratic civilization, it failed to happen. In many cases, what actually happened was the spread of the very sort of state that he believed provoked war: autocratic, authoritarian, and militaristic states. At the same time, liberal states themselves were not democratic role models in every way: several of them held on to vast empires, with colonies kept under coercive control (Long and Schmidt (eds) 2005). Woodrow Wilson himself was a staunch defender of racial hierarchy in the United States (Skowronek 2006).

The League of Nations never became the strong international organization that liberals hoped would restrain powerful and aggressively disposed states. Germany and Russia initially failed to sign the Versailles Peace Treaty, and their relationship to the League was always strained. Germany joined the League in 1926 but left in 1933. Japan also left at that time, while embarking on war in Manchuria. Russia finally joined in 1934, and was expelled in 1940 because of the war with Finland. But by that time the League was effectively dead. Although Britain and France were members from the start, they never regarded the League as an important institution and refused to shape their foreign policies with League criteria in mind. Most devastating, however, was the refusal of the United States Senate to ratify the covenant of the League (see Box 2.3). Isolationism had a long tradition in US foreign policy, and many American politicians were isolationists even if President Wilson was not; they did not want to involve their country in the entangling and murky affairs of Europe. So, much to Wilson's chagrin, the strongest state in the international system—his own—did not join the League. With a number of important states outside the League, including the most important, and with the two major powers inside the organization lacking any real commitment to it, the League never achieved the central position marked out for it in Wilson's blueprint.

BOX 2.3   The League of Nations

The League of Nations (1920–46) contained three main organs: the Council (fifteen members including France, the United Kingdom and the Soviet Union as permanent members) which met three times a year; the Assembly (all members) which met annually, and a Secretariat. All decisions had to be by unanimous vote. The underlying philosophy of the League was the principle of collective security which meant that the international community had a duty to intervene in international conflicts: it also meant that parties to a dispute should submit their grievances to the League. The centre-piece of the [League] Covenant was Article 16, which empowered the League to institute economic or military sanctions against a recalcitrant state. In essence, though, it was left to each member to decide whether or not a breach of the Covenant had occurred and so whether or not to apply sanctions.

Evans and Newnham (1992: 176)

FIGURE 2.2   Changes in industrial production 1929–30: contraction of world trade
Total imports of 75 countries 1929–33 (million gold US$)

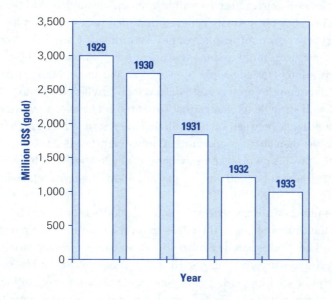

Based on Kindleberger (1973: 280)

Norman Angell's high hopes for a smooth process of modernization and interdependence also foundered on the harsh realities of the 1930s. The Wall Street crash of October 1929 marked the beginning of a severe economic crisis in Western countries that would last until the Second World War and would involve severe measures of economic protectionism. World trade shrank dramatically, and industrial production in developed countries declined rapidly to become only one-third of what it was a few years before (see Figure 2.2). In ironic contrast to Angell's vision, it was each country for itself, each country trying as best it could to look after its own interests, if necessary to the detriment of others—the 'jungle' rather than the 'zoo'. The historical stage was being set for a less hopeful and more pessimistic understanding of international relations (see web link 2.08).

Realism and the Twenty Years' Crisis

Liberal idealism was not a good intellectual guide to international relations in the 1930s. Interdependence did not produce peaceful cooperation; the League of Nations was helpless in the face of the expansionist power politics conducted by the authoritarian regimes in Germany, Italy, and Japan. Academic IR began to speak the classical realist language of Thucydides, Machiavelli, and Hobbes in which the grammar and the vocabulary of power was central.

The most comprehensive and penetrating critique of liberal idealism was that of E. H. Carr, a British IR scholar. In *The Twenty Years' Crisis* (1964 [1939]) Carr argued that liberal IR thinkers profoundly misread the facts of history and misunderstood the nature of international relations. They erroneously believed that such relations could be based on a harmony of interest between countries and people. According to Carr, the correct starting point is the opposite one: we should assume that there are profound conflicts of interest both between countries and between people. Some people and some countries are better off than others. They will attempt to preserve and defend their privileged position. The underdogs, the 'have-nots', will struggle to change that situation. International relations is, in a basic sense, about the struggle between such conflicting interests and desires. That is why IR is far more about conflict than about cooperation. Carr astutely labelled the liberal position 'utopian' as a contrast to his own position, which he labelled 'realist', thus implying that his approach was the more sober and correct analysis of international relations (see web links 2.10 and 2.11).

The other significant realist statement from this period was produced by a German scholar who fled to the United States in the 1930s to escape from the Nazi regime in Germany: Hans J. Morgenthau. More than any other European émigré scholar Morgenthau brought realism to the US, and with great success. His *Politics among Nations: The Struggle for Power and Peace*, first published in 1948, was for several decades the most influential American book on IR (Morgenthau 1960). There were other authors writing along the same realist lines: among the most important were Reinhold Niebuhr, George Kennan, and Arnold Wolfers. But Morgenthau gave the clearest summary of realism's core claims and had the widest appeal to IR scholars and their students (see web link 2.12).

For Morgenthau, human nature was at the base of international relations. And humans were self-interested and power-seeking and that could easily result in aggression. In the late 1930s, it was not difficult to find evidence to support such a view. Hitler's Germany, Mussolini's Italy, and Imperial Japan pursued blatantly aggressive foreign policies aimed at conflict, not cooperation. Armed struggle for the creation of *Lebensraum*, of a larger and stronger Germany, was at the core of Hitler's political programme. Furthermore, and ironically from a liberal perspective, both Hitler and Mussolini enjoyed widespread popular support, despite the fact that they were autocratic and even tyrannical leaders. Even the most horrendous component of Hitler's political project—elimination of the Jews—enjoyed much popular support (Goldhagen 1996).

Why should international relations be egoistic and aggressive? Observing the growth of fascism in the 1930s, Einstein wrote to Freud that there must be 'a human lust for hatred and destruction' (Ebenstein 1951: 802–4). Freud confirmed that such an aggressive impulse did indeed exist, and he remained deeply sceptical about the possibilities for taming it (see Box 2.4).

Another possible explanation draws on Christian religion. According to the Bible, humans have been endowed with original sin and a temptation for evil ever since Adam and Eve were thrown out of Paradise. The first murder in history is Cain's killing of his brother Abel out of pure envy. Human nature is plain bad; that is the starting point for realist analysis.

BOX 2.4	Freud's reply to Einstein

Freud's reply [to Einstein] drew on his theoretical work … We see this necessity for repression, Freud explained, in the imposition of discipline by parents over children, by institutions over individuals, and by the state over society. From this he deducted, and Einstein agreed, that a world government was needed to impose the necessary discipline on the otherwise dangerously anarchic international system. But whereas Einstein became a supporter of the United World Federalists and other groups working toward the establishment of world government, Freud doubted that humans have the requisite capacity to overcome their irrational attachments to national and religious groups. The father of psychoanalysis, therefore, remained deeply pessimistic about the prospects for fundamentally reducing the role of war in world politics.

Brown (1994: 10–11)

The second major element in the realist view concerns the nature of international relations. 'International politics, like all politics, is a struggle for power. Whatever the ultimate aims of international politics, power is always the immediate aim' (Morgenthau 1960: 29). There is no world government. On the contrary, there is a system of sovereign and armed states facing each other. World politics is an international anarchy. The 1930s and 1940s appeared to confirm this proposition. International relations was a struggle for power and for survival. The quest for power certainly characterized the foreign policies of Germany, Italy, and Japan. The same struggle, in response, applied to the Allied side during the Second World War. Britain, France, and the United States were the 'haves' in Carr's terms, the satisfied powers who wanted to hold on to what they already had, and Germany, Italy, and Japan were the 'have-nots'. So it was only natural, according to realist thinking, that the 'have-nots' would try and redress the international balance through the use of force.

Following realist analysis, the sole appropriate response to such attempts is the creation of countervailing power and the intelligent utilization of that power to provide for national defence and to deter potential aggressors. In other words, it was essential to maintain an effective balance of power as the only way to preserve peace and prevent war. This is a view of international politics that denies that it is possible to reorganize the 'jungle' into a 'zoo'. The strongest animals will never allow themselves to be captured and put in cages. Following the First World War, Germany was seen as proof of that truth. The League of Nations failed to put Germany in a cage. It took a world war, millions of casualties, heroic sacrifice, and vast material resources finally to defeat the challenges from Nazi Germany, Fascist Italy, and Imperial Japan. All of that might have been avoided if a realistic foreign policy based on the principle of countervailing power had been followed by Britain, France, and the United States right from the start of Germany's, Italy's, and Japan's sabre-rattling. Negotiations and diplomacy by themselves can never bring security and survival in world politics.

The third major component in the realist view is a cyclical view of history. Contrary to the optimistic liberal view that qualitative change for the better is possible, realism stresses continuity and repetition. Each new generation tends to make the same sort of mistake as previous generations. Any change in this situation is highly unlikely. As long as sovereign states are the dominant form of political organization, power politics will continue and states will have to look after their security and prepare for war. In other words, the Second World War was no extraordinary event; neither was the First World War. Sovereign states can live in peace with each other for long periods when there is a stable balance of power. But every now and then, that precarious balance will break down and war is likely to follow. There can, of course, be many different causes of such breakdown. Some realist scholars think that the Paris Peace Conference of 1919 contained the seeds of the Second World War because of the harsh conditions that the peace treaty imposed on Germany. But domestic developments in Germany, the emergence of Hitler, and many other factors are also relevant in accounting for that war.

In sum, the classical realism of Carr and Morgenthau combines a pessimistic view of human nature with a notion of power politics between states which exists in an international anarchy. They see no prospects of change in that situation; for classical realists, independent states in an anarchic international system are a permanent feature of international relations. The classical realist analysis appeared to capture the essentials of European politics in the 1930s and world politics in the 1940s far better than liberal optimism. When international relations took the shape of an East–West confrontation, or Cold War, after 1945 realism again appeared to be the best approach for making sense of what was going on.

The utopian liberalism of the 1920s and the realism of the 1930s–1950s represent the two contending positions in the first major debate in IR (see Figure 2.3).

The first major debate was clearly won by Carr, Morgenthau, and the other realist thinkers. Realism became the dominant way of thinking about international relations, not only among scholars, but also among politicians and diplomats. Morgenthau's summary of realism in his 1948 book became the standard introduction to IR in the 1950s and 1960s. Yet it is important to emphasize that liberalism did not disappear. Many liberals conceded that realism was the better guide to international relations in the 1930s and 1940s, but they saw this as an extreme and abnormal historical period. Liberals, of course, rejected the deeply pessimistic realist idea that humans were 'plain bad' (Wight 1991: 25) and they had some strong counter-arguments to that effect, as we shall see in Chapter 4. Finally, the post-war period was not only about a struggle for power and survival between the United States and the Soviet Union and their political–military alliances. It was also about cooperation and international institutions, such as the United Nations and its many special organizations. Although realism had won the first debate, there were still competing theories in the discipline that refused to accept permanent defeat.

FIGURE 2.3   First major debate in IR

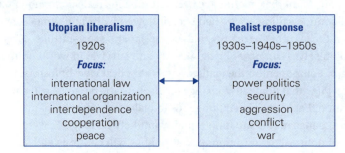

Utopian liberalism
1920s

Focus:

international law
international organization
interdependence
cooperation
peace

Realist response
1930s–1940s–1950s

Focus:

power politics
security
aggression
conflict
war

The Voice of Behaviouralism in IR

The second major debate in IR concerns methodology. In order to understand how that debate emerged, it is necessary to be aware of the fact that the first generations of IR scholars were trained as historians or academic lawyers, or were former diplomats or journalists. They often brought a humanistic and historical approach to the study of IR. This approach is rooted in philosophy, history, and law, and is characterized 'above all by explicit reliance upon the exercise of judgment' (Bull 1969). Locating judgement at the heart of international theory serves to emphasize the normative character of the subject which at its core involves some profoundly difficult moral questions that neither politicians nor diplomats nor anyone else who is involved can escape, such as the deployment of nuclear weapons and their justified uses, military intervention in independent states, and so forth. That is because the deployment and use of power in human relations, military power especially, always has to be justified and can thus never be divorced completely from normative considerations. This way of studying IR is usually referred to as the traditional, or classical, approach.

After the Second World War, the academic discipline of IR expanded rapidly. That was particularly the case in the United States, where government agencies and private foundations were willing to support 'scientific' IR research which they could justify as being in the national interest. That support produced a new generation of IR scholars who adopted a rigorous methodological approach. They were usually trained in political science, economics, or other social sciences, sometimes in mathematics and the natural sciences, rather than diplomatic history, international law, or political philosophy. These new IR scholars thus had a very different academic background and equally different ideas concerning how IR should be studied. These new ideas came to be summarized under the term 'behaviouralism' (see web link 2.14), which signified not so much a new theory as a novel methodology which endeavoured to be 'scientific' in the natural-science meaning of that term (see Box 2.5).

BOX 2.5	Behaviouralist science in brief

Once the investigator has mastered the existing knowledge, and has organized it for his purposes, he pleads a 'meaningful ignorance': 'Here is what I know; what do I not know that is worth knowing?' Once an area has been selected for investigation, the questions should be posed as clearly as possible, and it is here that quantification can prove useful, provided that mathematical tools are combined with carefully constructed taxonomic schemes. Surveying the field of international relations, or any sector of it, we see many disparate elements … wondering whether there may be any significant relationships between A and B, or between B and C. By a process which we are compelled to call 'intuition' … we perceive a possible correlation, hitherto unsuspected or not firmly known, between two or more elements. At this point, we have the ingredients of a hypothesis which can be expressed in measurable referents, and which, if validated, would be both explanatory and predictive.

Dougherty and Pfaltzgraff (1971: 36–7)

Just as scholars of science are able to formulate objective and verifiable 'laws' to explain the physical world, the ambition of behaviouralists in IR is to do the same for the world of international relations. The main task is to collect empirical data about international relations, preferably large amounts of data, which can then be used for measurement, classification, generalization, and, ultimately, the validation of hypotheses; i.e., scientifically explained patterns of behaviour. Behaviouralism is thus not a new IR theory; it is a new method of studying IR. Behaviouralism is more interested in observable facts and measurable data, in precise calculation, and the collection of data in order to find recurring behavioural patterns, the 'laws' of international relations. According to behaviouralists, facts are separate from values. Unlike facts, values cannot be explained scientifically. The behaviouralists were therefore inclined to study facts while ignoring values. The scientific procedure that behaviouralists support is laid out in Box 2.6.

The two methodological approaches to IR briefly described in the previous section, the traditional and the behavioural, are clearly very different. The traditional approach is a holistic one that accepts the complexity of the human world, sees international relations as part of the human world, and seeks to understand it in a humanistic way by getting *inside* it. That involves imaginatively entering into the role of statespeople, attempting to understand the moral dilemmas in their foreign policies, and appreciating the basic values involved, such as security, order, freedom, and justice. To approach IR in that traditional way involves the scholar in understanding the history and practice of diplomacy, the history and role of international law, the political theory of the sovereign state, and so forth. IR is in that view a broadly humanistic subject; it is not and could never be a strictly scientific or narrowly technical subject.

The other approach, behaviouralism, has no place for morality or ethics in the study of IR because that involves values, and values cannot be studied objectively; i.e., scientifically. Behaviouralism thus raises a fundamental question which continues to be discussed today: can we formulate scientific laws about international relations (and about the social world, the world of human relations, in general)? Critics emphasize what they see as a major mistake in that method: the mistake of treating human relations as an external phenomenon in the same general category as nature so that the theorist stands *outside* the subject—like an anatomist dissecting a cadaver. The anti-behaviouralists hold that the theorist of human affairs is a human being who can never divorce himself or herself completely from human

---

BOX 2.6   The scientific procedure of behaviouralists

The hypothesis must be validated through testing. This demands the construction of a verifying experiment or the gathering of empirical data in other ways … The results of the data-gathering effort are carefully observed, recorded and analyzed, after which the hypothesis is discarded, modified, reformulated or confirmed. Findings are published and others are invited to duplicate this knowledge-discovering adventure, and to confirm or deny. This, very roughly, is what we usually mean by 'the scientific method'.

Dougherty and Pfaltzgraff (1971: 37)

FIGURE 2.4   Second major debate in IR

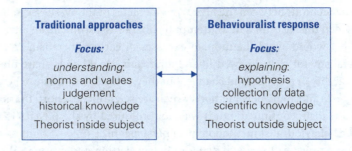

relations: he or she is always *inside* the subject (Hollis and Smith 1990; Jackson 2000). The scholar can strive for detachment and moral neutrality but can never succeed completely. Some scholars attempt to reconcile these approaches: they seek to be historically conscious about IR as a sphere of human relations while also trying to come up with general models that seek to explain and not merely understand world politics. Morgenthau might be an example of that. In studying the moral dilemmas of foreign policy, he is in the traditionalist camp; yet he also sets forth general 'laws of politics' which are supposed to apply at all times in all places, and that would appear to put him in the behaviouralist camp.

The behaviouralists did not win the second major debate in IR, but neither did the traditionalists (see Figure 2.4). After a few years of vigorous controversy, the second great debate petered out. A compromise resulted which has been portrayed as 'different ends of a continuum of scholarship rather than completely different games... Each type of effort can inform and enrich the other and can as well act as a check on the excesses endemic in each approach' (Finnegan 1972: 64). Yet behaviouralism did have a lasting effect in IR. That was largely because of the domination of the discipline after the Second World War by US scholars, the vast majority of whom supported the quantitative, scientific ambitions of behaviouralism. They also led the way in setting a research agenda focused on the role of the two superpowers, especially the United States, in the international system. That paved the way to new formulations of both realism and liberalism that were heavily influenced by behaviouralist methodologies. These new formulations—**neorealism** and **neoliberalism**—led to a replay of the first major debate under new historical and methodological conditions.

Neoliberalism: Institutions and Interdependence

Realism, having won the first major debate, remained the dominant theoretical approach in IR. The second debate, about methodology, did not immediately change that situation. After 1945, the centre of gravity in international relations was the Cold War struggle between the United States and the Soviet Union. The East–West rivalry lent itself easily to a realist interpretation of the world.

Yet during the 1950s, 1960s, and 1970s, a good deal of international relations concerned trade and investment, travel and communication, and similar issues which were especially prevalent in the relations between the liberal democracies of the West (see Table 2.1). Those relations provided the basis for a new attempt by liberals to formulate an alternative to realist thinking that would avoid the utopian excesses of earlier liberalism. We shall use the label 'neoliberalism' for that renewed liberal approach. Neoliberals share old liberal ideas about the possibility of progress and change, but they repudiate idealism. They also strive to formulate theories and apply new methods which are scientific. In short, the debate between liberalism and realism continued, but it was now coloured by the post-1945 international setting and the behaviouralist methodological persuasion.

In the 1950s, a process of regional integration was getting under way in Western Europe which caught the attention and imagination of neoliberals. By 'integration' we refer to a particularly intensive form of international cooperation. Early theorists of integration studied how certain functional activities across borders (trade, investment, etc.) offered mutually advantageous long-term cooperation. Other neoliberal theorists studied how integration fed on itself: cooperation in one transactional area paved the way for cooperation in other areas (Haas 1958; Keohane and Nye 1975) (see web link 2.21). During the 1950s and 1960s, Western Europe and Japan developed mass-consumption welfare states, as the United States had done already before the war. That development entailed a higher level of trade, communication, cultural exchange, and other relations and transactions across borders.

This provides the basis for sociological liberalism, a strand of neoliberal thinking which emphasizes the impact of these expanding cross-border activities. In the 1950s, Karl Deutsch and his associates argued that such interconnecting activities helped create common values and identities among people from different states and paved the way for peaceful, cooperative relations by making war increasingly costly and thus more unlikely. They also tried to measure the integration phenomenon scientifically (Deutsch et al. 1957).

In the 1970s, Robert Keohane and Joseph Nye further developed such ideas. They argued that relationships between Western states (including Japan) are characterized by complex interdependence: there are many forms of connections between societies in addition to the political relations of governments, including transnational links between business corporations. There is also an 'absence of hierarchy among issues'; i.e., military security does not dominate the agenda any more. Military force is no longer used as an instrument of foreign policy (Keohane and Nye 1977: 25). Complex interdependence portrays a situation that is

TABLE 2.1 OECD countries, total import/export, percentage of gross domestic product (GDP)

	1960	1970	1980	2000	2012
	%	%	%	%	%
Imports	11	13	19	23	28
Exports	11	13	18	22	28

Based on World Bank statistics

radically different from the realist picture of international relations. In Western democracies, there are other actors besides states, and violent conflict clearly is not on their international agenda. We can call this form of neoliberalism *interdependence liberalism*. Robert Keohane and Joseph Nye (1977) are among the main contributors to this line of thinking (see web link 2.22).

When there is a high degree of interdependence, states will often set up international institutions to deal with common problems. Institutions promote cooperation across international boundaries by providing information and by reducing costs. Institutions can be formal international organizations, such as the World Trade Organization (WTO) or European Union (EU) or Organization for Economic Cooperation and Development (OECD); or they can be less formal sets of agreements (often called regimes) which deal with common activities or issues, such as agreements about shipping, aviation, communication, or the environment. We can call this form of neoliberalism *institutional liberalism*. Oran Young (1986) and Robert Keohane (1989) are influential scholars in this area.

The fourth and final strand of neoliberalism—*republican liberalism*—picks up on a theme developed in earlier liberal thinking. It is the idea that liberal democracies enhance peace because they do not go to war against each other. It has been strongly influenced by the rapid spread of democratization in the world after the end of the Cold War, especially in the former Soviet satellite countries in Eastern Europe. An influential version of the theory of democratic peace was set forth by Michael Doyle (1983). Doyle finds that the democratic peace is based on three pillars: the first is peaceful conflict resolution between democratic states; the second is common values among democratic states—a common moral foundation; the final pillar is economic cooperation among democracies. Republican liberals are generally optimistic that there will be a steadily expanding 'Zone of Peace' among liberal democracies even though there may also be occasional setbacks (see web links 2.25 and 2.26).

These different strands of neoliberalism are mutually supportive in providing an overall consistent argument for more peaceful and cooperative international relations (see Table 2.2). They consequently stand as a challenge to the realist analysis of IR. In the 1970s, there was a general feeling among IR scholars that neoliberalism was on the way to becoming the dominant theoretical approach in the discipline. But a reformulation of realism by Kenneth Waltz (1979) once again tipped the balance towards realism. Neoliberal thinking could make convincing reference to relations between industrialized liberal democracies to argue its case about a more cooperative and interdependent world. But the East–West confrontation remained a stubborn feature of international relations in the 1970s and 1980s. The new reflections on realism took their cue from that historical fact.

TABLE 2.2 Variations of liberalism

THEORY	FOCUS
• Sociological liberalism	Cross-border flows, common values
• Interdependence liberalism	Transactions stimulate cooperation
• Institutional liberalism	International institutions, regimes
• Republican liberalism	Liberal democracies living in peace with each other

Neorealism: Bipolarity and Confrontation

Kenneth Waltz broke new ground in his book *Theory of International Politics* (1979), which sets forth a substantially different realist theory inspired by the scientific ambitions of behaviouralism. His theory is most often referred to as 'neorealism', and we shall employ that label. Waltz attempts to formulate 'law-like statements' about international relations that achieve scientific validity. He thus departs sharply from classical realism in showing virtually no interest in the ethics of statecraft or the moral dilemmas of foreign policy—concerns that are strongly evident in the realist writings of Morgenthau (see web links 2.30 and 2.31).

Waltz's focus is on the 'structure' of the international system and the consequences of that structure for international relations. The concept of structure is defined as follows. First, Waltz notes that the international system is anarchy; there is no worldwide government. Second, the international system is composed of like units: every state, small or large, has to perform a similar set of government functions such as national defence, tax collection, and economic regulation. However, there is one respect in which states are different and often very different: in their power, what Waltz calls their relative capabilities. Waltz thus draws a very parsimonious and abstract picture of the international system with very few elements. International relations is thus an anarchy composed of states that vary in only one important respect: their relative power. Anarchy is likely to endure, according to Waltz, because states want to preserve their autonomy.

The international system that came into existence after the Second World War was dominated by two superpowers, the United States and the Soviet Union; i.e., it was a bipolar system (see web link 2.31). The demise of the Soviet Union has resulted in a different system with several great powers but with the United States as the predominant power in the system; i.e., it is moving towards a multipolar system. Waltz does not claim that these few pieces of information about the structure of the international system can explain everything about international politics. But he believes that they can explain 'a few big and important things' (Waltz 1986: 322–47). What are they? First, great powers will always tend to balance each other. With the Soviet Union gone, the United States dominates the system. But 'balance-of-power theory leads one to predict that other countries … will try to bring American power into balance' (Waltz 1993: 52). Second, smaller and weaker states will have a tendency to align themselves with great powers in order to preserve their maximum autonomy. In making this argument, Waltz departs sharply from the classical realist argument based on human nature viewed as 'plain bad' and thus leading to conflict and confrontation. For Waltz, states are power-seeking and security conscious not because of human nature but rather because the structure of the international system compels them to be that way.

This last point is also important because it is the basis for neorealism's counter-attack against the neoliberals. Neorealists do not deny all possibilities for cooperation among states. But they do maintain that cooperating states will always strive to maximize their relative power and preserve their autonomy. In other words, just because there is cooperation, as for example in relations between industrialized liberal democracies (e.g., between the

United States and Japan), it does not mean that the neoliberal view has been vindicated. We shall return to the details of this debate in Chapter 4. Here we merely draw attention to the fact that in the 1980s, neorealism succeeded in putting neoliberalism on the defensive. Theoretical arguments were significant in this development. But historical events also played an important role. In the 1980s the confrontation between the United States and the Soviet Union reached a new level. US President Ronald Reagan referred to the Soviet Union as an 'evil empire', and in that hostile international climate, the arms race between the superpowers was sharply intensified. At about that time, the United States was also feeling increasing competitive pressure from Japan and, to some extent, from Europe too. Armed conflict between the liberal democracies was certainly not on the agenda; but there were 'trade wars' and other disputes between the Western democracies which appeared to confirm the neorealist hypothesis about competition between self-interested countries that were fundamentally concerned about their power position relative to each other.

During the 1980s, some neorealists and neoliberals came close to sharing a common analytical starting point that is basically neorealist in character; i.e., states are the main actors in what is still an international anarchy and they constantly look after their own best interests (Baldwin 1993). Neoliberals still argued that institutions, interdependence, and democracy led to more thoroughgoing cooperation than is predicted by neorealists. But many current versions of neorealism and neoliberalism were no longer diametrically opposed. In methodological terms there was even more common ground between neorealists and neoliberals. Both strongly supported the scientific project launched by the behaviouralists, even though republican liberals were a partial exception in that regard.

As indicated earlier, the debate between neorealism and neoliberalism can be seen as a continuation of the first major debate in IR. But unlike the earlier debate this one resulted in most neoliberals accepting most of the neorealist assumptions as starting points for analysis. Robert Keohane (1993; Keohane and Martin 1995) attempted to formulate a synthesis of neorealism and neoliberalism coming from the neoliberal side. Barry Buzan et al. (1993) made a similar attempt coming from the neorealist side. However, there is still no complete synthesis between the two traditions. Some neorealists (e.g., Mearsheimer 1993, 1995b) and neoliberals (e.g., Rosenau 1990) are far from reconciled to each other and keep arguing exclusively in favour of their side of the debate. The debate is, therefore, a continuing one (see web link 2.33).

International Society: The English School

The behaviouralist challenge was most strongly felt among IR scholars in the United States. The neorealist and neoliberal acceptance of that challenge also came predominantly from the American academic community. As indicated earlier, during the 1950s and 1960s, American scholarship completely dominated the developing but still youthful IR discipline. Stanley Hoffman made the point that the discipline of IR was 'born and raised in America', and he analysed the profound consequences of that fact for thinking and theorizing in IR (Hoffmann 1977: 41–59). Among the most important of such consequences is the fact that IR continues to be dominated by American scholars even though their pre-eminence may be declining. In the 1970s and 1980s, the IR agenda was preoccupied with the neoliberalism/neorealism debate. In the 1990s, after the end of the Cold War, American predominance in the discipline became less pronounced. IR scholars in Europe and elsewhere became more self-confident and less ready to accept an agenda largely written by US scholars.

In the United Kingdom, a school of IR had existed throughout the period of the Cold War which was different in two major ways. It rejected the behaviouralist challenge and emphasized the traditional approach based on human understanding, judgement, norms, and history. It also rejected any firm distinction between a strict realist and a strict liberal view of international relations. The IR school to which we refer is sometimes called 'the English School'. But that name is far too narrow: it overlooks the fact that several of its leading figures were not English and many were not even from the United Kingdom; rather, they were from Australia, Canada, and South Africa. For that reason, we shall use its other name: International Society. Two leading International Society theorists of the twentieth century are Martin Wight and Hedley Bull (see web links 2.34 and 2.35).

International Society theorists recognize the importance of power in international affairs. They also focus on the state and the state system. But they reject the narrow realist view that world politics is a Hobbesian state of nature in which there are no international norms at all. They view the state as the combination of a *Machtstaat* (power state) and a *Rechtsstaat* (constitutional state): power and law are both important features of international relations. It is true that there is an international anarchy in the sense that there is no world government. But international anarchy is a social and not an anti-social condition; i.e., world politics is an 'anarchical society' (Bull 1995) (see Box 2.7). International Society theorists also recognize the importance of the individual, and some of them argue that individuals are more important than states. Unlike many contemporary liberals, however, International Society theorists tend to regard IGOs and NGOs (intergovernmental and non-governmental organizations) as marginal rather than central features of world politics. They emphasize the relations of states and they play down the importance of transnational relations.

International Society theorists find that realists are correct in pointing to the importance of power and national interest. But if we push the realist view to its logical conclusion, states would always be preoccupied with playing the tough game of power politics; in a pure anarchy, there can be no mutual trust. That view is clearly misleading; there is warfare, but states

---

BOX 2.7   International Society

A *society of states* (or international society) exists when a group of states, conscious of certain common interests and common values, form a society in the sense that they conceive themselves to be bound by a common set of rules in their relations with one another, and share in the working of common institutions. My contention is that the element of a society has always been present, and remains present, in the modern international system.

Bull (1995: 13, 39)

are not continually preoccupied with each other's power, nor do they conceive of that power exclusively as a threat. On the other hand, if we take the liberal idealist view to the extreme, it means that all relations between states are governed by common rules in a perfect world of mutual respect and the rule of law. That view too is clearly misleading. Of course, there are common rules and norms that most states can be expected to observe most of the time; in that sense relations between states constitute an international society. But these rules and norms cannot by themselves guarantee international harmony and cooperation; power and the balance of power still remain very important in the anarchical society.

The United Nations system demonstrates how both elements—power and law—are simultaneously present in international society (see web links 2.36 and 2.37). The Security Council is set up according to the reality of unequal power among states. The great powers (the United States, China, Russia, Britain, France) are the only permanent members with the authority to veto decisions. That simply recognizes the reality of unequal power in world politics. The great powers have a de facto veto anyway: it would be very difficult to force them to do anything that they were not prepared to do. That is the 'realist power and inequality element' in international society. The General Assembly—by contrast with the Security Council—is set up according to the principle of international equality: every member state is legally equal to every other state; each state has one vote, and the majority rather than the most powerful prevails. That is the rationalist 'common rules and norms' element in international society. Finally, the UN also provides evidence about the importance of individuals in international affairs. The UN has promoted the international law of human rights, beginning with the Universal Declaration of Human Rights (1948). Today there is an elaborate structure of humanitarian law which defines the basic civil, political, social, economic, and cultural rights that are intended to promote an acceptable standard of human existence in the contemporary world. That is the cosmopolitan or solidarist element of international society.

For International Society theorists, the study of international relations is not about singling out one of these elements and disregarding the others. They do not seek to make and test hypotheses with the aim of constructing scientific laws of IR. They are not trying to explain international relations scientifically; rather, they are trying to understand it and interpret it. International Society theorists thus take a broader historical, legal, and philosophical approach to international relations. IR is about discerning and exploring the complex presence of all these elements and the normative problems they present to state leaders. Power and national interests matter; so do common norms and institutions. States are important, but so are human beings. Statesmen and stateswomen have a national responsibility to their own nation and its citizens; they have an international responsibility to observe and follow international law and respect the rights of other states; and they have a humanitarian responsibility to defend human rights around the world. But, as the crises in Somalia, Sudan, and elsewhere clearly demonstrated, carrying out these responsibilities in a justifiable way is no easy task (Jackson 2000). In sum, International Society is an approach which tells us something about a world of sovereign states where power and law are both present. The ethics of prudence and the national interest claim the responsibilities of statespeople alongside their duty to observe international rules and procedures. World politics is a world of states but it is

TABLE 2.3   International Society (the English School)

METHODOLOGICAL FOCUS	MAIN ELEMENTS IN THE INTERNATIONAL SYSTEM
Understanding	Power, national interest (realist element)
Judgement	Rules, procedures, international law (liberal element)
Values	Universal human rights, one world for all (cosmopolitan element)
Norms and historical knowledge	
Theorist inside subject	

also a world of human beings, and it will often be difficult to reconcile the demands and claims of both. The main elements of the International Society approach are summarized in Table 2.3.

The challenge posed by the International Society approach does not count as a new major debate. It should rather be seen as an extension of the first debate and a repudiation of the seeming behaviouralist triumph in the second debate. International Society builds on classical realist and liberal ideas, combining and expanding them in ways that provide an alternative to both. International Society adds another perspective to the first great debate between realism and liberalism by rejecting the sharp divisions between them. Although International Society scholars did not enter that debate directly, their approach clearly suggests that the difference between realism and liberalism is drawn too sharply; the historical world does not choose between power and law in quite the categorical way that the debate implies.

As regards the second great debate between the traditionalists and the behaviouralists, International Society theorists did enter that debate by firmly rejecting the latter approach and upholding the former approach (Bull 1969). International Society scholars do not see any possibility of the construction of 'laws' of IR on the model of the natural sciences. For them, that project is flawed: it is based on an intellectual misreading of the character of international relations. For International Society scholars, IR is entirely a field of human relations: it is thus a normative subject and it cannot be fully understood in non-normative terms. IR is about understanding, not explaining; it involves the exercise of judgement: putting oneself in the place of statespeople to try better to understand the dilemmas they confront in their conduct of foreign policy. The notion of an international society also provides a perspective for studying the issues of human rights and humanitarian intervention that figured prominently on the IR agenda at that time.

To sum up: International Society scholars emphasize the simultaneous presence in international society of both realist and liberal elements. There is conflict and there is cooperation; there are states and there are individuals. These different elements cannot be simplified and abstracted into a single theory that emphasizes only one explanatory variable—i.e., power. That would be a much too simple view of world politics and would distort reality. International Society theorists argue for a humanist approach that recognizes the simultaneous presence of all these elements, and the need for holistic and historical study of the problems and dilemmas that arise in that complex situation.

International Political Economy (IPE)

The academic IR debates presented so far are mainly concerned with international politics. Economic affairs play a secondary role. There is little concern with the weak states in the developing world. As we noted in Chapter 1, the decades after the Second World War were a period of decolonization. A large number of 'new' countries appeared on the map as the old colonial powers gave up their control and the former colonies were given political independence. Many of the 'new' states are weak in economic terms: they are at the bottom of the global economic hierarchy and constitute a 'Third [now developing] World'. In the 1970s, Third World (now developing) countries started to press for changes in the international system to improve their economic position in relation to developed countries. Around this time, neo-Marxism emerged as an attempt to theorize about economic underdevelopment in developing countries.

This became the basis for a third major debate in IR about international wealth and international poverty—i.e., about International Political Economy (IPE). IPE is basically about who gets what in the international economic and political system (see web links 2.41 and 2.42). The third debate takes the shape of a neo-Marxist critique of the capitalist world economy together with liberal IPE and realist IPE responses concerning the relationship between economics and politics in international relations (see Figure 2.5).

Neo-Marxism is an attempt to analyse the situation of developing countries by applying the tools of analysis first developed by Karl Marx. Marx, a famous nineteenth-century political economist, focused on capitalism in Europe; he argued that the bourgeoisie or capitalist class used its economic power to exploit and oppress the proletariat, or working class. Neo-Marxists extend that analysis to developing countries by arguing that the global capitalist economy controlled by the wealthy capitalist states is used to impoverish the world's poor countries. 'Dependence' is a core concept for neo-Marxists. They claim that countries in the developing world are not poor because they are inherently backward or undeveloped. Rather, it is because they have been actively underdeveloped by the rich countries of the developed world. Developing countries are subject to unequal exchange: in order to participate in the global capitalist economy they must sell their raw materials at cheap prices, and have to buy finished goods at high prices. In marked contrast, rich countries can buy low and sell high. It is important to emphasize that for neo-Marxists that situation is imposed upon poor countries by the wealthy capitalist states.

FIGURE 2.5   Third major debate in IR

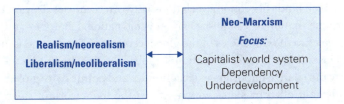

Andre Gunder Frank claims that unequal exchange and appropriation of economic surplus by the few at the expense of the many are inherent in capitalism (Frank 1967). As long as the capitalist system exists there will be underdevelopment in the Third (now developing) World. A similar view is taken by Immanuel Wallerstein (1974, 1983), who has analysed the overall development of the capitalist world system since its beginning in the sixteenth century. Wallerstein (see web link 2.45) allows for the possibility that some developing countries can 'move upwards' in the global capitalist hierarchy. But only a few can do that; there is no room at the top for everybody. Capitalism is a hierarchy based on the exploitation of the poor by the rich, and it will remain that way unless and until it is replaced.

The liberal view of IPE is very different and almost exactly the opposite. Liberal IPE scholars argue that human prosperity can be achieved by the free global expansion of capitalism beyond the boundaries of the sovereign state, and by the decline of the significance of these boundaries. Liberals draw from the economic analysis of Adam Smith and other classical liberal economists, who argue that free markets together with private property and individual freedom create the basis for self-sustaining economic progress for everybody involved. People would not conduct exchange on the free market unless it was to their benefit: 'Since the household always has the alternative of producing directly for itself, it need not enter into any exchange unless it benefits from it. Hence, no exchange will take place unless both parties do benefit from it' (Friedman 1962: 13–14). Thus, whereas Marxist IPE views international capitalism as an instrument for exploitation of developing countries by developed countries, liberal IPE views it as an instrument of progressive change for all countries regardless of their level of development (see web link 2.46).

Realist IPE is different again. It can be traced back to the thoughts of Friedrich List, a nineteenth-century German economist. It is based on the idea that economic activity should be put into the service of building a strong state and supporting the national interest. Wealth should thus be controlled and managed by the state; that statist IPE doctrine is often referred to as '**mercantilism**' or 'economic nationalism'. For mercantilists, the creation of wealth is the necessary basis for increased power of the state. Wealth is therefore an instrument in the creation of national security and national welfare. Moreover, the smooth functioning of a free market depends on political power. Without a dominant or hegemonic power, there can be no liberal world economy (Gilpin 1987: 72). The United States has had the role of hegemon since the end of the First World War. But beginning in the early 1970s, the US was increasingly challenged economically by Japan and by Western Europe. And according to realist IPE, that decline of US leadership has weakened the liberal world economy, because there is no other state that can perform the role of global hegemon.

These different views of IPE show up in analyses of three important and related IPE issues of recent years. The first issue concerns economic **globalization**; that is, the spread and intensification of all kinds of economic relations between countries. Does economic globalization undermine 'national' economies by erasing national borders and by subjecting national economies to the exigencies of the global economy? The second issue is about who wins and who loses in the process of economic globalization. The third issue concerns how we should view the relative importance of economics and politics. Are global economic relations ultimately controlled by states which set out the framework of rules that economic actors have to observe? Or are politicians increasingly subject to anonymous market forces over which they have lost effective control? Underlying many of these questions is the issue of state sovereignty: are the forces of global economics making the sovereign state obsolete? (See web links 2.50 and 2.51.) The three approaches to IPE come up with very different answers to these questions, as we shall see in Chapter 7.

In short, the third major debate further complicates the discipline of IR because it shifts the subject away from political and military issues and towards economic and social issues, and because it introduces the distinct socioeconomic problems of developing countries. It is not a debate as were the two IR debates discussed in the two previous sections. Rather, it is a marked expansion of the academic IR research agenda to include socioeconomic questions of welfare as well as political–military questions of security. Yet both realist and liberal traditions have specific views on IPE, and those views have been attacked by neo-Marxism. And all three perspectives are in rather sharp disagreement with each other: they take fundamentally different views of the international political economy in terms of both concepts and values. In that sense, we do indeed have a third debate. The debate was focused on North–South relations at first, but it has long since expanded to include IPE issues in all areas of international relations. There was no clear winner in the third debate, as we shall see in Chapter 7.

Dissident Voices: Alternative Approaches to IR

The debates introduced so far have concerned the established theoretical traditions in the discipline: realism, liberalism, International Society, and the theories of IPE. Currently a fourth debate on IR is under way. It involves various critiques of the established traditions by alternative approaches, sometimes identified as post-positivism (Smith et al. 1996). There have always been 'dissident voices' in the discipline of IR: philosophers and scholars who have rejected established views and tried to replace them with alternatives. But in recent years these voices have increased in number.

Two factors help explain that development. The end of the Cold War changed the international agenda in some fundamental ways. In place of a clear-cut East/West conflict dominated by two contending superpowers a number of diverse issues emerged in world politics, including, for example, state partition and disintegration, civil war, terrorism, democratization, national minorities, humanitarian intervention, ethnic cleansing, mass migration and refugee problems, environmental security, and so forth. An increasing number of IR scholars expressed dissatisfaction with the dominant Cold War approach to IR: the neorealism of Kenneth Waltz. Many IR scholars now take issue with Waltz's claim that the complex world of international relations can be squeezed into a few law-like statements about the structure of the international system and the balance of power. They also criticize Waltzian neorealism for its conservative political outlook; there is not much in neorealism that can point to change and the creation of a better world (see web link 2.56).

Post-Cold War developments do not fit well into a neorealist analysis. For example, the United States is today the preponderant power in the world, especially in terms of military strength. Neorealist logic dictates that other states will balance the United States because offsetting US power is a means of guaranteeing one's own security. Therefore, neorealists anticipate that the disappearance of the common enemy, the Soviet Union, will lead to intensified balance-of-power competition between old friends, both across the Atlantic and inside Western Europe (Fettweiss 2004; Paul et al. 2004). But this has not happened; there has been no major balancing of US power since the end of the Cold War. In order to understand that situation we are led towards different types of analysis of current international relations, including constructivism, some forms of liberalism, or even classical realism.

The events of 9/11 are also a problem for neorealism because that analysis is state-centric and focused on security threats between states while playing down the importance of non-state actors (see Chapter 11). Again, other approaches appear better suited to tackle the analysis of international terrorism. One such approach is liberalism, which recognizes the importance of non-state actors. But liberal analysis has also been challenged by post-Cold War developments. Francis Fukuyama (1989) optimistically expected the global victory of liberal democracy in a context of successful modernization of all countries. This has not happened; democracy has made progress but is also in dire states in many fragile states and also in the rising powers (Russia and China). At the same time, a financial crisis and sharp inequalities in the liberal West (Pikkety 2014) have raised questions as to the effectiveness of a liberal market economy.

In sum, developments since the end of the Cold War have pointed away from the theoretical convictions of neorealism and have also challenged the great optimism of many liberal views. New perspectives have emerged, both as regards theory; that is, *how* to best approach the study of IR (see web link 2.55), and as regards substantial issues; that is, *which* issues should be considered the most important ones for IR to study (Figure 2.6). We have chosen to present these developments in three chapters later in this volume.

Chapter 8 introduces social constructivism. Constructivists claim that neorealism and neoliberalism are 'materialist' theories; they focus on material power, such as military forces and economic capabilities. Constructivists argue that the international system is constituted by ideas, not material power. The chapter presents constructivist theories of IR. Chapter 9 considers post-positivist approaches, including post-structuralism, post-colonialism, and feminism. They criticize established theories on both methodological and substantial grounds, but they are not in agreement about what is the best replacement for the methods and theories that are now being rejected. Chapter 11 addresses key issues in contemporary IR: international terrorism; religion in IR; the environment; and new patterns of war and peace. They are rival answers to the question: what is the most important issue or concern in world politics now that the Cold War has come to an end, and IR's realist preoccupation with superpower rivalry and nuclear security along with it?

FIGURE 2.6   **A fourth major debate**

Social constructivism and the non-traditional issues and methodologies mentioned here have something in common: they claim that established traditions in IR fail to come to grips with the post-Cold War changes of world politics. These recent approaches should thus be seen as 'new voices' that are trying to point the way to an academic IR discipline that is more in tune with international relations at the start of a new millennium. In short, many scholars argue that a fourth IR debate has been thrown open in the 1990s between the established traditions on the one hand and these new voices on the other.

Which Theory?

This chapter has introduced the main theoretical traditions in IR. It is necessary to be familiar with theory, because facts do not speak for themselves. We always look at the world, consciously or not, through a specific set of lenses; we may think of those lenses as theory. Is development taking place in the developing world or is it underdevelopment? Is the world a more secure or a more dangerous place since the end of the Cold War? Are contemporary states more prone to cooperate or to compete with each other? Facts alone cannot answer these questions; we need help from theories. They tell us which facts are important and which are unimportant; that is, they structure our view of the world. They are based on certain values, and often they also contain visions of how we want the world to be. Early liberal thinking about IR, for example, was driven by the determination never to repeat the disaster of the First World War. Liberals hoped the creation of new international organizations would foster a more peaceful and cooperative world.

Because theory is necessary in thinking systematically about the world it is better to get the most important theories out in the open and subject them to scrutiny. We should examine their concepts, their claims about how the world hangs together, and what the important facts are; we should probe their values and visions. That is what we set out to do in the following chapters. The presentation of different theories always begs a big question: which theory is best? It may seem an innocent question, but it raises a number of difficult and complex issues. One answer is that the question about the best theory is not really meaningful, because different theories, such as realism and liberalism, are like different games, played by different people (Rosenau 1967; see also Smith 1997). If there was only one game, say tennis, we could easily find one winner by setting up a tournament. But when there is more than one game, say both tennis and golf, the golf player will not stop playing just because a tennis player comes along and claims that tennis is a much better game. Maybe the theories that most appeal to us are like the games that we most enjoy watching or playing.

Another answer to the question about the best theory is that, even if theories are in many ways different, it does make sense to rank them, just as it makes sense to point out the athlete of the year even if the candidates for that honour compete in very different athletic disciplines. What would be the criteria for identifying the best theory? We may think of several relevant criteria, among them:

- Coherence: the theory should be consistent; i.e., free of internal contradictions.
- Clarity of exposition: the theory should be formulated in a clear and lucid manner.

- Unbiased: the theory should not be based on purely subjective valuations. No theory is value-free, but the theory should strive to be candid about its normative premises and values.

- Scope: the theory should be relevant for a large number of important issues. A theory with limited scope, for example, is a theory about US decision making in the Gulf War. A theory with wide scope is a theory about foreign policy decision making in general.

- Depth: the theory should be able to explain and understand as much as possible of the phenomenon that it purports to tackle. For example, a theory of European integration has limited depth if it explains only some part of that process and much more depth if it explains most of it.

Other possible criteria could be set forth; but it must be emphasized that there is no objective way of choosing between the evaluative criteria. And it is clear that some criteria can load the dice in favour of some types of theory and against others. There is no simple way around the problem. A further complication is that people's values and political priorities play a role in choosing one theory ahead of another. It should also be remembered that cooperation between theories is possible; they can be combined in various ways (but not in every way!) in order to create stronger analytical frameworks (Howard 2010; Sil and Katzenstein 2010).

As textbook writers, we see it as our duty to present what we consider the most important theories in a way that draws out the strength of each theory but is also critical of its weaknesses and limitations. This book is not aimed at guiding the reader towards one single theory which we see as the best; it is aimed at identifying the pros and cons of several important theories in order to enable the reader to make his or her own well-considered choices from the available possibilities.

Conclusion

The foregoing traditional and alternative theories constitute the main analytical tools and concerns of contemporary IR. We have seen how the subject developed through a series of debates between different theoretical approaches. We noted that these debates were not conducted in splendid isolation from everything else; they were shaped and influenced by historical events, by the major political and economic problems of the day. They were also influenced by methodological developments in other areas of scholarship. These elements are summarized in Figure 2.1.

No single theoretical approach has clearly won the day in IR. The main theoretical traditions and alternative approaches that we have outlined are all actively employed in the discipline today. That situation reflects the necessity of different approaches to capture different aspects of a very complicated historical and contemporary reality. World politics is not dominated by one single issue or conflict; on the contrary, it is shaped and influenced by many different issues and conflicts. The pluralist situation of IR scholarship also reflects the personal preferences of different scholars: they often prefer particular theories for reasons that may have as much to do with their personal values and world views as with what takes place in international relations and what is required to understand those events and episodes.

KEY POINTS

- IR thinking has evolved in stages that are marked by specific debates between groups of scholars. The first major debate is between *utopian liberalism* and *realism*; the second debate is on method, between *traditional approaches* and *behaviouralism*. The third debate is between *neorealism/neoliberalism* and *neo-Marxism*; and an emerging fourth debate is between *established traditions* and *post-positivist alternatives*.

- The first major debate was won by the realists. During the Cold War realism became the dominant way of thinking about international relations not only among scholars but also among politicians, diplomats, and so-called 'ordinary people'. Morgenthau's (1960) summary of realism became the standard introduction to IR in the 1950s and 1960s.

- The second major debate is about method. The contenders are traditionalists and behaviouralists. The former try to understand a complicated social world of human affairs and the values fundamental to it, such as order, freedom, and justice. The latter approach, behaviouralism, finds no place for morality or ethics in international theory. Behaviouralism wants to classify, measure, and explain through the formulation of general laws like those formulated in the 'hard' sciences of chemistry, physics, etc. The behaviouralists seemed to triumph for a time but in the end neither side won the debate. Today both types of method are used in the discipline. There was a revival of traditional normative approaches to IR after the end of the Cold War.

- In the 1960s and 1970s, neoliberalism challenged realism by arguing that interdependence, integration, and democracy are changing IR. Neorealism responded that anarchy and the balance of power are still at the heart of IR.

- International Society theorists maintain that IR contains both 'realist' elements of conflict and 'liberal' elements of cooperation, and that these elements cannot be collapsed into a single theoretical synthesis. They also emphasize human rights and other cosmopolitan features of world politics, and they defend the traditional approach to IR.

- The third debate is characterized by a neo-Marxist attack on the established positions of realism/neorealism and liberalism/neoliberalism. This debate concerns IPE. It creates a more complex situation in the discipline because it expands the terrain towards economic issues and because it introduces the distinct problems of developing countries. There is no clear winner of the third debate. Within IPE, the discussion between the main contenders continues.

- Currently a fourth debate is under way in IR; it involves an attack on the established traditions by alternative approaches, sometimes identified as 'post-positivist alternatives'. The debate raises both methodological issues (i.e., *how* to approach the study of an issue) and substantial issues (i.e., *which* issues should be considered the most important ones). Some of these approaches also reject the scientific claims of neorealism and neoliberalism.

QUESTIONS

- Identify the major debates within IR. Why do the debates often linger on without any clear winner emerging?

- Which are the established theoretical traditions in IR? How can they be seen as 'established'?

- Why was early IR strongly influenced by liberalism?

- Seen over the long term, realism is the dominant theoretical tradition in IR. Why?

- Why do scholars have pet theories? What are your own theoretical preferences?

- Is it fair to put the label 'utopian liberalism' on the liberal politics of the 1920s? Why or why not?

GUIDE TO FURTHER READING

Angell, N. (1909). *The Great Illusion*. London: Weidenfeld & Nicolson.

Carr, E. H. (1964). *The Twenty Years' Crisis*. New York: Harper & Row.

Elman, C. and Elman, M. F. (2008). 'The Role of History in International Relations', *Millennium*, 37/2: 357–64.

Howard, P. (2010). 'Triangulating Debates Within the Field: Teaching International Relations Research Methodology', *International Studies Perspectives*, 11/4: 393–408.

Jackson, R. (2005). *Classical and Modern Thought on International Relations: From Anarchy to Cosmopolis*. New York: Palgrave Macmillan.

Knutsen, T. L. (1997). *A History of International Relations Theory*. Manchester: Manchester University Press.

Lawson, G. (2012). 'The Eternal Divide? History and International Relations', *European Journal of International Relations*, 18/2: 203–26.

Rengger, N. (2006). 'Theorizing World Politics for a New Century', *International Affairs*, 82/3: 427–30.

Schmidt, B. C. (1998). *The Political Discourse of Anarchy: A Disciplinary History of International Relations*. Albany, NY: SUNY Press.

WEB LINKS

Web links mentioned in the chapter, together with additional material including a case-study on how to analyse the world, can be found on the Online Resource Centre that accompanies this book.

www.oxfordtextbooks.co.uk/orc/jackson_sorensen6e/

PART 2

Classical Theories

Realism

▌ Summary

This chapter sketches the realist tradition in IR. The chapter takes note of an important dichotomy in realist thought between classical realism and contemporary realism, including strategic as well as structural approaches. Classical realists emphasize the normative aspects of realism as well as the empirical aspects. Most contemporary realists pursue a social scientific analysis of the structures and processes of world politics, but they are inclined to ignore norms and values. The chapter discusses both classical and social scientific strands of realist thought. It examines a recent theoretical debate among realist IR scholars concerning the relevance of the balance of power concept. It then reviews two critiques of realist doctrine: an International Society critique and a revisionist and emancipatory critique. The concluding section assesses the prospects for the realist tradition as a research programme in IR.

Introduction: Elements of Realism

Basic realist ideas and assumptions are: (1) a pessimistic view of human nature; (2) a conviction that international relations are necessarily conflictual and that international conflicts are ultimately resolved by war; (3) a high regard for the values of national security and state survival; and (4) a basic scepticism that there can be progress in international politics which is comparable to that in domestic political life (see web links 3.01 and 3.02). These pervasive ideas and assumptions steer the thought of most leading realist IR theorists, both past and present.

In realist thought, humans are characterized as being preoccupied with their own wellbeing in their competitive relations with each other. They desire to be in the driver's seat. They do not wish to be taken advantage of. They consequently strive to have the 'edge' in relations with other people—including international relations with other countries. In that regard at least, human beings are considered to be basically the same everywhere. Thus, the desire to enjoy an advantage over others and to avoid domination by others is universal. This pessimistic view of human nature is strongly evident in the IR theory of Hans Morgenthau (1965, 1985), who was the leading classical realist thinker of the twentieth century. He sees men and women as having a 'will to power'. That is particularly evident in politics and especially international politics: 'Politics is a struggle for power over men, and whatever its ultimate aim may be, power is its immediate goal and the modes of acquiring, maintaining, and demonstrating it determine the technique of political action' (Morgenthau 1965: 195).

Thucydides, Machiavelli, Hobbes, and indeed all classical realists share that view to a greater or lesser extent. They believe that the acquisition and possession of power, and the deployment and uses of power, are central preoccupations of political activity. International politics is thus portrayed as—above all else—'power politics': an arena of rivalry, conflict, and war between states in which the same basic problems of defending the national interest and ensuring the survival of the state, and the security of its people, repeat themselves over and over again.

Realists thus share a core assumption that the international state system is anarchy—i.e., a system with no higher, overarching authority; no world government. The state is the pre-eminent actor in world politics. International relations are primarily relations of states. All other actors in world politics—individuals, international organizations (IGOs), non-governmental organizations (NGOs), etc.—are either far less important or unimportant. The main point of foreign policy is to advance and defend the interests of the state. But states are not equal. On the contrary, there is an international hierarchy of power among states. The most important states in world politics are the great powers. International relations are understood by realists as primarily a struggle between the great powers for domination and security. Lesser and weaker powers are of secondary importance. They can only realistically adjust their policies and adapt their relations in response to the demands and expectations of the great powers.

The normative core of realism is national security and state survival: these are the values that drive realist doctrine and realist foreign policy. The state is considered to be essential for the good life of its citizens: without a state to guarantee the means and conditions of security human life is bound to be, in the famous phrase of Thomas Hobbes (1946: 82), 'solitary, poor, nasty, brutish and short'. The state is thus seen as a protector of its territory, of the population, and of their distinctive and valued way of life. The national interest is the final arbiter in judging foreign policy.

The fact that all states must pursue their own national interest means that other countries and governments can never be relied upon or completely trusted. All international agreements are provisional and conditional on the willingness of states to observe them. That makes treaties and all other conventions, customs, rules, laws, and so on between states merely expedient arrangements which can and will be set aside if they conflict with the vital interests of states. There are no international obligations in the legal or ethical sense of the word—i.e., bonds of mutual duty—between independent states. The only fundamental responsibility of statespeople is to advance and to defend the national interest by whatever means. That is nowhere stated more brutally than by Machiavelli in his famous book *The Prince* (see Box 3.3).

According to realist theory, international relations are always the same. That means that there can be no progressive change in world politics comparable to the developments that characterize domestic political life. That also means that realist IR theory is considered to be valid not only at particular times and places but also at all times, everywhere, because the foregoing basic facts of world politics never change. That, at any rate, is what most realists argue and evidently believe.

There is an important distinction in realist IR theory between **classical realism** and **social science realism**. Classical realism is one of the 'traditional' approaches to IR. It is basically a normative approach, and focuses on the core political values of national security and state survival. Classical realist thought has been evident in many different historical periods, from ancient Greece right down to the present time. Strategic and structural realism is basically a scientific approach. It is largely (although not exclusively) American in origin. Indeed, it has been and perhaps still is the most prominent IR theory in the United States, which is home to by far the largest number of IR scholars in the world.

Classical Realism

What is classical realism? Who are the leading classical realists? What are their key ideas and arguments? In this section we shall examine, briefly, the international thought of three outstanding classical realists of the past: (1) the ancient Greek historian Thucydides; (2) the Renaissance Italian political theorist Niccolò Machiavelli; and (3) the seventeenth-century English political and legal philosopher Thomas Hobbes. In the next subsection, we shall single out for special treatment the classical realist thought of the twentieth-century German–American IR theorist, Hans J. Morgenthau.

Thucydides

What we call international relations Thucydides saw as the inevitable competition and conflict between ancient Greek city-states (which together composed the cultural–linguistic civilization known as Hellas) and between Hellas and neighbouring non-Greek empires, such as Macedonia and Persia (see web links 3.04 and 3.05). Neither the states of Hellas nor their non-Greek neighbours were in any sense equal (Box 3.1). On the contrary, they were substantially unequal: there were a few 'great powers'—such as Athens, Sparta, and the Persian Empire, and many smaller and lesser powers—such as the tiny island statelets of the Aegean Sea. That inequality was considered to be inevitable and natural. A distinctive feature of Thucydides' brand of realism is thus its naturalist character. Aristotle said that 'man is a political animal'. Thucydides said in effect that political animals are highly unequal in their powers and capabilities to dominate others and to defend themselves. All states, large and small, must adapt to that given reality of unequal power and conduct themselves accordingly. If states do that, they will survive and perhaps even prosper. If states fail to do that, they will place themselves in jeopardy and may even be destroyed. Ancient history is full of many examples of states and empires, small and large, which were destroyed.

So Thucydides emphasizes the limited choices and the restricted sphere of manoeuvre available to rulers in the conduct of foreign policy. He also emphasizes that decisions have consequences; before any final decision is made, a decision maker should have carefully thought through the likely consequences, bad as well as good. In pointing that out, Thucydides is also emphasizing the ethics of caution and prudence in the conduct of foreign policy in an international world of great inequality, of restricted foreign-policy choices, and of ever-present danger as well as opportunity. Foresight, prudence, caution, and judgement are the characteristic political ethics of classical realism that Thucydides and most other classical realists are at pains to distinguish from private morality and the principle of justice. If a country and its government wish to survive and prosper, they better pay attention to these fundamental political maxims of international relations.

In his famous study of the Peloponnesian War (431–404 BCE), Thucydides (1972: 407) put his realist philosophy into the mouths of the leaders of Athens—a great power—in their dialogue with the leaders of Melos—a minor power—during a moment of conflict between the two city-states in 416 BCE. The Melians made an appeal to the principle of justice, which to them meant that their honour and dignity as an independent state should be respected by the powerful Athenians. But, according to Thucydides, justice is of a special kind in international relations. It is not about equal treatment for all, because states are in

---

BOX 3.1   International relations in ancient Greece

The Greeks established the Hellenic League . . . and placed it under the leadership of Sparta and Athens. Despite the semblance of Greek unity during the Persian Wars (492–77 BCE) there were serious conflicts between members of the League, mostly occasioned by the smaller city-states' fear of Athenian imperialism and expansion. Thus, after the Greek victories over the Persians, Athens' competitors, led by Sparta, formed a rival organization, the Peloponnesian League, an intricate alliance and collective security system designed to deter further Athenian expansion . . . A bitter competition over trade and naval supremacy between Corinth and Athens led ultimately to the Peloponnesian Wars involving the two military alliances.

Holsti (1988: 38–9)

BOX 3.2	**Thucydides on the strong and the weak**

The standard of justice depends on the equality of power to compel and that in fact the strong do what they have the power to do and the weak accept what they have to accept . . . this is the safe rule—to stand up to one's equals, to behave with deference to one's superiors, and to treat one's inferiors with moderation. Think it over again, then, when we have withdrawn from the meeting, and let this be a point that constantly recurs to your minds—that you are discussing the fate of your country, that you have only one country, and that its future for good or ill depends on this one single decision which you are going to make.

Thucydides (1972: 406)

fact unequal. Rather, it is about recognizing your relative strength or weakness, about knowing your proper place, and about adapting to the natural reality of unequal power. Thucydides, therefore, let the Athenians reply to the Melian appeal as set out in Box 3.2.

That is probably the most famous example of the classical realist understanding of international relations as basically an anarchy of separate states that have no real choice except to operate according to the principles and practices of power politics in which security and survival are the primary values and war is the final arbiter.

Machiavelli

Power (the Lion) and deception (the Fox) are the two essential means for the conduct of foreign policy, according to the political teachings of Machiavelli (1984: 66). The supreme political value is national freedom; i.e., independence. The main responsibility of rulers is always to seek the advantages and to defend the interests of their state and thus ensure its survival. That requires strength; if a state is not strong it will be a standing invitation for others to prey upon it; the ruler must therefore be a lion. That also requires cunning and—if necessary—ruthlessness in the pursuit of self-interest: the ruler must also be a fox. If rulers are not astute, crafty, and adroit they might miss an opportunity that could bring great advantages or benefits to them and their state. Even more importantly, they might fail to notice a menace or threat which if not guarded against might harm or even destroy them, their regime, and possibly even the state as well. That rulers must be both lions and foxes is at the heart of Machiavelli's (1984: 66) realist theory. Classical realist IR theory, therefore, is primarily a theory of survival (Wight 1966).

The overriding Machiavellian assumption is that the world is a dangerous place (see web link 3.06). But it is also, by the same token, an opportune place. If any political leader hopes to survive in such a world, he or she must always be aware of dangers, must anticipate them, and must take the necessary precautions against them. And if they hope to prosper, to enrich themselves, and to bask in the reflected glory of their accumulated power and wealth, it is necessary for them to recognize and to exploit the opportunities that present themselves and to do that more quickly, more skilfully, and—if necessary—more ruthlessly than any of their rivals or enemies (see Box 3.3). The conduct of foreign policy is thus an instrumental or 'Machiavellian'

> **BOX 3.3   Machiavelli on the Prince's obligations**
>
> A prince . . . cannot observe all those things for which men are considered good, for in order to maintain the state he is often obliged to act against his promise, against charity, against humanity, and against religion. And therefore, it is necessary that he have a mind ready to turn itself according to the way the winds of fortune and the changeability of [political] affairs require . . . as long as it is possible, he should not stray from the good, but he should know how to enter into evil when necessity commands.
>
> Machiavelli (1984: 59–60)

activity based on the intelligent calculation of one's power and interests as against the power and interests of rivals and competitors.

That shrewd and sober outlook is reflected in some typical Machiavellian maxims of realist statecraft, including the following: be aware of what is happening; do not wait for things to happen; anticipate the motives and actions of others; do not wait for others to act; and act before they do. The prudent state leader acts to ward off any threat posed by his or her neighbours. He or she should be prepared to engage in pre-emptive war and similar initiatives. The realist state leader is alert to opportunities in any political situation, and is prepared and equipped to exploit them.

Above all, according to Machiavelli, the responsible state leader must not operate in accordance with the principles of Christian ethics: love thy neighbour, be peaceful, and avoid war except in self-defence or in pursuit of a just cause; be charitable, share your wealth with others, always act in good faith, etc. Machiavelli sees these moral maxims as the height of political foolishness and irresponsibility; if political leaders act in accordance with Christian virtues, they are bound to come to grief and they will lose everything. Not only that, they will sacrifice the property and perhaps the freedom and even the lives of their citizens, who depend upon their statecraft. The implication is clear: if a ruler does not know or respect the maxims of power politics, his or her statecraft will fail and with it the security and welfare of the citizens who depend absolutely upon it. In other words, political responsibility flows in a very different vein from ordinary, private morality. The fundamental, overriding values are the security and the survival of the state; that is what must guide foreign policy.

Machiavelli's realist writings are sometimes portrayed (Forde 1992: 64) as 'manuals on how to thrive in a completely chaotic and immoral world'. But that view is somewhat misleading. The international world has its own morality of power. Rulers have responsibilities not merely to themselves or to their personal regimes but also to their country and its citizens: what Machiavelli, thinking of Florence, refers to as 'the republic'. This is the civic virtue aspect of Machiavellian realism: rulers have to be both lions and foxes because their people depend upon them for their survival and prosperity. That dependence of the people upon their ruler, and specifically upon the wisdom of his or her foreign policy, is owing to the fact that the people's fate is entangled with the ruler's fate. That is the normative heart not only of Machiavellian realism but also of classical realism generally.

Hobbes and the Security Dilemma

Thomas Hobbes thinks we can gain a fundamental insight into political life if we imagine men and women living in a 'natural' condition prior to the invention and institution of the sovereign state. He refers to that pre-civil condition as the '**state of nature**'. For Hobbes (1946: 82), the state of nature is an extremely adverse human circumstance in which there is a permanent 'state of war' 'of every man against every man'; in their natural condition every man, woman, and child is endangered by everybody else, life is constantly at risk, and nobody can be confident about his or her security and survival for any reasonable length of time. People are living in constant fear of each other. Hobbes characterizes that pre-civil condition as shown in Box 3.4. It is obviously not only desirable but also extremely urgent to escape from those intolerable circumstances at the earliest moment, if that is possible (see web link 3.07).

Hobbes believes there is an escape route from the state of nature into a civilized human condition, and that is via the creation and maintenance of a sovereign state. The means of escape is by men and women turning their fear of each other into rational joint collaboration with each other to form a security pact that can guarantee each other's safety. Men and women paradoxically cooperate politically because of their fear of being hurt or killed by their neighbours: they are 'civilized by fear of death' (Oakeshott 1975: 36). Their mutual fear and insecurity drive them away from their natural condition: the war of all against all. In other words, they are basically driven to institute a sovereign state not by their reason (intelligence) but, rather, by their passion (emotion). Their intelligence alone is insufficient to propel such action. With the value of peace and order firmly in mind, they willingly and jointly collaborate to create a state with a sovereign government that possesses absolute authority and credible power to protect them from both internal disorders and foreign enemies and threats. In the civil condition—i.e., of peace and order—under the protection of the state, men and women have an opportunity to flourish in relative safety; they no longer live under the constant threat of injury and fear of death. Being secure and at peace, they are now free to prosper. As Hobbes puts it, they can pursue and enjoy 'felicity'; i.e., happiness, well-being, etc. (Table 3.1).

However, that statist solution to the problem of the natural condition of humankind automatically poses a serious political problem. A peaceful and civilized life can only be enjoyed

---

BOX 3.4	Hobbes on the state of nature

In such condition, there is no place for industry; because the fruit thereof is uncertain: and consequently no culture of the earth, no navigation, nor use of the commodities that may be imported by sea; no commodious building . . . no arts; no letters; no society, and which is worst of all, continual fear, and danger of violent death; and the life of man, solitary, poor, nasty, brutish, and short.

Hobbes (1946: 82)

TABLE 3.1 Basic values of three classical realists

THUCYDIDES	MACHIAVELLI	HOBBES
Political fate	Political agility	Political will
Necessity and security	Opportunity and security	Security dilemma
Political survival	Political survival	Political survival
Safety	Civic virtue	Peace and felicity

within a state and it cannot extend beyond the state or exist between states. The very act of instituting a sovereign state to escape from the fearful state of nature among individual people simultaneously creates another state of nature between states. That poses what is usually referred to as 'the security dilemma' in world politics: the achievement of personal security and domestic security through the creation of a state is necessarily accompanied by the condition of national and international insecurity that is rooted in the anarchy of the state system.

There is no escape from the international security dilemma in the way that there is an escape from the personal security dilemma, because there is no possibility of forming a global state or world government. The main point about the **international state of nature** is that it is a condition of actual or potential war; there can be no permanent or guaranteed peace between sovereign states—no international peace. But there can be domestic peace—peace within the framework of the sovereign state—and the opportunities that only civil peace can provide for men and women to enjoy felicity. The state is organized and equipped for war in order to provide domestic peace for its subjects or citizens. Domestic peace can be realized in this way. International peace is an unrealizable dream and a dangerous illusion.

We can summarize the discussion thus far by briefly stating what these classical realists basically have in common. First, they agree that the human condition is a condition of insecurity and conflict that must be addressed and dealt with. Second, they agree that there is a body of political knowledge, or wisdom, to deal with the problem of security, and each of them tries to identify the keys to it. Finally, they agree that there is no final escape from this human condition, which is a permanent feature of human life. In other words, although there is a body of political wisdom—which can be identified and stated in the form of political maxims—there are no permanent or final solutions to the problems of politics— including international politics. There can be no enduring peace between states. This pessimistic and unhopeful view is at the heart of the IR theory of the leading classical realist of the twentieth century, Hans J. Morgenthau.

Morgenthau and Classical Realism

According to Morgenthau (1965), men and women are by nature political animals: they are born to pursue power and to enjoy the fruits of power. Morgenthau speaks of the *animus dominandi*: the human 'lust' for power (Morgenthau 1965: 192). The craving for power dictates a search not only for relative advantage but also for a secure political space—i.e., territory—to maintain oneself and to enjoy oneself free from the political dictates of others. The ultimate political space within which security can be arranged and enjoyed is, of course, the independent state. Security beyond the state and between states is impossible (see web links 3.08 and 3.09).

The human *animus dominandi* inevitably brings men and women into conflict with each other. That creates the condition of power politics which is at the heart of Morgenthau's realism (Box 3.5). 'Politics is a struggle for power over men, and whatever its ultimate aim may be, power is its immediate goal and the modes of acquiring, maintaining, and demonstrating it determine the technique of political action' (Morgenthau 1965: 195). Here, Morgenthau is clearly echoing Machiavelli and Hobbes. If people desire to enjoy a political space free from the intervention or control of foreigners, they will have to mobilize and deploy their power for that purpose. That is, they will have to organize themselves into a capable and effective state by means of which they can defend their interests. The anarchical system of states invites international conflict which ultimately takes the form of war (Box 3.6).

The struggle between states leads to the problem of justifying the threat or use of force in human relations (Box 3.6). Here we arrive at the central normative doctrine of classical realism. Morgenthau follows in the tradition of Thucydides and Machiavelli: there is one morality for the private sphere and another and very different morality for the public sphere. Political ethics allows some actions that would not be tolerated by private morality. Morgenthau is critical of those theorists and practitioners, such as American President Woodrow Wilson, who believed that it was necessary for political ethics to be brought into line with private ethics. For example, in a famous address to the US Congress in 1917,

BOX 3.5	Morgenthau on political morality

Realism maintains that universal moral principles cannot be applied to the actions of states in their abstract universal formulation, but that they must be filtered through the concrete circumstances of time and place. The individual may say for himself: '*fiat justitia, pereat mundus* (let justice be done even if the world perish)', but the state has no right to say so in the name of those who are in its care.

Morgenthau (1985: 12)

BOX 3.6	President Nixon on the balance of power (1970)

We must remember the only time in the history of the world that we have had any extended periods of peace is when there has been balance of power. It is when one nation becomes infinitely more powerful in relation to its potential competitor that the danger of war arises. So I believe in a world in which the United States is powerful. I think it will be a safer world and a better world if we have a strong, healthy United States, Europe, Soviet Union, China, Japan, each balancing the other, not playing one against the other, an even balance.

Quoted from Kissinger (1994: 705)

President Wilson said he could discern 'the beginning of an age in which it will be insisted that the same standards of conduct and of responsibility for wrong shall be observed among nations and their governments that are observed among the individual citizens of civilized states' (Morgenthau 1965: 180).

Morgenthau considers that outlook to be not only ill advised but also irresponsible; it is not only mistaken intellectually but also fundamentally wrong morally. It is a gross intellectual mistake because it fails to appreciate the important difference between the public sphere of politics on the one hand, and the private sphere or domestic life on the other hand. According to classical realists, the difference is fundamental. As indicated, Machiavelli made that point by noting that if a ruler operated in accordance with Christian private ethics he or she would come to grief very quickly because political rivals could not be counted on to operate in the same Christian way. It would thus be an ill-advised and irresponsible foreign policy; and all the people who depended on the policy would suffer from the disaster it created.

Such a policy would be reckless in the extreme, and would thus constitute an ethical failure because political leaders bear a very heavy responsibility for the security and welfare of their country and its people. They are not supposed to expose their people to unnecessary perils or hardships. Sometimes—for example, during crises or emergencies—it may be necessary to carry out foreign policies and engage in international activities that would clearly be wrong according to private morality: spying, lying, cheating, stealing, conspiring, and so on are only a few of the many activities that would be considered at best dubious and at worst evil by the standards of private morality. Sometimes, it may be necessary to trample on human rights for the sake of the national interest: during war, for example. Sometimes, it may be necessary to sacrifice a lesser good for a greater good or to choose the lesser of two evils. That tragic situation is, for realists, virtually a defining feature of international politics, especially during times of war. Here, Morgenthau is reiterating an insight into the ethically compromised nature of statecraft that was noted by the ancient Greek philosopher Plato (1974: 82, 121), who spoke of the 'noble lie': 'Our rulers will probably have to make considerable use of lies and deceit for the good of their subjects.'

For Morgenthau, the heart of statecraft is thus the clear-headed knowledge that political ethics and private ethics are not the same, that the former cannot be and should not be reduced to the latter, and that the key to effective and responsible statecraft is to recognize this fact of power politics and to learn to make the best of it. Responsible rulers are not merely free, as sovereigns, to act in an expedient way. They must act in full knowledge that the mobilization and exercise of political power in foreign affairs inevitably involves moral dilemmas, and sometimes evil actions. The awareness that political ends (e.g., defending the national interest during times of war) must sometimes justify morally questionable or morally tainted means (e.g., the targeting and bombing of cities) leads to situational ethics and the dictates of 'political wisdom': prudence, moderation, judgement, resolve, courage, and so on. Those are the cardinal virtues of political ethics. They do not preclude evil actions. Instead, they underline the tragic dimension of international ethics: they recognize the inevitability of moral dilemmas in international politics: that evil actions must sometimes be taken to prevent a greater evil (Table 3.2).

TABLE 3.2   Morgenthau's concept of statecraft

HUMAN NATURE (basic condition)	POLITICAL SITUATION (means and context)	POLITICAL CONDUCT (goals and values)
animus dominandi	Power politics	Political ethics (prudence, etc.)
Self-interest	Political power	Human necessities (security, etc.)
	Political circumstances	National interest
	Political skills	Balance of power

Morgenthau (1985: 4–17) encapsulates his IR theory in 'six principles of political realism'. As a conclusion to this section of the chapter we shall briefly summarize them.

- Politics is rooted in a permanent and unchanging human nature which is basically self-centred, self-regarding, and self-interested.

- Politics is 'an autonomous sphere of action' and cannot therefore be reduced to morals (as Kantian or liberal theorists are prone to do).

- Self-interest is a basic fact of the human condition. International politics is an arena of conflicting state interests. But interests are not fixed: the world is in flux and interests can change. Realism is a doctrine that responds to the fact of a changing political reality.

- The ethics of international relations is a political or situational ethics which is very different from private morality. A political leader does not have the same freedom to do the right thing that a private citizen has. That is because a political leader has far heavier responsibilities and very different responsibilities than a private citizen. The leader is *responsible to* the people (typically of his or her country) who depend on him or her; the leader is *responsible for* their security and welfare. The responsible state leader should strive to do the best that circumstances permit on that particular day. But in exercising political responsibility, a political leader may have to violate private morality to defend national security. Not only would that be justifiable, it may be absolutely necessary. During the Second World War, the British Government imprisoned many people of German and Italian ancestry without giving them a fair trial. This tough situation of political choice is the normative heart of classical realist ethics.

- Realists are therefore opposed to the idea that particular nations can impose their ideologies (e.g., democracy) on other nations. Realists oppose this because they see it as a dangerous activity that threatens international peace and security. It is fundamentally unwise as, ultimately, it could backfire and threaten the crusading country.

- Statecraft is a sober and uninspiring activity that involves a profound awareness of human limitations and human imperfections. That pessimistic knowledge of human beings as they are and not as we might wish them to be is a difficult truth that lies at the heart of international politics.

Schelling and Strategic Realism

Classical realists—including Thucydides, Machiavelli, Hobbes, and Morgenthau—provide a normative analysis as well as an empirical analysis of IR. Power is understood to be not only a fact of political life but also a matter of political responsibility. Indeed, power and responsibility are inseparable concepts. For example, the balance of power is not only an empirical statement about the way that world politics are alleged to operate. The balance of power is also a basic value: it is a legitimate goal and a guide to responsible statecraft on the part of the leaders of the great powers. In other words, for classical realists the balance of power is a desirable institution and a good thing to strive for because it prevents hegemonic world domination by any one great power. It upholds the basic values of international peace and security.

Since the 1950s and 1960s, new realist approaches have emerged that are a product of the quest for a social science of IR. Many current realists hold back from providing a normative analysis of world politics because it is deemed to be subjective and thus unscientific. That attitude to the study of values in world politics marks a fundamental divide between classical realists on the one hand and strategic realists and neorealists on the other. In this section, we shall examine **strategic realism**, which is exemplified by the thought of Thomas Schelling (1980, 1996). Schelling does not pay much attention to the normative aspects of realism, although he does notice their presence in the background. In the next section we shall turn to neorealism, which is associated most closely with Kenneth Waltz (1979). Waltz also tends to ignore the normative aspects of realism in his pursuit of a scientific theory.

Strategic realism focuses centrally on foreign-policy decision making. When state leaders confront basic diplomatic and military issues, they are obliged to think strategically—i.e., instrumentally—if they hope to be successful. Schelling (1980, 1996) seeks to provide analytical tools for strategic thought. He views diplomacy and foreign policy, especially of the great powers and particularly the United States, as a rational–instrumental activity that can be more deeply understood by the application of a form of logical analysis called 'game theory'. He summarizes his thought as shown in Box 3.7 (see web links 3.12, 3.13, and 3.14).

A central concept that Schelling employs is that of a 'threat': his analysis concerns how statespeople can deal rationally with the threat and dangers of nuclear war. For example, writing about nuclear deterrence, Schelling makes the important observation that:

> the efficacy of . . . [a nuclear] threat may depend on what alternatives are available to the potential enemy, who, if he is not to react like a trapped lion, must be left some tolerable recourse. We have come to realize that a threat of all-out retaliation . . . eliminates lesser courses of action and forces him to choose between extremes . . . [and] may induce him to strike first.

(Schelling 1980: 6–7)

This is a good example of strategic realism which basically concerns how to employ power intelligently in order to get our military adversary to do what we desire and, more importantly, to avoid doing what we fear. According to strategic realism, 'choosing between

BOX 3.7	Schelling on diplomacy

Diplomacy is bargaining: it seeks outcomes that, though not ideal for either party, are better for both than some of the alternatives . . . The bargaining can be polite or rude, entail threats as well as offers, assume a status quo or ignore all rights and privileges, and assume mistrust rather than trust. But . . . there must be some common interest, if only in the avoidance of mutual damage, and an awareness of the need to make the other party prefer an outcome acceptable to oneself. With enough military force a country may not need to bargain.

Schelling (1980: 168)

extremes' is foolish and reckless and is thus ill-advised because of the high levels of danger it involves. It should therefore be avoided.

For Schelling, the activity of foreign policy is a rational, enlightened activity. It is technically instrumental and thus free from moral choice. It is not primarily concerned about what is good or what is right. It is primarily concerned with the question: what is required for our policy to be successful? These questions are clearly similar to those posed above by Machiavelli. Schelling (1980) identifies and dissects with sharp insight various rational choice mechanisms, stratagems, and moves which, if followed by the principal actors, could generate collaboration and avoid disaster in a conflict-ridden world of nuclear-armed states. But Schelling does not base his instrumental analysis on an underlying political or civic ethics the way that Machiavelli does. The normative values at stake in foreign policy are largely taken for granted. That marks an important divide between classical realism on the one hand, and strategic realism and neorealism on the other.

One of the crucial instruments of foreign policy for a great power such as the United States is that of armed force. And one of the characteristic concerns of strategic realism is the use of armed force in foreign policy. Schelling devotes considerable thought to this issue. He observes an important distinction between brute force and coercion: 'between taking what you want and making someone give it to you'. He continues:

brute force succeeds when it is used, whereas the power to hurt is most successful when held in reserve. It is the threat of damage . . . that can make someone yield or comply.

(Schelling 1996: 169–70)

He adds that to make the use of our coercive apparatus effective 'we need to know what an adversary treasures and what scares him', and we also need to communicate clearly to him 'what will cause the violence to be inflicted and what will cause it to be withheld'. There should be no misunderstandings. The actors involved should be acutely aware of the dangers (costs) and opportunities (benefits) they face.

Schelling goes on to make a fundamentally realist point: for coercion to be effective, it 'requires that our interests and our opponent's [interests] are not absolutely opposed . . . coercion requires finding a bargain'. Coercion is a method of bringing an adversary into a bargaining relationship and getting the adversary to do what we want him or her to do without having to compel it—i.e., the use of brute force, which is usually far more difficult, far

<table>
<tr><td>**BOX 3.8**</td><td>**Schelling on the diplomacy of violence**</td></tr>
</table>

The power to hurt is nothing new in warfare, but . . . modern technology . . . enhances the importance of war and threats of war as techniques of influence, not of destruction; of coercion and deterrence, not of conquest and defense; of bargaining and intimidation . . . War no longer looks like just a contest of strength. War and the brink of war are more a contest of nerve and risk-taking, of pain and endurance . . . The threat of war has always been somewhere underneath international diplomacy . . . Military strategy can no longer be thought of . . . as the science of military victory. It is now equally, if not more, the art of coercion, of intimidation and deterrence . . . Military strategy . . . has become the diplomacy of violence.

Schelling (1996: 168, 182)

less efficient, and far more dangerous (see web links 3.15 and 3.16). Schelling (1996: 181) summarizes his analysis of the modern diplomacy of violence in Box 3.8.

There obviously are striking similarities between the realism of Machiavelli and that of Schelling. However, the strategic realism of Schelling (1980) does not usually probe the ethics of foreign policy; it merely presupposes basic foreign-policy goals without comment. The normative aspects of foreign policy and the justification of intelligent strategy in a dangerous world of nuclear-armed superpowers are intimated by his argument but largely hidden beneath the surface of his text. Schelling speaks quite readily of the 'dirty' and 'extortionate' heart of strategic realism. But he does not inquire why that kind of diplomacy could be called 'dirty' or 'extortionate', and he does not say whether that can be justified. The values at stake are largely assumed. Schelling's realism is fundamentally different from Machiavelli's realism in that important respect (Table 3.3).

Strategic realism thus presupposes values and carries normative implications. Unlike classical realism, however, it does not examine them or explore them. For example, Schelling (1980: 4) is well aware that rational behaviour is motivated not only by a conscious calculation of advantages but also by 'an explicit and internally consistent value system'. But the role of value systems is not investigated by Schelling beyond making it clear that behaviour is related to values, such as vital national interests. Values are taken as given and treated instrumentally. In other words, the fundamental point of behaving the way that Schelling suggests that foreign policymakers *ought* to behave is not explored, clarified, or even

TABLE 3.3   Realist statecraft: instrumental realism and strategic realism

	MACHIAVELLI'S RENAISSANCE STATECRAFT	**SCHELLING'S NUCLEAR STATECRAFT**
Mode	Instrumental realism	Strategic realism
Means	Strength and cunning	Intelligence, nerve and risk-taking
	Opportunism and luck	Logic and art of coercion
Goals	Security and survival	Security and survival
Values	Civic virtue	Value-neutral; non-prescriptive

addressed. He provides a strategic analysis but not a normative theory of IR. Here we come to a fundamental difference between Schelling and Machiavelli. For Machiavelli, the point was the survival and flourishing of the nation. Classical realists are explicitly concerned about the basic values at stake in world politics; they provide a political and ethical theory of IR. Most realists today are usually silent about them and seem to take them more or less for granted without commenting on them or building them into their IR theories. They limit their analyses to political structures and processes and they largely ignore political ends.

Waltz and Neorealism

The leading neorealist thinker is undoubtedly Kenneth Waltz (Table 3.4). Waltz's *Theory of International Politics* (1979) seeks to provide a scientific explanation of the international political system. He takes some elements of classical realism as a starting point—e.g., independent states existing and operating in a system of international anarchy. But he departs from that tradition by giving no account of human nature and by ignoring the ethics of statecraft. His explanatory approach is heavily influenced by economic models. A scientific theory of IR leads us to expect states to behave in certain predictable ways. In Waltz's view, the best IR theory is one that focuses centrally on the structure of the system, on its interacting units, and on the continuities and changes of the system. In classical realism, state leaders and their international decisions and actions are at the centre of attention. In neorealism, by contrast, the structure of the system that is external to the actors, in particular the relative distribution of power, is the central analytical focus. Leaders are relatively unimportant because structures compel them to act in certain ways. Structures more or less determine actions (Box 3.9). To that extent, Waltz's theory is a determinist theory.

According to Waltz's neorealist theory, a basic feature of international relations is the decentralized structure of anarchy between states. States are alike in all basic functional respects—i.e., in spite of their different cultures or ideologies or constitutions or histories, they all perform the same basic tasks. All states have to collect taxes, conduct foreign policy, maintain domestic order, and so on. States differ significantly only in regard to their greatly varying capabilities. In Waltz's own words, the state units of an international system are 'distinguished primarily by their greater or lesser capabilities for performing similar tasks . . . the structure of a system changes with changes in the distribution of capabilities across the

TABLE 3.4   Waltz's neorealist theory: structure and outcomes

INTERNATIONAL STRUCTURE	INTERNATIONAL OUTCOMES
(*state units and relations*)	(*effects of state competition*)
International anarchy	Balance of power
States as 'like units'	International recurrence and repetition
Unequal state capability	International conflict, war
Great power relations	International change

> ### BOX 3.9   Waltz on the importance of structure
>
> The ruler's, and later the state's, interest provides the spring of action; the necessities of policy arise from the unregulated competition of states; calculation based on these necessities can discover the policies that will best serve the state's interests; success is the ultimate test of policy, and success is defined as preserving and strengthening the state—structural constraints explain why the methods are repeatedly used despite differences in the persons and states who use them.
>
> Waltz (1979: 117)

system's units' (Waltz 1979: 97). In other words, international change occurs when great powers rise and fall and the balance of power shifts accordingly (see web link 3.18 and 3.19). A typical means of such change is great-power war. A good example of such fundamental change is the end of the Second World War, which involved the defeat and collapse of Germany and Japan, the decline of Britain and France, and the emergence and domination of the United States and the Soviet Union.

As indicated, the states that are crucially important for determining changes in the structure of the international system are the great powers. A balance of power between states can be achieved, but war is always a possibility in an anarchical system. Waltz distinguishes between bipolar systems—such as existed during the Cold War between the United States and the Soviet Union—and multipolar systems—such as existed both before and after the Cold War. Waltz believes that bipolar systems are more stable and thus provide a better guarantee of peace and security than do multipolar systems. 'With only two great powers, both can be expected to act to maintain the system' (Waltz 1979: 204). That is because in maintaining the system they are maintaining themselves. According to that view, the Cold War was a period of international stability and peace (Box 3.10).

Unlike Schelling's strategic realism, Waltz's neorealist approach does not provide explicit policy guidance to state leaders as they confront the practical problems of world politics. That is presumably because they have little or no choice, owing to the confining international structure in which they must operate. Waltz (1979: 194–210) does address the question of 'the management of international affairs'. However, that discussion is far more about the structural constraints of foreign policy than it is about what Schelling clearly understands as the logic and art of foreign policy.

Schelling operates with a notion of situated choice: the rational choice for the situation or circumstances in which leaders find themselves. The choice may be sharply confined by the circumstances but it is a choice nevertheless and it may be made intelligently or stupidly, skilfully or maladroitly, etc. Waltz's neorealism makes far less provision for statecraft and diplomacy. His argument is at base a determinist theory in which structure dictates policy. In this important respect, it is an explicit departure from classical realism, which focuses on the politics and ethics of statecraft (Morgenthau 1985). It is also a departure from Schelling, who assumes rational behaviour of statesmen and focuses centrally on strategic choice.

However, just beneath the surface of Waltz's neorealist text, and occasionally on the surface, there is a recognition of the ethical dimension of international politics

| BOX 3.10 | John Gaddis's portrait of the long bipolar peace during the Cold War |

1. The post-war bipolar system realistically reflected the facts of where military power resided at the end of World War II . . .

2. The post-1945 bipolar structure was a simple one that did not require sophisticated leadership to maintain it . . .

3. Because of its relatively simple structure, alliances in this bipolar system have tended to be more stable than they had been in the 19th century and in the 1919–1939 period. It is striking that the North Atlantic Treaty Organization has equalled in longevity the most durable of the pre-World War I alliances, that between Germany and Austria-Hungary; it has lasted almost twice as long as the Franco-Russian alliance, and certainly much longer than any of the tenuous alignments of the interwar period.

In short, without anyone's having designed it . . . the nations of the post-war era lucked into a system of international relations that because it has been based upon realities of power, has served the cause of order—if not justice—better than one might have expected.

Gaddis (1987: 221–2)

which is virtually identical to classical realism. The core concepts that Waltz employs have a normative aspect. For example, he operates with a concept of state sovereignty: 'To say that a state is sovereign means that it decides for itself how it will cope with its internal and external problems' (Waltz 1979: 96). Thus, state sovereignty means being in a position to decide, a condition which is usually signified by the term 'independence': sovereign states are postulated as independent of other sovereign states. But what is independence? Waltz (1979: 88) says that each state is formally 'the equal of all the others. None is entitled to command; none is required to obey'. But to say that states are 'equal' and that independence is an 'entitlement' is to take notice of a *norm* which is acknowledged; in this case the norm of 'equal' state sovereignty. Waltz also assumes that states are worth fighting for. That implies values: those of state security and survival. But unlike the classical realists, Waltz does not explicitly discuss those values. He simply takes them for granted.

Waltz (1979: 113) also operates with a concept of the national interest: 'each state plots the course it thinks will best serve its interests'. For classical realists the national interest is the basic guide of responsible foreign policy: it is a moral idea that must be defended and promoted by state leaders. For Waltz, however, the national interest seems to operate like an automatic signal commanding state leaders when and where to move. The difference here is: Morgenthau believes that state leaders are duty bound to conduct their foreign policies by reference to the guidelines laid down by the national interest, and they may be condemned for failing to do that; Waltz's neorealist theory hypothesizes that they will always do that more or less automatically. Morgenthau thus sees states as organizations guided by leaders whose foreign policies are successful or unsuccessful, depending on the astuteness and wisdom of their decisions. Waltz sees states as robots that respond to the structural constraints and dictates of the international system.

Similarly, Waltz (1979: 195) argues that the great powers manage the international system. Classical realists argue that they ought to manage the system and that they can be criticized when they fail to manage it properly—i.e., when they fail to maintain international order. The notion that the great powers must be 'Great Responsibles' is not only a traditional realist idea; it is also a core idea of the International Society approach (see Chapter 5). Great powers are understood by Waltz to have 'a big stake in their system' and for them management of the system is not only something that is possible but also something that is 'worthwhile'. It is perfectly clear that Waltz values international order. It is clear, too, that he is convinced that international order is more likely to be achieved in bipolar systems than in multipolar systems.

A distinctive characteristic of neorealism emerges at this point. Waltz wants to present a scientific *explanation* of international politics which is a big step beyond the political and moral theories of classical realism. He cannot avoid implying normative concerns, however, and he cannot escape from making what are implicitly normative assumptions. His entire theory rests on normative foundations of a traditional–realist kind. Thus, although he makes no explicit reference to values or ethics and avoids normative theory, the basic assumptions and concepts he uses and the basic international issues with which he is concerned are normative ones. In that respect, his neorealism is not as far removed from classical realism as his claims about scientific theory imply. This serves as a reminder that scientific explanations can frequently involve norms and values (see Chapter 9).

Mearsheimer, Stability Theory, and Hegemony

Both strategic realism and neorealism were intimately connected with the Cold War. They were distinctive IR theory responses to that special, if not unique, historical situation. Being strongly influenced by the behaviouralist revolution in IR (see Chapter 2) they both sought to apply scientific methods to the theoretical and practical problems posed by the conflict between the United States and the Soviet Union. Schelling tried to show how a notion of strategy based on game theory could shed light on the nuclear rivalry between the two superpowers. Waltz tried to show how a structural analysis could shed light on 'the long peace' (Gaddis 1987) that was produced by the bipolar rivalry between the United States and the Soviet Union during the Cold War (see web link 3.21). The end of the Cold War and the multipolar condition that emerged thus raises an important question about the future of realist theories that were developed during what could be regarded as an exceptional period of modern international history. In this section we shall address that question in connection with neorealism.

In a widely discussed essay, John Mearsheimer (1993) takes up the neorealist argument of Waltz (1979) and applies it to both the past and the future. He says that neorealism has continued relevance for explaining international relations; neorealism is a general theory that applies to other historical situations besides that of the Cold War. It is relevant to multipolar situations as much as to bipolar situations of world politics. He also argues that neorealism can be employed to predict the course of international history beyond the Cold War.

Mearsheimer builds on Waltz's (1979: 161–93) argument concerning the stability of bipolar systems as compared with multipolar systems (see web link 3.20). These two configurations are considered to be the main structural arrangements of power that are possible among independent states. As indicated, Waltz claims that bipolar systems are superior to multipolar systems because they provide greater international stability and thus greater peace and security. There are three basic reasons why bipolar systems are more stable and peaceful. First, the number of great-power conflicts is fewer, and that reduces the possibilities of great-power war. Second, it is easier to operate an effective system of deterrence because fewer great powers are involved. Finally, because only two powers dominate the system the chances of miscalculation and misadventure are lower. There are fewer fingers on the trigger. In short, the two rival superpowers can keep their eye steadily fixed on each other without the distraction and confusion that would occur if there were a larger number of great powers, as was the case prior to 1945 and arguably has been the case since 1990 (Mearsheimer 1993: 149–50).

The question Mearsheimer (1993: 141) poses is: what could be expected to happen when a bipolar system is replaced by a multipolar system? How would such a basic system change affect the chances for peace and the dangers of war in post-Cold War Europe? The answer Mearsheimer gives is as follows:

> the prospects for major crises and war in Europe are likely to increase markedly if . . . this scenario unfolds. The next decades in a Europe without the superpowers would probably not be as violent as the first 45 years of this century [an era of two world wars], but would probably be substantially more prone to violence than the past 45 years [the era of the Cold War].

(Mearsheimer 1993: 142)

What is the basis for that pessimistic conclusion? Mearsheimer (1993: 142–3) argues that the distribution and nature of military power are the main sources of war and peace and says, specifically, that 'the long peace' between 1945 and 1990 was a result of three fundamentally important conditions: the bipolar system of military power in Europe; the approximate military equality between the United States and the Soviet Union; and the reality that both of the rival superpowers were equipped with an imposing arsenal of nuclear weapons. The withdrawal of the superpowers from the European heartland would give rise to a multipolar system consisting of five major powers (Germany, France, Britain, Russia, and perhaps Italy) as well as a number of minor powers. That system would be 'prone to instability'. 'The departure of the superpowers would also remove the large nuclear arsenals they now maintain in Central Europe. This would remove the pacifying effect that these weapons have had on European politics' (Mearsheimer 1993: 143).

Thus, according to Mearsheimer (1993: 187), the Cold War between the United States and the Soviet Union 'was principally responsible for transforming a historically violent region into a very peaceful place' (Table 3.5). Mearsheimer argues that the demise of the

TABLE 3.5   Mearsheimer's neorealist stability theory

CONDITIONS OF STABLE BIPOLARITY	CONDITIONS OF UNSTABLE MULTIPOLARITY
• Europe during the Cold War	• Europe before 1945 and after 1990
• Two superpowers	• Several great powers
• Rough superpower equality	• Unequal and shifting balances of power
• Nuclear deterrence	• Conventional military rivalry
• Conquest is difficult	• Conquest is less difficult and more tempting
• Superpower discipline	• Great power indiscipline and risk-taking

bipolar Cold War order and the emergence of a multipolar Europe will produce a highly undesirable return to the bad old ways of European anarchy and instability and even a renewed danger of international conflict, crises, and possibly war. He makes the following highly controversial point:

The West has an interest in maintaining peace in Europe. It therefore has an interest in maintaining the Cold War order, and hence has an interest in the continuation of the Cold War confrontation; developments that threaten to end it are dangerous.

(Mearsheimer 1993: 332)

In the same vein as Waltz, Mearsheimer regards the behaviour of states as shaped if not indeed determined by the anarchical *structure* of international relations. He differs from Waltz, however, whom he characterizes as a 'defensive realist'; i.e., someone who recognizes that states must and do seek power in order to be secure and to survive, but who believe that excessive power is counterproductive, because it provokes hostile alliances by other states. For Waltz, it does not make sense, therefore, to strive for excessive power beyond that which is necessary for security and survival. Mearsheimer thus speaks of Waltz's theory as **'defensive realism'**.

Mearsheimer agrees with Waltz that anarchy compels states to compete for power. However, he argues that states seek hegemony, that they are ultimately more aggressive than Waltz portrays them. The goal for a country such as the United States is to dominate the entire system, because only in that way could it rest assured that no other state or combination of states would even think about going to war against it. All major powers strive for that ideal situation. But Mearsheimer qualifies his argument by noting that the planet is too big for global hegemony. The oceans are huge barriers. No state would have the necessary power. Mearsheimer, therefore, argues that states can only become the hegemon in their own region of the world. In the Western hemisphere, for example, the United States has long been by far the most powerful state. No other state—Canada, Mexico, Brazil—would even think about threatening or employing armed force against the United States.

Regional hegemons can see to it, however, that there are no other regional hegemons in any other part of the world. They can prevent the emergence and existence of a peer competitor. According to Mearsheimer, that is what the United States is trying to ensure. That is because a peer competitor might try to interfere in a regional hegemon's sphere of influence and control. For almost two centuries, since the Monroe Doctrine of 1823, the United States endeavoured to ensure that no great power intervened militarily in the Western hemisphere. As a great power for most of the past century and all of the present century, the United States has made great efforts to ensure that there is no regional hegemon in either Europe or East Asia, the two areas where there are other major powers or great powers and a potential peer competitor could emerge: Germany in Europe and China in East Asia. The United States confronted Imperial Germany in the First World War, Nazi Germany in the Second World War, and the Soviet Union in the Cold War, because if any of those states had gained hegemony in Europe it would be free to intervene in the Western hemisphere, and possibly threaten the security of the United States.

According to Mearsheimer, all states want to become regional hegemons. His neorealist theory postulates that Germany will become the dominant European state and that China will likely emerge as a potential hegemon in Asia. By the same theory, if that were to happen one would also expect the United States to react to try to prevent or undercut Chinese power in East Asia. Indeed, if China became a peer competitor the United States could be expected to go to great lengths to contain China's influence and prevent China from intervening in other regions of the world where American national interests are at stake. That is why he refers to his theory as '**offensive realism**', which rests on the assumption that great powers 'are always searching for opportunities to gain power over their rivals, with hegemony as their final goal' (Mearsheimer 2001: 29). Mearsheimer, like other realists, believes that his argument has general application to all places at all times. There has always been and there will always be a struggle between nation-states for power and domination in the international system. And there is nothing that anyone can do to prevent it. International struggle and conflict between great powers is inevitable. This is why the title of one of his books is *The Tragedy of Great Power Politics*.

Mearsheimer's theory of offensive realism has come in for criticism from many quarters. Some of those criticisms are levelled by liberal IR theorists. His theory of offensive realism has been criticized for failing to explain peaceful change and cooperation between great powers, such as between Britain and the United States for the past century and longer. Critics also argue, for example, that it fails to explain the emergence of the European Union, which involves the pooling of sovereignty by states in an international community. However, we shall be concerned only with selected criticisms from within realism itself. At least one potential regional hegemon has been involved in the process of European unification: Germany. Mearsheimer would explain that by the military presence of the United States in Europe, which checks Germany's military expansion. But from within his own theory one could ask: why do American armed forces remain in Europe long after the disintegration of the Soviet Union and in the absence of any other great power trying to dominate the region?

In fairness to Mearsheimer's argument about offensive realism, one could point to Russia's recent aggressive behaviour, orchestrated by Vladimir Putin, in relation to Ukraine and Georgia. In Georgia, Russia has intervened with armed force in support of ethnic separatists. In Ukraine, Russia has annexed the southern, Black Sea region of Crimea (which used to belong to Russia), and has intervened militarily in support of a war waged by ethnic Russian separatists against the Ukrainian army in eastern Ukraine. The United States has expressed profound concern about both instances of aggressive Russian behaviour, particularly in Ukraine. But Washington has refused to get directly involved militarily in either region. Some observers view the Russian intervention in Ukraine as evidence of a return of the Cold War in Eastern Europe.

A realist like Morgenthau would probably criticize Mearsheimer's argument for ignoring the responsibilities of statecraft, and for leaving the impression that states are conflicting power machines that behave without any human involvement as to their management or mismanagement. There are no misadventures, misunderstandings, or mistakes in the behaviour of great powers; there is no good or bad judgement, no miscalculation, etc. There is only power, conflict, war, hegemony, subjugation, and so on. That same criticism of a mechanistic model could, of course, also be directed against Waltz's defensive theory.

A related criticism of Mearsheimer's theory is its deficiency in empirical perceptiveness and subtlety. Mearsheimer sees no significant difference in the current and future power relationships between states in Western Europe as compared with those in East Asia. Here, it has been pointed out,

> he is at odds with that more famous realist, Henry Kissinger who, in his book *Does America Need a Foreign Policy?*, convincingly argues that for the foreseeable future there is little or no likelihood of the nations of Western Europe going to war with each other or with the United States, but that war is much more possible among the nations of Asia or between America and Asian powers.

(see web link 3.23; Sempa 2009: 90)

Mearsheimer's offensive realist theory has also been criticized for failing to look at historical experiences that are contrary to his thesis, or in other words for not being sufficiently open-minded and eclectic in seeking to explain relations between great powers and the balance of power. Eclecticism, however, means opening one's approach to the possibility of factors and forces not predicted by one's theory. Ultimately, eclecticism would transform theory into history, in the sense that it would seek to accurately describe events. That is not what neorealist theories are content with. Mearsheimer, like Waltz, wants to come up with explanations that satisfy the concept of a 'scientific' theory in accordance with philosophy of science criteria. How successful they have been in that regard is still being debated.

Neoclassical Realism

There has been an attempt recently to frame a realist theory that combines the best elements of neorealism with those of classical realism within one analytical framework. Like the versions of realism already discussed, this one rests upon the assumption that IR is basically an anarchical system. It draws upon neorealism, and that of Waltz in particular, by acknowledging the significance of the structure of the international state system and the relative power of states. It also draws upon classical realism, and Morgenthau and Kissinger in particular, by emphasizing the importance of leadership and foreign policy. **Neoclassical realism** departs from both of these basic realist approaches, however, by attempting to come up with a realist theory that can respond positively to some of the arguments associated with liberalism (see Chapter 4). Unlike the classical theories of realism discussed in this chapter, this is a recent approach. It remains to be seen whether it will become well established.

Advocates of neoclassical realism take a middle-of-the-road view: that state leadership operates and foreign policy is carried on within the overall constraints or 'broad parameters' of the anarchical structure of international relations (Rose 1998: 144). At first glance, the combination of neorealism and classical realism might appear to be contradictory. The determinist–materialist theory of Waltz seems to be at odds with the foreign-policy leadership and ethics of statecraft theory of Morgenthau and Kissinger.

As indicated in the section on classical realism, classical realists assume that the underlying condition of international relations is one of anarchy. They typically argue that foreign policy is always framed and carried out under the influences and constraints of international circumstances—defined by the presence and policies of foreign powers—whatever those circumstances happen to be at any particular time, whether threatening or promising, fluid or stable. They view international circumstances as the most important pressures on foreign policy. Statesmen and stateswomen are thus seen as necessarily having to deal with foreign powers in order to carry out their responsibilities for ensuring the security and survival of their country. Classical realists see that as the heavy moral responsibility of statesmen and stateswomen: the heart of classical realism is the ethics of statecraft.

Neoclassical realists are not content with that traditional or classical realist way of framing the problem. This is clearly evident by their acknowledgement of the significance of neorealism, and by their desire not to repudiate neorealism but rather to improve upon it by introducing elements which neorealists have left out of their analysis. Neoclassical realists clearly want to retain the structural argument of neorealism. But they also want to add to it the instrumental (policy or strategy) argument of the role of stateleaders, the responsibilities of power, on which classical realism places its emphasis (Table 3.6).

Neoclassical realists argue that 'anarchy gives states considerable latitude in defining their security interests, and the relative distribution of power merely sets parameters for grand strategy' (Lobell et al. 2009: 7). In other words, anarchy and the relative power of states do

TABLE 3.6   Classical realism, neorealism, and neoclassical realism

	CLASSICAL	NEOREALISM	NEOCLASSICAL
Anarchy	yes	yes	yes
State power	yes	yes	yes
Leadership	yes	no	yes
Statecraft ethics	yes	no	no
Domestic society	no	no	yes
Social science	no	yes	yes

not dictate the specific foreign policies of stateleaders. However, neoclassical realists also argue that 'leaders who consistently fail to respond to systemic incentives put their state's very survival at risk' (Lobell et al. 2009: 7). That is to say, international structure (anarchy and the balance of power) constrains states but it does not ultimately specify leadership policies and actions.

This way of portraying the structural situation in which stateleaders find themselves in their conduct of foreign policy—there are constraints of relative power but there is also latitude for choice—seems not very different from classical realism. The difference between the two concerns the interest in normative aspects of IR. Classical realists—like Morgenthau or Kissinger—will want to judge leadership success or failure in relation to ethical standards: do leaders live up to their responsibilities or not? Neoclassical realists focus on explaining what goes on in terms of the pressures of international structure on the one hand and the decisions made by stateleaders on the other. Neoclassical realism also seeks to introduce an element that all other realists ignore or downplay in their analyses: namely internal characteristics of states. Neoclassical realism:

seeks to explain why, how, and under what conditions the internal characteristics of states—the extractive and mobilization capacity of politic-military institutions, the influence of domestic societal actors and interest groups, the degree of state autonomy from society, and the level of elite or societal cohesion—intervene between the leaders' assessment of international threats and opportunities and the actual diplomatic, military, and foreign economic policies those leaders pursue.

(Lobell et al. 2009: 4)

That kind of analysis is inspired by liberal approaches to IR (see Chapter 4), which emphasize the importance of domestic conditions of countries in seeking to explain international relations and foreign policies. This contrasts sharply with all other realist approaches, including both neorealism and classical realism. The advantage of neoclassical realism is that an additional element which is relevant for explaining IR is included in the theory. The possible drawback is that the theory becomes less parsimonious, more complex, and more oriented towards including a large number of different elements in the analysis.

Rethinking the Balance of Power

For classical realists, probably the greatest responsibility of statesmen is the responsibility to maintain a balance of military power among the great powers. The point of doing so is to prevent any great power from getting out of control and attempting to impose its political and military will on everybody else. The two greatest examples in modern European history are French King Louis XIV's attempt to dominate Europe in the late seventeenth century, and Napoleon's attempt to do the same a century later. Both attempts ultimately failed. The other great powers at the time united to form military alliances that defeated each of those French bids for European hegemony.

Thus, in classical realist thinking, the balance of power is a valued political objective that promotes national security, upholds order among great powers, and makes the independence of states and their peoples possible. The Second World War can readily be seen in this light: Nazi Germany and Imperial Japan made a bid to impose their separate hegemonies on Europe and Asia; and Britain, the Soviet Union, and the United States formed an alliance to counter those attempts and restore a balance of power. The Cold War is generally portrayed as a bipolar balance of power based on nuclear weapons and often referred to as a balance of terror—between the United States and the Soviet Union.

Consequently, the end of the Cold War led many statesmen and scholars alike to envisage a new world order based on political freedom and economic progress which would not require any balance of terror. That hope did not last long. With the outbreak of various armed conflicts in the 1990s, some scholars began to speak of stable Cold War bipolarity being replaced by unstable post-Cold War multipolarity. That led to new IR scholarship which attempted to account for those post-Cold War conflicts in balance of power terms. More recently, it has been suggested that the conflict in Ukraine is evidence of a new cold war between Russia and the West (the United States and the European Union).

We can only summarize the main points of these arguments. Some scholars used the occasion to mount a root-and-branch assault on the relevance of classical balance of power theory to our understanding of world history (Wohlforth in Nexon 2009). They argued that many factors ignored by the theory—administrative capacity of hegemons, expansion of state membership in the international system, the societal unity or disunity of states, and the existence of international society norms—affect the existence of hegemons (hierarchy) and the degree of anarchy in the state system. Some argued that the new conflicts contradicted the classical proposition that the balance of power prevents hegemony (Wohlforth in Nexon 2009: 331). Others argued that the post-Cold War conflicts called for new conceptions of 'balance' and 'balancing' and thus for new theories of the balance of power.

Like many key concepts in IR, and perhaps even more than most, the balance of power has often proved to be not so easy to pin down. More than half a century ago, a leading American scholar identified how variously and differently the term 'balance of power' was employed in IR scholarship: in some cases the expression was used in contradictory ways (Haas 1953). That same difficulty has been noted in recent scholarship: 'While the balance of power concept is one of the most prominent ideas in the theory and practice of international relations, it is also one of the most ambiguous and intractable ones' (Paul et al. 2004: 29).

Yet, this underestimates the value and persistence of the concept, because there is substantial agreement among scholars on *two important* points that should be noted. First, the balance of power is understood as an international relationship that is so likely to occur, and is so widely occurring, that it appears to be virtually a natural phenomenon. There is thus a degree of predictability about it. Second, the balance of power assumes equilibrium of power among a small *number* of major states, where power is defined narrowly in terms of military capability. In other words, the balance of power is understood as a systemic and virtually mechanical condition of international relations which is likely to occur and recur when there are several military powers interacting. Since that system of powerful states seems likely to persist indefinitely, as a primary feature of international politics, balance of power theory can be expected to remain a central concept of IR theory.

Classical power balancing has by no means ended. It is not hard to find current examples of power balancing. Both China and Russia actively seek influence and control of their respective regions; Iran is attempting to change the balance of power in the Middle East in its favour. Yet, many realists did expect that the dominance of the winning side in the Cold War—the United States—would have been much more profoundly challenged by other great powers than has actually been the case (Fettweis 2004).

The European Union has proved remarkably successful in establishing what now looks like 'perpetual peace' between Germany and France, arguably the EU's greatest achievement. And peaceful cooperation between the European great powers in the EU did not end with the end of the Cold War and the disappearance of the common enemy, the Soviet Union. On the other hand, however, the emergence of a more belligerent Russia prepared to violate fundamental international norms in regard to Ukraine has provoked the European Union, along with the United States, to impose rather severe economic sanctions on Moscow. It has also involved increased military activities by NATO in Eastern Europe. It remains to be seen how long these new East–West tensions will last.

If classical power balancing has decreased in importance, what might have taken its place? This brings us to the distinction between a hard balance of power and a soft balance of power. The former is the classical realist concept of a balance of military power between major powers. The latter, on the other hand, is a more recent conception of liberal theorists. In this theory, the military power of states or international organizations—e.g., alliances—is not the main focus, as it is for both classical realists and International Society theorists. Rather, it emphasizes tacit or informal institutional collaboration or ad hoc cooperation among states for the purpose of joint security against a foreign threat. The concept clearly seeks to enlarge the focus of the balance of power, to include arrangements that are seen to be significant non-military ways in which major powers interact that cushion, assuage, or ease their relations which would otherwise be more antagonistic, uncompromising, and hostile.

The liberal notion of a soft balance of power has been the subject of much critical analysis. One important critique is the charge that the concept 'stretches' the notion of the balance of power to the point of making it so elastic and diverse that its core meaning is lost sight of (Nexon 2009). This is to criticize the concept for resting on what philosophers refer to as a 'category mistake', which is the error of overlooking or conflating categorical differences in bracketing phenomena together. The original concept of 'soft power' displays that problem, since the adjective 'soft' enlarges the noun 'power' to the point of characterizing such social elements as 'norms', 'laws', 'procedures', 'institutions', etc., as kinds or manifestations of power. Yet, conventionally understood, such terms belong within the normative category of authority (or right) and outside the instrumental or structural category of power. With such difficulties in mind, the concept of a soft balance of power has been criticized for being conceptually incoherent (Sartori 1984).

Where does this recent theory leave the balance of power concept? Some proponents of the soft balance of power argue that it encapsulates more of the ways that power is balanced.

It is thus more faithful to reality, more accurate, and more empirical. The critics in the section on strategic realism have already had their say, that soft power theory muddies the waters and confuses our understanding of the balance of power, rather than enhancing it. We leave it to our readers to decide. What is clear, however one decides, is that the balance of power theory in IR is still very much alive, which is why we have discussed it at considerable length (see esp. Paul et al. 2004; Wohlforth in Nexon 2009).

Two Critiques of Realism

The dominance of realism in IR during the second half of the twentieth century, especially in the United States, provoked a substantial literature that criticizes many of its core assumptions and arguments (see web link 3.30). As indicated in Chapter 2, realism itself rose to a position of academic pre-eminence in the 1940s and 1950s by effectively criticizing the liberal idealism of the interwar period. Neorealism has been involved in a renewed debate with liberalism. We shall investigate that debate in Chapter 4. Here we shall confine our discussion to two important critiques of realism: an International Society critique and an emancipatory critique.

The International Society tradition (see Chapter 5) is critical of realism on two counts. First, it regards realism as a one-dimensional IR theory that is too narrowly focused. Second, it claims that realism fails to capture the extent to which international politics is a dialogue of different IR voices and perspectives. The International Society tradition is not critical of every aspect of realist thought in IR. On the contrary, International Society scholars acknowledge that classical realism provides an important angle of vision on world politics. They agree that there is a strain in human nature that is self-interested and combative. They share a focus of analysis in which states loom large. They operate with a conception of international relations as anarchical. They agree that power is important and that international relations consist significantly of power politics. They also agree that international theory is in some fundamental respects a theory of security and survival. They recognize that the national interest is an important value in world politics. In short, International Society scholars incorporate several elements of realism into their own approach.

However, they do not believe that realism captures all of IR or even its most important aspects. They argue that realism overlooks, ignores, or plays down many important facets of international life. It overlooks the cooperative strain in human nature. It ignores the extent to which international relations form an anarchical *society* and not merely an anarchical system. States are not only in conflict, but also they share common interests and observe common rules which confer mutual rights and duties. Realism ignores other important actors besides states, such as human beings and NGOs. Realism plays down the extent to which the relations of states are governed by international law. It also plays down the extent to which international politics are progressive; i.e., cooperation instead of conflict can prevail in some circumstances. International Society theorists recognize the importance of the national interest as a value, but they refuse to accept that it is the only value that is important in world politics.

Martin Wight (1991), a leading representative of the International Society approach, places a great deal of emphasis on the character of international politics as a historical dialogue between three important philosophies/ideologies: realism (Machiavelli), rationalism (Grotius), and revolutionism (Kant). In order to acquire a holistic understanding of IR it is necessary, according to Wight, to comprehend the dialectical relations of these three basic normative perspectives (see Chapter 5).

At least one leading classical realist appears to agree with Wight. In a monumental study of diplomacy, the American scholar and statesman Henry Kissinger (1994: 29–55) explores the long-standing and continuing dialogue in diplomatic theory and practice between the foreign-policy outlook of pessimistic realism and that of optimistic liberalism. For example, Kissinger discerns that dialogue in the contrasting foreign policies of US Republican President Theodore Roosevelt and Democratic President Woodrow Wilson in the early twentieth century. Roosevelt was 'a sophisticated analyst of the balance of power' while Wilson was 'the originator of the vision of a universal world organization, the League of Nations'. Both perspectives have shaped American foreign policy historically. That dialogue between realism and liberalism is not confined to past and present American foreign policy; it is also evident historically in British foreign policy. Kissinger contrasts the politically cautious and pragmatic nineteenth-century British foreign policy of Conservative Prime Minister Benjamin Disraeli and the morally aroused and interventionist foreign policy of his Liberal counterpart, William Gladstone. Kissinger implies that both these perspectives have a legitimate place in American foreign policy and in British foreign policy, and that neither of them should be ignored. Here, then, is an implied criticism of realism by a famous classical realist: that it is inclined to ignore or at least to downplay the liberal and democratic voice in world affairs.

We thus have reason to ask whether Kissinger should be classified as a realist at all. Is he a secret member of the International Society school? We believe Kissinger should be regarded as a classical realist. Although he portrays the Wilsonian voice in American foreign policy and the Gladstonian voice in British foreign policy as legitimate and important, it is abundantly clear from his lengthy analysis that his preferred basis for any successful foreign policy for the United States and Britain is the realist outlook disclosed by Roosevelt and Disraeli, with whom Kissinger strongly identifies.

International Society scholars can thus be criticized for failing to recognize that while the liberal voice is important in world politics, the realist voice is always first in importance. That is because it is the best perspective on the core problem of IR: war. According to realists, difficult times such as war demand hard choices that realists are better able to clarify than any other IR scholars or practitioners. Liberals—according to classical realists—tend to operate on the assumption that foreign-policy choices are easier and less dangerous than they really may be: they are the foremost theorists of peaceful, prosperous, and easy times. For realists the problem with that is: what shall we do when times are difficult? If we follow the liberals, we may fail to respond adequately to the challenge with appropriate hard choices and we may thus place ourselves—and those who depend on our policies and actions—at risk. In other words, realism will always be resorted to during times of crisis when hard choices have to be made.

An alternative and very different critique of realism is that of **emancipatory theory**. Because realism has been such a dominant IR theory, emancipatory theorists direct their energies into providing what they consider to be a root-and-branch critique of realist assumptions and arguments. That is intended to pave the way for a complete reconceptualization of IR. Their critique of realism is central to their project of global human emancipation. Echoing Marxists of an earlier period, emancipatory theorists argue that IR theories should seek to grasp correctly how men and women are prisoners of existing international structures. IR theorists should indicate how they can be liberated from the state and from other structures of contemporary world politics that have the effect of oppressing them and thus preventing them from flourishing as they would otherwise. A central aim of emancipatory theory, then, is the transformation of the realist state-centric and power-focused structure of international politics. The goal is human liberation and fulfilment. The role of the emancipatory IR theorist is to determine the correct theory for guiding the practice of human liberation.

An emancipatory critique of realism has been developed by Ken Booth (1991). Booth (1991: 313–26) builds his critique on a familiar realist view of the 'Westphalian system'; 'a game' that is 'played by diplomats and soldiers on behalf of statesmen'. The 'security game' that states learned to play was 'power politics, with threats producing counter-threats, alliances, counter-alliances and so on'. In IR, that produced an 'intellectual hegemony of realism': a conservative or 'status quo' theory based on the security and survival of existing states, and focused on strategic thinking in which the concept of military (sometimes nuclear) threats was the core of realist thought. In other words, Booth is specifically criticizing strategic realism associated with thinkers such as Thomas Schelling (1980), discussed in the section on strategic realism.

Booth claims that the realist game of power politics and military (including nuclear) strategy is obsolete because security is now a local problem within disorganized and sometimes failed states. It is no longer primarily a problem of national security and national defence. Security is now more than ever both cosmopolitan and local at the same time: a problem of individual humans (e.g., citizens in failed states) and of the global community of humankind (facing, for example, ecological threats or nuclear extinction). Security is different in scope; it is also different in character: emancipation is the freeing of people (as individuals and groups) from those physical and human constraints which stop them carrying out what they would freely choose to do. War and the threat of war is one of those constraints, together with poverty, poor education, political oppression, and so on. Security and emancipation are two sides of the same coin. Emancipation, not power or order, produces true security (Booth 1991: 319). Implicit in this argument is the Kantian 'categorical imperative': the moral idea 'that we should treat people as ends and not means. States, however, should be treated as means and not ends' (Booth 1991: 319). In other words, people always come first; states are merely expedient instruments or tools that can be discarded if they are no longer useful.

In a similar vein, Andrew Linklater (1989) disputes the realist view of IR and offers an alternative emancipatory perspective to take its place (Box 3.11). Both Booth and Linklater

> **BOX 3.11** | **Linklater's emancipatory vision of global politics**
>
> A new framework for world politics, based on:
>
> 1. the construction of a 'global legal and political system' which goes beyond the state and 'affords protection to all human subjects';
>
> 2. the decline of self-interest and competitiveness which, according to realist thinking, sustains the state and fosters international conflict and ultimately war;
>
> 3. the rise and spread of human generosity that transcends state boundaries and extends to people everywhere;
>
> 4. the consequent development of a community of humankind to which all people owe their primary loyalty.
>
> Linklater (1989: 199)

claim that world politics can be constructed along these universal solidaristic lines, with IR theorists leading the way. Not only that: they also claim that this social movement away from the anarchical society based on states and power politics and towards a cosmopolitan idea of global human security is well under way. The consequence of that for IR is clear: realism is becoming obsolete as a theoretical approach for studying IR, and irrelevant as a practical attitude to world politics.

The realist response to such emancipatory critiques could be expected to include some of the following observations. Linklater's and Booth's declaration of the death of the independent state and thus of the anarchical state system, like the famous mistaken announcement of the death of Mark Twain, is premature. People across the world in their almost countless millions continue to cling to the state as their preferred form of political organization. We need only recall the powerful attraction of self-determination and political independence based on the state for the peoples of Asia, Africa, and the Middle East during the demise of European colonialism and for the peoples of Eastern Europe during the demise of the Soviet empire. When states fragment—as in the case of Yugoslavia at the end of the Cold War—the fragments turn out to be new (or old) states—e.g., Slovenia, Croatia, Bosnia, Kosovo. In historical terms all these major movements towards the sovereign state occurred recently—i.e., in the late twentieth or early twenty-first centuries. Security continues to be based primarily on the state and the state system. It is not based on a global political–legal organization—such an entity does not exist; nor is there any indication that it will exist in the foreseeable future.

Where security is based on other social organizations, such as the family or the clan, as sometimes happens in Africa and some other parts of the world, that is because the local state has failed as a security organization. People are trying to make the best of a bad situation. Their own state has failed them, but that does not mean they have given up on the state. What they want is what the people of many other countries already have: a developed and democratic state of their own. What they do not want is a 'global legal and political system' such as Linklater describes: that would be scarcely distinguishable from Western colonialism from which they have just escaped.

It is also necessary to mark the continuing significance of the major states. Realists underline the centrality of great powers in world politics. Great-power relations shape the international relations and influence the foreign policies of most other states. That is why realists concentrate their attention on the great powers. There is little reason to doubt that the United States, China, Japan, Russia, Germany, France, Britain, India, and a few other core states will continue to perform leading roles in world politics. There also is little reason to doubt that the people of the world depend on those states, before all others, for maintaining international peace and security. There is nobody else to provide that fundamental service.

Research Prospects and Programme

Realism is a theory, first about the security problems of sovereign states in an international anarchy, and second about the problem of international order. The normative core of realism is state survival and national security. If world politics continues to be organized on the basis of independent states with a small group of powerful states largely responsible for shaping the most important international events, then it seems clear that realism will continue to be an important IR theory. The only historical development that could render it obsolete is a world historical transformation that involved abandoning the sovereign state and the anarchical state system. That does not appear very likely in the foreseeable future.

This chapter has discussed the main strands of realism; a major distinction was made between classical realism on the one hand and strategic realism and neorealism on the other. Which strand of realism contains the most promising research programme? John Mearsheimer (1993) says that neorealism is a general theory that applies to other historical situations besides that of the Cold War. He argues that neorealism can be employed to predict the course of international history after the Cold War. We have noted that neorealism formulates a number of important questions about the distribution of power in the international system and the power balancing of the leading powers. Yet, we have also emphasized some limitations of neorealist theory, especially as regards the analysis of cooperation and integration in Western Europe after the end of the Cold War. Some neorealists think that these patterns of cooperation can be addressed without major difficulty through the further development of neorealist analysis (see, for example, Grieco 1997). From a more sceptical view, neorealism (and also strategic realism) appears closely tied to the special historical circumstances of the East–West conflict: (1) a bipolar system based on two rival superpowers (the United States and the Soviet Union) each implacably opposed to the other and prepared to risk nuclear war for the sake of its ideology; and (2) the development of nuclear weapons and the means to deliver them to any point on earth.

Since the end of the Cold War the Soviet Union has disappeared and the bipolar system has given way to one in which there are several major powers. The United States is arguably now the only superpower. This remains the case even though Putin's Russia seems to challenge it. It seems clear, however, that Russia in the twenty-first century is a belligerent regional (Eastern European) power and is no longer a world power in the way that it once was. With the rise of China, however, the current pre-eminent position of the United States in international relations might be expected to come to an end at some point in the not too distant future. That still remains to be seen.

Nuclear weapons remain in existence, of course, but the tight Cold War controls on them may have been loosened. There are a number of states, besides the United States, Russia, and China, which possess or may soon possess (in the case of Iran) nuclear arms. There is now an even greater danger of the spread of nuclear weapons than there was during the Cold War. Some strategic realists (such as Schelling) might see that development as dangerous, because there would be more fingers on the nuclear weapons trigger. However, Waltz views such a development as reducing risk of war and increasing the prospects of peace. That is because every nuclear power is mutually terrified and thus unlikely to risk a nuclear conflagration. Thus, nuclear proliferation is conducive to bringing about a more peaceful world. Different realists clearly can hold different views on matters of supreme importance in world politics.

We believe that all the various strands of realism we have presented continue to have important insights to offer in the analysis of international relations. But there are some important issues of the post-Cold War state system that the narrower focus of strategic realism and neorealism cannot so readily come to grips with. Among those are four key issues: (1) the emergence of the United States as an unrivalled great power following the demise of the Soviet Union, and the reduced significance of Russia as compared with its predecessor, the Soviet Union; (2) the threat posed by peripheral 'rogue states' which are prepared to threaten regional peace and security but are not in a position to threaten the global balance of power; (3) the problems posed by 'failed states' and the issue of great-power responsibility for the protection of human rights around the world; and (4) the security crisis presented by acts of international terrorism which threaten the personal security of citizens as much as or even more than either the national security of states or international peace and security. The two most significant developments, in that regard, have been the 11 September 2001 attacks on New York and Washington DC, which led to the prolonged wars in Iraq and Afghanistan, and the more recent emergence and expansion of ISIL in the Middle East, particularly Syria and Iraq.

We believe that leaves classical and neoclassical realism with the most promising future research programmes. A plausible research strategy for post-Cold War realism, therefore, would involve an attempt to understand the role of an unrivalled but also benign paramount power in an international system that must face several fundamental problems: the protection of global peace and security; the coming to grips with 'rogue states' and 'failed states' on the periphery of the state system; the prevention of violent and fanatical terrorists (ISIL) from establishing themselves as separate, outwardly hostile and inwardly abusive, jihadist states; and the protection of citizens, particularly those of Western countries, from international terrorism.

That research strategy would have to be revised, of course, with the emergence of China as a great power equal to the United States. That change would correspondingly invite a research strategy that focused centrally on bipolarity. One might conclude that the world had returned to a new version of the Cold War. That would probably be a mistake. Insofar as China has been transforming itself into a major player in the liberal world economy as well as a major player in international politics as a 'responsible' great power, this would not be a return to the bipolarity of the Cold War. Were this scenario to happen, as seems likely, a research question for that emerging bipolar system might be: 'How does the new bipolarity differ from the Cold War bipolarity?'

KEY POINTS

- Realists usually have a pessimistic view of human nature. Realists are sceptical that there can be progress in international politics that is comparable to that in domestic political life. They operate with a core assumption that world politics consists of an international anarchy of sovereign states. Realists see international relations as basically conflictual, and they see international conflicts as ultimately resolved by war.

- Realists believe that the goal of power, the means of power, and the uses of power are central preoccupations of political activity. International politics is thus portrayed as 'power politics'. The conduct of foreign policy is an instrumental activity based on the intelligent calculation of one's power and one's interests as against the power and interests of rivals and competitors.

- Realists have a high regard for the values of national security, state survival, and international order and stability. They usually believe that there are no international obligations in the moral sense of the word—i.e., bonds of mutual duty—between independent states. For classical realists there is one morality for the private sphere and another and very different morality for the public sphere. Political ethics allows some actions that would not be tolerated by private morality.

- Realists place a great deal of importance on the balance of power, which is both an empirical concept concerning the way that world politics are seen to operate and a normative concept: it is usually a structural concept of a system of states, but it is also a legitimate goal and a guide to responsible statecraft on the part of the leaders of the great powers. It keeps great powers under control, and upholds the basic values of peace and security.

- Structural realists employ the concepts bipolar system and multipolar system, and many see bipolarity as more conducive to international order.

- Neoclassical realists seek to combine the neorealist argument of Waltz with the classical realist arguments of Morgenthau and Kissinger. They also seek to incorporate the concept of domestic statehood and society which is a characteristic feature of liberalism.

- Some IR theorists employ the distinction between a hard balance of power and a soft balance of power. The former is the classical realist concept of a balance of military power between major powers. The latter, on the other hand, is a more recent, liberalistic conception of a many-faceted and more diverse balance of power.

- Schelling seeks to provide analytical tools for strategic thought. He views diplomacy and foreign policy, especially of the great powers and particularly the United States, as a rational–instrumental activity that can be more deeply understood by the application of a form of mathematical analysis called 'game theory'. Coercion is a method of bringing an adversary into a bargaining relationship and getting the adversary to do what we want him or her to do without having to compel it—i.e., employ brute force, which, in addition to being dangerous, is usually far more difficult and far less efficient.

- Neorealism is an attempt to explain international relations in scientific terms by reference to the unequal capabilities of states and the anarchical structure of the state system, and by focusing on the great powers whose relations determine the most important 'outcomes' of international politics. A scientific theory of IR leads us to expect states to behave in certain predictable ways. Waltz and Mearsheimer believe that bipolar systems are more stable and thus provide a better guarantee of peace and security than multipolar systems. According to that view, the Cold War was a period of international stability and peace.

- The International Society tradition is critical of realism on two counts. First, it regards realism as a one-dimensional IR theory that is too narrowly focused. Second, it claims that realism fails to capture the extent to which international politics is a dialogue of different IR voices and perspectives. Emancipatory theory claims that power politics is obsolete because security is now a local problem within disorganized and sometimes failed states, and at the same time is a cosmopolitan problem of people everywhere regardless of their citizenship. It is no longer exclusively or even primarily a problem of national security and national defence.

? QUESTIONS

- Realists are pessimistic about human progress and cooperation beyond the boundaries of the nation-state. What are the reasons given for that pessimism? Are they good reasons?

- Why do realists place so much emphasis on security? Does that make sense? How important is security in world politics?

- Identify the major differences between the classical realism of Hans Morgenthau and the neorealism of Kenneth Waltz. Which approach is best suited for analysing international relations after the Cold War?

- Outline the main arguments for and against NATO expansion. State your own position including supporting arguments.

- How does the new bipolarity differ from Cold War bipolarity?

- Is the role of Putin's Russia in Ukraine evidence of a new cold war?

- Does the concept of a soft balance of power make sense?

- Does the argument of neoclassical realism contain a basic contradiction?

- What is the emancipatory critique of realism? Does it make sense?

→ GUIDE TO FURTHER READING

Kaufman, S., Little, R., and Wohlforth, W. (eds) (2007). *The Balance of Power in World History*. London: Palgrave Macmillan.

Kennan, G. (1954). *Realities of American Foreign Policy*. Princeton, NJ: Princeton University Press.

Kissinger, H. (1994). *Diplomacy*. New York: Simon & Schuster.

Kissinger, H. (2014). *World Order: Reflections on the Character of Nations and the Course of History*. London: Penguin.

Lobell, S., Ripsman, N., and Taliaferro J. (2009). *Neoclassical Realism, the State, and Foreign Policy*. Cambridge: Cambridge University Press.

Machiavelli, N. (1984). *The Prince*, trans. P. Bondanella and M. Musa. New York: Oxford University Press.

Mearsheimer, J. (2001). *The Tragedy of Great Power Politics*. New York: W. W. Norton.

Paul, T. V., Wirtz, J., and Fortmann, M. (eds) (2004). *Balance of Power Theory and Practice in the 21st Century*. Stanford, CA: Stanford University Press.

Schelling, T. (1980). *The Strategy of Conflict*. Cambridge, MA: Harvard University Press.

Schweller, R. L. (2006). *'Unanswered Threats': Political Constraints on the Balance of Power*. Princeton, NJ: Princeton University Press.

Waltz, K. N. (1979). *Theory of International Politics*. New York: McGraw-Hill.

Williams, M. C. (2007). *Realism Reconsidered: The Legacy of Hans Morgenthau in International Relations*. Oxford: Oxford University Press.

WEB LINKS

Web links mentioned in the chapter, together with additional material including a case-study on NATO expansion, can be found on the Online Resource Centre that accompanies this book.

www.oxfordtextbooks.co.uk/orc/jackson_sorensen6e/

CHAPTER 4

Liberalism

▮ Summary

This chapter sets forth the liberal tradition in IR. Basic liberal assumptions are: (1) a positive view of human nature; (2) a conviction that international relations can be cooperative rather than conflictual; and (3) a belief in progress. In their conceptions of international cooperation, liberal theorists emphasize different features of world politics. Sociological liberals highlight transnational non-governmental ties between societies, such as communication between individuals and between groups. Interdependence liberals pay particular attention to economic ties of mutual exchange and mutual dependence between peoples and governments. Institutional liberals underscore the importance of organized cooperation between states; finally, republican liberals argue that liberal democratic constitutions and forms of government are of vital importance for inducing peaceful and cooperative relations between states. The chapter discusses these four strands of liberal thought and a debate with neorealism to which it has given rise. The concluding section evaluates the prospects for the liberal tradition as a research programme in IR.

Introduction: Basic Liberal Assumptions

The previous chapter introduced the realist tradition, with its focus on power and conflict. This chapter is about the sharply contrasting liberal view. How can liberals be 'optimistic' about IR? Why do they see a more peaceful world down the road? What are their arguments and beliefs?

The liberal tradition in IR is closely connected with the emergence of the modern liberal state. Liberal philosophers, beginning with John Locke in the seventeenth century, saw great potential for human progress in modern civil society and capitalist economy, both of which could flourish in states which guaranteed individual liberty. Modernity projects a new and better life, free of authoritarian government, and with a much higher level of material welfare (Box 4.1).

The process of modernization unleashed by the scientific revolution led to improved technologies and thus more efficient ways of producing goods and mastering nature. That was reinforced by the liberal intellectual revolution which had great faith in human reason and rationality. Here is the basis for the liberal belief in progress: the modern liberal state invokes a political and economic system that will bring, in Jeremy Bentham's famous phrase, 'the greatest happiness of the greatest number' (see web link 4.03).

Liberals generally take a positive view of human nature. They have great faith in human reason and they are convinced that rational principles can be applied to international affairs. Liberals recognize that individuals are self-interested and competitive up to a point. But they also believe that individuals share many interests and can thus engage in collaborative and cooperative social action, domestically as well as internationally, which results in greater benefits for everybody at home and abroad. In other words, conflict and war are not inevitable; when people employ their reason they can achieve mutually beneficial cooperation not only within states but also across international boundaries. Liberal theorists thus believe that human reason can triumph over human fear and the lust for power. But they disagree about the magnitude of the obstacles on the way to human progress (Smith 1992: 204). For some liberals it is a long-term process with many setbacks; for others, success is just around

---

BOX 4.1	**Modernization**

Between 1780 and 1850, in less than three generations, a far-reaching revolution, without precedent in the history of Mankind, changed the face of England. From then on, the world was no longer the same. The Industrial Revolution transformed Man from a farmer-shepherd into a manipulator of machines worked by inanimate energy . . . [It] opened up a completely different world of new and untapped sources of energy such as coal, oil, electricity and the atom. From a narrow technological point of view, the Industrial Revolution can be defined as the process by which a society gained control of vast sources of inanimate energy; but such a definition does not do justice to this phenomenon . . . as regards its economic, cultural, social and political implications.

Cipolla (1977: 7–8)

the corner. However, all liberals agree that in the long run cooperation based on mutual interests will prevail. That is because modernization constantly increases the scope and the need for cooperation (Zacher and Matthew 1995: 119) (see Figure 4.1).

The belief in progress is a core liberal assumption. But it is also a point of debate among liberals (see Pollard 1971: 9–13). How much progress? Scientific and technological for sure, but also social and political? What are the limits of progress? Are there any limits? Progress for whom? A small number of liberal countries or the entire world? The scope and degree of liberal optimism as regards progress has fluctuated over time. Many early liberals were inclined to be thoroughly optimistic; we have also noted the surge of utopian liberalism around the First World War. After the Second World War, however, liberal optimism became more muted. Robert Keohane, for example, cautiously notes that liberals at a minimum believe 'in at least the possibility of cumulative progress' (Keohane 1989: 174). Yet, there was another surge of liberal optimism after the end of the Cold War, propelled by the notion of 'the end of history' based on the defeat of communism and the expected universal victory of liberal democracy (Fukuyama 1989, 1992). However, the terrorist attacks in New York and Washington of 11 September 2001, followed by the attacks in Madrid, London, and elsewhere, are a setback for liberal optimism.

Progress for liberals is always progress for individuals. The core concern of liberalism is the happiness and contentment of individual human beings. John Locke (see web link 4.05) argued that states existed to underwrite the liberty of their citizens and thus enable them to live their lives and pursue their happiness without undue interference from other people. In contrast to realists, who see the state first and foremost as a concentration and instrument of power, a *Machtstaat*, liberals see the state as a constitutional entity, a *Rechtsstaat*, which establishes and enforces the rule of law that respects the rights of citizens to life, liberty, and property. Such constitutional states would also respect each other and would deal with each other in accordance with norms of mutual toleration. That argument was expanded by Jeremy Bentham—an eighteenth-century English philosopher—who coined the term 'international law'. He believed that it was in the rational interests of constitutional states to adhere to international law in their foreign policies (Rosenblum 1978: 101). The argument was further expanded by Immanuel Kant, an eighteenth-century German philosopher. He thought that a world of such constitutional and mutually respectful states—he called them

FIGURE 4.1   Classical liberalism

FOCUS:

freedom, cooperation, peace, progress

EARLY THINKERS:

Locke (1632–1704)	Bentham (1748–1832)	Kante (1724–1804)
The rule of law	Liberal states respect	'Republics will establish
'*Rechtsstaat*'	international law	perpetual peace'

FIGURE 4.2   Basic liberal assumptions

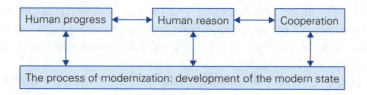

'republics'—could eventually establish 'perpetual peace' in the world (Gallie 1978: 8–36). Figure 4.1 summarizes the focus of leading classical liberal thinkers.

In summary, liberal thinking is closely connected with the emergence of the modern constitutional state. Liberals argue that modernization is a process involving progress in most areas of life. The process of modernization enlarges the scope for cooperation across international boundaries. Progress means a better life for at least the majority of individuals. Humans possess reason, and when they apply it to international affairs greater cooperation will be the end result (see Figure 4.2).

In Chapter 2, we presented the utopian or idealist liberalism of the 1920s. This chapter focuses on liberal theory after the Second World War. It is useful to divide post-war liberalism into four main strands of thinking: **sociological liberalism**; **interdependence liberalism**; **institutional liberalism**; and **republican liberalism** (Nye, Jr 1988: 246; Keohane 1989: 11; Zacher and Matthew 1995: 121). The following sections of this chapter will focus on each one in turn. It will not be possible to address all the relevant scholarly works or to demonstrate in detail how contemporary liberal thought builds on classical liberal thinking. Our focus will be on important contributions that represent each of these strands. We have chosen this division into four major strands because we find that they bring out the most important aspects of current liberal ideas about international relations.

Sociological Liberalism

For realists, IR is the study of relations between the governments of sovereign states. Sociological liberalism rejects this view as too narrowly focused and one-sided. IR is not only about state–state relations; it is also about transnational relations; i.e., relations between people, groups, and organizations belonging to different countries. We should note that this emphasis on society as well as the state, on many different types of actors and not just national governments, has led some to identify liberal thought by the term 'pluralism'.

Transnational relations are considered by sociological liberals to be an increasingly important aspect of international relations (see web links 4.09 and 4.10). James Rosenau defines transnationalism as follows: 'the processes whereby international relations conducted by governments have been supplemented by relations among private individuals, groups, and societies that can and do have important consequences for the course of events' (Rosenau 1980: 1). In focusing on transnational relations, sociological liberals return to an old theme in liberal thinking: the notion that relations between people are more cooperative and more supportive of peace than are relations between national governments. Richard Cobden, a leading nineteenth-century liberal thinker, put the idea as follows: 'As little intercourse betwixt the Governments, as much connection as possible between the nations of the world' (Cobden 1903: 216; Taylor 1957: 49); by 'nations' Cobden was referring to societies and their membership.

During the 1950s, Karl Deutsch was a leading figure in the study of transnational relations. He and his associates attempted to measure the extent of communication and transactions between societies. Deutsch argues that a high degree of transnational ties between societies leads to peaceful relations that amount to more than the mere absence of war (Deutsch et al. 1957). It leads to a security community: 'a group of people which has become "integrated" '. Integration means that a 'sense of community' has been achieved; people have come to agree that their conflicts and problems can be resolved 'without resort to large-scale physical force' (Deutsch et al. 1957: 5). Such a security community has emerged, argues Deutsch, among the Western countries in the North Atlantic area. He lists a number of conditions that are conducive to the emergence of security communities: increased social communication; greater mobility of persons; stronger economic ties; and a wider range of mutual human transactions.

Many sociological liberals hold the idea that transnational relations between people from different countries help create new forms of human society which exist alongside or even in competition with the nation-state. In a book called *World Society*, John Burton (1972) proposes a 'cobweb model' of transnational relationships. The purpose is to demonstrate how any nation-state consists of many different groups of people that have different types of external ties and different types of interest: religious groups, business groups, labour groups, and so on. In marked contrast, the realist model of the world often depicts the system of states as a set of billiard balls; i.e., as a number of independent, self-contained units (Figure 4.3). According to sociological liberals such as Burton, if we map the patterns of communication and transactions between various groups, we will get a more accurate picture of the world because it would represent actual patterns of human behaviour rather than artificial boundaries of states (see web link 4.14).

FIGURE 4.3 **The billiard ball model and the cobweb model**

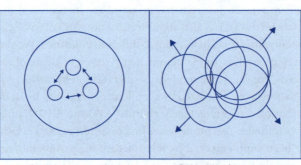

Billiard balls collide

Cobweb of groups:
conflicts muted

Burton implies that the cobweb model points to a world driven more by mutually beneficial cooperation than by antagonistic conflict. In this way the cobweb model builds on an earlier liberal idea about the beneficial effects of cross-cutting or overlapping group memberships. Because individuals are members of many different groups, conflict will be muted if not eliminated; overlapping memberships minimize the risk of serious conflict between any two groups (Nicholls 1974: 22; Little 1996: 72).

James Rosenau has further developed the sociological liberal approach to transnational relations (Rosenau 1990, 1992). He focuses on transnational relations at the macro level of human populations in addition to those conducted at the micro level by individuals (Box 4.2). Rosenau argues that individual transactions have important implications and consequences for global affairs. First, individuals have greatly extended their activities owing to better education and access to electronic means of communication as well as foreign travel. Second, states' capacity for control and regulation is decreasing in an ever more complex world. The consequence is a world of better informed and more mobile individuals who are far less tied than before to 'their' states. Rosenau thus sees a profound transformation of the international system that is underway: the state-centric, anarchic system has not disappeared but a new 'multi-centric world has emerged that is composed of diverse "sovereignty-free" collectivities which exist apart from and in competition with the state-centric world of "sovereignty-bound" actors' (Rosenau 1992: 282). Rosenau thus supports the liberal idea that an

---

BOX 4.2	**The importance of individuals in global politics**

Citizens have become important variables . . . in global politics . . . [for] at least five reasons:

1. The erosion and dispersion of state and governmental power.

2. The advent of global television, the widening use of computers in the workplace, the growth of foreign travel and the mushrooming migrations of peoples, the spread of educational institutions . . . has enhanced the analytic skills of individuals.

3. The crowding onto the global agenda of new, interdependence issues (such as environmental pollution, currency crises, the drug trade, AIDS, and terrorism) has made more salient the processes whereby global dynamics affect the welfare and pocketbooks of individuals.

4. The revolution of information technologies has made it possible for citizens and politicians literally to 'see' the aggregation of micro actions into macro outcomes. People can now observe support gather momentum as street rallies, the pronouncements of officials, the responses of adversaries, the comments of protesters . . . and a variety of other events get portrayed and interpreted on television screens throughout the world.

5. This new-found capacity of citizens to 'see' their role in the dynamics of aggregation has profoundly altered . . . possibly even reduced, the extent to which organization and leadership are factors in the mobilization of publics . . . Leaders are increasingly becoming followers because individuals are becoming increasingly aware that their actions can have consequences.

Rosenau (1992: 274–6)

increasingly pluralist world, characterized by transnational networks of individuals and groups, will be more peaceful. In some respects it will be a more unstable world, because the old order built on state power has broken down; but only rarely will conflicts lead to the use of force, because the numerous new cosmopolitan individuals that are members of many overlapping groups will not easily become enemies divided into antagonistic camps.

A recent analysis by Moisés Naím (2013a) also stresses the diffusion of power towards the micro-level. His argument is that the conventional holders of power in political, military, corporate 'macro-structures' of power are increasingly being undermined and challenged by 'micropowers'—'insurgents, fringe political parties, innovative start-ups, hackers, loosely organized activists, upstart citizen media outlets, leaderless young people in city squares, and charismatic individuals who seem to have "come from nowhere" are shaking up the old order' (2013b: 1). The rise of micropowers, Naím argues, is due to three 'revolutions'. The 'More revolution' means that many more people are living longer and healthier lives and that makes them more difficult to 'regiment and control' (2013a: 58). The 'Mobility revolution' implies that people are able to move around a lot more than earlier: they cross borders, they communicate globally, and they easily switch loyalties of any kind. Finally, the 'Mentality revolution' concerns the aspiration of the rapidly growing middle classes all around the world. They shake off traditional values, take nothing for granted, and they do not easily defer to authorities.

Another recent statement of sociological liberalism was made by Phil Cerny (2010). He underlines the many ways in which the distinction between 'domestic' and 'international' is being challenged, leading to a transformation of the state (see Box 4.3). Where these processes will eventually lead remains uncertain; Cerny outlines four different major scenarios, ranging from 'rosy' and cooperative towards 'hegemonic' and more conflict-prone.

We can summarize sociological liberalism as follows. IR is not only a study of relations between national governments; IR scholars also study relations between private individuals, groups, and societies. Overlapping interdependent relations between people are bound to be more cooperative than relations between states because states are exclusive and, according to sociological liberalism, their interests do not overlap and cross-cut. A world with a large number of transnational networks will thus be more peaceful.

BOX 4.3	Phil Cerny on state transformation

What we are seeing is not the disappearance of the state but the actual transformation of the state, its absorption into transnational webs of politics and power, and the reconstruction of the notion of 'statehood' itself along multilevel, multinodal lines. The key driving force in this transformation and reconstruction will be transnationally linked groups of political actors engaging in crosscutting competition and coalition-building behaviour, exploiting the growing institutional loopholes of global politics, constructing new power games, creating new networks, and changing people's perceptions of how world politics works by changing the parameters and dynamics of who gets—and should get—what, when, and how.

Cerny (2010: 22–3)

Interdependence Liberalism

Interdependence means mutual dependence: peoples and governments are affected by what happens elsewhere, by the actions of their counterparts in other countries. Thus, a higher level of transnational relations between countries means a higher level of interdependence. This also reflects the process of modernization, which usually increases the level of interdependence between states. The twentieth century, especially the period since 1950, has seen the rise of a large number of highly industrialized countries. Richard Rosecrance (1986, 1995, 1999) has analysed the effects of these developments on the policies of states. Throughout history, states have sought power by means of military force and territorial expansion. However, for highly industrialized countries, economic development and foreign trade are more adequate and less costly means of achieving prominence and prosperity. That is because the costs of using force have increased and the benefits have declined. Why is force less beneficial for states and trade increasingly so? The principal reason, according to Rosecrance, is the changing character and basis of economic production, which is linked to modernization. In an earlier age, the possession of territory and ample natural resources were the key to greatness. In today's world that is no longer the case; now a highly qualified labour force, access to information, and financial capital are the keys to success (see web link 4.18).

The most economically successful countries of the post-war period are the 'trading states' such as Japan and Germany. They have refrained from the traditional military–political option of high military expenditure and economic self-sufficiency; instead, they have chosen the trading option of an intensified international division of labour and increased interdependence. Many small countries are also 'trading states'. For a long time the very large countries, most notably the former Soviet Union and the United States, pursued the traditional military–political option, thereby burdening themselves with high levels of military expenditure. That has changed in recent decades. According to Rosecrance, the end of the Cold War has made that traditional option less urgent and thus less attractive. Consequently, the trading-state option is increasingly preferred even by very large states (see web links 4.15 and 4.16).

Basically, these liberals argue that a high division of labour in the international economy increases interdependence between states, and that discourages and reduces violent conflict between states. There still remains a risk that modern states will slide back to the military option and once again enter into arms races and violent confrontations. But that is not a likely prospect. It is in the less developed countries that war now occurs, according to Rosecrance, because at lower levels of economic development land continues to be the dominant factor of production, and modernization and interdependence are far weaker.

During the Second World War, David Mitrany (1966) set forth a **functionalist theory of integration**, arguing that greater interdependence in the form of transnational ties between countries could lead to peace. Mitrany believed, perhaps somewhat naïvely, that cooperation should be arranged by technical experts, not by politicians. The experts would devise solutions to common problems in various functional areas: transport, communication, finance, and so on. Technical and economic collaboration would expand when the participants discovered the mutual benefits that could be obtained from it. When citizens saw the welfare improvements that resulted from efficient collaboration in international organizations, they would transfer their loyalty from the state to international organizations. In that way, economic interdependence would lead to political integration and to peace (see web link 4.20).

Ernst Haas developed a so-called neofunctionalist theory of international integration that was inspired by the intensifying cooperation that began in the 1950s between the countries of Western Europe. Haas builds on Mitrany. But he rejects the notion that 'technical' matters can be separated from politics. Integration has to do with getting self-interested political elites to intensify their cooperation. Integration is a process whereby 'political actors are persuaded to shift their loyalties . . . toward a new center whose institutions possess or demand jurisdiction over the preexisting national states' (Haas 1958: 16). This 'functional' process of integration depends on the notion of 'spillover', when increased cooperation in one area leads to increased cooperation in other areas. Spillover would ensure that political elites marched inexorably towards the promotion of integration. Haas saw that happening in the initial years of West European cooperation in the 1950s and early 1960s.

From the mid-1960s, however, West European cooperation entered a long phase of stagnation and even backsliding. That was due primarily to President de Gaulle of France, who opposed the limitations on French sovereignty that resulted from interdependence. Functional and neofunctional theory did not allow for the possibility of setbacks in cooperation; integration theorists had to rethink their theories accordingly. Haas concluded that regional integration ought to be studied in a larger context: 'theory of regional integration ought to be subordinated to a general theory of interdependence' (Haas 1976: 179) (see Figure 4.4).

FIGURE 4.4   Major EU institutions

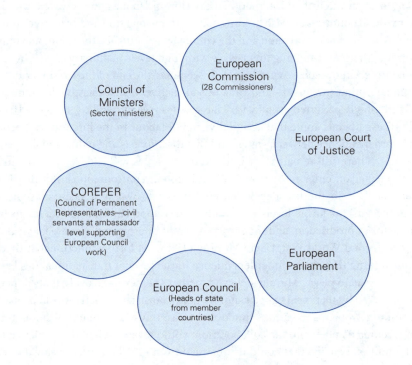

It was indeed such a general theory of interdependence that was attempted in the next phase in liberal thinking. But we should also note that theories of integration have seen a revival since the 1990s due to a new momentum in West European cooperation (Wiener and Dietz 2004; Hix 2005; Telò 2007). A core issue in these recent studies concerns whether integration is best explained by a liberal, neofunctionalist approach, or by a realist approach emphasizing national interest. We return to that debate between liberals and realists in the section 'Neorealist Critiques of Liberalism'.

An ambitious attempt to set forth a general theory of what they called 'complex interdependence' was made in the late 1970s in a book by Robert Keohane and Joseph Nye, Jr, *Power and Interdependence* (1977, 2001). They argue that post-war 'complex interdependence' is qualitatively different from earlier and simpler kinds of interdependence. Previously, international relations were directed by stateleaders dealing with other stateleaders. The use of military force was always an option in the case of conflict between those national leaders. The 'high politics' of security and survival had priority over the 'low politics' of economics and social affairs (Keohane and Nye, Jr 1977: 23). Under conditions of complex interdependence, however, that is no longer the case, and for two reasons. First, relations between states nowadays are not only or even primarily relations between stateleaders; there are relations on many different levels via many different actors and branches of government. Second, there is a host of transnational relations between individuals and groups outside of the state. Furthermore, military force is a less useful instrument of policy under conditions of complex interdependence (see web links 4.24 and 4.25).

Consequently, international relations are becoming more like domestic politics: 'Different issues generate different coalitions, both within governments and across them, and involve different degrees of conflict. Politics does not stop at the water's edge' (Keohane and Nye, Jr 1977: 25). In most of these conflicts military force is irrelevant. Therefore, power resources other than military ones are of increasing importance; for example, negotiating skills. Finally, under complex interdependence states become more preoccupied with the 'low politics' of welfare and less concerned with the 'high politics' of national security (Keohane and Nye, Jr 1977: 24–6; Nye, Jr 1993: 169).

We typify the receding old realist world and the advancing new world of complex interdependence in Table 4.1.

TABLE 4.1 Types of international relations

REALISM	COMPLEX INTERDEPENDENCE
• States dominant actors and coherent units	• Transnational actors increasingly important. States not coherent units
• Force usable and effective	• Military force less useful. Economic and institutional instruments more useful
• Military security dominates the agenda	• Military security less important. Welfare issues increasingly important

Based on Keohane and Nye, Jr (1977)

Complex interdependence clearly implies a far more friendly and cooperative relationship between states. According to Keohane and Nye, Jr (1977: 29–38), several consequences follow. First, states will pursue different goals simultaneously and transnational actors, such as NGOs and transnational corporations, will pursue their own separate goals free from state control. Second, power resources will most often be specific to issue areas. For example, in spite of their comparatively small size, Denmark and Norway will command influence in international shipping because of their large merchant and tanker fleets, but that influence does not easily translate to other issue areas. Third, the importance of international organizations will increase. They are arenas for political actions by weak states, they animate coalition formation, and they oversee the setting of international agendas.

Where do we locate complex interdependence in time and space? On the time dimension, it appears to be connected with social modernization or what Keohane and Nye, Jr (1977: 227) call 'the long-term development of the welfare state', which picked up speed after 1950. In space, complex interdependence is most evident in Western Europe, North America, Japan, Australia, and New Zealand: in short, the industrialized, pluralist countries (Keohane and Nye, Jr 1977: 27). The relevance of complex interdependence grows as modernization unfolds, and it is thus especially applicable to the relations between advanced Western countries. Keohane and Nye are nevertheless at pains to emphasize that realism is not irrelevant or obsolete:

It is not impossible to imagine dramatic conflict or revolutionary change in which the use of threat of military force over an economic issue or among advanced industrial countries might become plausible. Then realist assumptions would again be a reliable guide to events.

(Keohane and Nye, Jr 1977: 28)

In other words, even among industrialized countries of the West an issue could still become 'a matter of life and death' (Keohane and Nye, Jr 1977: 29), because even that world is still in some basic respects a world of states. In that eventuality, realism would be the more relevant approach to events.

Realists claim that any issue can become a matter of life and death in an anarchic world. Interdependence liberals will reply that that is too simplistic and that a large number of issues on the international agenda are important bread-and-butter items in line with the complex interdependence assumptions. Therefore, interdependence liberals suggest a compromise:

The appropriate response to the changes occurring in world politics today is not to discredit the traditional wisdom of realism and its concern for the military balance of power, but to realize its limitations and to supplement it with insights from the liberal approach.

(Nye, Jr 1990: 177)

Interdependence liberals are thus more balanced in their approach than some other liberals for whom everything has changed for the better and the old world of violent conflict, unbridled state power, and the dictatorship of the national interest is gone forever. However, in adopting this middle-of-the-road position, interdependence liberals face the problem of deciding exactly how much has changed, how much remains the same, and what the precise implications are for IR. We return to this debate later in the chapter (for analyses of interdependence and conflict, see Mansfield and Pollins (eds) 2003).

Meanwhile, interdependence liberalism can be summarized as follows. Modernization increases the level and scope of interdependence between states. Under complex interdependence, transnational actors are increasingly important, military force is a less useful instrument, and welfare—not security—is becoming the primary goal and concern of states. That means a world of more cooperative international relations.

Institutional Liberalism

This strand of liberalism picks up on earlier liberal thought about the beneficial effects of international institutions. In Chapter 2, we noted Woodrow Wilson's vision about transforming international relations from a 'jungle' of chaotic power politics to a 'zoo' of regulated and peaceful intercourse. This transformation was to be achieved through the building of international organizations, most importantly the League of Nations (see web link 4.27). Present-day institutional liberals are less optimistic than their more idealist predecessors. They do agree that international institutions can make cooperation easier and far more likely, but they do not claim that such institutions can by themselves guarantee a qualitative transformation of international relations, from a 'jungle' to a 'zoo'. Powerful states will not easily be completely constrained. However, institutional liberals do not agree with the realist view that international institutions are mere 'scraps of paper', that they are at the complete mercy of powerful states. International institutions are more than mere handmaidens of strong states. They are of independent importance, and they can promote cooperation between states (Keohane 1989; Acharya and Johnston 2007; Jönsson and Tallberg 2008).

What is an international institution? According to institutional liberals, it is an international organization, such as NATO or the European Union (EU); or it is a set of rules which governs state action in particular areas, such as aviation or shipping. These sets of rules are also called 'regimes'. Often the two go together; the trade regime, for example, is shaped primarily by the World Trade Organization (WTO). There may also be regimes without formal organizations; for example, the Law of the Sea conferences held under the auspices of the United Nations (UN) do not have a formal international organization. Institutions can be universal, with global membership, such as the UN, or they can be regional (or subregional), such as the EU. Finally, we should note that there is an additional type of international institution which is of a more fundamental kind, such as state sovereignty or the balance of power. These fundamental institutions are not what institutional liberals focus on; but they are main objects of study for International Society theorists, as we shall see in Chapter 5.

Institutional liberals claim that international institutions help promote cooperation between states. In order to evaluate that claim, an empirical measure of the extent of institutionalization among states is devised. The degree to which these international institutions have helped advance cooperation is then assessed. The extent of institutionalization can be measured on two dimensions: scope and depth. 'Scope' concerns the number of issue areas in which there are institutions. Are they only in a few crucial economic areas, such as trade and investment, or are they in many other economic, as well as in military and socio-political, areas? For assessing the 'depth' of institutionalization, three measures have been suggested:

- **Commonality:** the degree to which expectations about appropriate behaviour and understanding about how to interpret action are shared by participants in the system.

- **Specificity:** the degree to which these expectations are clearly specified in the form of rules.

- **Autonomy:** the extent to which the institution can alter its own rules rather than depending on outside agents (i.e., states) to do so.

(From Keohane 1989: 4; see also Peters 2011)

It is clear that a thorough analysis of the scope and depth of institutionalization among a group of states is a substantial research task. A complete absence of institutionalization is highly unlikely; there will always be some rules of coordination. The difficulty is to determine the exact level of institutionalization. One way of doing that is to look at a group of states where we immediately believe that the scope and depth of institutionalization are high and then evaluate the ways in which institutions matter. One such group of states is Europe, especially the European Union countries (see web link 4.30). EU countries cooperate so intensively that they share some functions of government, for example in agricultural and industrial policies; they have established the regulatory framework for a single market in the economic sector, and they are in the process of intensifying their cooperation in other areas. EU Europe, in other words, is a good test case for examining the importance of institutions. Institutional liberals do claim that institutions have made a significant difference in Western Europe since the end of the Cold War (Keohane et al. 1993). Institutions acted as 'buffers' which helped absorb the 'shocks' sent through Western Europe by the end of the Cold War and the reunification of Germany (see web link 4.29).

The institutional liberal view can be set against that of neorealist analysis. Neorealists argue that the end of the Cold War is most likely to bring the return of instability to Western Europe which could lead to a major war. It threatens to be a repetition of the first half of the twentieth century. Peace in Europe during the Cold War rested on two pillars that made up the balance of power between the United States and the Soviet Union. They were, first, bipolarity with its stable distribution of military power and, second, large arsenals of nuclear weapons almost entirely monopolized by those superpowers. With the revival of multipolarity, however, instability and insecurity is sharply increased. At the root of all this is the anarchic structure of the international system. According to neorealist John Mearsheimer, '[a]narchy has two principal consequences. First, there is little room for trust among states . . . Second, each state must guarantee its own survival since no other actor will provide its security' (Mearsheimer 1993: 148).

The argument made by institutional liberals (Keohane et al. 1993) is that a high level of institutionalization significantly reduces the destabilizing effects of multipolar anarchy identified by Mearsheimer. Institutions make up for lack of trust between states. They do that by providing a flow of information between their member states, which consequently are much less in the dark about what other states are doing and why. Institutions thus help reduce member states' fear of each other. In addition, they provide a forum for negotiation between states. For example, the European Union has a number of fora with extensive experience in negotiation and compromise, including the Council of Ministers, the European Commission, and the European Parliament. Institutions provide continuity and a sense of stability. They foster cooperation between states for their mutual advantage. For example, European states can use the EU machinery to try to ensure that other parties will respect commitments already made. Institutions help 'create a climate in which expectations of stable peace develop' (Nye, Jr 1993: 39). The constructive role of institutions as argued by institutional liberals is summarized in Box 4.4.

Current research on international institutions focuses on the challenges that these institutions face in an increasingly globalized world. On the one hand, there is a growing need for the regulation and management that they provide; on the other hand, they are lacking in both power and legitimacy necessary for taking on heavy responsibilities (see Box 4.5).

In this context, focus is also on the factors that account for the demand for institutional cooperation and integration. One major position in this debate emphasizes the crucial role

---

BOX 4.4   Institutional liberalism: the role of institutions

- Provide a flow of information and opportunities to negotiate;
- Enhance the ability of governments to monitor others' compliance and to implement their own commitments—hence their ability to make credible commitments in the first place;
- Strengthen prevailing expectations about the solidity of international agreements.

Based on Keohane (1989: 2; see also Mitchell 2006)

BOX 4.5   Transnational conflicts and international institutions

International institutions are overtaxed in a double sense: their basis of legitimacy is too small for the responsibilities they are supposed to carry out; but, in view of the magnitude of global problems, what they do is not enough. Many of the post-war international institutions have been supplemented with, or replaced by, new institutions that intervene more deeply into the affairs of national societies. These institutions increasingly exercise independent political authority and violate the principle of non-intervention, which, in turn, leads to serious problems of legitimacy and public acceptance. At the same time, international institutions are too weak, for example, to regulate international financial markets or to effectively combat climate change and its impacts. As a result growing societal and national resistance to these institutions has begun to emerge in conjunction with transnational disputes over international affairs.

Zürn (2011)

of state interests; that position is labelled 'liberal intergovernmentalism' (Moravcsik 1999b). Another major position is neofunctional theory which focuses on international cooperation driven by functional challenges; that is, some tasks are better attended to by international cooperation than by states alone and that works in favour of more cooperation. A recent version of neofunctionalism attempts to create a revised analytical framework that makes room for both 'intergovernmental' and 'functional' elements (Niemann 2006). At the same time, there is now more focus on issues connected with leadership (Beach 2010; Paterson et al. 2010) and with democracy and legitimacy (Eriksen 2009).

Institutional liberalism can be summarized as follows. International institutions help promote cooperation between states and thereby help alleviate the lack of trust between states and states' fear of each other which are considered to be the traditional problems associated with international anarchy. The positive role of international institutions for advancing cooperation between states continues to be questioned by realists. We return to that debate below.

Republican Liberalism

Republican liberalism is built on the claim that liberal democracies are more peaceful and law-abiding than are other political systems. The argument is not that democracies never go to war; democracies have gone to war as often as have non-democracies. But the argument is that democracies do not fight each other. This observation was first articulated by Immanuel Kant (1992 [1795]) in the late eighteenth century in reference to republican states rather than democracies. It was resurrected by Dean Babst in 1964 and it has been advanced in numerous studies since then. One liberal scholar even claims that the assertion that democracies do not fight each other is 'one of the strongest nontrivial or non-tautological statements that can be made about international relations' (Russett 1989: 245). This finding, then, is the basis of the present optimism among many liberal scholars and policy-makers concerning the prospects of long-term world peace (see web link 4.35). Their reasoning goes as follows. Because the number of democracies in the world has increased rapidly in recent years (see Table 4.2), we can look forward to a more peaceful world with international relations characterized by cooperation instead of conflict (parts of this section draw on Sørensen 2008a).

TABLE 4.2   Democracy's progress

The Freedom House 2014 Index Classification of Free Countries (with more than one million inhabitants)

(1 = Highest Rating)	
Australia	Ireland
Austria	Italy
Bahamas	Japan

(continued)

TABLE 4.2   Democracy's progress *(continued)*

Barbados	Lithuania
Belgium	Netherlands
Canada	New Zealand
Chile	Norway
Costa Rica	Poland
Cyprus	Portugal
Czech Republic	Slovakia
Denmark	Slovenia
Dominica	Spain
Estonia	Sweden
Finland	Switzerland
France	United Kingdom
Germany	United States
	Uruguay

average rating: 1.5

Belize	Israel
Croatia	Mauritius
Ghana	Mongolia
Grenada	Taiwan
Hungary	

average rating: 2.0

Argentina	Romania
Benin	Samoa
Brazil	Senegal
Bulgaria	Serbia
Greece	South Africa
Latvia	South Korea
Namibia	Suriname
Panama	Trinidad and Tobago

average rating: 2.5

Botswana	Jamaica
Dominican Republic	Lesotho
El Salvador	Peru
India	

Based on data from www.freedomhouse.org The index employs one dimension for political rights and one dimension for civil liberties. For each dimension, a seven-point scale is used, so that the highest-ranking countries (that is, those with the highest degree of democracy) are one-ones (1–1s) and the lowest ranking countries are seven-sevens (7–7s). Countries with an average rating between 1 and 2.5 are considered free.

Why are democracies at peace with one another? The answer to that question has been most systematically addressed by Michael Doyle (1983, 1986) (see web links 4.36 and 4.37). Doyle based his argument on the classical liberal treatment of the subject by Immanuel Kant. There are three elements behind the claim that democracy leads to peace with other democracies. The first is the existence of domestic political cultures based on peaceful conflict resolution. Democracy encourages peaceful international relations because democratic governments are controlled by their citizens, who will not advocate or support wars with other democracies.

The second element is that democracies hold common moral values which lead to the formation of what Kant called a 'pacific union'. The union is not a formal peace treaty; rather, it is a zone of peace based on the common moral foundations of all democracies. Peaceful ways of solving domestic conflict are seen as morally superior to violent behaviour, and this attitude is transferred to international relations between democracies. Freedom of expression and free communication promote mutual understanding internationally, and help to assure that political representatives act in accordance with citizens' views.

Finally, peace between democracies is strengthened through economic cooperation and interdependence. In the pacific union it is possible to encourage what Kant called 'the spirit of commerce': mutual and reciprocal gain for those involved in international economic cooperation and exchange.

Of the different strands of liberalism considered in this chapter, republican liberalism is the one with the strongest normative element. For most republican liberals, there is not only confidence but also hope that world politics is already developing and will develop far beyond rivalry, conflict, and war between independent states. Republican liberals are optimistic that peace and cooperation will eventually prevail in international relations, based on progress towards a more democratic world. Not only that (and here the normative element shows itself clearly), they see it as their responsibility to promote democracy worldwide, for in so doing they are promoting peace, which is one of the most fundamental of all political values.

The end of the Cold War helped launch a new wave of democratization; that led to growing liberal optimism as regards the future of democracy. Yet, most liberals are well aware of the fragility of democratic progress. When republican liberals examine the conditions for a democratic peace in the light of recent democratic transformations in Eastern Europe, Latin America, and Africa, the evidence is not supportive of any profound optimism. With regard to the first condition (see Figure 4.5), it is evident that a democratic culture with norms of peaceful conflict resolution has not yet taken root in the new democracies. Democratic norms must be ingrained before the domestic basis of the democratic peace will be secure, and such development of the political culture usually takes a long time. There will be setbacks; some countries will revert to non-democratic forms of rule. For example, Russia took a step backwards in 2004 and is now classified by Freedom House as a 'Not Free' country (see web links 4.43 and 4.46).

As regards the second condition, peaceful relations have indeed developed between the consolidated democracies of the West. There is reason to hope that most of the new democracies of Eastern Europe will come to be included in this zone—provided that there are no

FIGURE 4.5   **Republican liberalism: three conditions of peace among liberal democracies**

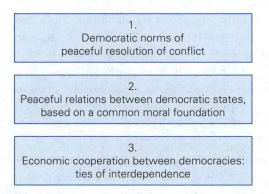

severe setbacks in their further democratization. The democracies of the global South are more problematic in that regard. The foundations between the global North and South are not strong. During the Cold War, the United States was hostile and even aggressive towards some southern democracies; e.g., the Dominican Republic in the early 1960s and Chile in the early 1970s. This reflected American determination to defend its perceived economic and security interests in its competition with the Soviet Union (for further analysis, see Sørensen 2008a: 131–59). Today, there can still be divisions and mistrust between old and new democracies.

Turning to the final condition, economic cooperation and interdependence is highly developed among the consolidated democracies of the West. At least some of the new democracies of Eastern Europe are integrated into these economic networks through membership of the European Union; e.g., Poland, Hungary, and the Czech Republic. Yet, the complex negotiations about EU enlargement demonstrate the considerable difficulties involved in close economic cooperation between countries at highly different levels of development. For the democracies of the South, continued one-sided economic dependence on the North rather than interdependence is the order of the day, even two decades after the end of the Cold War. That relation of basic inequality augurs less well for the development of peaceful relations even if both parties have democratic governments.

In short, the emergence of a global pacific union embracing all the new and old democracies is not guaranteed. Indeed, most of the new democracies fail to meet at least two of the three conditions for a democratic peace identified above. And instead of exhibiting further progress, they may backslide towards authoritarian rule. Most republican liberals are therefore less optimistic than was Francis Fukuyama when he predicted 'the end of history as such: that is, the end point of mankind's ideological evolution and the universalization of Western liberal democracy as the final form of human government' (1989: 4) (see web link 4.47). Most liberals argue that there is a democratic 'zone of peace' among the consolidated liberal democracies, including Western Europe, North America, and Japan. But the expansion of that zone is far from assured (Russett 1993: 138).

Most republican liberals thus emphasize that democratic peace is a dynamic process rather than a fixed condition. A pacific union does not spring into existence between countries as soon as they meet a minimum definition of democracy. Peace is built on all three foundation stones (Figure 4.5) only over a long period of time. There can be setbacks. There can even be reversions to non-democratic rule. There is a weakness even in this qualified republican liberal argument, however. Republican liberals need to specify the exact ways in which democracy leads to peace, and they need to sort out in more precise terms when there is a democratic peace between a group of democracies and why. In that context a more thorough evaluation of the current processes of democratization is necessary. There are already a number of contributions that address these issues (Souva and Prins 2006; Harrison 2010; Hook 2010; Hegre 2014).

At the same time, there is a dark side to the relationship between democracy and peace. It concerns the fact that established liberal democracies have gone to war rather frequently over the last decade; the wars in Iraq and Afghanistan are prominent examples of this. This kind of 'democratic war' does not disprove the democratic peace theory discussed here, but it is a powerful reminder of the readiness of established democracies to go to war against non-democracies for a number of different reasons, be it security concerns, economic interests, or humanitarian principles. Critics of republican liberalism emphasize this point in order to make clear that the connection between liberal democracy and peace is not as clear-cut as some liberal theorists will have us believe (Hobson et al. 2011: 147–85).

Republican liberalism can be summarized as follows. Democracies do not go to war against each other owing to their domestic culture of peaceful conflict resolution, their common moral values, and their mutually beneficial ties of economic cooperation and interdependence. These are the foundation stones upon which their peaceful relations are based. For these reasons, an entire world of consolidated liberal democracies could be expected to be a peaceful world.

We have already introduced a number of specific points where realists are sceptical of liberalism. Realists are sceptical about this version of liberalism too. Behind their disbelief is a larger debate which sets liberalism against realism in IR. The core question in that debate is: can a liberal world escape the perils of anarchy? Will a more liberal world, with more democracies, with a higher level of interdependence, and with more international institutions, mean that anarchy is eclipsed? Will it mean that war is permanently ended? The next two sections take up the most important debates between liberals and neorealists.

Neorealist Critiques of Liberalism

Liberalism's main contender is neorealism. We saw in Chapter 2 that the first major debate in IR was between idealist liberalism and pessimist realism. The debate between liberalism and realism continues to this day. We shall see that this debate has created divisions in the liberal camp. There is now a group of 'weak liberals' who have moved closer to the realist camp; and there is a group of 'strong liberals' who continue to support a more distinctively liberal view of world politics.

A main point of contention in previous debates between liberals and realists around the time of the Second World War concerned 'human nature'. We have seen that liberals generally take a positive view of human nature, whereas realists tend to hold a negative view: they see human beings as capable of evil. This issue was at the core of Hans Morgenthau's realist critique of liberals. The substance of this critique can be expressed as follows: 'You have misunderstood politics because you have misestimated human nature' (Waltz 1959: 40).

These diverging views of human nature continue to separate realists from liberals. But 'human nature' is no longer a major point of debate for two reasons. First, it was increasingly realized among neorealists as well as liberals that human nature is highly complex. It is behind 'good' things as well as 'bad' things: peace and war, philanthropy and robbery, Sunday schools and brothels. Our attention must therefore shift to the social and political context to help us explain when humans (having the potential for being good as well as bad) will behave in one way or another way (Waltz 1959: 16–41). Second, there was the influence from the behavioural movement in political science. That influence led scholars away from the study of human actions and their 'internal' moral qualities and capabilities towards the analysis of observable facts and measurable data in the 'external' world; i.e., overt evidence of patterns of human behaviour. How should scholars conceive of the external world? How should we view history?

We noted earlier that classical realists have a non-progressive view of history. States remain states in spite of historical change. They continue to reside in an unchanging anarchical system. Anarchy leads to self-help: states have to look after themselves; nobody will do it for them. To be secure, they arm themselves against potential enemies; one state's security is another state's insecurity. The result can be an arms race and, eventually, war. That was the case 2,000 years ago. According to neorealists, it is still the case today, because the basic structure of the state system remains the same. History is 'the same damn things over and over again' (Layne 1994: 10).

For liberals, however, history is at least potentially progressive. We identified the main conditions of liberal progress earlier and summarized them in the four major strands of liberal thought. Neorealists are not impressed. They note that such 'liberal' conditions have existed for a long time without being able to prevent violent conflict between states. For example, economic interdependence is nothing new. As a percentage of world gross national product (GNP), world exports in 1970 were below the 1880–1910 level (Table 4.3). Put differently, the rapid increase in world trade between 1950 and 1975 which liberals view as the great era of interdependence was nothing more than a recovery from abnormally low levels of interdependence caused by two world wars and the Great Depression in the first half of the twentieth century.

Financial flows reveal a similar story. Measured as a percentage of GNP, total foreign investment from Western developed countries was much higher over the entire period from 1814 to 1938 than during the 1960s and 1970s. International banking has been important for more than two centuries (Thompson and Krasner 1989). In sum, economic interdependence is nothing new, and in the past it has done little to prevent wars between states, such as the Second World War.

Neorealists are also critical of the role that liberals attach to international institutions. While states cooperate through institutions, they still do it solely on the basis of their own

TABLE 4.3   Trade as percentages of world GNP, various years

YEAR	WORLD EXPORTS/WORLD GNP
1830	4.6
1840	5.7
1850	6.8
1860	9.3
1870	9.8
1880	11.4
1890	11.1
1900	10.4
1910	10.4
1913	11.4
1950	8.1
1960	9.2
1970	10.0
1980	16.9
2002	23.8
2010	27.9

Based on tables in Thompson and Krasner (1989: 199, 201) and www.OECD.org

decision and self-interest. The strong prevail in international relations. Institutions are no more than theatre stages where the power play unfolds. But the play has been written by the playwright: the states. Institutions are not important in their own right (Mearsheimer 1995b: 340). Finally, as we indicated, neorealists are critical of republican liberalism (Gowa 1999). They emphasize that there is always the possibility that a liberal or democratic state will revert to authoritarianism or another form of non-democracy. Furthermore, today's friend might very well turn out to be tomorrow's enemy, whether or not they are a democracy.

There is thus a common thread running through the realist critique of the various strands of liberalism: the persistence and permanence of anarchy and the insecurity that that involves. According to neorealists, anarchy cannot be eclipsed. Anarchy means that even liberal states must contemplate the possibility that their liberal friends will perhaps someday turn against them. 'Lamentably, it is not possible for even liberal democracies to transcend anarchy' (Mearsheimer 1993: 123). No amount of sociological, interdependence, institutional, or republican liberalism can do the trick. And, as long as anarchy prevails, there is no escape from self-help and the security dilemma. Liberal optimism is not warranted.

The Retreat to Weak Liberalism

Liberals have reacted to these neorealist objections in basically two different ways. One group is somewhat defensive, accepting several realist claims including the essential point about the persistence of anarchy. We shall call this group '**weak liberals**'. Another group, whom we shall call the '**strong liberals**', will not budge; they claim that the world is changing in some fundamental ways which are in line with liberal expectations. Note that the labels 'weak' and 'strong' say nothing about the solidity of the arguments made. They are purely descriptive labels, indicating different degrees of disagreement with realism.

The work of Robert Keohane, one of the leading scholars in the debate between liberals and neorealists, illustrates how a liberal adjusted to realist critiques. As indicated, his early work with Joseph Nye, Jr (Keohane and Nye, Jr 1971) is characteristic of sociological liberalism. In that work, they draw an important distinction between a 'state-centric' paradigm and a 'world politics' paradigm; the former's focus is on 'interstate interactions' whereas the latter's focus is on 'transnational interactions' in which non-governmental actors play a significant role (1971: xii, 380). The implication is that world politics is changing dramatically from a state system to a transnational political system. That argument is an example of strong liberalism.

This sociological liberal view was popular in the early 1960s; realists were on the defensive. But sociological liberalism appeared to be a prisoner of history and the circumstances of the time. It turned out that the flutter of transnational relations upon which sociological liberals built their argument could only develop smoothly within a framework created by dominant American power (Little 1996: 78). That was true for a period following the Second World War. Then came a period when American power appeared to wane; the country was tied up in a difficult and unpopular war in Vietnam. There was also trouble on the economic front: President Nixon terminated the dollar's convertibility into gold in 1971. The United States' political and economic distress sent shock waves through the entire international system. That put realism back on the offensive; if sociological liberalism only worked within a realist framework of power, progress had hardly gone very far.

Keohane turned his attention away from transnational relations and back towards states. The result was the theory of complex interdependence described earlier. This analysis was a movement in the direction of realism: the primary importance of states was acknowledged. But it was unclear to what extent realism should be supplemented with liberal insights. Keohane increasingly focused his analysis on international institutions. That brought him one step closer to neorealism. The analytical starting point is now clearly realist. States are the major actors, the international system is anarchical, and the power of states is highly significant. The strong can prevail over the weak. Still, as we saw above, a liberal core remained, namely the idea that international institutions can facilitate cooperation.

Even though this brand of liberalism is fairly close to a neorealist position, most such realists remained dissatisfied with the revised and very much weakened liberal thesis. They claim that Keohane as well as several other liberal institutionalists overlook one crucial item, that of relative gains. 'Gains' are benefits that accrue to participants that cooperate (Figure 4.6). Institutional liberals claim that institutions facilitate cooperation and thus make it less likely that states will cheat on each other. That is because international institutions are transparent. They provide information to all member states and they thus foster an environment in which it is easier for states to make reliable commitments. Neorealists reply that cheating is not the main problem in negotiation between states. The main

FIGURE 4.6   Absolute and relative gains

Absolute gains	As long as we do well it doesn't matter if others do even better.
	Example: The United States economy grows by 25% over the next decade; China grows by 75%.

Relative gains	We will do our best, but number one priority is that the others don't get ahead of us.
	Example: The United States economy grows by 10% over the next decade; China grows by 10.3%.

The American that chooses the latter scenario over the first is concerned with relative gains.

problem is relative gains. States must worry that other states gain more from cooperation than they do themselves. Neorealists claim that institutional liberals take no account of that problem; they 'ignore the matter of relative gains . . . in doing so, they fail to identify a major source of state inhibitions about international cooperation' (Grieco 1993: 118) (see web link 4.48).

This neorealist critique led Keohane to emphasize a qualification which further moderated his liberal position. That qualification concerned the conditions for cooperation between states. The single most important condition is the existence of common interests between states (Keohane 1993: 277). If states have interests in common they will not worry about relative gains. In such situations, institutions can help advance cooperation. In the absence of common interests, states will be competitive, apprehensive, and even fearful. In those circumstances, institutions will not be of much help.

This way of responding to the neorealist critique does make the liberal position less vulnerable to realist attacks, and it does help us to understand why there can be cooperation under anarchy. But it leads liberalism closer and closer to neorealism: less and less remains of a distinctive and genuine liberal theory. In other words, liberal institutionalism is open to the criticism that it is merely neorealism 'by another name' (Mearsheimer 1995a: 85). Keohane has recognized the close familiarity between institutional theory and neorealism (Keohane 2002). However, the end of the Cold War and the rapid growth of globalization gave a strong boost to a more pronounced liberal posture.

The Counter-attack of Strong Liberalism

The neorealist attack on liberal theory looks strong. Their spare and parsimonious theory builds on two basic assumptions: history is 'the same damn things over and over again'; there is anarchy leading to insecurity and the risk of war. A terse and bold starting point makes for strong statements. But parsimony can also be a weakness, because so many things are not taken into consideration. Can we really seriously believe that nothing has changed in international relations over the past several hundred years? Neorealism, as one experienced observer noticed, 'manages to leave most of the substance of the field [of IR] outside the straitjacket' (Hoffmann 1990). In order to argue for such a bald thesis, you have to close your eyes to a lot of things.

That is where '**strong liberals**' begin their counter-attack on neorealism. They maintain that qualitative change has taken place. Today's economic interdependence ties countries much closer together; economies are globalized (see Figure 4.3 and Box 4.6); production and consumption take place in a worldwide marketplace. It would be extremely costly in welfare terms for countries to opt out of that system (Holm and Sørensen 1995; Cerny 2010). Today, there is also a group of consolidated liberal democracies for whom reversion to authoritarianism is next to unthinkable, because all major groups in society support democracy. These countries conduct their mutual international relations in new and more cooperative ways. For them there is no going back; historical change is irreversible. 'Strong liberals' include Rosenau (2003), Slaughter (2004), Ikenberry (2009), and Cerny (2010).

Neorealists do not insist that there has been no change at all; but they do maintain that such change has not led to the disappearance of anarchy. The self-help system of states remains in place. In that fundamental respect, the realist analysis continues to apply. From this fact, neorealists draw the conclusion that there is a huge difference between domestic and international politics. In domestic affairs there is 'authority, administration and law', while international politics 'is the realm of power, struggle, and of accommodation' (Waltz 1979: 113). Strong liberals, however, dispute that crucial premise: the assertion that anarchy—as understood by realists—remains in place. Strong liberals do not argue that anarchy has been replaced by hierarchy; that a world government has been created or is in the making. Rather, they argue that anarchy is a far more complex international relationship than is recognized by neorealists, and they question the conclusions that neorealists draw from the existence of anarchy.

What does it mean that there is anarchy in the international system? It means that there is no single, overarching government. It does not mean that there is no government at all. It

---

BOX 4.6 **Globalization in practice**

First, information is now universally available, in real time, simultaneously, in every financial centre of the world. Second, technology has tied all the principal countries and world financial and banking centres together into one integrated network. Few countries or parts of the world can any longer remain insulated from financial shocks and changes, wherever they may occur. Third, technology has made possible the establishment of a new, comprehensive system and highly efficient world market to match lenders and borrowers, to pool resources and share risks on an international scale without regard to boundaries.

Blumenthal (1988)

follows that the distinction between domestic and international politics is not as clear as neorealists claim. The fact is that some states lack an effective and legitimate system of government; e.g., Cameroon, Chad, Zimbabwe, and Somalia. The fact also is that some groups of states are acquiring a governmental system; e.g., the EU. Politics is not 'stopping at the water's edge'. Anarchy does not necessarily mean complete absence of legitimate and effective authority in international politics.

Strong liberals take their cue from that reality. International politics need not be a 'raw anarchy' with fear and insecurity all around. There can be significant elements of legitimate and effective international authority. And strong liberals see examples in the international relations of firmly consolidated, liberal democracies, because here we have combined the key elements of sociological liberalism, interdependence liberalism, institutional liberalism, and republican liberalism. One way of characterizing these relations is by Karl Deutsch's term, 'security communities'. The consolidated liberal democracies of Western Europe, North America, and Japan constitute a security community (Singer and Wildavsky 1993; Adler and Barnett 1998). It is extremely unlikely—indeed, it is unthinkable—that there will be violent conflict between any of these countries in the future.

Strong liberals thus underline the need for a more nuanced view of peace and war. Peace is not merely the absence of war, as most realists believe. There are different kinds or degrees of peace. The 'warm peace' between the countries of the security community of liberal democracies is far more secure than the 'cold peace' between, say, the United States and the Soviet Union during the height of the Cold War (Boulding 1979; Adler and Barnett 1996). A more nuanced view of war is also required. War has changed dramatically in the course of history. War has grown more and more destructive, spurred by technological and industrial development, culminating in the two world wars of the twentieth century. In addition, there is now the risk of unlimited destruction through nuclear war. Strong liberals argue that these developments increase the incentives for states to cooperate (Mueller 1990, 1995); neorealists do not deny that nuclear weapons help decrease the risk of war (Waltz 1993). But strong liberals go one step further. They argue that large-scale war has moved 'toward terminal disrepute because of its perceived repulsiveness and futility' (Mueller 1990: 5; Mueller 2009) (Box 4.7).

BOX 4.7	The obsolescence of major war

Duelling and slavery no longer exist as effective institutions and have faded from human experience except as something one reads about in books . . . There are signs that, at least in the developed world . . . [war] . . . has begun to succumb to obsolescence. Like duelling and slavery, war does not appear to be one of life's necessities—it is not an unpleasant fact of existence that is somehow required by human nature or by the grand scheme of things. One can live without it, quite well in fact. War may be a social affliction, but in important respects it is also a social affliction that can be shrugged off.

John Mueller (1990: 13)

Strong liberals, then, argue that in important parts of the world anarchy does not produce the insecurity that realists claim. Peace is fairly secure in many important places. There are two main types of peace in the world today. The first type is among the heavily armed powers, especially the nuclear powers, where total war threatens self-destruction. It rests primarily (but not solely) on the balance created by military power. It is the least secure peace. The second main type of peace is among the consolidated democracies of the OECD. This is a far more secure, 'liberal' peace, predicated upon liberal democratic values, a high level of economic interdependence, and a dense network of institutions facilitating cooperation (Lipson 2003; Mandelbaum 2004).

For these reasons, strong liberals remain optimistic about the future. They argue that genuine progress is possible, and that it is taking place in important parts of the world. There is no world government, of course, but in several areas the world has moved far beyond the neorealist condition of raw anarchy, with all its negative consequences for international relations. Liberals thus appear better equipped than most realists when it comes to the study of change as progress. Whereas many realists always see more of the same in international relations, namely anarchy and power politics, most liberals have a notion of modernization and progress built into their theoretical foundation which makes them more receptive to the study of social, economic, institutional, and political change (Figure 4.7). The end of the Cold War has boosted the liberal position; the world seems to be moving in a more liberal direction. At the same time, liberals are less well prepared for lack of progress or retrogress. For example, we saw how liberal theories of integration did not allow for setbacks in the process of cooperation in Europe. In the developing world a number of very poor countries have experienced lack of development and even in some instances state collapse. Liberal

FIGURE 4.7 Prospects for war and peace

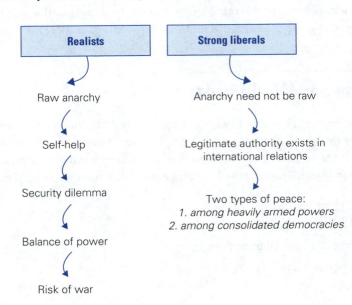

theory has difficulty in handling such cases because it is fundamentally based on a conception of irreversible modernization (Sørensen 2011). It is the beneficial consequences of that process that are the core theme of liberal thinking. Consequently, when that process does not take place for some reason or when it backfires, liberal analysis falters.

Also, liberals are not as precise in their claims as are realists. How much has actually changed? How secure is a democratic peace? What is the exact link between the various liberal elements in international relations—such as democracy or transnational relations—and more peaceful and cooperative relations between governments? Liberals have problems with these questions. That is because liberals try to theorize historical change, which is by its very nature complex, fluid, open-ended, and thus uncertain in the course it will take.

Recent liberal thinking has gone to work on these problems. Andrew Moravcsik has set forth a reformulation of liberal theory that attempts to be 'non-ideological and non-utopian' (Moravcsik 1997: 513) (see web link 4.49). The fundamental actors in international politics are rational individuals and private groups. The policies of states represent what individuals and groups in society (and inside the state apparatus) want. In other words, government policy reflects the preferences of different combinations of groups and individuals in domestic society. In the international system, each state seeks to realize its preferences—to get what it wants—under the constraints imposed by the preferences of other states.

This reformulation of liberal theory avoids prior assumptions about the prevalence of cooperation over conflict or the unavoidability of progress. At the same time, it contains both a 'domestic' component (state preferences) and an international, 'systemic' component (state preferences constrained by other states). The core element in the theory is the set of preferences pursued by states. The preferences may be influenced by liberal factors. To the extent that they are, peace and cooperation may follow. To the extent that they are not, conflict may prevail. According to Moravcsik, there are three major variants of liberal theory: ideational, commercial, and republican. Republican liberalism, for example, 'stresses the impact on state behaviour of varying forms of domestic representation and the resulting incentives for social groups to engage in rent seeking' (Moravcsik 1997).

Liberalism and World Order

Another recent attempt by strong liberals to update liberal thinking is the theory of 'structural liberalism' by Daniel Deudney and G. John Ikenberry (1999; see also Ikenberry 2009). They seek to characterize the major features of the Western order; that is, the relations between Western liberal democracies. Five elements of that order are singled out:

- security co-binding;
- penetrated reciprocal hegemony;
- semi-sovereign and partial great powers;
- economic openness; and
- civic identity.

Security co-binding refers to the liberal practice of states locking one another into mutually constraining institutions, such as NATO. That organization has joint force planning, coordinated military command structures, and a network for making political and military decisions. Penetrated reciprocal hegemony is the special way in which the United States leads Western order. The US is an open and diverse political system that is also receptive to pressures from its partners. Transnational and trans-governmental political networks play an increasing role in this.

Semi-sovereign and partial great powers refer to the special status of Germany and Japan. They have imposed constraints on themselves as great powers; an important part of this is that they have foregone the acquisition of nuclear weapons. The features of these 'trading states' are an anomaly seen from neorealism, but from a liberal view they are an integrated part of Western political order. Economic openness is another major aspect of the Western liberal order. In a world of advanced industrial capitalism, the benefits from absolute gain derived from economic openness are so great that liberal states try to cooperate so as to avoid the incentive to pursue relative gains. Finally, civic identity expresses common Western support for the values of political and civil liberties, market economics, and ethnic toleration.

Deudney and Ikenberry (1999) argue that these features of the Western liberal order are so strong and entrenched that they will survive the collapse of the common external threat, the Soviet Union. In short, the liberal order rests on a liberal foundation, not on a particular balance of power or a certain external threat.

It is possible to question the liberal optimism in Deudney and Ikenberry's (1999) analysis. The coming to power of George W. Bush in the United States and the US security strategy focused on a 'war on terrorism' has strained relations across the Atlantic (Ikenberry 2002). According to one (realist) commentator (Kagan 2003), Europeans and Americans live in different worlds in the sense that they have very different views of world order: 'Americans are from Mars and Europeans are from Venus', says Kagan, meaning that Europeans live in a 'Kantian world' of 'peace and relative prosperity', whereas the

United States remains mired in history, exercising power in an anarchic Hobbesian world where international laws and rules are unreliable, and where true security and the defense and promotion of a liberal order still depend on the possession and use of military might.

(Kagan 2003: 3)

The question is whether Kagan overstates the differences between Europe and the United States. There is no prospect whatsoever that the transatlantic disagreements will lead to violent conflict: the security community based on liberal values, interdependence, and common institutions remains in place. So instead of a confrontation between the US and Europe, the disagreement is sooner about the best ways of confronting the terrorist threat. In the US, the neoconservative strategy of aggressively confronting states thought to have 'weapons of mass destruction' (WMDs) has so far dominated; in Europe, there is stronger support for the view that 'the best response to transnational terrorist networks is networks of cooperating government agencies' (Nye, Jr 2003: 65). During the presidency of Barack Obama, Europe and the US once again began working together more closely.

Nevertheless, these events illustrate that there are tensions in the liberal view of world order. What values should a liberal foreign policy seek to realize? The answer from Liberal International is clear: 'Freedom, responsibility, tolerance, social justice, and equality of opportunity' (Liberal International 1997). Of course, liberals will seek freedom. But freedom is no uniform entity; Isaiah Berlin (1969) pursued a now classical distinction between negative and positive liberty. Negative liberty is an individual sphere of autonomy, of non-interference of state authorities of any kind. The core element in this kind of freedom is property rights: liberty is a right that flows from property in one's own person; property of person and possessions is a crucial condition for liberty and happiness. The critical task of political authority is to ensure these rights (see web link 4.53).

According to Berlin (1969), positive liberty, by contrast, is the liberty of 'being one's own master'. Positive freedom is only possible when certain conditions are met: one must have health, economic resources, education, and so on. To be really free, individuals must have more than that afforded by negative liberty, and the state should take care to provide such conditions for all.

Individuals are not states and domestic conditions are not like the conditions in the international system. Even so, we can trace the presence of negative and positive liberty in liberal internationalism (Sørensen 2006, 2011). Negative liberty emphasizes a Liberalism of Restraint, of holding back, of providing room for states to conduct their own affairs unobstructed by others. Non-intervention as a core element in the classical institution of sovereignty emphasizes negative liberty: let states choose on their own, but also let them take responsibility if they fail. International institution-building and international law is also part of a Liberalism of Restraint: it entails the fencing-in of raw power and the principle of negotiation to resolve discord.

Positive liberty, by contrast, points to a different kind of liberal internationalism. It forms the basis for a Liberalism of Imposition, of going out and radically changing the world in order to provide the universal basis for the 'good (i.e., liberal) life'. Woodrow Wilson's dictum of 'making the world safe for democracy' is Liberalism of Imposition; so is John Kennedy's willingness to 'pay any price, bear any burden . . . to assure the success of liberty' (inauguration speech). President Bush declared that the US and the UK 'seek the advance of freedom and the peace that freedom brings'. Charles Krauthammer has identified this Liberalism of Imposition as the motive behind the wars in Afghanistan and Iraq (Krauthammer 2004: 11). In sum, Liberalism of Restraint wants to live and let live, to quietly sort out differences via negotiation and collaboration, to persuade via the argument rather than via the sword. Liberalism of Imposition sees this as much too defensive and ineffective; it wants to go out and forcefully change the world in a liberal direction, using force when necessary. Both liberalisms have a home in liberal thinking. It is quite clear that in the face of the world's problems, a Liberalism of Restraint can be too little (i.e., not solving the problems), and a Liberalism of Imposition can be too much (i.e., undermining the liberal values it seeks to promote; cf. Sørensen 2011).

We do not have space in the present context to further pursue this liberal dilemma. Our point here is a simple one: with liberal values preponderant in the present world order, the contradictions of liberalism cannot fail to be further exposed and sharpened. When this happens, foreign policies of liberal states will increasingly be confronted with the question of how to master this core tension in liberalism. Those who favour restraint must point to ways to avoid this from leading to quiet acceptance of massive human suffering. Those who favour imposition must point to ways of ensuring the result will not be illiberal outcomes and illegitimate policies. In sum, this essential dilemma in liberalism is a central key to appreciating the challenges faced by a liberal foreign policy.

Liberalism: The Current Research Agenda

With the end of the Cold War some traditional issues on the liberal research agenda have been endowed with a new urgency. More than previously, it is now important to know precisely how democracy leads to peace, and to understand the exact extent to which new democracies need to be consolidated in order to secure a democratic peace. The concept of the 'security community' proposed by Karl Deutsch (Deutsch et al. 1957) requires further development. This notion is helpful in emphasizing that peace is more than merely the absence of war. However, it is less precise than it ought to be as an effective research tool (Lindberg 2005; Harrison 2010; Hook 2010; Hegre 2014).

A similar urgency of need for more solid knowledge pertains to international institutions. Newer institutions, such as the Organization for Security and Cooperation in Europe (OSCE) and the World Trade Organization (WTO), have appeared on the world stage. Older institutions, such as the **North Atlantic Treaty Organization (NATO)**, are changing significantly. (Core questions regarding the emergence, change, and effects of institutions were set forth in the section on institutional liberalism in this chapter.)

Sociological and interdependence liberals have emphasized the importance of the development of transnational relations. It appears that this process is continuing with increasing intensity, at least among some countries (Scholte 2005; Cerny 2010). In Western Europe, it has helped foster a policy of integration with qualitatively new elements: states are pooling their sovereignty in order to improve their collective capacity for regulation (Pollack 2005; Paterson et al. 2010). At the same time, even in Western Europe, continued successful integration is not a certain prospect (Webber 2014; Soros 2014).

Tensions in the liberal view of world order were discussed in the section 'Liberalism and World Order'. As already indicated, the atrocities of 11 September 2001 presented a challenge to liberal IR theory. Mass murder terrorism, such as the attacks on New York and Washington DC, is obviously a very ominous threat to the physical security of citizens of Western liberal democracies, especially the United States (see web links 4.59 and 4.60). It clearly is the case that easy movement of people across international boundaries around the world has a dark side. Some individuals may exploit that freedom to plot and carry out acts of mass murder against citizens of the country in which they are residing. That new security threat demands greater police and intelligence surveillance within countries. That could extend to infringing some of the civil liberties associated with liberal democracy—as in the case of the US PATRIOT Act passed in the aftermath of the attacks (Waldron 2003). It also demands greater security at international borders and other entry points to countries. That could extend to closer inspection of the international transport of goods. It could interfere with the open borders advocated by liberals. At the same time, however, the event could also strengthen international cooperation between countries that perceive a terrorist threat to the security of their citizens. This has happened in connection with the terrorist attacks on New York and Washington DC. The main point is: such events may oblige theorists to rethink their theories, and that includes liberals and liberalism.

Finally, liberal theory is challenged by the comprehensive financial crisis that plagues liberal states in the OECD world. The challenge is that 'free markets' do not merely bring benefits; they also involve large risks of speculation, unemployment, and stagnation. We return to this aspect of liberalism in Chapter 7.

In sum, all students of IR need to take note of the processes of change that are taking place, and to evaluate the possible consequences for international relations. That is an important lesson that liberal IR theory teaches us.

KEY POINTS

- The theoretical point of departure for liberalism is the individual. Individuals plus various collectivities of individuals are the focus of analysis; first and foremost states, but also corporations, organizations, and associations of all kinds. Liberals maintain that not only conflict but also cooperation can shape international affairs.

- Liberals are basically optimistic: when humans employ their reason they can arrive at mutually beneficial cooperation. They can put an end to war. Liberal optimism is closely connected with the rise of the modern state. Modernization means progress in most areas of human life, including international relations.

- Liberal arguments for more cooperative international relations are divided into four different strands: sociological liberalism, interdependence liberalism, institutional liberalism, and republican liberalism.

- Sociological liberalism: IR not only studies relations between governments; it also studies relations between private individuals, groups, and societies. Relations between people are more cooperative than relations between governments. A world with a large number of transnational networks will be more peaceful.

- Interdependence liberalism: modernization increases the level of interdependence between states. Transnational actors are increasingly important, military force is a less useful instrument, and welfare, not security, is the dominant goal of states. That 'complex interdependence' signifies a world of more cooperative international relations.

- Institutional liberalism: international institutions promote cooperation between states. Institutions alleviate problems concerning lack of trust between states and they reduce states' fear of each other.

- Republican liberalism: democracies do not go to war against each other. That is due to their domestic culture of peaceful conflict resolution, to their common moral values, and to their mutually beneficial ties of economic cooperation and interdependence.

- Neorealists are critical of the liberal view. They argue that anarchy cannot be eclipsed and therefore that liberal optimism is not warranted. As long as anarchy prevails, there is no escape from self-help and the security dilemma.

- Liberals react differently to these neorealist objections. One group of 'weak liberals' accepts several neorealist claims. Another group, 'strong liberals', maintains that the world is changing in fundamental ways that are in line with liberal expectations. Anarchy does not have the exclusively negative consequences that neorealists claim: there can be positive anarchy that involves secure peace between consolidated liberal democracies.

? QUESTIONS

- Liberals are optimistic about human progress, cooperation, and peace. What are the reasons given for that optimism? Are they good reasons?

- Has international history been as progressive as liberals claim? Use examples.

- Identify the arguments given by the four strands of liberalism discussed in this chapter. Is any strand of liberalism more fundamentally important, or are all strands equally important?

- What arguments can you make, for and against, the assertion that democracy has made striking progress in the world during the past decade?

- Realists argue that anarchy cannot be transcended. Strong liberals say it can. Who is right and for which reasons?

- Was 11 September 2001 a setback for liberal ideas?

- Think of one or two research projects based on liberal theory.

- Identify the tensions in the liberal view of world order. How can these tensions be mastered in the formulation of liberal politics?

→ GUIDE TO FURTHER READING

Cerny, P. G. (2010). *Rethinking World Politics: A Theory of Transnational Neopluralism.* Oxford: Oxford University Press.

Doyle, M. (2012). *Liberal Peace: Selected Essays.* Abingdon: Routledge.

Dunne, T. and Flockhart, T. (eds) (2013). *Liberal World Orders.* Oxford: Oxford University Press.

Griffiths, M. (2011). *Rethinking International Relations Theory.* Basingstoke: Palgrave Macmillan.

Hook, S. W. (ed.) (2010). *Democratic Peace in Theory and Practice.* Kent, OH: Kent State University Press.

Ikenberry, G. J. (2009). 'Liberal Internationalism 3.0: America and the Dilemmas of Liberal World Order', *Perspectives on Politics*, 7/1: 71–87.

Keohane, R. O. and Nye, Jr, J. S. (2001). *Power and Interdependence: World Politics in Transition*, 3rd edn. New York: Longman.

Moravcsik, A. (2008). 'The New Liberalism', in C. Reus-Smit and D. Snidal (eds), *The Oxford Handbook of International Relations*. Oxford: Oxford University Press, 235–54.

Paterson, W. E., Nugent, N., and Egan, M. P. (2010). *Research Agendas in EU Studies: Stalking the Elephant*. Basingstoke: Palgrave Macmillan.

Sørensen, G. (2011). *A Liberal World Order in Crisis: Choosing Between Imposition and Restraint*. Ithaca, NY: Cornell University Press.

WEB LINKS

Web links mentioned in the chapter, together with additional material including a case-study on the democratic peace, can be found on the Online Resource Centre that accompanies this book.

www.oxfordtextbooks.co.uk/orc/jackson_sorensen6e/

CHAPTER 5

International Society

▌ Summary

The International Society tradition of IR—sometimes labelled the 'English School' (Buzan 2014)—is an approach to world politics that focuses on international history, ideas, structures, institutions, and values. The basic assumptions and claims are: (1) at the heart of the subject are people and basic values such as independence, security, order, and justice; (2) IR scholars are called upon to interpret the thoughts and actions of the people involved with international relations; (3) international anarchy is an important concept but not an exclusive premise—International Society scholars argue that world politics is not merely an international system, it is an '**anarchical society**' with distinctive rules, norms, and institutions that statespeople are involved with in their conduct of foreign policy; (4) they view states not as autonomous entities in themselves, like machines, instead, they see them as human organizations—statespeople wield the power of states and are responsible for their policies and actions; (5) International Society incorporates notions of both a pluralist society of multiple sovereign states, and a solidarist world society of the human population on the planet.

Basic International Society Approach

According to a leading exponent of this approach (Wight 1991: 1), international politics 'is a realm of human experience' with its own distinctive characteristics, problems, and language. To study IR means 'entering this tradition', 'joining in the conversation', and reflecting on that experience with the aim of understanding it in proper academic terms. The main substantive point of this approach is that international relations ought to be understood as a 'society' of mutually recognizing states and not merely as a 'system' of competing and conflicting powers. It is distinctive from other societies by having **sovereign states** as its primary, although not exclusive, membership.

Hedley Bull (1969: 20) summarized the 'traditional' or 'classical' International Society approach as follows: it derives from 'philosophy, history and law' and it 'is characterized above all by explicit reliance upon the exercise of judgement' (see Box 5.1 and web link 5.02). By 'the exercise of judgement', Bull meant that IR scholars should fully understand that foreign policy sometimes presents difficult moral choices to the statespeople involved: choices between rival political values and goals; choices that may involve the use of armed force and may therefore bring about physical destruction and human suffering for the people caught up in it. A difficult foreign-policy choice in this regard would be the decision to go to war or the decision to engage in humanitarian intervention. Examples of such decisions are discussed later in this chapter.

The traditional International Society approach seeks to avoid the stark choice between (1) state egotism and conflict; and (2) human goodwill and cooperation presented by the debate between realism and liberalism. On the one hand, International Society scholars reject classical realists' pessimistic view of states as self-sufficient and self-regarding political organizations that relate to each other and deal with each other only on an instrumental basis of narrow self-interest—international relations conceived as an unchanging state 'system' that is prone to recurrent discord, conflict, and—sooner or later—war. On the other hand, they reject classical liberalism's optimistic view of international relations as a developing world community that is inevitably moving in the direction of unparalleled human progress and perpetual peace, a condition which would be increasingly indistinguishable from domestic peace and prosperity.

The International Society tradition is a middle way in classical IR scholarship; it occupies a position between classical realism and classical liberalism and develops that into a separate and distinctive IR approach. It regards international relations as a **society of states** in which

BOX 5.1	Classical International Society approach

- Human-focused
- Interpretive
- Normative
- Historical-concrete

the principal actors are statespeople who are specialized in the practice of statecraft. It views statecraft as a very important human activity that encompasses foreign policy, military policy, trade policy, diplomatic communication, intelligence-gathering and spying, forming and joining military alliances, threatening or engaging in the use of armed force, negotiating and signing peace treaties, entering into commercial agreements, joining and participating in international organizations, and engaging in countless international contacts, interactions, transactions, and exchanges. The discussion so far can be summarized: international relations consist of the foreign-oriented policies, decisions, and activities of statespeople who act on behalf of territory-based political systems that are independent of each other and subject to no higher authorities than themselves; i.e., sovereign states.

'International organizations', 'non-governmental organizations', 'multinational corporations', and so forth are important human organizations that are also involved in international relations. But they are subordinate to sovereign states. They cannot operate completely independently of those states, because sovereign states collectively control all the territory of the planet. That is why International Society theorists consider sovereign states to be the foundation of world politics; hence, the basic images of the 'system of states' and the 'society of states' that International Society scholars employ in their thinking and research.

International politics is understood to be the special branch of politics that is lacking in hierarchical authority—i.e., there is no world 'government' that is above sovereign states. To that extent, International Society scholars agree with classical realists. However, there are still common interests, rules, institutions, and organizations that are created and shared by states and which help to shape the relations of states. That international social condition is summed up by Hedley Bull's (1995) phrase 'the anarchical society': a worldwide social order of independent states. Within that concept, Bull also drew an important distinction between an **international system** and an **international society** (see Box 5.2).

The more international relations constitute a *society* and the less international relations merely compose a *system* is an indication of the extent to which world politics forms a distinctive human civilization with its own norms and values. For example, during the Cold War, the international society between the United States and the Soviet Union was reduced to being not much more than a system in which the foreign policy of each side was based on its calculation about the intentions and capabilities of the other side, particularly as regards nuclear weapons (see web link 5.11). After the Cold War, however, Russia became more

---

BOX 5.2   International system, international society

A system of states (or international system) is formed when two or more states have sufficient contact between them, and have sufficient impact on one another's decisions to make the behaviour of each a necessary element in the calculations of the other. A society of states (or international society) exists when a group of states, conscious of certain common interests and common values, form a society in the sense that they conceive themselves to be bound by a common set of rules in their relations with one another and share in the working of common institutions.

Bull (1995: 9–13)

involved with the Western-centred world of international organizations such as the G-8 (Group of Eight—the United States, Japan, Germany, Britain, France, Italy, Russia, and Canada); the Organization of Economic Cooperation and Development (OECD); the International Monetary Fund (IMF); the European Bank for Reconstruction and Development (EBRD); the Organization of Security and Cooperation in Europe (OSCE); and the North Atlantic Treaty Organization (NATO). In order to do that, Russia had to take on board common interests and observe, however imperfectly, the common values and obligations of those international organizations—in short, Russia had to become a reliable citizen of Western-centred international society. More recently, however, Russia put its involvement with those international organizations in jeopardy by interfering with the territorial sovereignty of Ukraine, for example, by annexing Crimea and by supplying military assistance to separatists in the eastern part of the country.

Another important set of distinctions are the concepts of **realism**, **rationalism**, and **revolutionism** (Wight 1991). These are three different ways of looking at the relations of states. The first concept views states as power agencies that pursue their own interests. It thus conceives of international relations solely as instrumental relations devoid of morality or law. That is the realist view of Machiavelli (see web link 5.04). The second concept views states as legal organizations that operate in accordance with international law and diplomatic practice (see web links 5.15 and 5.16). It thus conceives of international relations as rule-governed activities based on the mutually recognized authority of sovereign states. That is the rationalist view of Grotius (see web link 5.05). The third concept downplays the importance of states and places the emphasis on human beings. Humans are seen to compose a primordial 'world community' or 'community of humankind' that is more fundamental than the society of states. This is the revolutionist view of Kant (see web links 5.06 and 5.07).

According to Martin Wight (1991), IR cannot be adequately understood through any one of these conceptualizations alone. IR can only be adequately understood through all of them together. If properly carried out, the International Society approach should be an exploration of the conversation or dialogue between these three different theoretical perspectives. Realists, rationalists, and revolutionists each represent a distinctive normative position, or 'voice', in a continuing dialogue about the conduct of foreign policy and other international human activities. That will be set out in the next section.

All three voices broadcast the fact that international relations are basically human activities concerned with fundamental values. Two of the most fundamental are given special attention by Hedley Bull (1995): **international order** and **international justice**. By 'international order', Bull means 'a pattern or disposition of international activity that sustains' the basic goals of the society of states. By 'international justice' he means the moral rules which 'confer rights and duties upon states and nations', such as the right of self-determination, the right of non-intervention, and the right of all sovereign states to be treated on a basis of equality (Bull 1995: 78). These two basic values of the International Society tradition will be discussed in a later section.

Two international values that are closely related to order and justice are given special emphasis by John Vincent (1986): state sovereignty and human rights. On the one hand, states are supposed to respect each other's independence; that is the value of state sovereignty and non-intervention. On the other hand, international relations involve not only states but also human beings who possess human rights regardless of the state of which they happen to be a citizen (see web links 5.26, 5.27, and 5.29). There can be and sometimes is a conflict between the right of non-intervention and human rights. When that happens, which of these values should have priority? If human rights are being massively violated from within a state, does the government retain its right of non-intervention? In such circumstances, is there a norm of humanitarian intervention to provide security for people and protect their human rights (see web links 5.30 and 5.33)? How should sovereign rights and human rights be balanced? This is one of the basic value conflicts of international relations that became prominent after the Cold War.

The traditional International Society approach presents two main answers to these questions. The first answer is *pluralist*, stressing the importance of state sovereignty. According to this view, rights and duties in the international society are conferred upon sovereign states; individuals have only the rights given to them by their own states or recognized by the society of states. Therefore, the principles of respect for sovereignty and non-intervention always come first. The second answer given by the International Society approach to the above questions is *solidarist*, stressing the importance of individuals as the ultimate members of international society. Human rights take precedence over the rights of sovereign states, just as human beings existed long before sovereign states were thought of. On this view, there is at least a right and probably also a duty for states to conduct armed intervention if that is deemed necessary to mitigate extreme cases of human suffering inside a country.

In summary, the traditional International Society approach views world politics as a human world. That means that it is attuned to the normative aspects and value dilemmas of international relations; that also means that the approach is basically situational or historical. World politics is open to all the potential that human beings have for improving their lives, including the progress and peace that classical liberals emphasize. But world politics is exposed, as well, to all the shortcomings and limitations that human beings exhibit, with all the possibilities of risk, uncertainty, danger, conflict, and so on that that implies; including the insecurity and disorder emphasized by classical realists. The International Society approach refuses to choose between liberal optimism and realist pessimism; that may be its main strength (see Table 5.1).

TABLE 5.1   Basic International Society approach

Core concepts	Human beings
	Solidarism
	State sovereignty
	Pluralism
	International structure
	State system
	System of states
	Society of states
Basic values	Order
	Justice

Some contemporary 'English School' theorists have moved away from the traditional approach of Martin Wight and Hedley Bull, who emphasized the role of ideas, norms, and values in IR, and closer to the social science approach to IR exemplified by the work of Kenneth Waltz, which emphasizes international structure (see Chapter 3). Barry Buzan (2004) seeks to develop a more sophisticated analysis of the structure of international society. By 'structure' is meant the encompassing framework and underlying foundation of international relations, the very basis of the existence of either an international system or an international society. For Waltz, international structure was the underpinning power relations of sovereign states. For Buzan, international structure is sustained by a number of 'primary institutions' of international society. The master institutions are: sovereignty; territoriality; diplomacy; great power management; equality of people; market; nationalism; and environmental stewardship (Buzan 2004: 187). It is clear that a full analysis of these institutions and their interplay is a demanding task; the concluding chapter of his book is a first attempt at such an investigation.

The International Society approach refuses to place all the emphasis on one main conceptual angle of vision or line of argument, as for instance to choose between liberal optimism and progressivism and realist pessimism and conservatism. The main strength of the International Society approach for studying international relations is its comprehensiveness, and arguably also its subtlety, which results from its being open and receptive to the strong points of other approaches, particularly realism and liberalism. It is also receptive to the basic elements of international law and the major events and episodes of international history. That openness enables it to get closer to the empirical complexities of international relations, and to gain a deeper appreciation of the normative dilemmas and difficulties of statecraft, foreign policy, and diplomatic relations. In being so open-minded, however, it invites the dangers of excessive complexity and perhaps even the risk of incoherence in its arguments and analyses. Those strengths and weaknesses will become apparent in the exposition that follows.

The Three Traditions

Martin Wight (1991) taught that the leading ideas of the most outstanding classical theorists of IR—theorists such as Machiavelli, Grotius, and Kant—fall into three basic categories: realist, rationalist, and revolutionist. **Realists** are those who emphasize and concentrate on the aspect of 'international anarchy'; **rationalists** are those who emphasize and concentrate on the aspect of 'international dialogue and intercourse'; and **revolutionists** are those who emphasize and concentrate on the aspect of 'moral unity' of humankind (Wight 1991: 7–8). Wight considered these to be the foundational ideas of international relations. Wight sees IR as a never-ending dialogue between realist, rationalist, and revolutionist ideas. One cannot plausibly suppose IR can be reduced to realism or to rationalism or to revolutionism without creating theoretical biases and blind spots.

None of these ideas is 'true' and none is 'false'. They represent different basic outlooks on world politics that compete with each other. Each is incomplete in that it only captures one aspect or dimension of international relations. Each by itself is an inadequate theory of IR. But together they play an indispensable role in IR theory. Realism is the 'controlling' or disciplining factor, revolutionism is the 'vitalizing' or energizing factor, and rationalism is the 'civilizing' or moderating factor in world politics. However, there is a tendency—but only a tendency—for International Society theorists to listen most carefully to the moderate voice of Grotian rationalism.

Realism is the doctrine that rivalry and conflict between states is 'inherent' in their relations. Realists emphasize 'the element of anarchy, of power politics, and of warfare' (Wight 1991: 15–24). Realism concentrates on the actual—what is—rather than the ideal—what ought to be. It involves the avoidance of wishful thinking and 'the frank acceptance of the disagreeable side of life'. Realists, therefore, tend to be pessimistic about human nature: humankind is divided into 'crooks and fools', and realists survive and succeed by outsmarting the crooks and taking advantage of those who are stupid or naive. That implies that world politics cannot progress but always remains basically the same from one time or place to another. Realism taken to the extreme is denial of an international society; what exists is a Hobbesian state of nature. The only political society and, indeed, moral community is the state. There are no international obligations beyond or between states.

Revolutionists identify themselves with universal human fulfilment however defined; e.g., common humanity (Kant), or the world proletariat (Marx), or the liberal end of history (Fukuyama 1989). They assume 'the moral unity' of human society beyond the state (Wight 1991: 8–12). They are 'cosmopolitan' rather than state-centric thinkers; solidarists rather than pluralists; and their international theory has a progressive and even a missionary character in that it aims at changing the world for the better and forever. Revolutionary social change to bring about a universal condition that is conducive to human fulfilment (however that may be defined) is the ultimate goal. History has a purpose; human beings have a destiny. Revolutionists are optimistic about human nature: they believe in human perfectibility.

The ultimate purpose of international history is to enable humans to achieve fulfilment and freedom. For Kant, revolution involved instituting a universal system of constitutional states—'Republics'—that could jointly build perpetual peace. For Marx, revolution involved destroying the capitalist state, overthrowing the class system upon which it was based, and instituting a classless world society. For Fukuyama, revolution involved overcoming pessimism, fear, and the bondage of states, and finding fulfilment in the realm of human freedom and world unity. When that was finally achieved, humanity would not only be liberated but also reunited. Revolutionism taken to the extreme is a claim that the only real society on earth is a world society consisting of every human being; that is, humankind.

Rationalists believe that humans are reasonable, can recognize the right thing to do, and can learn from their own and from others' mistakes (Wight 1991: 14–24). People can intelligently manage to live together even when they share no common government, as in the anarchical condition of international relations. The rationalist world view when taken to the extreme—if it is possible to push to the limit that which is the soul of moderation—is an accommodating world of mutual respect, concord, and the rule of law between states. In this way, rationalism defines a 'middle road' of international politics, separating the conservative realists on one side from the progressive revolutionists on the other (Table 5.2).

TABLE 5.2 **Wight's three IR traditions**

REALISM	RATIONALISM	REVOLUTIONISM
Anarchy	Society	Humanity
Power politics	Evolutionary change	Revolutionary change
Conflict and warfare	Peaceful coexistence	Global community
Pessimism	Hope without illusions	Utopianism

Based on Wight (1991: 47)

Order and Justice

Martin Wight was essentially an historian of ideas who reflected on the dynamic interplay of foundational concepts and assumptions in international relations. Hedley Bull, on the other hand, was primarily a philosopher of world politics who tried to work out a systematic theory of international society. Both Wight and Bull saw IR theory as a branch of political theory under the influence of history. They believed it was only possible to theorize IR within the context of concrete historical events and episodes.

The main point of the anarchical society, according to Bull (1995: 16–19), is promotion and preservation of international *order*, which is defined as 'a pattern or disposition of international activity that sustains those goals of the society of states that are elementary, primary or universal'. He identifies four such goals: (1) preservation of international society; (2) upholding the independence of member states, maintaining peace, and helping to secure the normative foundations of all social life, which includes 'the limitation of violence' (expressed in the laws of war); (3) 'the keeping of promises' (expressed in the principle of reciprocity); and (4) 'the stability of possession' (expressed in the principle of mutual recognition of state sovereignty). According to Bull, these are the most fundamental goals of the anarchical society.

Bull distinguishes three kinds of order in world politics (Bull 1995: 3–21). The first kind is 'order in social life', which is an essential element of human relations regardless of the form taken; the second is 'international order', which is order between states in a system or society of states; and the last is 'world order', which is order among humankind as a whole. He goes on to say that 'world order is more fundamental and primordial than international order because the ultimate units of the great society of all mankind are not states . . . but individual human beings'. States and the society of states are merely temporary—i.e., historical—arrangements of human relations, but 'individual human beings . . . are permanent and indestructible in a sense in which groupings of them . . . are not'. That is a cosmopolitan or solidarist inclination of Bull's IR theory. But most of Bull's analysis is concerned with states and the society of states: it is pluralist rather than solidarist.

The responsibility for sustaining international order—order between states—belongs to the great powers, and is achieved by 'managing their relations with one another'. Bull adds the important qualifier that this is not an empirical statement about what great powers actually do. Rather, it is a normative statement of their special role and responsibility in world politics. He notes that 'great powers, like small powers, frequently behave in such a way as to promote disorder rather than order' (Bull 1995: 199–201). That, of course, happened on two major occasions in the twentieth century and shook the foundations of world politics: the First World War (1914–18) and the Second World War (1939–45).

Bull argued that during the 1960s and early 1970s the United States and the Soviet Union made some attempt to act 'as responsible managers of the affairs of international society as a whole'. The Cold War at times produced international order. But he also said that at certain other times during the Cold War, specifically in the late 1970s and early 1980s, the two superpowers behaved more like 'the great irresponsibles', as they were prepared to sacrifice international order for the sake of their own interests (Bull and Watson 1984: 437). That is the context for the reflections made by President Gorbachev in 1985 (see Box 5.3).

Bull's argument on the balance of power comes very close to that of a moderate realist in Wight's terms. He employed history to draw some important distinctions; for example, between a 'simple balance of power' and a 'complex balance of power'. The former corresponds roughly to the realist concept of bipolarity; the latter corresponds roughly to the realist concept of multipolarity. In the same vein, he went on to use historical illustrations to distinguish between a general balance of power and a local balance of power, and between an objective balance of power and a subjective balance of power. The general balance of power between the United States and the Soviet Union during the Cold War could be distinguished from the local balance of power between Israel and the Arab states in the Middle East, or between India and Pakistan in South Asia.

The objective balance of power is a factual reality, but the subjective balance is a matter of belief and even faith: the doctrine and hope of promoting and maintaining a balance of power to achieve and maintain the value of international order. Writing in the 1970s, Bull (1995: 109) noted that there was no general agreement between the great powers that the maintenance of the balance of power was a common objective, much less a valuable goal for them to pursue. That is misleading, however, because the Soviet Union and the United States did in fact work out rules between themselves for regulating nuclear weapons and other military aspects of their relationship: they collaborated in the pursuit of nuclear peace, and in so doing they disclosed a recognition of shared interests and at least a minimal sociability in their Cold War relationship (Hoffmann 1991).

BOX 5.3	President Gorbachev on Soviet–US collaboration (1985)

You asked me what is the primary thing that defines Soviet–American relations. I think it is the immutable fact that whether we like one another or not, we can either survive or perish only together. The principal question that must be answered is whether we are at last ready to recognize that there is another way to live at peace with each other and whether we are prepared to switch our mentality and our mode of acting from a warlike to a peaceful track.

Quoted from Kissinger (1994: 790)

Hedley Bull also uses historical and contemporary illustrations to make his argument about the nature of war in an anarchical society. Since 1945, international society has succeeded in limiting interstate war but not intrastate war. Wars between great powers have been almost non-existent—except for 'wars fought "by proxy" between the superpowers', such as the Korean War or the Vietnam War (Bull 1995: 187). Bull notes that 'international war, as a determinant of the shape of the international system, has declined in relation to civil war', which he attributed largely to the Cold War stand-off between the superpowers, but which could also be attributed to the norms of the UN Charter, which outlaw aggressive war, and to international public opinion which stands behind them. These 'wars of a third kind' (Holsti 1996) have occurred since 1945 and even more since the end of the Cold War. They include revolutionary wars, wars of national liberation, civil wars, secessionist wars, and so forth. They are often 'asymmetrical' wars because they usually involve non-state actors and raise questions of human rights abuses and, therefore, of humanitarian responsibility in war, discussed later in this chapter. Bull died before our era of armed terrorists and wars against terrorism, but these wars, best exemplified by the recent war against the Islamic State of Iraq and the Levant (ISIL), are perhaps the best examples thus far of asymmetrical warfare.

Hedley Bull notes (1995: 179) that war between states is often contrasted unfavourably with peace between states, but that can be misleading. He points out that 'the historical alternative to war between states was more ubiquitous violence', such as the social anarchy that existed during the European medieval era before modern states monopolized the activity and means of warfare (see Chapter 1). Historically, the state system has sought to suppress such violence by restricting warfare to armed combat between states. So the monopoly of war by states has promoted the value of order (Box 5.4). Here, again, the contemporary era of wars of a third kind are particularly vivid and very apt illustrations of Bull's point about the dangers of social anarchy.

Perhaps the anarchy Bull feared returned after the Cold War in the form of the war against terrorism. The post-Cold War determination of states, particularly the United States and its NATO allies, to suppress international terrorism is a strong indication of their desire to maintain their monopoly of war and thereby uphold international order.

BOX 5.4   Bull's rationalist conception of war as an institution

War is organized violence carried on by political units against each other . . . We should distinguish between war in the loose sense of organized violence which may be carried out by any political unit (a tribe, an ancient empire, a feudal principality, a modern civil faction) and war in the strict sense of international or interstate war, organized violence waged by sovereign states. Within the modern states system only war in the strict sense, international war, has been legitimate; sovereign states have sought to preserve for themselves a monopoly of the legitimate use of violence . . . In any actual hostilities to which we can give the name 'war', norms or rules, whether legal or otherwise, invariably play a part.

Bull (1995: 178)

That is even more evident in the war against ISIL (2014–), which was occurring at the time of writing. ISIL is a terrorist organization that tries to strike fear in ordinary people by whatever means available, including roadside bombs, suicide bombers, kidnappings, murder, torture, and similar methods. However, ISIL is also something more than that. More than any other recent terrorist organization, ISIL seeks to conquer and control large *territories* in Syria and Iraq and turn their military conquests into an Islamic state modelled on a traditional Islamic caliphate. It would be ironic if ISIL were successful in that regard, because it would then be a kind of 'state' rather than decentralized and loosely coordinated terrorism— although a state that would be hostile to the institutions and norms of the modern state system, and a state that the outside world would find it difficult, if not impossible, to tolerate.

According to Bull, international society involves concerns not only about order but also about *justice*. He identifies various conceptions of justice, but he draws particular attention to the distinction in international relations between *commutative justice* and *distributive justice*. Commutative justice is about procedures and reciprocity. It involves 'a process of claim and counter-claim' among states. States are like firms in the marketplace; each firm does its best to succeed within the framework of economic competition. That presupposes a level playing field: all firms play by the same rules of the market; all states play by the same rules of international society. Justice is fairness of the rules of the game: the same rules are applied in the same way to everybody. The rules of the game are expressed by international law and diplomatic practices. That is commutative justice, the principal form of international justice (Table 5.3).

Distributive justice is about goods. It involves the issue of how goods should be distributed between states, as 'exemplified by the idea that justice requires a transfer of economic resources from rich countries to poor'. International distributive justice is the idea that the world's poor cannot be abandoned simply because they live in a foreign country; on the contrary, they deserve special treatment, such as development aid, which can address their misfortune or plight. That means that not all states play by the same rules: the rich and the strong have special obligations to the poor and the weak who have special rights. This form of justice takes a back seat to commutative justice because sovereign states are usually understood as the most appropriate framework within which issues of distributive justice ought to be resolved; in other words, distributive justice is usually understood as an issue of domestic politics rather than international politics. However, during the twentieth and twenty-first centuries, issues of distributive justice have grown in importance as the globe has shrunk and the plight of unfortunate peoples in foreign countries has become more immediately apparent. It indicates a tendency towards greater solidarism in international relations.

TABLE 5.3 Order and justice

ORDER	JUSTICE
Order in social life	Human justice
International order	Interstate justice
World order	World justice

Bull distinguishes three levels of justice in world politics: 'international or interstate justice', which basically involves the notion of equal state sovereignty; 'individual or human justice', which basically involves ideas of human rights; and 'world justice', which basically involves 'what is right or good for the world as a whole', as evident, for example, in global environmental standards. Historically, the interstate level has usually prevailed in world politics. In the late twentieth and early twenty-first century, the latter two levels of justice became more prominent, but they did not overtake the interstate level, the level at which most issues of justice in world politics are still addressed.

Bull ends his discussion of order and justice by considering the relative weight of these two values in world politics. In his comparison, order is seen to be more fundamental: 'it is a condition for the realization of other values' (Bull 1995: 93). Order is prior to justice, because without order, justice becomes more difficult (if not impossible) to achieve. Bull makes a point of saying that that is a general statement, but in any particular case justice may come first. An example is the international justice of self-determination and state sovereignty for colonized peoples in Asia and Africa that was widely regarded as morally taking precedence over the international order of Western colonialism in those parts of the world. Bull's main point is that world politics involves questions of both order and justice, and that international relations cannot be adequately understood by focusing on either value to the exclusion of the other.

Empire and World Society

International Society scholars have been devoting increased attention to the ideas of empire and world society, both of which are solidarist concepts that stand in contrast to the pluralist notion of an international society of sovereign states. An 'empire' may be defined as a hierarchical system between an imperial government and its various dependencies, in which sovereignty is held exclusively by that government and is exercised as supremacy or dominion over its dependencies. In the era before decolonization, large areas of the non-Western world were dominated and ruled by European empires, such as the British Empire or the French Empire, each of which had numerous colonies in Asia, Africa, and elsewhere.

Martin Wight devoted some attention to the concept and history of empire. His most important work was a comprehensive study of the overall constitutional framework of the modern British Empire as it existed immediately before the start of the era of decolonization (Wight 1952). Wight's theory of empire was never fully developed: imperialism does not feature as a systematic category in his IR theory. However, he did indicate in some detail how the later British Empire was legally constructed and how it operated, showing rather clearly the fundamental conceptual difference between an imperial system and a system or society of states. Wight provided some leads to follow up in the analysis of empire. One such lead was the British Empire as a global political system. Britain exercised imperial sovereignty over as many as sixty separate dependencies at the high watermark of the British Empire in the late nineteenth and early twentieth centuries.

The United States is sometimes understood in similar terms of global imperialism. The American government has formal defence agreements with numerous countries scattered around the world which provide the United States with military access to local bases—airports, harbours, etc. It is possible to argue that this contemporary global defence system constitutes an 'empire' not unlike the earlier British Empire. Martin Wight's analysis, which contrasts imperial systems with state systems, would not lead to that conclusion. A recent study by Andrew Hurrell (2007) raises the interesting question of 'empire reborn'. But he questions whether the United States' global military presence around the world could be understood as an empire directly comparable, say, to the British Empire. To Hurrell, the main difference is: Britain formally exercised sovereignty over most of its overseas dependencies. American military bases in foreign countries exist as a result of agreements between their independent governments and Washington. Those bilateral and multilateral arrangements are entirely consistent with the worldwide society of sovereign states. American global military power cannot rest on old-fashioned imperialism. It must rest on international agreements with selected locally sovereign states of a worldwide international society.

That brings us to the idea of a world society. This term refers to common interests and shared values that link 'all parts of the human community' (Bull 1995: 269–70). It is important to differentiate world society and world empire. The former makes reference to the universal community of humankind as Bull defines it. The latter refers to world government by one imperial sovereign to which the population of the world is ultimately subject. World society is often understood as existing in parallel with international society. Whereas international society is pluralist and rests on sovereign states, world society, by contrast, is solidarist and rests on the community of humankind and the 'cosmopolitan culture of late modernity' (Dunne et al. 2010). As defenders of humankind and protectors of human rights, sovereign states have an increasingly important place in acknowledging and upholding world society. This argument was already evident in the International Society theory of R. J. Vincent (1986) and Hedley Bull (1995). It has been expanded in subsequent International Society scholarship (Dunne and Wheeler 1999).

World society is seen to be manifested in various international organizations with a humanitarian purpose, particularly the protection of human rights. The UN Charter and its related declarations and conventions are typically seen as having laid the groundwork for the protection of human rights around the world. Subsequent 'layers' of cosmopolitan norms have been added via various human rights regimes, both global and regional. The most significant is the Council of Europe, which established a European Court of Human Rights. The jurists of that court can review cases brought to them on appeal from the final decisions of national courts of member states of the Council of Europe—if those states have acceded to that legal process. In those cases, the judgments of national supreme courts can be overturned by the European Court of Human Rights, as well as upheld by them. Regional war crimes tribunals, with a limited period of existence, have also been created in the past two decades to prosecute war crimes committed in former Yugoslavia, Rwanda, and Cambodia. Individuals accused of having committed acts of genocide and other flagrant human rights violations have been brought before those tribunals, and some of them have been found guilty and have been punished in accordance with international law.

Since the end of the Cold War, a permanent tribunal—the International Criminal Court (ICC)—has been established, whose enacting Rome Statute has been endorsed by a large number of sovereign states, although by no means all of them. Three permanent members of the UN Security Council have refused to become parties to the Rome Statute: the United States, Russia, and China. Their absence registers a significant division of international society and the limits of its solidarity on the matter of humanitarian law enforcement. However, there can be no doubt that world society has become an increasingly significant feature of international relations.

Some International Society scholars argue that such developments register a 'clear shift from an international society to a world society' (Armstrong 1999). That suggests incompatibility between an international society and a world society: progress towards the latter constitutes movement away from the former. It would seem to mean that the spread of humanitarianism and human rights marks a decline of state sovereignty, and the right of non-intervention. It may even point to the transformation of international society into a world society with shared values and common interests and concerns. That would be a shift—presumably irreversible—from rationalism to revolutionism in Martin Wight's terms, or from pluralism to solidarism in Hedley Bull's terms.

Other scholars point out that the human rights regimes of contemporary world society have not come into existence independently from the society of states. On the contrary, they have been brought into existence by the humanitarian concerns and efforts of member states of international society, especially—although not exclusively—by the Western democracies (Jackson 2006). It has been argued that sovereign states, particularly Western states, are not only the principal authors of international human rights law, but they are also the principal protectors of human rights. As Bull argued (Bull 1995), that suggests an international society based on state sovereignty is not inconsistent with a world society of human rights.

However we choose to interpret this development, world society can be understood as a further humanitarian stage in the evolution or transformation of international society. That stage might be defined historically as starting with the post-World War II era of the UN and European human rights regimes and as evolving, thus far, into the post-Cold War era of the ICC and the several regional and temporary war crimes tribunals. Scholars who study human rights (Dunne and Wheeler 1999) also draw our attention to the importance of international humanitarian NGOs in the creation and development of a worldwide regime of human rights. The spread of a world society is seen as coterminous with the rise of international human rights NGOs in the era following the Second World War.

Statecraft and Responsibility

The International Society approach leads to the study of normative choices in foreign policy with which responsible statespeople are confronted (Jackson 2000). We can discern at least three distinctive dimensions or levels of responsibility which correspond to Wight's three traditions noted above: (1) devotion to one's own nation and the well-being of its citizens; (2) respect for the legitimate interests and rights of other states and for international law; and (3) respect for human rights (Table 5.4).

TABLE 5.4   Four dimensions of responsibility

	RESPONSIBLE TO WHOM?	RESPONSIBLE FOR WHAT?
National	Our citizens	National security
International	Other states	International peace

National Responsibility

According to this conception, statespeople are responsible for the well-being of their citizens. National security is the foundational value they are duty-bound to protect. This standard for evaluating foreign policies gives rise to Machiavellian precepts, such as: always put your nation and its citizens first; avoid taking unnecessary risks with their security and welfare; collaborate with other countries when it is advantageous or necessary but avoid needless foreign entanglements; and do not subject your population to war unless it is absolutely necessary. These normative considerations are characteristic of a system of autonomous states; i.e., realism.

What is the basis for claiming that statespeople are only responsible for defending the national interest? The answer can be derived from a familiar theory of political obligation which regards the state as a self-contained political community that is morally and legally superior to any international associations it may subsequently join. States are seen to have no international obligations that come before their national interests: international law and international organizations are merely instrumental considerations in determining the national interest of states (see web link 5.17). In other words, states are good international citizens because it is in their national interests.

International Responsibility

According to this conception, statespeople have foreign obligations deriving from their state's membership of international society, which involves rights and duties as defined by international law. This interstate standard for evaluating foreign policies gives rise to Grotian precepts, such as: recognize that other states have international rights and legitimate interests which deserve respect; act in good faith; observe international law; and comply with the laws of war. These normative considerations are characteristic of a pluralist society of states based on international law; i.e., rationalism (see Box 5.5).

BOX 5.5	**President Franklin Roosevelt on international responsibility (1945)**

Nothing is more essential to the future peace of the world than continued cooperation of the nations which had to muster the force necessary to defeat the conspiracy of the Axis powers to dominate the world. While the great states have a special responsibility to enforce the peace, their responsibility is based upon the obligations resting upon all states, large and small, not to use force in international relations except in defence of law.

Cited in Kissinger (1994: 427)

What is the normative basis for believing that statespeople have a separate responsibility to international society and its members? The usual answer comes from a conception of international obligation: states are not isolated or autonomous political entities, responsible only to their own people. On the contrary, states are related to each other, and they acknowledge the sovereignty of each other by the activities of recognition, diplomacy, commerce, and so on. States consequently have foreign obligations to other states and to international society as a whole from which they reciprocally and jointly obtain important rights and benefits. That is the heart of the traditional International Society approach.

Humanitarian Responsibility

According to this conception, statespeople are first and foremost human beings and as such they have a fundamental obligation to respect human rights not only in their own country but also in all countries around the world. This cosmopolitan standard for evaluating foreign policies gives rise to Kantian precepts, such as: always remember that people in other countries are human beings just like yourself; respect human rights; give sanctuary to those who are fleeing from persecution; assist those who are in need of material aid which you can supply at no sacrifice to yourself; and in waging war, spare non-combatants. These normative considerations are characteristic of a solidarist world society based on the community of humankind; i.e., revolutionist.

This cosmopolitan criterion of responsible statecraft obviously goes well beyond international responsibility. What is the normative basis for believing that statespeople are responsible for human rights around the world? The usual answer derives from a theory of human obligation: before one can be a citizen of a state and a member of its government, one must be a human being. We are all born as humans but we are each made into citizens of different countries. The traditional way of expressing one's obligations as a human being is by claiming that there is a 'natural law', a universal law of reason and of conscience, and 'natural rights'—what we now call 'human rights'—which statespeople no less than any other people are duty-bound to respect (Box 5.6).

If these criteria and precepts are mutually operative standards of conduct, it becomes clear that we should expect normative dilemmas and conflicts to be a feature of contemporary statecraft. It is equally clear that all three of these dimensions of responsibility must be a focus of analysis. To reduce responsible statecraft to only one or two of these dimensions

BOX 5.6	Russian Foreign Minister Andrei Kozyrev on humanitarian responsibility

Wherever threats to democracy and human rights occur, let alone violations thereof, the international community can and must contribute to their removal . . . Such measures are regarded today not as interference in internal affairs but as assistance and cooperation ensuring everywhere a 'most favoured regime' for the life of the peoples—one consistent with each state's human rights commitments under the UN Charter, international covenants and other relevant instruments.

Quoted from Weller (1993)

is to carry out at best a partial analysis and at worst a biased account that would underestimate the normative complexity of international relations and consequently the actual difficulty of making normatively defensible choices in foreign policy. No criterion can predictably trump all other considerations in all circumstances. There is an underlying normative **pluralism** from which statespeople cannot escape, which IR scholars should not ignore, and which perhaps is what Wight (1991) is referring to when he says he encountered all three perspectives when he canvassed his own mind on such questions.

Humanitarian Responsibility and War

One way to look into humanitarian responsibility is by reference to intervention and war, which has been a striking feature of international society in the period since the end of the Cold War. Human rights became widely recognized in international relations after the Second World War in reaction to the atrocities committed during that war. The UN Charter consequently makes room not only for state sovereignty but also for human rights. The Preamble expresses the UN's 'faith in fundamental human rights'. One of the four 'purposes' of the UN is 'promoting and encouraging respect for human rights and for fundamental freedoms for all without distinction as to race, sex, language, or religion' (Art. 1, 3). The primary purpose of the UN, however, has always been to maintain or restore 'international peace and security' (Art. 1, 1).

The vital articles which justify the use of armed force by the UN and its member states (Arts 39–51) make no mention of humanitarian justification or human rights. The UN's justification for employing armed force is confined to maintaining international peace and security (Art. 39) and 'the inherent right of individual or collective self-defense' (Art. 51). The human security of populations inside of sovereign states is the exclusive responsibility of their governments. The protection of human rights by means of international military intervention is not among the UN Charter justifications for the lawful and legitimate waging of war; quite the opposite. There is what could be called a 'legal firewall' in the charter between human rights and the authority to employ armed force. The charter does not mention human rights in its war-authorizing articles (Chapter 7, Arts 39–51). Instead, it lays great emphasis on 'the sovereign equality' of its member states and their obligation to 'refrain in their international relations from the threat or use of force against the territorial integrity or political independence of any state' (Art. 2).

That rule of restraint has been seen, particularly by non-Western, ex-colonial states, as the fundamental norm of a pluralistic international society and as their main defence against neo-imperialism (de facto Western empires) and neo-colonialism (de facto Western colonies). Western states and the United States in particular are not only concerned about human rights but they are also in positions of great military strength, enabling them to engage in acts of armed intervention in Africa and similar developing areas of the world to protect such rights. Since most, although by no means all, humanitarian crises have occurred in non-Western countries that are militarily weak, their governments have little choice but to invoke what they see as the fundamental norm of non-intervention whenever they become candidates for armed humanitarian intervention by Western governments. Russia and China have tended to support those non-Western countries and also to view Art. 2 as a fundamental norm of international society.

Since the end of the Cold War, the UN Security Council has, nonetheless, passed resolutions which authorize the use of armed force to address major humanitarian crises inside member states which are seen to present a threat to international peace and security. Among the countries targeted by these resolutions have been Iraq, Somalia, Haiti, Kosovo (Serbia), East Timor (Indonesia), and Libya. These resolutions connect human rights to international peace and security and in so doing can be interpreted as establishing a solidarist international society norm of humanitarian intervention and humanitarian war. In other words, they have the effect of overriding, *in practice*, the 'firewall' separation in the UN Charter between the recognition of human rights and the lawful and legitimate use of armed force. These Security Council resolutions have been adopted in spite of the fact that the Charter still remains the same as it was when the UN was founded in 1945.

The absence in the UN Charter of articles that *explicitly* authorize the use of armed force to protect human rights or for other humanitarian purposes has been seen by many Western countries, by some other countries, and by humanitarian NGOs as a deficiency that ought to be corrected. This justification of war has come to be known as the **Responsibility to Protect** doctrine (Evans 2008). Proponents of the doctrine have accordingly sought to justify the international use of armed force beyond 'self-defence' and 'international peace and security' by adding 'military intervention for human protection purposes' (see Box 5.7). That solidarist norm of human protection by military force would be invoked whenever there was 'serious and irreparable harm occurring to human beings, or imminently likely to occur'. That would be triggered by 'large scale loss of life, actual or apprehended' produced by 'deliberate state action, or state neglect or inability to act, or a failed state situation'. It would also be triggered by 'large scale "ethnic cleansing," actual or apprehended'. States where such human catastrophes occurred could no longer hide behind their sovereignty (see web link 5.29).

Proponents of the solidarist norm of armed humanitarianism also argue that human protection by armed force is made necessary by the emergence of various kinds of 'asymmetrical warfare' in the post-Cold War era (Gross 2010). Such warfare includes internal or civil wars, armed anarchy within failed states, forced expulsion of unwanted populations usually in the form of 'ethnic cleansing', and, of course, terrorism. None of those activities are addressed by

| BOX 5.7 | The Responsibility to Protect (R2P): core principles |

A. State sovereignty implies responsibility, and the primary responsibility for the protection of its people lies with the state itself.

B. Where a population is suffering serious harm, as a result of internal war, insurgency, repression or state failure, and the state in question is unwilling or unable to halt or avert it, the principle of non-intervention yields to the international responsibility to protect.

the UN Charter in its articles dealing with armed conflict. That is often seen as a deficiency which ought to be corrected for the sake of protecting humanity under international law.

The clearest case to date of an instance of humanitarian responsibility in war explicitly justified by the Responsibility to Protect doctrine is the 2011 intervention in Libya by NATO air forces (and a few others) to protect the country's civilian population from armed attack by the violent regime of Muammar Gaddafi. The intervention was authorized by UN Security Council Resolution 1973. The air power of NATO and some of its members, particularly France, Britain, and the United States, was authorized 'to protect civilians and civilian populated areas' of Libya that were under attack by armed forces loyal to Gaddafi. NATO carried out its mission and helped bring an end to the humanitarian crisis (Box 5.8). It is worth noting, however, that Libya subsequently deteriorated into a condition of armed anarchy and warfare that is characteristic of a failed state.

The adoption of this solidarist norm of humanitarian intervention and war remains controversial and many states continue to object to it. Yet, the humanitarian concerns which it reflects are beyond question. There can be no doubt that many states fail, some to an alarming degree, in their responsibility to protect the human rights of their populations, or they are militarily incapable of protecting them, or they lack the will. Some even launch armed attacks on their own populations. And there can be no doubt that this has raised great humanitarian concern, not only among many individuals or NGOs but also among some very important international organizations and an increasing number of sovereign states, including some of the major powers.

Nevertheless, there are important normative issues posed by the Responsibility to Protect doctrine when analysed from a pluralist international society perspective. The first and most recurrent objection is the claim that it undermines the norm of non-intervention as enshrined in Art. 2 of the UN Charter. That undoubtedly is the main objection of

---

BOX 5.8	**United Nations Security Council Resolution 1973 (2011) on Libya**

Determining that the situation in the Libyan Arab Jamahiriya continues to constitute a threat to international peace and security, *Acting* under Chapter VII of the Charter of the United Nations,

1. *Demands* the immediate establishment of a ceasefire and a complete end to violence and all attacks against, and abuses of, civilians;

2. *Stresses* the need to intensify efforts to find a solution to the crisis which responds to the legitimate demands of the Libyan people;

3. *Demands* that the Libyan authorities comply with their obligations under international law, including international humanitarian law, human rights and refugee law and take all measures to protect civilians and meet their basic needs, and to ensure the rapid and unimpeded passage of humanitarian assistance;

4. *Authorizes* Member States that have notified the Secretary-General, acting nationally or through regional organizations or arrangements, and acting in cooperation with the Secretary-General, to take all necessary measures . . . to protect civilians and civilian populated areas under threat of attack in the Libyan Arab Jamahiriya.

| BOX 5.9 | **Prime Minister David Cameron | London Conference on Libya Speech | 29 March 2011** |

Let me welcome you all to London.

Foreign Ministers from more than 40 countries—from America to Asia—from Europe to Africa—from the United Nations to the Arab world. All here to unite with one purpose: to help the Libyan people in their hour of need.

Today is about a new beginning for Libya—a future in which the people of Libya can determine their own destiny, free from violence and oppression.

But the Libyan people cannot reach that future on their own.

They require three things of us.

First, we must reaffirm our commitment to UN Security Council Resolutions 1970 and 1973 and the broad alliance determined to implement it.

Second, we must ensure the delivery of humanitarian aid where it is needed, including to newly liberated towns.

And third, we must help the Libyan people plan for their future after the conflict is over.

These are the three goals of this London Conference.

non-Western governments who fear that the doctrine will weaken their authority and open the way to neo-colonial military interference in their part of the world. The second objection is the claim that the doctrine involves a significant and troubling expansion of the right of war beyond the restrictions placed upon it by the UN Charter in 1945. The third objection is the concern that the doctrine runs the risk of deeply dividing the great powers. The fourth objection is the concern that humanitarian intervention will be abandoned by Western states that engage in it, if casualties among their own soldiers increase to the point where the intervention will not be supported by their publics. That could leave the target country in even greater turmoil, which arguably happened in Libya (Box 5.9).

This emergent solidarist norm of justifiable war remains a controversial development and cannot yet be regarded as a universal standard accepted by virtually every member state of the UN. What is beyond doubt, however, is the fact that humanitarianism and human rights have become important justifications for armed intervention and war by the UN, by many of its significant member states, and by prominent international organizations such as NATO and the EU. The solidarist conception of international society has thus become manifest with regard to one of the most vital subjects of international relations, namely the lawful and legitimate use of armed force.

Critiques of International Society

Several major criticisms can be made of the International Society approach to IR. First, there is the realist critique that the evidence of international norms as determinants of state policy and behaviour is weak or non-existent. Second, there is the liberal critique that the International

Society tradition downplays domestic politics—e.g., democracy—and cannot account for progressive change in international politics. Third, there is the IPE critique that it fails to give an account of international economic relationships. Finally, there are several solidarist critiques that emerge from within the International Society tradition itself that focus on its limitations—perhaps its failure—as a theory to come to grips with an emerging postmodern world.

The realist critique of the International Society approach rests on a deep scepticism of an 'international society', as Hedley Bull (1995: 13) characterizes it namely as a group of states that 'conceive themselves to be bound by a common set of rules in their relations with one another, and share in the working of common institutions'. Realists believe states are bound only by their own national interests. Where is the evidence, realists ask, that states are also 'bound by certain rules . . . that they should respect one another's claims to independence, that they should honour agreements into which they enter, and that they should be subject to certain limitations in exercising force against one another' (Bull 1995: 13). States may respect such rules, but only because it is in their own interest. When there is conflict between international obligations and national interests the latter will always win, because the fundamental concern of states is always their own advantage, and ultimately their own security and survival.

The International Society approach is not as soft a target as the realist critique claims. As pointed out, realism is built into the approach as one of its three basic elements. Wight (1966) characterizes IR as a 'theory of survival', which is an acknowledgement of the primacy of states, their right to exist, and the legitimacy of their interests. But the International Society approach does not stop there. It emphasizes that states bind themselves to other states via treaties, and that the justification for that can be more than merely self-interest (realism), or even enlightened self-interest (moderate realism). It emphasizes that states have legitimate interests that other states recognize and respect; it also emphasizes that states recognize the general advantages of observing a principle of reciprocity in international affairs (rationalism). Likewise, it notices that states do not observe treaties only when it is in their best interests to do so. Rather, they enter into treaty commitments with caution because they know that they are binding themselves to the terms of such treaties. If states really acted the way realists claim, there would be no binding treaties, because no state could be expected to keep their promise when it was no longer in their interest to do so. Yet, binding treaties are commonplace in world politics.

Liberals have directed most of their critical attention at realism, and the debate between liberals (or idealists) and realists was the most conspicuous IR debate of the twentieth century. However, one implied liberal critique is the lack of interest of International Society theorists in the role of domestic politics in international relations. Like realists, International Society theorists are not inclined to investigate the domestic aspects of foreign policy. A second implied liberal critique derives from the claim that liberal democracies are more peace-loving than non-democratic political systems. Here, republican liberals are criticizing not only realists but also—by implication—International Society theorists who tend to ignore the subject. A third implied liberal critique is the inability of the International Society approach to account for progressive change in international relations. Wight (1966: 33) claims that domestic politics is a sphere of progressive change, but that international politics is a sphere of recurrence and repetition and IR is thus basically a 'theory of survival'. This view is identical to that of realism.

The main criticism that IPE scholars direct at the International Society approach is its neglect of economics and the social-class aspect of international relations. International Society scholars have only a limited defence against such a criticism, because the fact is that Martin Wight and Hedley Bull give their overwhelming attention to international politics and largely ignore international economics. There is little explicit discussion of economic issues in their writings. However, economics are not entirely ignored. Wight (1991) includes in his definition of rationalism the idea of 'commerce' as one of the basic relations between sovereign states. Bull (1995) explores the role of 'economic factors in international relations' and specifically of 'multinational corporations', 'regional economic associations', and 'transnational society'. Robert Jackson (1990) investigates the role of 'international development assistance', 'Third World debt', and the obstacles and hurdles that existing international society based on state sovereignty puts in the way of developing countries.

Undoubtedly the most significant international society contribution to the study of international economics is by James Mayall (1982). For him, international society has an economic dimension of real significance. In his way of thinking, there is the basis of an economic community in the international society, which binds states together in a complex web of economic ties and mutual interdependence. This is registered in international economic organizations, such as the General Agreement on Tariffs and Trade (GATT) and its successor the World Trade Organization (WTO), the IMF, and the World Bank. He argues that this international economic community even links together in a common global enterprise the economically developed countries (the North) and the developing countries (the South).

The 'transnational society' critique basically argues that international society conceived in terms of a 'society of states' is deficient because it fails to take into account 'the transnational activities of individuals, firms, interest associations and social groups' (Peterson 1992). The state 'does not monopolize the public sphere' and, accordingly, the relations of states do not exhaust international relations. These transnational actors and activities should be neither underestimated nor overestimated: they 'coexist' with sovereign states and interstate relations. International relations are both public and private. There is an international 'civil society' that consists of various transnational actors, but the operation of that society 'relies on the state' to provide 'the conditions under which it can flourish' (Peterson 1992). Those conditions include peace, security, and reciprocity—in other words, Bull's basic goals of international order. International Society scholars would consequently argue that transnational actors and activities are ultimately dependent upon favourable international conditions—peace, stability, lawfulness, free movement of goods and people, etc.—which only states and the society of states can bring about (see Tables 5.5 and 5.6).

TABLE 5.5 Three traditional critiques of International Society

REALISM	**LIBERALISM**	**IPE**
Weak evidence of norms	Ignores domestic society	Ignores economics
Interests dominate	Ignores democracy	Ignores developing world
	Ignores progress	

TABLE 5.6   Three solidarist critiques of International Society

TRANSNATIONAL SOCIETY	GLOBAL SOCIETY	GLOBAL INJUSTICE
State and non-state	Anti-statist	Anti-statist
Transnational activities	Complex global relations	Global protection racket
International civil society	World society	Human wrongs
Public-private coexistence		World injustice

That pinpoints the debate between the traditional International Society theorists of IR (see Box 5.3 and Table 5.3) and their transnational critics. The question is: how significant are these conditions, and how important is the state in providing them (see web link 5.17)? It is hard to see any practical and viable alternative to the state at present. If the state is the only institution that can provide peace, security, and reciprocity, then the transnational critique loses relevance and becomes merely an added, secondary feature of international society which is still, basically, a society of states. If transnational society flourishes in the conditions of the society of states, the transnational critique is less a critique of the traditional International Society approach than an amendment or modest reform which expands on that approach by including secondary features that paint a more complete picture.

The 'global society' critique basically argues that International Society is deficient because it operates with 'a fundamentally state-centric approach' which regards states as actors 'akin to individuals', and neglects 'the complex social relations which bind individuals and states' (Shaw 1992). International Society theory is really a thinly disguised ideology which serves the purpose of justifying the system of sovereign states. The core of this critique is the Marxist claim that there is a primary world society in existence in relation to which the society of states is secondary and subordinate. World society is the basic structure. The society of states is only a 'superstructure', to borrow a Marxist term. International Society theorists dispense an 'ideology' of state primacy, the national interest, the law of nations, and so on, which conceals that underlying materialist 'reality'.

A response that International Society theorists might make to Shaw's critique is to point to the way that statespeople actually conceive of and exercise responsibility in world politics, which is by giving priority first to their own citizens (national responsibility), second to other states (international responsibility), and only third to human beings, regardless of their citizenship or to the world as a whole. In other words, the ethic of pluralism is more significant than that of solidarism in shaping and taking responsibility in world politics. This response probably would not satisfy Shaw because it fails to address the basis of his critique, which is Marxist materialism. The reader has to decide whether the state and, by extension, the society of states, is more or less important than other international relations in world politics, such as economic relationships.

The 'global injustice' critique acknowledges that state interests and concerns still have primacy in world politics, but goes on to make a cosmopolitan critique of the morality, or rather the immorality, of the sovereign state. Ken Booth (1995) argues that international society conceived in terms of a 'society of states' sacrifices human beings on the altar of the sovereign state (see web link 5.33). Statism is the problem rather than the solution as far as human well-being is concerned (Table 5.6). Booth thus extends Shaw's critique by arguing that statespeople, far from acting responsibly, have created an exclusive club—the society of states—whose rules of equal sovereignty and non-intervention exist to serve their own self-ish interests at the expense of a suffering humanity. International Society theorists, by trying to understand and appreciate the difficult choices that statespeople face, actually end up by apologizing for their actions and being 'fetishizers [sic] of Foreign Offices' (Booth, quoted from Wheeler 1996).

However, this critique ignores or plays down the goal of international order and coexistence without which, arguably, there can be no global justice. It also ignores the fact that Hedley Bull was anything but an apologist when it came to the misconduct of the great powers, and specifically the United States and the Soviet Union, which he said were 'not well suited to fulfil the normative requirements of great powerhood' (Bull 1984).

The Current Research Agenda

Since the end of the Cold War, the research agenda of International Society has expanded and changed to a degree. Not only has there been a shift of scholarly concern in the direction of justice, but there has also been a movement away from a concern about international justice and towards a concern about human justice. There has also been an enlargement of the subject to include issues of world justice—such as environmental protection or the law of the sea—and the question of what shape International Society might take in the future if state sovereignty ceases to be the foundation institution of world politics as it has been for the past three or four centuries. Finally, there has been a methodological critique which seeks to move away from that classical approach towards a more strictly social science approach to the subject.

This raises the age-old question of state sovereignty. We still live in a world of sovereign states and there is a strong feeling, in our age of democracy, that countries should govern themselves and should not be governed by foreigners, whether they are colonial powers or international organizations. However, the same democratic age has produced numerous declarations of human rights which reduce, at least in theory, the sphere of state sovereignty. John Vincent observes that 'boundaries' between domestic societies, and international society became 'fuzzier' in the last half of the twentieth century with the accumulation of many international declarations and conventions on human rights (Vincent 1990). In other words, there is an ambiguous and confusing relation in international law today between the responsibilities of national citizenship on the one hand, and universal human rights on the other. A leading item on the research agenda of International Society has been the analysis of that ambiguity in contemporary world politics.

John Vincent and Peter Wilson (1993) argue in more reformist International Society terms that a new idea of 'international legitimacy' is emerging because the international law of human rights 'opens up the state to scrutiny from outsiders and propels us beyond non-intervention'. There is a 'new order of things', an interdependent and transnational world that is 'nudging international society in the direction of a world society'. They argue that the pluralist society of states based on the principle of non-intervention 'has now been replaced by a much more complex world'. They call for a cosmopolitan or solidarist theory of International Society 'which recognizes that the principle of non-intervention no longer sums up the morality of states'. Another area where we can see an expanding research agenda is 'the greening' of International Society theory (Hurrell and Kingsbury 1992). It is often believed that the environment presents normative problems to which international society cannot respond in the usual terms of state sovereignty and international law. For example, Robert Goodin (1990) considers 'that the traditional structure of international law—guided as it is by notions of autonomous national actors with strong rights that all other national actors similarly share—is wildly inappropriate to many of the new environmental challenges'. This argument suggests that traditional international society based on state sovereignty is beyond its useful life, and now serves more as an obstacle than an asset as far as addressing world environmental problems is concerned.

Traditional International Society theorists argue that the society of states is more flexible and adaptable than that critique implies. They see no reason why international society cannot be made greener by conventional means of international environmental law and international environmental organizations. Indeed, only if sovereign states get involved will environmental problems gain the recognition and environmental norms the respect they deserve. On that view, international law has not obstructed or even discouraged environmental concerns; on the contrary, it has been employed and adjusted to accommodate and, indeed, to promote such concerns (Birnie 1992) by fitting them into the practices of state sovereignty. As the above discussion indicates, there has been an enlargement of the scope of International Society theory well beyond its traditional focus on state sovereignty and the society of states.

Hedley Bull (1995: 254–66) speculates on whether the classical society of states based on state sovereignty 'may be giving place to a secular reincarnation of the system of overlapping or segmented authority that characterized medieval Christendom' (see Chapter 1). He sees preliminary evidence of such a trend in 'five features of contemporary world politics': (1) the regional integration of states, such as the European Union; (2) the disintegration of states, such as the break-up of the Soviet Union and former Yugoslavia; (3) the expansion of private international violence, such as the rise of international terrorism; (4) the growth of transnational organizations, including the rise of multinational corporations; and (5) the increasing 'unification' of the world by means of advancing technology, such as the spread of electronic communications.

Richard Falk (1985) responds to Bull's theory of neo-Medievalism by arguing that a fundamental transformation of international organization is taking place that involves 'the reorganization of international life'. It has 'two principal features—increased central guidance and increased roles for non-territorial actors'. Bull disagreed with Falk's revolutionist assessment: 'there is no clear evidence that in the next few decades the states system is likely to give place to any of the alternatives to it that have been nominated'.

However, Bull did emphasize 'that there is now a wider world political system of which the states system is only a part'. That larger system is a 'world-wide network of interaction' that embraces not only states but also other political actors, both 'above' the state and 'below' it. In short, the difference between Falk and Bull on the question of the future of International Society is a matter of scholarly discernment concerning the same body of evidence. Falk judges world politics to be in a process of fundamental, revolutionary change. Bull judges world politics to be in a process of evolutionary adaptation. The reader will have to make up his or her own mind as to which of these theorists is closer to getting it right.

Lastly, there has been a methodological shift from the classical approach of Martin Wight and Hedley Bull towards a more strictly social science approach to the subject. The emphasis here is on international society as a distinctive 'form of social structure'. This approach 'is about finding sets of analytical constructs with which to describe and theorise about what goes on in the world, and in that sense it is a positivist approach' (Buzan 2014: 79). At this point, the study of international society is not very different from some realist approaches, as discussed in Chapter 3.

 KEY POINTS

- The International Society approach is a middle way in classical IR scholarship: it occupies a place between classical realism and classical liberalism and builds that place into a separate and distinctive IR approach. It regards international relations as a 'society' of states in which the principal actors are statespeople who are specialized in the art of statecraft.

- A system of states is formed when two or more states have sufficient contact between them to make the behaviour of each a necessary element in the calculations of the other. A society of states exists when a group of states form a society in the sense that they conceive themselves to be bound by a common set of rules in their relations with one another.

- Some International Society scholars argue that we should think of the system of states and the society of states as two dimensions of a more fundamental and more comprehensive international structure which underpins them.

- IR is a never-ending dialogue between realism, rationalism, and revolutionism. Realism emphasizes anarchy and power politics. Rationalism emphasizes society and international law. Revolutionism emphasizes humanitarianism, human rights, and human justice.

- The main point of international society is the promotion and preservation of international order. The responsibility for sustaining order between states belongs to the great powers.

- International society also involves concerns about justice. Commutative justice is the principal form of international justice. But issues of distributive justice are of increasing importance on the international agenda.

- Pluralist international society evolved largely out of the disintegration of European empires. The question has been asked whether empires may be coming back into existence.

- Pluralist international society may be evolving, at least in some respects, into a solidarist world society.

- Statespeople face difficult dilemmas because of the different kinds of responsibility that they have to consider. There are three distinctive dimensions of responsibility: national, international, and humanitarian.

- War raises perhaps the most difficult issues of humanitarian responsibility.

- Critics argue that international society is becoming more, some would say far more, than merely a society of states. They point to the rise of human rights, the globalization of the world economy, the growth of environmentalism, and similar developments in international relations.

QUESTIONS

- What are the core elements of the International Society approach?

- Is there a more basic structure of international relations that underpins both the system of states and the society of states, as some International Society scholars argue?

- What is the difference between order and justice in world politics? Is Hedley Bull correct in claiming that order comes before justice?

- Explain the basic differences between pluralist international society and solidarist international society.

- Does the concept of empire have any application to contemporary international society?

- Can war be justified in terms of international humanitarian responsibility?

- Some International Society theorists argue that human rights have become of increased importance in world politics since the end of the Cold War. Are they correct? What is the evidence in favour of such a view?

- International Society theorists are sometimes accused of being realists in disguise. Is that accusation warranted?

- Is international society moving beyond a pluralist society of sovereign states and increasingly becoming a solidarist world society in response to globalization, environmentalism, and other processes of transformation?

- Is the structural approach to the theory of international society another version of realism?

GUIDE TO FURTHER READING

Armstrong, D. (1999). 'Law, Justice and the Idea of World Society', *International Affairs*, 75/3: 547–61.

Bull, H. (1995). *The Anarchical Society: A Study of Order in World Politics*, 2nd edn. London: Macmillan.

Buzan, B. (2004). *From International to World Society?* Cambridge: Cambridge University Press.

Buzan, B. (2014). *An Introduction to the English School of International Relations*. Cambridge: Polity Press.

Dunne, T. and Wheeler, N. (1999). *Human Rights in Global Politics*. Cambridge: Cambridge University Press.

Evans, G. (2008). *The Responsibility to Protect*. Washington, DC: Brookings Institution.

Hurrell, A. (2007). *On Global Order: Power, Values and the Constitution of International Society*. Oxford: Oxford University Press.

Jackson, R. H. (2000). *The Global Covenant: Human Conduct in a World of States*. Oxford: Oxford University Press.

Keene, E. (2002). *Beyond the Anarchical Society*. Cambridge: Cambridge University Press.

Vincent, R. J. (1986). *Human Rights in International Relations*. Cambridge: Cambridge University Press.

Wight, M. (1991). *International Theory: The Three Traditions*. Leicester: Leicester University Press.

Williams, J. and Little, R. (2006). *Anarchical Society in a Globalized World*. New York: Palgrave Macmillan.

WEB LINKS

Web links mentioned in the chapter, together with additional material including a case-study on the existence of an international society, can be found on the Online Resource Centre that accompanies this book.

www.oxfordtextbooks.co.uk/orc/jackson_sorensen6e/

CHAPTER 6

International Political Economy: Classical Theories

▌ Summary

This chapter is about the relationship between politics and economics, between states and markets in world affairs. Ultimately, International Political Economy (IPE) is about wealth and poverty, about who gets what in the international economic and political system. The most important classical theories in this area are mercantilism, economic liberalism, and neo-Marxism. They are 'theories' in the very broad sense of a set of assumptions and values from which the field of IPE can be approached. We present each of these theories in some detail; the next chapter moves on to the most important debates between them.

Introduction: What is IPE?

In some fundamental ways, our lives are about political economy. To survive, we need food, clothes, and many other goods. Most of us obtain these provisions in the marketplace, paying for them with money we have earned. A modern market is based on political rules (if not, it would be a 'Mafia market' based on threats, bribes, and force). Political rules and regulations constitute a framework within which the market functions. At the same time, economic strength is an important basis for political power. If economics is about the pursuit of wealth, and politics about the pursuit of power, the two interact in complicated and puzzling ways (Polanyi 1957; Gilpin 1987, 2001). It is this complex interplay in the international context between politics and economics, between states and markets, which is the core of IPE (see web links 6.02 and 6.03).

The theoretical traditions introduced in earlier chapters have issues of war and peace, of conflict and cooperation between states, as their main subject of study. IPE shifts our attention to issues of wealth and poverty, and to who gets what in the international system. The present chapter is also different from the previous ones in that it does not focus on a single theoretical tradition. Instead, it introduces the three most important classical theories within the field of IPE; the next chapter adds the major current theories and debates. This approach reflects the development of the discipline of IR in which IPE has emerged as a field of study in its own right. Some scholars even argue that IPE is the more comprehensive discipline and that IR should consequently be seen as a subfield of IPE. Alternatively, both IR and IPE could be subfields within a broader discipline of International Studies (Strange 1995). Many economists believe that methods and theories from the discipline of economics can be applied in other areas of human affairs, including politics and IR. Many political scientists will argue against this tendency to reduce politics to a branch of economics. This debate is fundamentally about which theories and which research questions are the most important.

As we saw in Chapter 2, a core normative argument for the establishment of the academic discipline of IR at the beginning of the twentieth century was that it should help promote a more peaceful world. The focus on war and peace continued during the 1950s and 1960s in the context of the Cold War. For those academics, as well as politicians whose international outlook was shaped by the experiences of two world wars this was a natural choice of focus. French President (and General) Charles de Gaulle, for example, considered economic affairs 'quartermaster's stuff' and 'low politics', which could be looked after by lesser minds while statesmen such as himself took care of the 'high politics', which concerned the larger issues of war and peace.

There is another reason for this attitude. It concerns the nature of economic activity in modern society: the separation between a political sphere of the state and an economic sphere of the market is a feature of modern, capitalist society. As we shall see in the section on economic liberalism, liberals hold that the economic system works most efficiently when left to itself, free from political interference. But this liberal idea should not be taken to mean that economics and politics have nothing to do with each other. The term 'free market' does not imply freedom from politics. Many kinds of political regulation concerning contracts, consumer and producer protection, taxation, working conditions, and so on make up the framework within which the 'free market' functions. Politics and economics are entangled in complex ways, even in the most liberal 'free market' economies.

In the 1950s and 1960s, one could easily get the impression that many IR scholars committed the misunderstanding of separating economics and politics. For a long time, economics and politics in international relations were seen as almost totally isolated from each other, as qualitatively different activities being studied with qualitatively different approaches. As one scholar pointed out in 1970, international economics and international politics were 'a case of mutual neglect' (Strange 1970). But this sharp distinction between politics and economics was from the beginning of the 1970s increasingly questioned.

Why the change of attitude? First, the system that politicians had set up to foster economic growth and international exchange after the Second World War—the so-called **Bretton Woods** system—showed signs of crisis (see web link 6.06). In particular, the United States was in economic difficulties which grew out of its deep involvement in the Vietnam War (1961–73). To halt the drain on US gold reserves, the gold-convertibility of the American dollar had to be abandoned. That measure was taken by American President Richard Nixon. In other words, political measures were taken that changed the rules of the game for the economic marketplace (Box 6.1). The oil crisis from 1973 onwards contributed to a sense of lost invulnerability. In times of economic crisis, it usually becomes clearer that politics and economics hang together. Second, decolonization had created a new group of politically weak and economically poor states in the international system. Most newly independent countries were far from satisfied with their subordinate position in the international economic system. At the UN during the 1970s, they called for a 'New International Economic Order'; i.e., political proposals designed to improve the economic position of Third World (now developing) countries in the international system (see web links 6.07 and 6.08). Although far less important than the Bretton Woods foreign-exchange crisis, these proposals did reveal how the economic position of countries in the international order is closely connected to political measures. Finally, the end of the Cold War also underlined the connection between politics and economics. After 1989, Eastern Europe and the former Soviet

---

BOX 6.1	The Bretton Woods system

The rules of Bretton Woods . . . provided for a system of fixed exchange rates. Public officials, fresh from what they perceived as a disastrous experience with floating rates in the 1930s, concluded that a fixed exchange rate was the most stable and the most conducive to trade ... The rules further encouraged an open system, by committing members to the convertibility of their respective currencies into other currencies and to free trade . . .

On August 15, 1971, President Nixon—without consulting the other members of the international monetary system and, indeed, without consulting his own State Department—announced his new economic policy: henceforth, the dollar would no longer be convertible into gold, and the United States would impose a 10 per cent surcharge on dutiable imports. August 15, 1971, marked the end of the Bretton Woods period.

Spero (1985: 37, 54)

Union began to be reintegrated in the international system created by the West. They wanted both political integration, such as membership of Western organizations, and economic integration, meaning more intensive links of economic interdependence with the advanced economies of Western Europe, North America, and Japan.

In summary, there is a complex relationship between politics and economics, between states and markets, that IR has to be able to grasp. That relationship is the subject of IPE. We need different theoretical ways of approaching the connection between politics and economics. From the possible theories to choose from (Balaam and Dillman 2010; Watson 2014), we have selected three theories which most scholars see as the main theories of IPE: mercantilism, economic liberalism, and Marxism. These are 'theories' in the very broad sense of a set of assumptions and values from which the field of IPE can be approached. As will be apparent, the outlook of mercantilism has much in common with realism, while economic liberalism is an addition to liberal theory. These two theories thus represent views on IPE that are basically realist and liberal. Marxism has its own original theoretical position and we will spend a little more time on that because the Marxist approach has not been previously presented.

Mercantilism

We begin with mercantilism because this theory is intimately connected to the establishment of the modern, sovereign state during the sixteenth and seventeenth centuries. Mercantilism was the world view of political elites that were at the forefront of building the modern state (see web link 6.11). They took the approach that economic activity is and should be subordinated to the primary goal of building a strong state. In other words, economics is a tool of politics, a basis for political power. That is a defining feature of mercantilist thinking. Mercantilists see the international economy as an arena of conflict between opposing national interests, rather than an area of cooperation and mutual gain. In brief, economic competition between states is a 'zero-sum game' where one state's gain is another state's loss. States have to be worried about relative economic gain, because the material wealth accumulated by one state can serve as a basis for military–political power which can be used against other states. We should notice the close affinity between this mercantilist way of thinking and neorealist thought about competition between states in an anarchic realm.

Economic rivalry between states can take two different forms (Gilpin 1987: 32). The first is called defensive or 'benign' mercantilism: states look after their national economic interests because that is an important ingredient of their national security; such policies need not have overly negative effects on other states. The other form, however, is aggressive or 'malevolent' mercantilism. Here, states attempt to exploit the international economy through expansionary policies; for example, the imperialism of European colonial powers in Asia and Africa. Mercantilists thus see economic strength and military–political power as complementary, not competing goals, in a positive feedback loop. The pursuit of economic strength supports the development of the state's military and political power; and military–political power enhances and strengthens the state's economic power.

This contrasts sharply with the liberal view introduced in Chapter 4. Liberals posit a radically different choice—the pursuit of economic prosperity through free trade and open economic exchange versus the pursuit of power by the means of military force and territorial expansion. In other words, states can choose the road of economic development and trade and thus become 'trading states', as did West Germany and Japan after the Second World War. Or they can choose the road of military force and territorial expansion and thus base their prominence on military power, as did Russia under Communist rule. Mercantilists reject that liberal view. More national wealth and more military–political power are complementary stratagems that serve the same fundamental end: a stronger, more powerful state. A choice between the two appears only in specific situations; one example is the limits that Western powers put on economic exchange with the Eastern Bloc during the Cold War. Here, the West makes an economic sacrifice for reasons of military security. Mercantilists see that as an extraordinary situation. Normally, wealth and power can be pursued simultaneously, in mutual support.

Mercantilists maintain that the economy should be subordinate to the primary goal of increasing state power: politics must have primacy over economics. But the content of the concrete policies recommended to serve that goal has changed over time. Sixteenth-century mercantilists noted how Spain benefitted from the supply of gold and silver bullion from the Americas; that led them to call for the acquisition of bullion as the main road to national wealth. However, when the Netherlands emerged as the leading country in Europe, not through the acquisition of bullion, but mainly because of its vast overseas trading empire, mercantilists started to emphasize trade and the creation of the largest possible trade surplus as the road to national prosperity. Ever since Britain obtained a leading role in world politics through industrialization, mercantilists have underlined the need for countries to industrialize as the best way to obtain national power. Mercantilism has been particularly popular in countries that lagged behind Britain in industrial development; they felt an urgent need to catch up industrially in order to compete with Britain (Box 6.2). That catching-up could not be left to market forces; it called for political measures to protect and develop local industry.

BOX 6.2   Basic mercantilist assumptions

Anglo-American *theory* instructs Westerners that economics is by nature a 'positive sum game' from which all can emerge as winners. Asian *history* instructs many Koreans, Chinese, Japanese, and others that economic competition is a form of war in which some win and others lose. To be strong is much better than to be weak; to give orders is better than to take them. By this logic, the way to be strong, to give orders, to have independence and control, is to keep in mind the difference between 'us' and 'them'. This perspective comes naturally to Koreans (when thinking about Japan), or Canadians (when thinking about the United States), or Britons (when thinking, even today, about Germany), or to Chinese or Japanese (when thinking about what the Europeans did to their nations).

Fallows (1994: 231)

TABLE 6.1 **Mercantilism summarized**

Relationship between economics and politics:	Politics decisive
Main actors/units of analysis:	States
The nature of economic relations:	Conflictual, a zero-sum game
Economic goals:	State power

Mercantilism has been advocated by some eminent politicians and economists. Alexander Hamilton, one of the founding fathers of the United States, was a strong proponent of mercantilism in the form of protectionist policies aimed at promoting domestic industry in the United States. Another eloquent spokesman for mercantilism was Friedrich List, a German economist (see web link 6.12). In the 1840s he developed a theory of 'productive power' which stressed that the ability to produce is more important than the result of producing. In other words, the prosperity of a state depends not primarily on its store of wealth, but on the extent to which it has developed its 'powers of production':

A nation capable of developing a manufacturing power, if it makes use of the system of protection, thus acts quite in the same spirit as the landed proprietor did who by the sacrifice of some material wealth allowed some of his children to learn a production trade.

(List 1966: 145)

Recent mercantilist thinking focuses on the successful 'developmental' states in East Asia: Japan, South Korea, Taiwan, and China. They emphasize that economic success has always been accompanied by a strong, commanding role for the state in promoting economic development. In Japan, for example, the Japanese state has played a very comprehensive role in the economic development of the country. The state has singled out strategic industries, protected them from outside competition, and supported their development even by regulating the competition between firms. We shall have more to say about these theorists in the next chapter.

In summary, mercantilism posits the economy as subordinate to the polity and, particularly, the government. Economic activity is seen in the larger context of increasing state power. The organization that is responsible for defending and advancing the national interest, namely the state, rules over private economic interests. Wealth and power are complementary, not competing goals. Economic dependence on other states should be avoided as far as possible. When economic and security interests clash, security interests have priority (Table 6.1).

Economic Liberalism

Economic liberalism emerged as a critique of the comprehensive political control and regulation of the economic affairs that dominated European state building in the sixteenth and seventeenth centuries; i.e., mercantilism. Economic liberals reject theories and policies that subordinate economics to politics. Adam Smith (1723–90), the father of economic liberal-ism, believed that markets tend to expand spontaneously for the satisfaction of human needs—provided that governments do not interfere (see web link 6.15). He builds on the body of liberal ideas summarized in Chapter 4. These core ideas include the rational indi-vidual actor, a belief in progress and an assumption of mutual gain from free exchange. But Smith also adds some elements of his own to liberal thinking, including the key notion that the economic marketplace is the main source of progress, cooperation, and prosperity. Political interference and state regulation, by contrast, are uneconomical, retrogressive, and can lead to conflict.

Liberal economics has been called 'a doctrine and a set of principles for organizing and managing economic growth, and individual welfare' (Gilpin 1987: 27). It is based on the notion that if left to itself the market economy will operate spontaneously according to its own mechanisms or 'laws'. These laws are considered to be inherent in the process of eco-nomic production and exchange. One example is the 'law of comparative advantage' devel-oped by David Ricardo (1772–1823). He argued that free trade—i.e., commercial activities that are carried on independently of national borders—will bring benefits to all participants because free trade makes specialization possible and specialization increases efficiency and thus productivity (see web link 6.17). Paul Samuelson summarized the argument as follows:

Whether or not one of two regions is absolutely more efficient in the production of every good than is the other, if each specializes in the product in which it has a comparative advantage (greatest relative efficiency), trade will be mutually profitable to both regions.

(Samuelson 1967: 651)

In a world economy based on free trade, all countries will benefit through specialization and global wealth will increase (Box 6.3).

Economic liberals thus reject the mercantilist view that the state is the central actor and focus when it comes to economic affairs. The central actor is the individual as a consumer and a producer. The marketplace is the open arena where individuals come together to exchange goods and services. Individuals are rational in pursuing their own economic interests, and when they apply that rationality in the marketplace, all participants gain. Economic exchange via the market is thus a positive-sum game: everybody gains more than

---

BOX 6.3   A liberal view

Under a system of perfectly free commerce, each country naturally devotes its capital and labour to such employments as are most beneficial to each. The pursuit of individual advantage is admi-rably connected with the universal good of the whole. By stimulating industry, by rewarding inge-nuity, and by using most efficaciously the peculiar powers bestowed by nature, it distributes labour most effectively and most economically: while, by increasing the general mass of produc-tions, it diffuses general benefit and binds together, by one common tie of interest and inter-course, the universal society of nations throughout the civilized world.

Ricardo (1973: 81)

TABLE 6.2   Liberalism summarized

Relationship between economics and politics:	Economics autonomous
Main actors/units of analysis:	Individuals and private firms
The nature of economic relations:	Cooperative, a positive-sum game
Economic goals:	Maximum individual and social well-being

they put in because of increased efficiency. Individuals and companies would not be active in the marketplace unless it were to their benefit. Liberal economists find that this view of individuals as rational and self-seeking (wanting to make themselves better off) can be used as a starting point for understanding not only market economics but also politics. That particular perspective goes under the name of rational choice theory. Liberals thus reject the mercantilist zero-sum view where one state's economic gain is necessarily another state's economic loss. The road to human prosperity, then, goes through the unfettered expansion of the free market economy, capitalism, not only in each country but also across international boundaries (Table 6.2).

There is a recurring debate among economic liberals, however, about the extent to which political interference by governments may be necessary. Early economic liberals called for **laissez-faire**; i.e., for the freedom of the market from all kinds of political restriction and regulation. Yet, even the early economic liberals were aware of the need for a politically constructed legal framework as a basis for the market. Laissez-faire does not mean the absence of any political regulation whatsoever; it means that the state shall only set up those minimal underpinnings that are necessary for the market to function properly. This is the classical version of economic liberalism. At the present time this view is also put forward under labels such as 'conservatism' or 'neoliberalism'; the content however is basically the same. The 'conservative/neoliberal' economic policies of Margaret Thatcher in Britain and of Ronald Reagan in the United States were both based on classical laissez-faire doctrines.

Economic liberals have from early on been aware that in some cases the market may not work according to expectations of efficiency and mutual gain; such cases are usually called instances of 'market failure'. Political regulation may be necessary to correct or avoid market failures. Some economic liberals thus argue for a larger degree of state interference in the market. John Stuart Mill was in many ways a laissez-faire economic liberal, but he was also critical of the extreme inequalities of income, wealth, and power that he observed in nineteenth-century Britain. That made him call for limited state action in some areas, including education and relief for the poor. In the 1930s, John Maynard Keynes, the leading economist of the early twentieth century, went one step further (see web link 6.21). According to Keynes, the market economy is a great benefit to people, but it also entails potential evils of 'risk, uncertainty and ignorance'. That situation could be remedied through improved political management of the market. Keynes thus argued in favour of a market which was 'wisely managed' by the state (Keynes 1963: 321).

This positive view of the state amounted to a major shift in liberal economic doctrine. Keynesian ideas paved the way for a significantly reformed liberal theory: one which was still based on a market economy, but with a considerable degree of state interference and direction. That Keynesian view was popular in Europe in the decades following the Second World War. In the 1980s, however, the pendulum swung back to classical laissez-faire liberalism. One major reason for this renewed liberal faith in the unfettered market is the belief that economic globalization will bring prosperity to all. We shall return to that issue in the next chapter.

In summary, economic liberals argue that the market economy is an autonomous sphere of society which operates according to its own economic laws. Economic exchange is a positive-sum game and the market will tend to maximize benefits for the rational, self-seeking individuals, the households, and the companies that participate in market exchange. The economy is a sphere of cooperation for mutual benefit among states as well as among individuals. The international economy should thus be based on free trade. Classical liberal economists view the role of the state as that of leaving the market alone, including international markets as well as national markets: laissez-faire. However, some twentieth- and twenty-first-century economic liberals favour increased state involvement in the marketplace.

Marxism

The political economy of the nineteenth-century German philosopher and economist Karl Marx represents in many ways a fundamental critique of economic liberalism. We saw above that economic liberals view the economy as a positive-sum game with benefits for all. Marx rejected that view. Instead, he saw the economy as a site of human exploitation and class inequality. Marx thus takes the zero-sum argument of mercantilism and applies it to relations of classes instead of relations of states. Marxists agree with mercantilists that politics and economics are closely intertwined; both reject the liberal view of an economic sphere operating under its own laws. But where mercantilists see economics as a tool of politics, Marxists put economics first and politics second. For Marxists, the capitalist economy is based on two antagonistic social classes: one class, the bourgeoisie, owns the means of production; the other class, the proletariat, owns only its labour power which it must sell to the bourgeoisie. But labour puts in more work than it gets back in pay; there is a surplus value appropriated by the bourgeoisie. That is capitalist profit and it is derived from labour exploitation.

Even if a capitalist economy controlled by the bourgeoisie is exploitative of labour, Marx did not see the growth of capitalism as a negative or retrogressive event. On the contrary, capitalism means progress for Marx in two ways: first, capitalism destroys previous relations of production, such as feudalism, which were even more exploitative, with peasants subsisting under slave-like conditions. Capitalism is a step forward in the sense that labour is free to sell its labour power and seek out the best possible pay. Second, and most important for Marx, capitalism paves the way for a socialist revolution where the means of production will be placed under social control for the benefit of the proletariat who are the vast majority.

The Marxist view is materialist: it is based on the claim that the core activity in any society concerns the way in which human beings produce their means of existence. Economic production is the basis for all other human activities, including politics. The economic basis consists, on the one hand, of the forces of production; i.e., the technical level of economic activity (e.g., industrial machinery versus artisan handicraft). On the other hand, it consists of the relations of production; i.e., the system of social ownership which determines actual control over the productive forces (e.g., private ownership versus collective ownership). Taken together, forces of production and relations of production form a specific mode of production, for example capitalism, which is based on industrial machinery and private ownership (Box 6.4). The bourgeoisie, which dominates the capitalist economy through control of the means of production, will also tend to dominate in the political sphere because according to Marxists economics is the basis of politics (see web link 6.31).

This brings us to the Marxist framework for the study of IPE. First, states are not autonomous; they are driven by ruling-class interests, and capitalist states are primarily driven by the interests of their respective bourgeoisies. This means that struggles between states, including wars, should be seen in the economic context of competition between capitalist classes of different states. For Marxists, class conflict is more fundamental than conflict between states. Second, as an economic system, capitalism is expansive: there is a never-ending search for new markets and more profit. Because classes cut across state borders class conflict is not confined to states; instead, it expands around the world in the wake of capitalism. Such expansion first took the form of imperialism and colonization, but it continued after the colonies had been granted independence. It now takes the form of economic globalization led by giant transnational corporations. The history of IPE can thus be seen by Marxists as the history of capitalist expansion across the globe.

Lenin, the Communist leader of the Russian Revolution of 1917, analysed this process. He argued that the process of capitalist expansion must always be unequal or uneven, between countries, industries, and firms. For example, Britain was ahead of Germany for most of the eighteenth and nineteenth centuries. Consequently, Britain had secured for itself a vast colonial empire whereas Germany had very little. At the beginning of the twentieth century, however, Germany was catching up economically and Britain was declining. Therefore, Lenin noted, Germany wanted a redivision of international spheres of influence, according to the new relative strength of the countries. That demand led to war between

---

BOX 6.4   A Marxist view

Modern industry has converted the little workshop of patriarchal master into the great factory of the industrial capitalist. Masses of laborers, crowded into the factory, are organized like soldiers. As privates of the industrial army they are placed under the command of a perfect hierarchy of officers and sergeants. Not only are they slaves of the bourgeois class, and of the bourgeois state; they are daily and hourly enslaved by the machine, by the overlooker, and above all, by the individual bourgeois manufacturer himself. The more openly this despotism proclaims gain to be its end and aim, the more petty, the more hateful and the more embittering it is.

Marx and Engels (1955 [1848]: 17)

> **BOX 6.5** **Lenin and the law of uneven development**
>
> There can be no other conceivable basis under capitalism for the division of spheres of influence . . . than a calculation of the strength of the participants in the division, their general economic, financial, military strength, etc. And the strength of these participants in the division does not change to an equal degree, for under capitalism the development of different undertakings, trusts, branches of industry, or countries cannot be even.
>
> Lenin (1999 [1917]: 116)

Germany and Britain. Such disparities and conflicts will always develop under capitalist conditions, argued Lenin. That is the 'law of uneven development' (Box 6.5).

The notion of uneven development points to the need for an historical analysis of capitalist expansion. A Marxist analysis must therefore also be clear about history. Events must always be analysed in their specific historical context. For example, there was high economic interdependence between countries around the time of the First World War; there is also high economic interdependence between many countries today. But we need to look at the precise nature of that interdependence in its historical context in order to be able to understand the processes taking place and their significance for international relations; interdependence around the First World War was often arm's-length import/export relations between independent companies. Today, it is frequently integrated circuits of production between subsidiaries of the same transnational company; a Ford car, for example, contains parts produced in many different countries. Such global networks of production make for a different and closer type of economic integration than traditional imports and exports between separate companies.

The difference between Marxist and realist analysis should be brought to attention. Both views agree on the perennial competition and conflict between states. But realists explain this by pointing to the existence of independent states in a condition of anarchy. Therefore, the struggle between states has been taking place for several millennia, ever since the emergence of states (i.e., independent political units) on the world stage. Marxists reject that view as abstract and unhistorical. It is abstract because there is no concrete specification for the social forces that actually sustain conflict between states. These social forces, so the Marxists claim, are exactly the ruling classes of capitalists (and their allies); they ultimately control and determine what 'their' states do. When states are rivals and sometimes come into conflict it is because they pursue the economic and political interests for international dominance and control sought after by the ruling classes (Box 6.6).

The realist view is also unhistorical, according to Marxists. This is because realists see history as always repeating itself; it is 'the same damned things over and over again'; states competing in anarchy. Marxists argue that conflict between states varies substantially across history. Conflict between capitalist states—and ultimately between capitalist ruling classes—is, of course, connected to the capitalist historical era. Consequently, competition and conflict of earlier historical phases require a different explanation, tying it in with the contest between the social forces of those periods of feudalism and antiquity.

BOX 6.6	A neo-Marxist view

It is widely believed that the United States and other developed capitalist countries contribute more capital to the underdeveloped countries than they receive from them. Nonetheless, all available statistics . . . show precisely the opposite . . . For the seven largest Latin American countries . . . the United States Department of Commerce's conservatively calculated figures for the years 1950 to 1961 indicate $2,962 million of investment flows on private account out of the United States and remittances of profits and interest of $6,875 million; adding American public loans and their Latin American servicing between the same years still leaves a conservatively calculated net capital outflow of $2,081 million *to* the United States.

Frank (1971: 237–8)

Realists argue that the Marxist view of the state is reductionist; that is, it reduces the state to a simple tool in the hands of the ruling classes, with no will of its own. States are strong actors in their own right. They embody powerful institutions, they control the means of violence (army, police), and they have substantial economic resources. It is simply wrong to view the state as a mere instrument for others. More recent Marxist analysis has conceded this point. The state has some autonomy from the ruling classes, but it is a *relative* autonomy; the basic function of the capitalist state remains the safeguarding of the capitalist system. Yet, within this general framework, the state should not be reduced to a simple tool of others (Carnoy 1984: ch. 4).

Current Marxist thinking has developed this view further. Robert Cox is a prominent neo-Marxist analyst of world politics and political economy (Cox 1996). Cox begins with the concept of historical structures, defined as 'a particular configuration of forces' (Cox 1996: 97). These historical structures are made up of three categories of forces that interact: material capabilities, ideas, and institutions. Note how Cox moves away from the traditional Marxist emphasis on materialism through the inclusion of ideas and institutions. In the next step, historical structures are identified at three different levels; they are labelled 'social forces', 'forms of state', and 'world orders', as outlined in Figure 6.1 (see web link 6.37).

The term 'social forces' is shorthand for the process of capitalist production. An analysis of this aspect will inform us about the present state of development of the capitalist economy on a global scale. 'Forms of state' point to the ways in which states change in the interplay

FIGURE 6.1   Cox's analytical framework

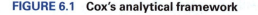
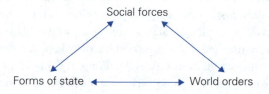

Social forces

Forms of state ←→ World orders

with the social forces of capitalist development. The term 'world orders' refers to the current organization of international relations, including relations between major states and groups of states, the status of international law, and international institutions.

In sum, Cox theorizes a complex interplay between politics and economics, specified as the interaction between social forces, forms of state, and world orders. The task for the analyst is to find out how these relationships play out in the current phase of human history. It is not possible to present Cox's analysis of these matters fully here, but the gist of his argument is as follows (Cox 1992). As regards the social forces of capitalism, they are currently involved in an intense process of economic globalization, meaning an internationalizing of production as well as migration movements from South to North. Globalization has been driven by market forces, but Cox foresees that new social movements critical of globalization will grow increasingly strong and this will open a new phase of struggle between social forces concerning the control and regulation of economic globalization.

As regards forms of state, there is variation between states because they link into the global political economy in different ways. States compete for advantage, but they do it on the premise that integration in the global economy is unavoidable. The dominant forces in capitalist states 'concur in giving priority to competitiveness in the global economy and in precluding interventions by whatever authority that are not consistent with this aim' (Cox 2002: 34). Non-territorial power is becoming more important for states; they compete for markets and economic opportunities across the globe. Transnational corporations and civil society organizations operating across borders (i.e., NGOs) are of increasing importance.

Finally, as regards world order, the long-term tendency will be for replacement of the current global US dominance. Several scenarios are possible; one is an international order of 'conflicting power centres' (Cox 1996: 114) structured around leading states or groups of states, such as the EU in Europe and China and Japan in East Asia (see Chapter 7). Another possibility is a 'post-hegemonic order' (Cox 1992: 142) where states agree on rules and norms of peaceful cooperation for mutual benefit and a common framework for the resolution of possible conflicts. Robert Cox's framework is one example of a recent development of neo-Marxist analysis; we shall return in the next chapter to some of the issues he takes up.

Another major neo-Marxist analysis comes from Immanuel Wallerstein (1974, 1979, 1983, 2004, 2013). His starting point is the concept of **world system analysis**. World systems need not physically include the whole world; they are unified areas characterized by particular economic and political structures. The concept thus ties economics and politics together: a world system is characterized by a certain economic and a certain political structure with the one depending on the other. In human history, there have been two basic varieties of world systems: 'world empires' and 'world economies'. In world empires, such as the Roman Empire, political and economic control is concentrated in a unified centre. World economies, in contrast, are tied together economically in a single division of labour; but politically, authority is decentralized, residing in multiple polities, in a system of states. Wallerstein's key focus is the analysis of the modern world economy, characterized by capitalism (see web link 6.35).

The capitalist world economy was established in 'the long sixteenth century' (1450–1640). It was based on an international division of labour that covered Europe first, but soon expanded to the Western hemisphere and later also to other parts of the world. Within this division of labour, a process of specialization took place; this happened in a somewhat accidental way at first; for a number of reasons north-west Europe was in a better position to diversify its agriculture and to connect it with industrial advance in textiles and shipping. So the capitalist world economy is built on a hierarchy of core areas, peripheral areas, and semi-peripheral areas. The core areas contain the advanced and complex economic activities (mass-market industries and sophisticated agriculture). Furthermore, these activities are controlled by an indigenous bourgeoisie. Peripheral areas are at the bottom of the hierarchy; they produce staple goods such as grain, wood, sugar, and so on. They often employ slavery or coerced labour; what little industrial activity exists is mostly under the external control of capitalists from core countries. Semi-peripheral areas are economically mixed; they are a middle layer between the upper stratum of core countries and the lower stratum of peripheral countries.

A basic mechanism of the capitalist world economy is unequal exchange. Economic surplus is transferred from the periphery to the core. Surplus is appropriated from low-wage, low-profit producers in the periphery to high-wage, high-profit producers in the core. This transfer is further accentuated by the emergence of strong state machineries in the core and weak state machineries in the periphery. Strong states can enforce unequal exchange on weak ones. Thus capitalism 'involves not only appropriation of surplus value by an owner from a laborer, but an appropriation of surplus of the whole world-economy by core areas. And this was as true in the stage of agricultural capitalism as it is in the stage of industrial capitalism' (Wallerstein 1979: 18).

In the process of unequal exchange, tensions are created in the system. The semi-periphery has an important function in this regard. It provides an element of political stability, because the core countries are not facing unified opposition; the semi-periphery acts as a buffer or shock absorber. At the same time, the world economy is not entirely static; any single area of the system may change place from periphery to semi-periphery, from semi-periphery to core, and vice versa. Furthermore, the types of commodities involved in core and peripheral economic activities respectively are subject to dynamic change. Technological advance means that the concrete content of what is 'advanced economic activity' always changes. At one point it was textiles; in a later phase it was industrial machinery; today, it is information- and bio-technology together with financial and other services. But Wallerstein emphasizes that the capitalist system as such does not change: it remains a hierarchy of core, semi-periphery, and periphery, characterized by unequal exchange.

Wallerstein sees the end of the Cold War and the destruction of the Soviet Bloc as a consequence of the development of the capitalist world economy. However, the long-term prospect is the demise of the capitalist system, because the contradictions of that system are now unleashed on a world scale. Success, not failure, is the real threat to global capitalism; when the possibilities for expansion are all used up, the never-ending quest for more profit will lead to new crises in the world capitalist economy which sooner or later will spell its transformation.

TABLE 6.3   Marxism summarized

Relationship between economics and politics:	Economics decisive
Main actors/units of analysis:	Classes
The nature of economic relations:	Conflictual, zero-sum
Economic goals:	Class interests

There are some similarities between Wallerstein's world systems analysis of capitalism and Waltz's neorealist analysis of the international system. Both focus on the system rather than on single units or countries; what happens to countries very much depends on their position in the system. Both see the system as a hierarchy with strong states in the top and weak states in the bottom. But from here the differences take over: Waltz's focus is on relative political–military power in a condition of anarchy; Wallerstein's focus is first and foremost economic power and capability which is then connected with political power. Wallerstein analyses the historical development of capitalism from the sixteenth century onwards, putting economics first and politics second. Waltz analyses the international balance of power in the twentieth century, putting power politics first and economics second. The reader is encouraged to speculate about the advantages and drawbacks of each theory.

It is clear that the contributions from Wallerstein and Cox add a number of nuances to Marxist analysis. In the present context, however, we need to focus on the main thrust of the Marxist approach as compared with liberalism and mercantilism. This basic Marxist view can be summarized as follows: the economy is a site of exploitation and inequality between social classes, especially the bourgeoisie and the proletariat. Politics is to a large extent determined by the socio-economic context. The dominant economic class is also dominant politically. That means that in capitalist economies the bourgeoisie will be the ruling class. Global capitalist development is uneven and bound to produce crises and contradictions, between both states and social classes (Table 6.3). Marxist IPE thus concerns the history of global capitalist expansion, the struggles between classes and states to which it has given rise around the world, and how a revolutionary transformation of that world might come about.

Conclusion

In an overall summary of this chapter, it is helpful to summarize the three classical theories by combining the information in Boxes 6.3, 6.5, and 6.10. That information is contained in Table 6.4.

In the next chapter, we shall introduce the main debates to which the principal IPE theories have given rise in order to convey an impression of the kind of questions and issues that are currently being discussed in IPE.

TABLE 6.4   Three theories of IPE

	MERCANTILISM	ECONOMIC LIBERALISM	MARXISM
Relationship between economics and politics:	Politics decisive	Economics autonomous	Economics decisive
Main actors/units of analysis:	States	Individuals	Classes
The nature of economic relations:	Conflictual, zero-sum game	Cooperative, positive-sum game	Conflictual, zero-sum game
Economic goals:	State power	Maximum individual and social well-being	Class interests

KEY POINTS

- The relationship between politics and economics, between states and markets, is the subject matter of International Political Economy (IPE). There are three main theories of IPE: mercantilism, economic liberalism, and Marxism.

- Mercantilism posits the economy as subordinate to politics. Economic activity is seen in the larger context of increasing state power: the national interest rules over the marketplace. Wealth and power are complementary, not competing, goals; but excessive economic dependence on other states should be avoided. When economic and security interests clash, security interests have priority.

- Economic liberals argue that the market economy is an autonomous sphere of society, operating according to its own economic laws. Economic exchange is a positive-sum game and the market will tend to maximize benefits for individuals, households, and companies. The economy is a sphere of cooperation for mutual benefit, among states as well as among individuals.

- In the Marxist approach, the economy is a site of exploitation and inequality between social classes, especially the bourgeoisie and the proletariat. Politics is to a large extent determined by the socio-economic context. The dominant economic class is also dominant politically. IPE concerns the history of global capitalist expansion and the struggles between classes and states to which it has given rise. Capitalist development is uneven and bound to produce new crises and contradictions, between both states and social classes.

QUESTIONS

- What is IPE and why is it important?

- Give the core arguments made by the three main theories of IPE: mercantilism, economic liberalism, and Marxism. Which theory, if any, is the best one? Why?

- Politics is in control of economics, say mercantilists. Economics is the basis for everything else, including politics, say Marxists. How should we settle this dispute?

- Economic liberals argue that economic exchange is a positive-sum game. In the Marxist approach the economy is a site of exploitation and inequality. Who is correct?

- Do security interests always have priority over economic matters, as mercantilists claim?

- Compare Waltz and Wallerstein. Who has the better theory?

- In terms of practical politics, do states today follow liberal recommendations, or can we find examples of mercantilist or even Marxist policies?

→ GUIDE TO FURTHER READING

Balaam, D. N. and Dillman, B. (2014). *Introduction to International Political Economy*, 6th edn. London: Pearson Education.

Cox, R. W. (1987). *Production, Power and World Order: Social Forces in the Making of History*. New York: Columbia University Press.

Cox, R. W. with Schechter, M. G. (2002). *The Political Economy of a Plural World: Critical Reflections on Power, Morals, and Civilization*. London: Routledge.

Gilpin, R. (2001). *Global Political Economy: Understanding the International Economic Order*. Princeton, NJ: Princeton University Press.

Polanyi, K. (1957). *The Great Transformation: The Political and Economic Origins of Our Time*. New York: Farrar Rinehart.

Schwartz, H. (2009). *States versus Markets: The Emergence of a Global Economy*, 3rd edn. London: Macmillan.

Wallerstein, I. (2004). *World-Systems Analysis: An Introduction*. Durham, NC: Duke University Press.

⊕ WEB LINKS

Web links mentioned in the chapter, together with additional material including a case-study on the interplay between politics and economics, can be found on the Online Resource Centre that accompanies this book.

www.oxfordtextbooks.co.uk/orc/jackson_sorensen6e/

PART 3

Contemporary Approaches and Debates

CHAPTER 7

International Political Economy: Contemporary Debates

▌ Summary

This chapter presents three important debates in IPE. The first debate concerns power and the relationship between politics and economics. Is politics in charge of economics or is it the other way around? This argument is crucial to our understanding of who has power in the world today. The second debate concerns development and underdevelopment in the developing world. A number of developing countries are today successful modernizers, including China, India, and Brazil, but that does not mean we can expect modernization to succeed everywhere. The third debate is about the nature and extent of economic globalization. How extensive is economic globalization, who drives the process, and who benefits from it? In the light of the financial crisis, there is a discussion about the viability of the US/Western model of capitalist development.

Introduction: The Complex Landscape of IPE

The previous chapter presented three classical theories of IPE. They have deep historical roots, but the current versions of them were developed in the 1970s and 1980s. They continue to be under construction, of course, and to develop in many new directions. At the same time, different theories, inspired by social constructivism (see Chapter 8) or post-positivism (see Chapter 9) have entered the field of IPE; a recent analysis identified no less than 19 different 'traditions of thought' in IPE (Watson 2014). This means that many of the theoretical disputes we have introduced in other chapters are also on the table among IPE-scholars (Cohen 2014). For example, many IPE-scholars support the enterprise of 'hard science', of explaining on the basis of quantitative data collection and rigorous empirical testing. Others prefer a qualitative historical approach where the theorist puts herself inside the subject in an attempt to understand the moral dilemmas and the values that drive actors to move in certain directions (see Chapter 2). Several other scholars maintain that these positions can be combined and that a constructive 'middle ground' can be found (Ravenhill 2008).

All these theories attempt to tackle a large number of different subjects, including trade, production, finance, corporations, institutions, varieties of capitalism, and a host of other issues. This diversity gives rise to long and complex debates about the appropriate delimitation of IPE (what should be studied) and about the best ways of approaching the various issues. It has also been suggested to change the name of the field of study from IPE to GPE (Global Political Economy). The two names cover the same topics; we will, as do many scholars, stay with the name of IPE.

We cannot begin to give full coverage of all theories and subjects of IPE in context of one chapter; that would require a separate book. For such specialization, there are a great many IPE-introductions to choose from (for example, Hulsemeyer 2010; O'Brien and Williams 2013; Underhill 2014). What we can do here is to offer an overview of major contemporary debates in IPE and the various theoretical views which drive these debates. We need help from theories in order to organize and clarify our analysis of IPE; but since any theory elucidates some part of reality and leaves others in the dark, there is a risk that it can act as blinkers, leading us in the wrong direction. Note also that theories make normative commitments; they each have specific preferences as to how politics and economics ideally should be related.

The first debate concerns power and the relationship between politics and economics. Is politics in charge of economics or is it the other way around? For mercantilists, states control markets; politics is in control of economics. Liberals recognize the influence of politics, but they consider the market an autonomous sphere of society, which has a dynamic of its own. For Marxists, the class forces emerging from the capitalist economy are the basic drivers of both economic and political development. Why is this debate important? Because it fundamentally affects our understanding of who has power in the world today and thus drives the major changes in the global economy.

The second debate concerns development and underdevelopment in the developing world. Liberals emphasize the constructive role of market forces for economic development;

mercantilists point to the leading role of the state in the process. Marxists point to the ties of dependency and exploitation that hamper development in Third World (the term used by many Marxists for 'developing world'). Today, this discussion takes place in a new context; a number of developing countries, including China, India, Brazil, and several others have had high rates of economic growth for a long period and appear to be successful modernizers. They throw a new light on the debate about the conditions that promote or impede a process of development.

The third debate is about the nature and extent of economic globalization. How extensive is economic globalization, who drives the process, and who benefits from it? For liberals, it is a market-driven process with great potential to bring benefits to all. For mercantilists, states are basically in charge of globalization and heavily influence who gets what from the process. Marxists see globalization as an uneven, hierarchical process where the advanced industrialized countries benefit the most. This debate presently takes places in a context of increasing inequality between and inside countries; it is also informed by the serious financial crisis which broke out in 2008 and has led to a discussion about the viability of the current model of capitalism in the United States and Western Europe.

Power and the Relationship between Politics and Economics

A world characterized by capitalism and economic globalization must rest on a stable framework of liberal rules and regulations. Mercantilists argue that such a framework can only be provided by a hegemon; that is, a dominant military and economic power. In the absence of such a power, liberal rules cannot be created and enforced around the world. That is basically the theory of hegemonic stability which is indebted to mercantilist thinking about politics being in charge of economics (see web links 7.01 and 7.02). But **hegemonic stability theory** is not exclusively mercantilist. There is also a liberal element: the dominant power does not merely manipulate international economic relations for its own sake; it creates an open world economy based on free trade which is to the benefit of all participating states and not only the hegemon. The version of the theory we present here was first set forth by Charles Kindleberger (1973) and then further developed by Robert Gilpin (1987) and informed by several recent debates (Clark 2011) (see web link 7.34).

Why is the theory of hegemonic stability important? Because if it is true, we must expect international markets to be dependent on the existence of a liberal dominant power. In the absence of such a hegemon, an open world economy will be much more difficult to sustain. There is a risk that economic relations will deteriorate into nationalistic, self-interested, protectionist competition, as they did during the world economic crisis of the 1930s, when countries pursued national policies the effect of which was 'beggar your neighbour'. The United States was already the largest economic power, but it was not willing to take on the hegemonic responsibility of creating and maintaining a liberal world economic order. That willingness emerged only after the Second World War, which put an end to American isolationism. The question for today is whether there is a leading power, a hegemon, in the world economy and whether there is a stable framework in place for the process of economic globalization. We return to this issue below; but will first provide some background to the history of US hegemony.

The Second World War elevated the United States to a position of nearly unrivalled world leadership. A majority of American politicians recognized that the United States had to take on responsibility for creating a liberal world market economy after the war. With Europe and Japan in ruins and Britain exhausted, there was no other post-war power to perform that global capitalist role. In short, for a liberal economic world order to come into being, the mere capability of a dominant power is not enough; there must also be a willingness to take on the task. Finally, there must be a commitment to sustain a liberal order once it has been created: to support it not only in good times when the world economy is expanding but also in bad times when it is in recession and participating states may be tempted to beggar their neighbours.

What kinds of power resources are necessary for a hegemon to perform its role? The question is not an easy one to answer, because it involves the complex issue of the fungibility of power. A power resource is fungible if it can be used across several areas. For example, military force is not only useful on the battlefield; it can also be used as a lever in other areas of foreign policy. The United States has employed its military power to provide security to Western Europe against the Soviet threat. That situation has given the United States influence in Europe in other areas, such as trade policies. The provision of military security thus paves the way for leverage in economic areas. In the IR debate about these issues, the claim is that the fungibility of military power is decreasing (Nye, Jr 1990, 2011). We will return to the issue later in this section. Here, it is sufficient to say that a dominant state needs a number of different power resources to perform the role of hegemon. In addition to military power, according to Keohane (1984: 32), it requires control over four sets of world economic resources: raw materials, capital, markets, and the hegemon's competitive advantage in the production of goods that can command a very high value.

Why is a hegemon required in order to create and maintain a liberal world economy? Might we not expect that smaller, less powerful states will also be interested in a liberal world economy because that is to the benefit of all? Why would they not cooperate to sustain such an economy? What is the use, then, for a dominant liberal power? According to the theory of hegemonic stability, the need for a hegemon has to do with the nature of the goods that it provides. A liberal world economy is a so-called public or collective good; that is, a good or a service which, once supplied, creates benefits for everybody. **Public goods** are characterized by non-excludability; i.e., others cannot be denied access to them. The air that we breathe is an example of such a good. A lighthouse is another example of a public good; so is a road or a pavement.[1] The elements of a liberal world economy, such as a currency system for international payments, or the possibility to trade in a free market, are examples of public goods. Once created, they are there for the benefit of all.

---

[1] Yet we know that some roads are closed off, unless a toll is paid; still, many roads are public goods. For further discussion on the difficulties with the distinction see, for example, Hardin (1982).

The problem with public goods is underprovision and what the economists call 'free riding'; i.e., making use of the goods without paying for them. Why should anyone sustain the cost to provide such a good in the first place if it is there to be used at no cost, once it is supplied? Existing public goods invite free riding. That is where the hegemon comes in: such a dominant power is needed to provide those goods and to deal with problems created by free riders, for example by penalizing them. Why would the hegemon do that? Because it has a huge stake in the system.

There are two major historical examples of liberal hegemons: Great Britain during the late nineteenth and early twentieth century; and the United States after the Second World War (see web link 7.05). Britain was a global trading power and imperial power and, as such, had a profound interest in maintaining an open world economy based on free trade. Britain lost its position of hegemony in the early twentieth century when other powers began to rival and surpass it, particularly Germany and the United States. After the Second World War, the United States took the lead in setting up new institutions of a reformed liberal world economy: the IMF, the World Bank, the General Agreement on Tariffs and Trade (GATT, now replaced by the WTO), and OECD. This set of institutions and the agreements on financial stability was called the Bretton Woods system, named after the small town in the US where the agreement was made in 1944.

It was clearly in the United States' own interest to restore the liberal world economy based on new institutions which it could largely control. As the world's dominant industrial power, an open world economy was of great benefit to the US because it gave America better access to foreign markets. Helping in the rebuilding of Western Europe and Japan was also important for American security reasons in its Cold War struggle with the Soviet Union. The United States was not interested in an unstable world, susceptible to Soviet influence, because that would be a threat to the United States' political and economic interests. However, it can be argued that there was also an altruistic element in the American effort. The Marshall Plan helped post-war reconstruction get under way. The US accepted unequal treatment by its partners; Japan was allowed to maintain a limited access to its domestic market; Western Europe was allowed to continue its policies of subsidy and protectionism in agriculture.

By the late 1950s or early 1960s, the economies of Western Europe and Japan had been rebuilt. The huge US economic lead was disappearing; Japan and Western Europe were catching up economically. There was a growing deficit in the American balance of payments. By the 1970s, the US started running trade deficits for the first time in the post-war era. US policies became more oriented towards national interests. Instead of sustaining the post-1945 liberal world economy, the US adopted protectionist measures to support its own economy. America began to act as a 'predatory hegemon' (John Conybeare, quoted from Gilpin 1987). In other words, the US became more concerned about its own national interests, began to lose sight of its role as the defender of an open world economy, and perhaps even started to exploit its power position. It was a new era characterized by 'increasing protectionism, monetary instability, and economic crisis' (Gilpin 1987: 351).

However, the economic crises of the 1970s and 1980s never went very deep and did not threaten the viability of the Western economic order. The end of the Cold War meant a new, tremendous boost, for that order. The Soviet Union folded, and so did the Eastern system of planned economies. Almost all countries were now eager to join the Western system of capitalism and economic globalization. Many did so with great success and in recent years China and other states have been catching up economically. Twenty-five years ago, China accounted for 3.8 per cent of the global GDP and the United States stood for 25 per cent. Today, the Chinese share is 15.4 per cent and the US share is 19.3 per cent (Quandl 2014). It is clear that China and other modernizing states are in a process of catching up economically. To what extent will this threaten US hegemony, and will it mean a crisis for the global capitalist order as predicted by some observers? (See Figure 7.1.)

Let us look at the issue of US power first. Several observers dispute the idea that US economic power has declined substantially (Nye, Jr 2002). The United States remains very strong in traditional power resources (military, economy, technology, territory). There has been a relative decline in the overall economic terms but that was probably inevitable given the great disparities of earlier days. The US continues to lead the world in areas of high-technology innovation and competition (Table 7.1). Furthermore, as indicated, the US is especially strong in the most advanced, information-rich industries, which now count more in terms of economic power than industrial capacity. And, finally, the US also remains strong in non-material power resources, such as 'popular culture' with universal appeal; e.g., films, television, Internet, and so on. Liberal values in line with American ideology also permeate international institutions such as the IMF and the WTO. That gives the United States a substantial amount of **soft power** (see Box 7.1).

If we accept these arguments, we are led to the conclusion that US hegemony is still very much in place (see web links 7.09 and 7.10). This is confirmed in a recent analysis which argues that the wide range of US power resources gives the United States the position of 'history's most complete global hegemon' (Brown 2013: 24). The problem with this view is that is focuses only on the power resources a country has in different areas so that the leading power is the one with the greatest power portfolio. But a successful hegemon does not merely possess great power in terms of resources; it is also able and willing to put these resources to use in the creation of an effective and stable world economy. Here, the US track record is less spectacular, both before and after the end of the Cold War.

FIGURE 7.1   US hegemony and global capitalist order.

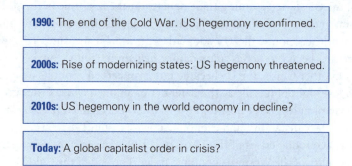

1990: The end of the Cold War. US hegemony reconfirmed.

2000s: Rise of modernizing states: US hegemony threatened.

2010s: US hegemony in the world economy in decline?

Today: A global capitalist order in crisis?

TABLE 7.1   Power resources of major countries/regions

SOURCE OF POWER	US	RUSSIA	EUROPE	JAPAN	CHINA
Tangible:					
Basic resources	strong	strong	strong	*medium*	strong
Military	strong	*medium*	*medium*	*weak*	strong
Economic	strong	*medium*	strong	*medium*	strong
Science/ technology	strong	*weak*	strong	strong	*weak*
Intangible:					
National cohesion	strong	*medium*	*weak*	strong	strong
Universalistic culture	strong	*medium*	strong	*medium*	*medium*
International institutions	strong	*medium*	strong	*medium*	*medium*

Modified from Nye, Jr (2002: 35–40; see also Brown 2013)

So power resources are not the problem. The problem is about the United States rising to the task of assuming responsibility for the liberal world economy (for a similar line of reasoning, see Nye, Jr 2002, 2011). More recently, such criticism has also been voiced against the Republican administration of George W. Bush and the Democratic administration of Barack Obama; the US remains the world's supreme power but does not fill the role of enlightened leadership. Instead, US policy is more narrowly focused on satisfying domestic interest groups (see web link 7.08). The financial crisis that began in 2008 first broke out in the US. A credit bubble, which was related to the housing sector and to leading financial institutions, burst, and three out of the five major Wall Street-based brokers folded. The charge against the US government is that it has been too preoccupied with securing a high level of domestic activity and too little concerned with sound regulation against excessive financial speculation (Wade 2008). Focusing on trade, Ian Campbell has complained about the lack of leadership (see Box 7.2).

BOX 7.1	Soft power

A country may obtain the outcomes it wants in world politics because other countries want to follow it, admiring its values, emulating its example, aspiring to its level of prosperity and openness. In this sense, it is just as important to set the agenda in world politics and attract others as it is to force them to change through the threat or use of military or economic weapons. This aspect of power—getting others to want what you want—I call soft power.

Nye, Jr (2002: 9)

> ### BOX 7.2   No leadership in the world economy
>
> The world no longer has a leader in economic policymaking. Nowhere is that lack of leadership more evident than in trade. The failure of the ministerial summit meeting of the WTO in Cancun, Mexico in September was prepared by the prior positions adopted by the main players: the United States, the European Union and developing countries. The positions of all were characterized by hypocrisy. Perhaps the greatest hypocrisy, however, was that of the United States, which preaches the merits of free trade more strongly than almost any other country and yet spends tens of billions of dollars to prevent its own markets from being free and has taken fresh measures in recent years to discriminate against other countries' producers . . . Developing countries that depend utterly on agriculture are forced to compete with a US agricultural sector that is hugely subsidized. Yet the United States constantly urges countries to open their own markets and allow freer access to US goods and services.
>
> Campbell (2004: 111)

The Marxist position as set forth by Robert Cox agrees that the relative economic decline of the US presents problems for a stable economic order. But he follows the Italian Marxist Antonio Gramsci by emphasizing the ideological dimension of hegemony (see web links 7.03 and 7.04). A stable hegemonic order is based on a shared set of values and understandings derived 'from the ways of doing and thinking of the dominant social strata of the dominant state' (Cox 1996: 517). In other words, US hegemony was based not only on material power but also on consent; i.e., a model of society that other countries found attractive and wanted to emulate. This line of thought is close to the liberal idea about soft power (Box 7.1), but it also underlines a notion of power as resources combined with the ability and willingness to employ these resources in the construction of a stable world economy. Furthermore, many Marxists see US hegemony as a vehicle for control over weaker states by the bourgeoisies of the US and other leading Western countries in ways that were to the economic and political benefit of the West. From this perspective, the liberal world economy is a misnomer for economic and political control of the world by a Western capitalist elite for its own benefit.

Today, there is a new debate about US power. While some think we are living in an age of US empire, others believe that American power is rather fragile and unstable (Hardt and Negri 2000; Mann 2003; Boggs 2005; Münkler 2005; Buzan 2011). On the basis of the above reflections we can try to settle this dispute. On the one hand, the United States certainly remains number one in terms of power resources; that is the basis for US strength. It should be added that many emphasize military power as the area with most pronounced US dominance. But coercion is a less useful instrument after the end of the Cold War because the common enemy has gone and there is no pressing threat to interstate peace. On the other hand, the United States has not recently been consistently able and willing to put these resources to good use and for that reason several observers find that there is a crisis in the world economy rather than a stable hegemonic order; that is the basis for US weakness.

In this situation, is the global capitalist order then in crisis as indicated in Figure 7.1? The optimistic view is that the system of governance has actually worked pretty well, even in the face of financial crisis: 'The evidence suggests that global governance structures adapted and responded to the 2008 financial crisis in a robust fashion. They passed the stress test' (Drezner 2012: 18). But how can governance work if the dominant state does not fulfil its role as hegemonic leader? An earlier analysis by Robert Keohane helps answer this question. He argues that hegemonic power helped establish international cooperation in such areas as finance, trade, and oil. When US power declined, however, cooperation did not break down, as the theory of hegemonic stability would expect. Keohane concludes that hegemonic power may have been important for the initial establishment of cooperation. But once the necessary international institutions are set up, they have a staying power of their own, they operate on their own, and they are able to promote further cooperation even in the circumstances of hegemonic decline. In other words, we should 'recognize the continuing impact of international regimes on the ability of countries with shared interests to cooperate' (Keohane 1984: 216).

The sceptics are not convinced about the healthy situation of the present order. They stress that, today, 'global governance is more fractured and turbulent than it has been for many decades' (Wade 2013: 104). There are several reasons for this but the major problem is that 'for the first time in seven decades, we live in a world without global leadership' (Bremmer 2012: 3).

What can we learn from these discussions about the larger debate concerning the relationship between politics and economics? First, while mercantilism is correct in pointing to the need for a political framework as a foundation for economic activity, it does not mean that there is a one-way relationship in which politics is in control of economics. The economic sphere has a dynamic of its own and unequal economic development between states reshuffles the basis for political power. There is a logic of politics and a logic of economics which influence each other, but economics is not entirely controlled by politics and vice versa. This relationship is summarized in Figure 7.2.

Second, the relative decline of the US has not meant a total breakdown of the liberal world economy, but it is also clear that the current neoliberal regime of regulation needs to be modified in order to create more economic stability. This raises the question about how much leadership and political management is necessary in order to secure a well-functioning global economic order.

FIGURE 7.2   Politics and economics

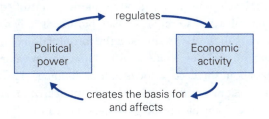

TABLE 7.2   Politics and economics in theories of IPE

	TRUE CLAIM	**FALSE CLAIM**
Mercantilism	Political actors create a framework for economic activity	Politics is in full control of economics
Marxism	Economics affects and influences politics	Economics determines politics
Liberalism	The market has an economic dynamic of its own	The market is an autonomous sphere of society

Finally, the policies of a leading power may be altruistic in the sense that it accepts responsibility for international tasks which others cannot look after, but there will almost always be an important element of self-interest involved. There is a benign as well as a malign aspect of hegemony. The issue of which aspect will dominate cannot be decided beforehand; it must depend on an analysis of each concrete case (see web link 7.12).

In conclusion, one cannot say that politics is in full control of economics, as mercantilists will have us believe; but it is true that political regulation creates the framework for economic activity. Nor can it be said that economics determines politics, as many Marxists claim; but it is true that economic dynamics affect and influence political power. The liberal claim that the market economy is an autonomous sphere of society is misleading; but it is true that once political regulation has created a market economy, that economy has a dynamic of its own. There is a complex relationship between politics and economics, as shown in Table 7.2.

Liberalism, Marxism, and mercantilism have each revealed an important aspect of the political–economic relationship. They also disclose distinct shortcomings: they cannot stand alone. We need elements of each theory in order to investigate the complex relationship between politics and economics.

Development and Underdevelopment in the Developing World

Questions about problems in the developing world (in Asia, Africa, and Latin America) were hardly ever asked before the 1950s. When they were asked it was in terms of colonial development, because most developing countries were colonies controlled by European states. The development of colonies was an imperial issue but not strictly an international issue. Decolonization, beginning in the 1950s, marked the introduction of development research on a larger, international scale. 'New' states in Africa and Asia became members of the UN and raised their voices about the need to focus on development. The Cold War confrontation between East and West meant that each side was interested in cultivating closer links with the developing world to the disadvantage of the other side.

It was economic liberals who spearheaded development research in the West. Their various contributions were given the label '**modernization theory**'. The basic idea was that developing countries should be expected to follow the same developmental path taken earlier by the developed countries in the West: a progressive journey from a traditional, pre-industrial, agrarian society towards a modern, industrial, mass-consumption society. Development meant overcoming barriers of pre-industrial production, backward institutions, and parochial value systems which impeded the process of growth and modernization. Many economic liberals take note of a dualism in developing countries; i.e., a traditional sector still rooted in the countryside and an emerging modern sector concentrated in the cities. The two sectors exist in relative isolation from each other. The only significant linkage is that the traditional sector functions as a reservoir of labour for the modern sector. This spread of development dynamics from the modern sector to the traditional sector is a core problem in getting economic development underway (Lewis 1970).

Economic liberals, or modernization theorists as they are often called in the development debate, endeavour to identify the full range of impediments to modernization as well as all factors that promote modernization. Economic liberals underscore the need for an open economy, free of political interference, to help generate the large amounts of investment that is required to foster sustained economic growth and development (Lal 1983). A famous modernization theory by W. W. Rostow (1960, 1978) specifically stressed that the 'take-off', the crucial push in moving from traditional towards modern, is characterized by a marked increase in modern-sector investment, to a minimum of 10 per cent of the gross national product (see web link 7.13). Another critical element concerns the relationship of developing countries with the world market. Close market relations with the developed countries are seen to have a positive developmental effect on developing world economies. Foreign trade is viewed as a road to market expansion and further growth of the modern sector. Foreign direct investment in the developing world by transnational corporations (TNCs) brings in much needed modern technology and production skills. The economic liberal theory can be summarized as shown in Figure 7.3.

The liberal understanding of development was subjected to increasing criticism during the 1960s and 1970s. That was partly in reaction to the lack of progress in many developing countries at that time. While growth rates in the developed world reached unprecedented highs in the post-war decades, many developing countries had difficulties in getting economic development underway. Their economies refused to 'take off'. That naturally led to increasing dissatisfaction with modernization theory (see web link 7.14).

FIGURE 7.3   The liberal economic development theory

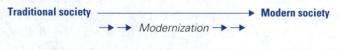

Traditional society ⟶ Modern society
→ → *Modernization* → →

Essential modernization factors:
- a market economy, free of political interference
- a growing rate of economic investment
- foreign direct investment

The most radical critique of economic liberals came from neo-Marxist underdevelopment theory, which is also known as **dependency theory**. It draws on classical Marxist analysis. But it is different from classical Marxism in a basic respect. Unlike Marx, dependency theorists do not expect capitalist development to take root and unfold in the developing world in the same way that capitalism first took place in Western Europe and North America. And, unlike Soviet Marxism, dependency theorists do not support a Soviet model with its centralized and highly authoritarian system. Instead, they argue in favour of a socialist model that is more decentralized and democratic. Their main aim, however, is not so much the formulation of alternative development models to those of capitalism or economic liberalism. Rather, it is to critique the dependency form that capitalist development is seen to take in the developing world (for general overviews, see Kay 1989; Hettne 1995). In short, dependency theory is an attack on late capitalism. It is an effort to provide the theoretical tools by which developing countries can defend themselves against globalizing capitalism.

We saw earlier that for economic liberals 'traditional society' was the place where all countries started their process of development and modernization. Dependency theory rejects that view. The starting point for dependency theory is not tradition; it is underdevelopment. Underdevelopment is not a condition which once characterized all countries. It is a process within the framework of the global capitalist system to which developing countries have been subjected: they have been underdeveloped as an intentional by-product of the development of the West. Underdevelopment is the process by which capitalist forces expand to subdue and impoverish the developing world. Earlier forms of society in the developing world may have been undeveloped; but underdevelopment begins only with the arrival of global capitalism. That is, global capitalism in one single process generates development and wealth (in the industrialized world) and underdevelopment and poverty (in the developing world).

Under such adverse global conditions, how can development be brought to the developing world? Radical dependency theorists, such as Andre Gunder Frank (1969, 1977) and Samir Amin (1976, 1990), do not hesitate to argue that developing countries have to cut off, or at least severely limit, their ties to the capitalist world market. Through reliance on their own strength, as well as mutual cooperation, their real economic development becomes possible, outside the reach of capitalist world market exploitation. Moderate dependency theorists, such as Fernando Henrique Cardoso (Cardoso and Faletto 1979), are less severe in their critique of the capitalist world market. They argue that some progress in the developing world is possible even given the ties of external dependence on the capitalist West. We can summarize the radical dependency view as shown in Box 7.3 (see also Evers and Wogau 1973).

Radical dependency theory came under fire during the 1970s and went into decline (see web links 7.20 and 7.22). A number of countries in South East Asia, most notably the 'Four Tigers' (South Korea, Taiwan, Singapore, and Hong Kong), experienced rapid economic growth combined with world market integration. That was a blow to dependency theory's prediction of stagnation and misery and seemed to support liberal modernization theory. Furthermore, dependency theory severely downplayed domestic factors in their analyses, such as the role of the state and social forces. To some extent, the world systems analysis by Wallerstein set forth in Chapter 6 has an answer to such critiques. Wallerstein builds on

BOX 7.3	Dependency theory of underdevelopment

1. Underdevelopment is caused by factors external to the poor countries. Developing countries are dominated by foreign interests originating in the developed West.

2. Underdevelopment is not a phase of 'traditional society' experienced by all countries. Both development and underdevelopment are results of a single process of global capitalist development.

3. Underdevelopment is due to external, primarily economic, forces; these forces result in crippled and distorted societal structures inside developing countries.

4. To overcome underdevelopment, a delinking from external dominance is required.

ideas from dependency theory about unequal exchange and underdevelopment in the periphery. But in his view some countries, such as the 'Four Tigers', may well move ahead; other countries will simply move in the opposite direction and, overall, hierarchy and unequal exchange continues to characterize the capitalist world economy. Furthermore, Wallerstein would protest against labelling his analysis as economistic; economics and politics affect each other in a dialectical interaction (see also Tausch and Köhler 2002).

In any case, the 1980s saw a strong revival of economic liberal ideas in development thinking. Ronald Reagan's presidency in the US and Margaret Thatcher's administration in the UK both promoted liberal policies that emphasized the role of free market forces and the downsizing of state bureaucracies and state regulations. Developing countries were encouraged to pursue similar policies (Toye 1987).

Yet, the late 1980s and early 1990s also saw the return of ideas based on mercantilist thinking. Mercantilism has not set forth a brief and clear statement about developing world progress comparable to the ones formulated by economic liberals and dependency theorists. But there is a broad and diverse mercantilist tradition in development which has gained new strength in recent years. The mercantilist view of development strikes a balance between economic liberal and dependency views. Whereas economic liberals argue in favour of world market integration in order to promote development, and dependency theorists argue for delinking, mercantilists suggest a middle road. Raul Prebisch (1950) and Gunnar Myrdal (1957) had already argued in the 1950s against free trade based on comparative advantage. The economic benefits which liberals said would accrue to the South according to the theory of comparative advantage were not forthcoming. Basically, that was owing to a long-term decline in the terms of trade for the South's traditional exports.[2] In other words, those export commodities lost much of their previous value on world markets, whereas industrial and increasingly high-technology imports still cost the same or even more. Therefore, it was necessary to actively promote industrialization in the South, even if such industry may be comparatively high-cost in the initial phase. If liberal comparative advantage can be

---

[2] 'Terms of trade' is the ratio of export and import prices. When developing countries receive less for their raw material exports and have to pay more for import of industrialized goods, their terms of trade deteriorate.

TABLE 7.3   Development or underdevelopment in sub-Saharan Africa?

PROGRESS	DEPRIVATION
HEALTH	
Between 1960 and 2009, life expectancy at birth increased from 40 to 56 years.	There is only one doctor for every 5,025 people, compared with 658 as a world average, and 368 for the OECD countries.
In the last two decades, the proportion of the population with access to safe water significantly increased—from 48 per cent in 1990 to 64 per cent in 2013.	More than 24 million people are infected with HIV, over 70 per cent of all those infected in the world.
EDUCATION	
During the past two decades, adult literacy increased from 53 per cent to 64 per cent.	At the primary level, more than 32 million boys and girls are still out of school.
Between 1998 and 2012, the net enrolment ratio at the primary level increased from 57 per cent to 77 per cent, and at the secondary level from 20 per cent to 33 per cent.	Only little over half of the entrants to grade 1 persist to the last grade of primary.
INCOME AND POVERTY*	
Over the period 1975–2010 (ex. 2006, 2007, 2009), four countries—Botswana, Cape Verde, Lesotho, and Mauritius—had an annual GDP growth rate of more than 3 per cent.	About 223 million people do not get enough to eat. 70 per cent of the population in sub-Saharan Africa is living on less than 2 dollars a day.
CHILDREN	
Over the past four decades, the infant mortality rate dropped from 155 per thousand live births to 64.	About 29 million children in the region are malnourished, and 14 per cent of babies are underweight.

Sources: World Bank (2014); Joint United Nations Programme on HIV/AIDS (UNAIDS) (2014); Food and Agriculture Organization of the United Nations (FAO) (2013)

*Total population in sub-Saharan Africa (2013): 936 million; GNP per capita (2013): US$1,008

criticized, so can dependency ideas about delinking. Modern mercantilists thus suggest a compromise between the extremes of economic autonomy and full integration into the global capitalist economy (Table 7.3).

A second core area of development where the mercantilists strike a balance concerns the market and the state. Economic liberals argue that free market forces and a minimal role for the state are best for the promotion of economic development. Mercantilists reply that there may be serious flaws in the alleged efficiency of the market (Weiss 1988: 177). Yet, mercantilists recognize that excessive state intervention can involve 'bureaucratic failures' (White 1984: 101) and they do not support the dependency view where there is no significant role at all for market forces. If too much is left to market forces, there is the danger of market failure; for example, monopolies may be created in some areas so that there is no competition among producers; or there may be negative side-effects due to unregulated production, such as pollution. Yet, if too much is left to state regulation, the result may be bureaucratic failures that are 'red tape' problems of high cost and inefficiency. The actual balance between state and market will vary across societies and within the same society over time (White 1984; Chang 2002). The recent years of prolonged economic crisis in Japan are an indication that after many years of successful growth the political and bureaucratic establishment is unable or unwilling—because there are vested political and economic interests in the current system—to devise new strategies for viable economic development.

Another example of the mercantilist middle road in development thinking concerns the role of TNCs (Rugman and Doh 2008). Economic liberals often see TNCs as 'engines of growth', bringing progress and prosperity to the South; dependency theory, in contrast, frequently sees TNCs as 'the devil incorporated' (Streeten 1979). Mercantilists note that TNCs have the potential for benefitting developing world progress, but only under certain conditions. In weak states with undeveloped local economies, TNCs will totally dominate the host country and that is not helpful for the strengthening of local industry; the TNCs will be local monopolists. In stronger states with some local industry, TNC investment can assist in upgrading local undertakings technologically and otherwise, and thus significantly assist in developing the host economy (Nixson 1988; Dicken 2011). In other words, TNCs on their own will not bring economic development to the South; there has to be a counterweight in the form of local industry and a host government strong enough to oversee TNC activity (see web links 7.28 and 7.29). We can summarize the modern mercantilist view of development as shown in Box 7.4.

Modern mercantilism in many ways appears to offer a sensible strategy for economic development. Yet, it is not without weaknesses. To follow the path advocated by modern mercantilists, the states of the South need a fairly high political–administrative capacity; otherwise they will not be able to undertake sophisticated state interventions and regulations of the economy. Even if there are a number of states with such developmental strength in East Asia and elsewhere, it is clear that the majority of states in the South are not very strong (Brock et al. 2011). For example, in sub-Saharan Africa, corrupt and self-interested state elites are part of the development problem rather than part of the solution. Under such

---

BOX 7.4   Modern mercantilism

1. It strikes a balance between national autonomy and international integration; i.e., between incorporation into the world market and self-reliance.

2. It strikes a balance between state and market; i.e., between free market forces and state regulation.

3. Foreign direct investment by TNCs can be a strong modernization factor, but only provided that TNCs are counterbalanced by local industry and host government supervision.

circumstances, there is little hope of success for the modern mercantilist strategy. Indeed, mercantilist policies might even lead to greater problems by creating conditions in which corruption can flourish (see web link 7.30).

It ought to be clear from this brief introduction that the problems concerning development and underdevelopment in the developing world continue to provoke debate among scholars who hold different theoretical positions. The popularity of the main positions has waxed and waned yet the development problem remains in place; some 870 million people are chronically malnourished (FAO 2012), and 1.22 billion live on less than $1.25 per day (World Bank 2014). Economic liberals are right in claiming that a free market economy can be a powerful force promoting growth and modernization; but it is not true that an unregulated market will more or less automatically lead to optimum development for individuals and states in the long run. Dependency theorists have a point when they emphasize how relations of dependence shape and impact progress in the developing world. But they are wrong in claiming that integration in the world market must lead to underdevelopment and that developed, Western countries are no more than imperialist exploiters. Modern mercantilism appears to strike a sensible middle road between state and market, between autonomy and integration. But mercantilists tend to rely too much on prudent manoeuvring by developing world states, many of which are quite weak and are led by self-serving and often highly corrupt elites.

In sum, and not surprisingly, each of the main theoretical positions has insights concerning the development problem, and each has blind spots, as shown in Table 7.4.

In recent years, the debate on development has grown more complex (Payne 2005). The major theories discussed above claim relevance for development problems everywhere; that is, they are general theories. But there are specific problems in many regions and countries, due to particular historical experiences and variation in local conditions. When the Cold War ended, liberals generally expected that both the former planned economies in the East and the developing countries in the South would embark on an intensified process of modernization which would eventually turn them into system like those in the West: liberal market economies and liberal democracies (Fukuyama 1989), but the liberal view of a one-way street to modernity has not been confirmed by events so far.

TABLE 7.4 The development problem in theories of IPE

	TRUE CLAIM	**FALSE CLAIM**
Liberalism	A free market economy promotes growth and development	An unregulated market will lead to the best result for individuals and states
Dependency theory	Dependence shapes Third World development	Integration in the world market must lead to underdevelopment
Modern mercantilism	Development benefits from a sensible mix of state and market, autonomy and integration	Governments are always able to regulate the economy in an optimum fashion

The roads taken by today's rising powers are not copies of the West. They combine their own peculiar versions of capitalism with political and social systems which are in many ways fundamentally different from the liberal West. China is perhaps the most prominent example of this but the tendency applies to other modernizers as well. That has opened up a new debate about different models or varieties of capitalist development. The debate began with reflections on types of capitalism in the West (Hall and Soskice 2001); in this part of the world the major distinction is between 'liberal market economies' such as the United States and the United Kingdom, and 'coordinated market economies', for example, Germany and Sweden. But these distinctions will clearly not do when we look at the variety of modernizing states around the world because they differ on several other dimensions. Most importantly, it has become clear that capitalism can be combined with non-democratic rule, a possibility not discussed in relation to Western varieties of capitalism.

There is no agreement about how to categorize the present capitalist diversity in the world. Barry Buzan and George Lawson suggest a typology of four major types of capitalism (Buzan and Lawson 2014). There are two democratic types, 'liberal democratic capitalism' (e.g., United States), and 'social democratic' (e.g., Germany), and two non-democratic types, 'competitive authoritarian' (e.g., Russia, Venezuela) and 'state bureaucratic' (e.g., China). Markets dominate in the liberal democratic type; states are highly present in the state bureaucratic type. Charles Kupchan (2012: 86–145) suggests further distinctions among the non-democratic capitalist systems. In addition to 'communal autocracy' (China) and 'paternal autocracy' (Russia), he also includes 'tribal autocracy', where political community is primarily defined by tribe and clan (e.g., the Persian Gulf sheikdoms). Kupchan also identifies 'the theocrats' (the Muslim systems in the Middle East) and 'the strongmen' (the African systems with few checks on the power of the leaders), and, finally, 'the populists', made up of the left-wing populist regimes of Latin America.

It is clear that such a great variety of models must affect the discussion about economic development. When the Cold War ended, we thought there was no alternative to the Western model of capitalist development. We must now appreciate that capitalist development can take place in a variety of forms under very different political conditions. The good news is that there are different possible roads to modernity. The bad news is that the non-democratic varieties of capitalism suffer from severe corruption problems and a host of other difficulties that makes it hard to project whether they will be viable systems in the long run. The Chinese economic model, for example, is based on rapid export growth and cheap labour. Export growth of this magnitude cannot continue and the supply of cheap labour is declining. China wants to graduate into high-tech industries, but these activities are heavily dominated by foreign firms and the demand from developed countries is slow. Two fundamental additional downsides of the Chinese model are environmental degradation and increasing inequality.

China will surely not fall apart; it remains a robust system in many ways. But the example demonstrates how 'the economic development problem' is becoming increasingly differentiated because a large number of dissimilar capitalist systems face a variety of different problems connected to the various peculiar models of development that they are pursuing. To this should be added that there are a number of fragile states in the world today with ineffective political systems, frail economies, and great divisions in the population which often lead to violent domestic conflict (e.g., Somalia, Sudan, Afghanistan, the Congo, Chad, Haiti, Iraq). They present a specific development challenge because the basic conditions of domestic peace and order are not in place.

Increasingly, then, there is no simple liberal, mercantilist, or Marxist answer to the development problem. It is rather the case that different countries face their own set of problems. Some have been successful in bringing about economic growth and reducing poverty; in that sense they are no longer 'traditional' or even 'underdeveloped' societies, but they face a number of development problems anyway. Development is not about finally arriving somewhere and then sitting down to rest; processes of development rather solve some problems while they create others in the process of doing so. In that sense, all countries are developing countries, including the so-called advanced capitalist states that have their own problems, as we shall see in the next section. At the same time, there are a number of fragile states at the bottom, with very serious challenges. They are cases of what may be called 'blocked development'. That is not a situation of complete stagnation or standstill; it doesn't mean that nothing ever happens. What it does mean is that attempts at political, economic, and social development are liable to remain erratic, with progress always combined with setbacks (Brock et al. 2011: 43).

What is Economic Globalization and Who Benefits?

The phenomenon of globalization has received a great deal of attention from IPE. Globalization is the spread and intensification of economic, social, and cultural relations across international borders (see web links 7.33 and 7.35). This means that globalization covers almost everything; it concerns economics, politics, technology, communication, and more. Such a concept of globalization is very difficult to theorize; in social science one cannot have a theory about 'everything', because different aspects of reality have to be analysed in different ways. So, in order to move on, it is helpful to 'unpack' the concept; that is, to look at different major aspects of globalization. Because this is a chapter on IPE, we shall concentrate on the economic aspect of globalization, but it should be remembered that this is only one, albeit very important, aspect of globalization. It is related to interdependence, which was discussed in Chapter 4.

A growing level of economic interconnection between two national economies, for example, in the form of more external trade or foreign investment, is one aspect of economic globalization. We might call it 'intensified interdependence'. But there is an additional aspect which signifies a shift towards a truly global economic system. Intensified economic interdependence involves more of the same in the sense that economic intercourse between national economies increases. True economic globalization, however, involves a qualitative shift towards a world economy that is no longer based on autonomous national economies; rather, it is based on a consolidated global marketplace for production, distribution, and consumption. In this latter case, the single global economy 'dominates' the numerous national economies contained within it (Hirst and Thompson 1992: 199). Some scholars call this process 'deep integration' (Dicken 2011), in contrast to intensified interdependence which can be seen as 'shallow integration'. Deep integration is first and foremost organized by TNCs. They increasingly organize the production of goods and services on a global scale. The various segments of production, from development and design to manufacture and assembly, are each placed in locations that offer the best conditions for that particular segment in terms of labour cost, input availability, proximity of markets, and so on (Table 7.5). At the same time, TNCs set up networks with local firms that act as suppliers and subcontractors (see web links 7.35, 7.37, and 7.42).

Globalization is pushed by several factors: the most important is technological change which is driven by relentless economic competition between firms. The measures taken by states (e.g., trade and finance liberalization) are also important catalysts. The three main theoretical approaches to IPE are in agreement that economic globalization is taking place. But they disagree about the actual content of the process (shallow or deep integration); they also disagree about the consequences of economic globalization for states. Many economic liberals have an optimistic view of economic globalization. One example is the famous American economist, Milton Friedman, who celebrates the fact that it is now 'possible to produce a product anywhere, using resources from anywhere, by a company located anywhere, to be sold anywhere' (Friedman 1993). That is because states no longer interfere with production and consumption the way they used to. According to John Naisbitt (1994), such a world offers tremendous economic opportunities: the possibilities for economic advance are 'far greater than at any time in human history', not only for companies and institutions but also for individuals and families (Naisbitt 1994: 59; see also Friedman 2005; for an overview of literature on the effects of globalization, see Osland 2003). Globalization also means that the component parts of the world become smaller and far more numerous. Small is beautiful not only in the economic sphere but also in the political sphere. This process has profound consequences for the state. In a unified global economy, small, flexible, economic players can grow increasingly powerful as national economies become obsolete. As globalization progresses, says Naisbitt, people become more and more conscious of their 'tribal' identities (e.g., language and culture), and that is driving the

TABLE 7.5 Two aspects of economic globalization

ECONOMIC GLOBALIZATION	*'More of the same'*	*Indicator:* **Global exports (as per cent of GDP)**	
		1990:	2012:
		19 per cent	30 per cent
	'Qualitative shift'	*Indicator:* **Related-party trade (as per cent of total US trade, 2013)**	
		Exports:	Imports:
		30 per cent	50 per cent

Source: World Bank (2014); US Department of Commerce 2014

formation of an increasing number of smaller countries. Naisbitt foresees 1,000—maybe even 2,000—countries by sometime in the twenty-first century. That would entail the decline and fall of the nation-state as we have known it for the past several centuries.

The idea that the Westphalian nation-state is becoming too small for some things and too big for other things in an era of globalization resonates with many economic liberals. They argue that the nation-state is pressured 'from above' in the sense that globalization creates cross-border activities which states are no longer able to control on their own—such as global economic transactions and environmental problems. And the nation-state is also pressured 'from below': there is a trend towards ever-stronger identification with the local community where people live their daily lives (Archer et al. 2007). The economic liberal view of economic globalization and its consequences can be summarized as shown in Box 7.5.

Mercantilists have not formulated a view of globalization that rivals the economic liberal analysis in scope and ambition. But there is what could be termed a mercantilist position in the globalization debate. The position is highly critical of the economic liberal analysis, as regards both the content of economic globalization and the supposed consequences for the nation-state. Mercantilists remain unconvinced that a qualitative shift towards a global economic system has taken place. In other words, they do not believe there is a phenomenon called 'globalization'. Instead, they see economic globalization as 'more of the same'; a process of intensified interdependence between national economies. Furthermore, they argue that trade and investment flows between countries were at a very high level before the First World War. In other words, there is little news in the fact of economic interdependence (see web link 7.39). Mercantilists also reject the claim made by many economic liberals that corporations have lost their national identity in pursuit of their ambition to become truly global economic players (Table 7.6). Instead, mercantilists argue, states and their national corporations remain 'closely linked' in spite of the noteworthy increase in world trade and investment flows since the end of the Second World War (Kapstein 1993: 502; for an overview of the debate, see Sørensen 2004; Dicken 2011).

Mercantilists thus reject the idea that nation-states are being pressured and are somehow losing out in the process of economic globalization. They say liberals fail to take into account the increased capacity of nation-states to respond to the challenges of economic globalization. The technological developments that foster globalization have also helped increase the state's capacity for regulation and surveillance. States are stronger than ever in

---

BOX 7.5   Economic liberals' view of globalization

1. Economic globalization means a qualitative shift towards a global economic system.

2. Economic globalization will bring increased prosperity to individuals, families, and companies.

3. The nation-state loses power and influence as it is pressed from above and from below.

TABLE 7.6   Selected top-100 TNCs, ranked by transnationality index

CORPORATION	HOME ECONOMY	INDUSTRY	TRANSNATIONALITY INDEX*
Top 5			
Nestlé SA	Switzerland	Food, beverages and tobacco	97.1
Anglo American plc	United Kingdom	Mining & quarrying	95.9
Anheuser-Busch InBev NV	Belgium	Food, beverages and tobacco	93.3
Linde AG	Germany	Chemicals	91.0
Bottom 5			
Wal-Mart Stores Inc	United States	Retail and trade	36.1
EDF SA	France	Utilities (electricity, gas, and water)	34.0
Statoil ASA	Norway	Petroleum	30.0
China National Offshore Oil Corp.	China	Petroleum	18.6
CITIC Group	China	Diversified	17.1

Based on UNCTAD 2013 annex-table 28:

http://unctad.org/en/pages/DIAE/World%20Investment%20Report/Annex-Tables.aspx

*The 'transnationality index' is calculated from the average ratios of foreign assets to total assets, foreign sales to total sales, and foreign employment to total employment.

their capacity to extract economic surplus, such as taxes, from their citizens. Their ability to control and regulate all kinds of activities in society has also increased dramatically. The long-term trend is towards more, not less, state autonomy. And lastly, the sovereign state remains the preferred form of political organization around the world. No serious competitor has emerged. We can summarize the realist–mercantilist view of economic globalization as shown in Box 7.6.

The neo-Marxist view of economic globalization differs from that of both economic liberalism and mercantilism. We shall concentrate on the neo-Marxist contribution of Robert Cox which contains both aspects introduced above. Economic globalization involves both intensified interdependence and a qualitative shift towards a global economy (for a different neo-Marxist analysis of globalization, see Rosenberg 2005). According to Cox, there is a new global economy that exists alongside that classical capitalist world economy, but the tendency is that the former 'incrementally supersedes' the latter (Cox 1994: 48). Cox finds that in the process of economic globalization nation-states have lost substantial power over the economy. However, the continued process of economic globalization requires the political framework provided by nation-states; in particular, it requires 'the military-territorial power of an enforcer' (Cox 1994: 54). The United States

---

BOX 7.6	The realist–mercantilist view of globalization

1. Economic globalization is 'more of the same'; i.e., intensified economic interdependence—nothing much new in that.
2. Corporations do not lose their national identities because they are global payers; they remain tied to their home countries.
3. The nation-state is not threatened by globalization; the state's capacity for regulation and surveillance has increased rather than decreased.

---

has assumed that role. But America is beset by a contradiction between decreasing economic strength and increasing projection of military power on a world scale. Being the world's 'policeman' requires a strong economic base, but that is diminishing under the pressures of economic globalization. The macro-regions (headed by the US in North and South America, by China in East Asia, and by the European Union in Europe) are the new political–economic frameworks of capital accumulation. Yet, the macro-regions continue to be part of the larger, global economic system.

Robert Cox and other neo-Marxists thus stress the uneven, hierarchical nature of economic globalization. The global economy is characterized by dependence rather than interdependence. Economic power is increasingly concentrated in the leading industrialized countries, including the United States, Japan, and the states of Western Europe. This means that economic globalization will not benefit the impoverished masses of developing countries. Nor will it improve the living standards of the poor in highly industrialized countries. For that situation to change, social forces from below, such as workers and students, will have to be successful in their struggle to reclaim political control over the economic forces of globalization (Cox 1994). In short, globalization is a form of capitalism, and as such it perpetuates capitalist class domination and the exploitation of poor people around the world. We can summarize the neo-Marxist view of economic globalization as set forth by Robert Cox (Box 7.7) (see web link 7.46).

The debate on economic globalization is not easily settled because each of the three theoretical positions outlined above can point to some empirical evidence that supports their

---

BOX 7.7	The neo-Marxist view of globalization

1. Economic globalization is both 'intensified interdependence' and the creation of a global economy.
2. Nation-states remain important regulators of globalization, but they are losing power over the economy. In response, they form macro-regions.
3. Economic globalization is an uneven, hierarchical process, where economic power is increasingly concentrated in leading industrialized countries.

views (see web links 7.40 and 7.45). It is true, as economic liberals claim, that globalization has the potential of bringing increased prosperity to individuals and companies; but it is also true, as emphasized by neo-Marxists, that current processes of globalization are uneven and may have little to offer large groups of underprivileged people. Economic liberals are perhaps correct in claiming that globalization is a challenge to the nation-state; but it is equally true, as stressed by mercantilists, that states remain strong players and that they have proved themselves able to adapt to many new challenges. Neo-Marxists correctly emphasize that 'intensified interdependence' and the creation of a global economy are simultaneously present. On that issue, however, economic liberals and mercantilists are too one-sided—they emphasize either one or the other aspect of globalization. In sum, we can, again, find useful insights in each of the theoretical positions, but also weak components in each (see Table 7.7).

There is no doubt about the existence of sharp inequalities in today's world. At the turn of the twenty-first century, the richest 20 per cent of the world's population had:

- 86 per cent of world GDP—the bottom fifth had 1 per cent.
- 82 per cent of world export markets—the bottom fifth had 1 per cent.
- 68 per cent of foreign direct investment—the bottom fifth had 1 per cent.
- 74 per cent of world telephone lines—the bottom fifth had 1.5 per cent.
- 93.3 per cent of all Internet users—the bottom fifth had 0.2 per cent.

(UNDP 1999: 3)

It is important to understand that the poorest countries—and people—are in difficulty not because of economic surplus being taken from them by the rich; rather, it is because they are marginalized participants in the process of economic globalization. Their markets are not attractive to foreign investors because people's purchasing power is low; political institutions are inefficient and corrupt, so there is a lack of stability and political order.

TABLE 7.7 Economic globalization and theories of IPE

	TRUE CLAIM	FALSE CLAIM
Economic liberalism	Economic globalization has the potential to bring increased prosperity to all.	Economic globalization benefits everybody.
	Economic globalization challenges the state.	Economic globalization spells the demise of the state.
Realist mercantilists	States adapt to challenges of economic globalization. States remain strong players.	States are in full control of economic globalization. Economic globalization is merely more interdependence.
Neo-Marxism	Economic globalization is an uneven, hierarchical process.	Economic globalization benefits only a tiny minority.

There is a clear relationship between measures of inequality and progress in terms of industrialization. When industrialization began in earnest in Western Europe in the nineteenth century, the gap between the richest and the poorest fifth in the world was not very large; it stood at 3 to 1 in 1820. Today, the gap is much more dramatic; it stood at 74 to 1 at the turn of the century (UNDP 1999: 3; see also Box 7.8).

Ironically, the poorest countries are not excluded from the global economic system. They are integrated in the sense that much of what they produce is agricultural goods or raw materials for export. As much as 30 per cent of sub-Saharan Africa's GDP goes to export. But demand for what they have to offer has been stagnant; so have prices. Upgrading to more advanced products has proved difficult because of domestic political and economic conditions. At the same time, restricted access to global markets for Africa's agricultural products has added to the problem.

Meanwhile, the debate about inequality has focused increasingly on the richest part of the world, the advanced capitalist countries in North America and Europe (see web link 7.47). It comes in the wake of the financial crisis that broke out in 2008. The crisis began with a 'housing bubble' in the United States: when the high real estate prices started dropping, people could no longer refinance their mortgages, triggering a financial collapse. Behind this was a neoliberal period of lax regulation where financial institutions had perverse incentives to 'take excessive risk when financial markets are buoyant' (Crotty 2009: 564); that is, to maximize the flow of loans whether they were sound or not in order to profit from sales and mortgage securitization. At the same time, a 'derivatives bubble' emerged on the basis of financial products so complex and opaque they could not be priced correctly because the connection between the paper and the underlying real value could no longer be pinned down (Wade 2008). Financial profits were huge: the US financial sector is responsible for only 5 per cent of total employment; but at its peak, in 2004, it accounted for 40 per cent of total profits (Weismann 2013).

The neoliberal period which began with Ronald Reagan and Margaret Thatcher in the early 1980s and culminated in the financial crisis has led to a vast increase of inequality

---

BOX 7.8   Absolute and extreme poverty

Absolute poverty is defined as the lack of access to basic needs—such as food, water, shelter, and sanitation—over a period that is long enough to cause serious harm. *Extreme* poverty is commonly measured as the percentage of a population living on the equivalent of US$1.25 per day or less. The United Nations' Millennium Development Goal of halving—between 1990 and 2015—the proportion of people living in extreme poverty was achieved in 2010, in large part due to progress in China. At a global level, however, 1.22 billion people—or 21 per cent—were still living in extreme poverty in 2010, while 2.4 billion were living on less than US$2 per day.

Source: World Bank Poverty and Equity Data
http://povertydata.worldbank.org/poverty/home/
http://www.worldbank.org/en/topic/poverty/overview#1

in the advanced capitalist countries, in particular the United States. In the US, the 1 per cent richest took home about 9 per cent of total income in the mid-seventies; today, they take home more than 23 per cent. Meanwhile, huge sections of the middle class have stood still. Median incomes have been stagnating in real terms for more than three decades; and technological change reduces the amount of less-skilled middle-class jobs; together with outsourcing of jobs in context of globalization, the middle class is increasingly squeezed (Fukuyama 2012). Europe and Japan display similar problems even if overall inequality is a bit lower. The old American dream of working one's way up has been shattered: today, access to capital gains is much more lucrative than hard work (Pikkety 2014).

These developments have sparked a new debate about the benefits and downsides of economic globalization. Dani Rodrik argues that we cannot pursue the current version of economic globalization and simultaneously uphold democracy and national determination. If what he calls hyperglobalization continues, the only way to preserve democracy is to create a strong form of global governance, even a world state. That is not realistic, or even desirable, in Rodrik's view, because the vast majority of people want to maintain their attachment to the nation-state. His suggestion is instead that hyperglobalization is reigned in and replaced by a less freewheeling system of economic exchange which is better regulated and in more harmony with national economic and political objectives (Rodrik 2011).

This re-ignites the discussion about economic globalization among the major theoretical perspectives: to which extent should our view of globalization be informed by liberal, mercantilist, or Neo-Marxist views? One way of approaching this problem is theoretical eclecticism; that is, the combination of insights from different theories in order to construct new frameworks for analysing the complexities of IPE. A book by Rudra Sil and Peter Katzenstein (2010) introduces this way of theorizing in their review of five studies in IPE (Box 7.9). On this view, we need a variety of different theories in order to understand the complex interplay between economics and politics.

BOX 7.9	Theoretical eclecticism in IPE

The five studies collectively make a strong case for the promise of eclecticism in analysing different facets of the global political economy. Seabrooke offers a novel analysis that connects domestic politics to states' relative position in global finance. Sinclair examines the various mechanisms and processes through which rating agencies have acquired power in the global financial system. Woll enquires into the changes in politics and perceptions accompanying the liberalization of telecommunications and air transport. Jabko studies the evolution of a distinctive political strategy that enabled key actors to promote market liberalization while engineering support for supranational governance structures. And Stubbs explores the connections between war-fighting and preparations for war, on the one hand, and the dynamic growth experienced by seven East Asian economies, on the other.

Sil and Katzenstein (2010: 148)

Conclusion: The Future of IPE

The issues of wealth and poverty raised by IPE are of increasing importance in world politics. The traditional focus of IR is on war and peace. But the danger of war between states, particularly great-power war, appears to be in decline for reasons discussed elsewhere in this book. Violent conflict nowadays takes place mainly inside states, especially inside weak states. That violence is bound up with problems of development and underdevelopment, one of the core issues in IPE; in other words, even when we look at the traditional core issue of IR, that of armed conflict, IPE is of increasing importance. IPE also addresses the issue of sovereign statehood: the national economy is a crucially important resource base for the nation-state. When national economies are being integrated into a global economy in the course of economic globalization, the basis of modern statehood might be expected to change in significant ways. As indicated above, that raises new problems concerning the relationship of states and markets and the ability of states to control and regulate the process of economic globalization. IPE opens up several new research agendas, some of which move away from IR as traditionally understood. Such themes as 'international business', 'micro- and macro-economics', 'economic geography', 'international finance and banking', and 'economic history' are all part of IPE. Such research paths are a good reminder that IR involves a host of other issues studied by additional sub-disciplines of the vast area of social science.

We have been able to introduce only the main theoretical approaches in IPE and to sketch the research agenda of a very large research territory. What we call 'economic liberalism' is a discipline in its own right, comprising the study of micro-and macro-economics (Keohane 2009). Marxism is a vast theoretical edifice with many different empirical orientations and a variety of schools. We have been able to introduce only a few of them. The literature on hegemonic stability, development, and underdevelopment in the developing world, and on economic globalization has grown to immense proportions with a large number of different contributions. However, we do believe that we have singled out the most important theories and the most important debates. We have also argued in favour of drawing on elements of all three classical theories of IPE. No single theory can stand alone; it needs to be combined with insights from the others. Only in that way can we expect to develop a comprehensive and well-founded IPE.

KEY POINTS

- We focus on three large debates. The first debate concerns power and the relationship between politics and economics. Is politics in charge of economics or is it the other way around? The second debate is about development and underdevelopment in the developing world. Is development under way everywhere? The third debate concerns the nature and extent of economic globalization; who drives the process and who benefits from it? These debates are informed by the three major theoretical positions in IPE: liberalism, mercantilism, and neo-Marxism.

- Who has power in the world today and thus drives the major changes in the global economy? In terms of the strongest portfolio of power resources, the United States remains the leading state. But power is also about the ability and willingness to take on the role of enlightened leadership and thus put the power resources to good use. Here, the US is lacking and for that reason several observers argue that there is a crisis in the world economy.

- The issues of wealth and poverty raised by IPE are of increasing importance in world politics. The traditional focus of IR is on war and peace; but the danger of war between states appears to be in decline. Violent conflict nowadays takes place mainly inside states, especially inside weak states. That violence is intimately bound up with problems of development and underdevelopment, one of the core issues in IPE. At the same time, today's rising powers are not copies of the West and there is a fresh debated about different versions of capitalism in the world.

- IPE also raises the problems of development and change of sovereign statehood in a very direct manner. The national economy is a crucially important resource basis for the nation-state. When national economies are in a process of being integrated into a global economy in the context of economic globalization the whole basis for modern statehood changes in a critical way. At present, both rich and poor countries have an increasing problem with inequality and that raises the question whether economic globalization should continue in its present form.

? QUESTIONS

- Should we support the claim that a hegemon is needed in order to create a liberal world economy?

- Is the United States currently the leading power in the world? In which fields is the US strong and in which areas is it weak?

- What is 'soft power' and which countries have it?

- Define the development problem in the developing world and discuss how it should be analysed. Which theory is most helpful?

- Can the development problem be solved for all countries?

- What are the pros and cons of different varieties of capitalism? Discuss with reference to two or three examples.

- What is economic globalization? What are the benefits and drawbacks of economic globalization? What are the implications for sovereign statehood?

- Dani Rodrik wants to seriously modify the current model of economic globalization. As advisor to the UN, which model would you support and why?

→ GUIDE TO FURTHER READING

Dicken, P. (2011). *Global Shift: Reshaping the Global Economic Map in the 21st Century*, 6th edn. New York: The Guilford Press.

Nye, J. S., Jr (2011). *The Future of Power*. New York: Public Affairs.

O'Brien, R. and Williams, M. (2013). *Global Political Economy: Evolution and Dynamics*. Basingstoke: Palgrave Macmillan.

Panitch, L. and Gindin, S. (2013). *The Making of Global Capitalism: The Political Economy of American Empire*. London: Verso.

Ravenhill, J. (ed.) (2011). *Global Political Economy*, 3rd edn. Oxford: Oxford University Press.

Rodrik, D. (2011). *The Globalization Paradox: Why Global Markets, States, and Democracy Can't Coexist*. Oxford: Oxford University Press.

Underhill, G. R. D. (2015). *Political Economy and Global Governance: Theories, Issues, and Dynamics*. Basingstoke: Palgrave Macmillan.

Willis, K. (2011). *Theories and Practices of Development*, 2nd edn. London: Routledge.

WEB LINKS

Web links mentioned in the chapter, together with additional material including a case-study on the financial crisis, can be found on the Online Resource Centre that accompanies this book.

www.oxfordtextbooks.co.uk/orc/jackson_sorensen6e/

Social Constructivism

▌ Summary

This chapter introduces the social constructivist theory of IR. We first clarify where constructivism comes from and why it has established itself as an important approach in IR. Constructivism is examined as both a meta-theory about the nature of the social world and a substantial theory of IR. Several examples of constructivist IR theory are presented, followed by reflections on the strengths and weaknesses of the approach.

Introduction

The focus of social constructivism (in shorthand: constructivism) is on human awareness or consciousness and its place in world affairs. Much IR theory, and especially neorealism, is materialist; it focuses on how the distribution of material power, such as military forces and economic capabilities, defines balances of power between states and explains the behaviour of states. Constructivists reject such a one-sided material focus. They argue that the most important aspect of international relations is social, not material. Furthermore, they argue that this social reality is not objective, or external, to the observer of international affairs. The social and political world, including the world of international relations, is not a physical entity or material object that is outside human consciousness. Consequently, the study of international relations must focus on the ideas and beliefs that inform the actors on the international scene as well as the shared understandings between them (see web link 8.01).

The international system is not something 'out there' like the solar system. It does not exist on its own. It exists only as an intersubjective awareness, or a common understanding, among people; in that sense the system is constituted by ideas, not by material forces. It is a human invention or creation not of a physical or material kind but of a purely intellectual and ideational kind. It is a set of ideas, a body of thought, a system of norms, which has been arranged by certain people at a particular time and place.

If the thoughts and ideas that enter into the existence of international relations change, then the system itself will also change, because the system consists of thoughts and ideas. That is the insight behind the oft-repeated phrase by constructivist Alexander Wendt: 'anarchy is what states make of it' (1992: 394). The claim sounds innocent but the potential consequences are far reaching: suddenly the world of IR becomes less fixated in an age-old structure of anarchy; change becomes possible in a big way because people and states can start thinking about each other in new ways and thus create new norms that may be radically different from the old ones.

This chapter introduces the constructivist theory of IR. We first clarify where constructivism comes from and why it has established itself as an important approach in IR over a short period of time. The nature of constructivist theory is examined: is it a meta-theory about the nature of the social world or is it a substantial theory of IR, or is it both? That leads to a brief presentation of the constructivist contributions to IR theory and some reflections on the strengths and weaknesses of the approach.

The Rise of Constructivism in IR

Beginning in the 1980s, constructivism has been becoming an increasingly significant approach, especially in North American IR (see web links 8.05 and 8.10). During the Cold War there was a clear pattern of power balancing between two blocs, led by the United States and the Soviet Union respectively. After the end of the Cold War and following the dissolution of the Soviet Union, the situation turned much more fluid and open. It soon became obvious that the parsimonious neorealist theory was not at all clear about future developments of the balance of power. Neorealist logic dictates that other states will equate with the US because offsetting US power is a means of guaranteeing one's own security; such equalizing will lead to the emergence of new great powers in a multipolar system. But since the end of the Cold War, this has not happened; Waltz (2002) argues that it will eventually happen 'tomorrow'—a prediction that is now more than a decade old. Another neorealist, Christopher Layne, speculates that it could take some fifty years before Japan and Germany seriously start to be equated with the US (1993), but he also insists that some forms of equating with the US are already taking place (2006). The constructivist claim is that neorealist uncertainty is closely connected to the fact that the theory is overly spare and materialist; and constructivists argue that a focus on thoughts and ideas leads to a better theory about anarchy and power balancing (see web link 8.16).

Some liberals (see Chapter 4) have basically accepted neorealist assumptions as a starting point for analysis; they are, of course, vulnerable to much of the critique directed against neorealism by constructivists. Other liberals did begin to focus more on the role of ideas after the Cold War ended. When Francis Fukuyama (1989) proclaimed 'the end of history', he was endorsing the role of ideas and especially the progress of liberal ideas in the world. But he and other liberals are mostly interested in the concrete advance of liberal, democratic government in the world. Even if constructivists are sympathetic to several elements of liberal thinking, their focus is less on the advance of liberal ideas; it is on the role of thinking and ideas in general.

So the historical context (i.e., the end of the Cold War) and the theoretical discussion between IR scholars (especially among neorealists and liberals) helped set the stage for a constructivist approach. And constructivism became especially popular among North American scholars, because that environment was dominated by the neorealist/neoliberal approaches. In Europe, the International Society approach (see Chapter 5) had already to a significant extent included the role of ideas and the importance of social interaction between states in their analysis. In that sense, there was less intellectual space in Europe for constructivists to fill out.

At the same time, constructivists were inspired by theoretical developments in other social science disciplines, including philosophy and sociology. In sociology, Anthony Giddens (1984) proposed the concept of **structuration** as a way of analysing the relationship between structures and actors (see web link 8.02). According to Giddens, structures (i.e., the rules and conditions that guide social action) do not determine what actors do in any mechanical way; an impression one might get from the neorealist view of how the structure of anarchy constrains state actors. The relationship between structures and actors involves intersubjective understanding and meaning. Structures do constrain actors, but actors can also transform structures by thinking about them and acting on them in new ways. The notion of structuration, therefore, leads to a less rigid and more dynamic view of the relationship between structure and actors. IR constructivists use this as a starting point for suggesting a less rigid view of anarchy.

We have noted some recent historical and theoretical developments that help explain the rise of social constructivism in IR. But constructivism has deeper roots; it is not an entirely new approach. It also grows out of an old methodology that can be traced back at least to the eighteenth-century writings of the Italian philosopher Giambattista Vico (Pompa 1982). According to Vico, the natural world is made by God, but the historical world is made by Man (Pompa 1982: 26). History is not some kind of unfolding or evolving process that is external to human affairs. Men and women make their own history. They also make states which are historical constructs. States are artificial creations and the state system is artificial too; it is made by men and women and if they want to, they can change it and develop it in new ways (see web link 8.03).

Immanuel Kant is another forerunner of social constructivism (Hacking 1999: 41). Kant argued that we can obtain knowledge about the world, but it will always be subjective knowledge in the sense that it is filtered through human consciousness (see web link 8.04). Max Weber emphasized that the social world (i.e., the world of human interaction) is fundamentally different from the natural world of physical phenomena. Human beings rely on 'understanding' of each other's actions and assigning 'meaning' to them. In order to comprehend human interaction, we cannot merely describe it in the way we describe a physical phenomenon, such as a boulder falling off a cliff; we need a different kind of interpretive understanding, or *verstehen* (Morrison 1995: 273–82). Is patting another person's face a punishment or a caress? We cannot know until we assign meaning to the act. Weber concluded that 'subjective understanding is the specific characteristic of sociological knowledge' (Weber 1977: 15). Constructivists rely on such insights to emphasize the importance of 'meaning' and 'understanding' (Fierke and Jørgensen 2001).

Constructivism as Social Theory

We can distinguish between theories at different levels of abstraction. Social theory is the more general theory about the social world, about social action, and about the relationship between structures and actors. Such theory is relevant for the entire field of social science. Substantive IR theory, by contrast, is theory about some aspect of international relations. Constructivism is both a social theory and a number of different substantive theories of IR; this section is about constructivism as a social theory; the next section is about constructivist theories of IR.

In social theory, constructivists emphasize the social construction of reality. Human relations, including international relations, consist of thoughts and ideas and not essentially of material conditions or forces. This is the philosophically idealist element of constructivism which contrasts with the materialist philosophy of much social science **positivism** (see Chapter 9). According to constructivist philosophy, the social world is not a given: it is not something 'out there' that exists independently of the thoughts and ideas of the people involved in it. It is not an external reality whose laws can be discovered by scientific research and explained by scientific theory, as positivists and behaviourists argue. The social and political world is not part of nature. There are no natural laws of society or economics or politics. History is not an evolving external process that is independent of human thought and ideas. That means that sociology or economics or political science or the study of history cannot be objective 'sciences' in the strict positivist sense of the word.

Everything involved in the social world of men and women is made by them. The fact that it is made by them makes it intelligible to them. The social world is a world of human consciousness: of thoughts and beliefs, of ideas and concepts, of languages and discourses, of signs, signals, and understandings among human beings, especially groups of human beings, such as states and nations. The social world is an intersubjective domain: it is meaningful to people who made it and live in it, and who understand it precisely because they constructed it and they are at home in it.

The social world is in part constructed of physical entities; note that the quote by Wendt mentions 'material resources' among those elements that constitute social structures (Box 8.1). In that sense materialism is a part of constructivism. But it is the ideas and beliefs concerning those entities that are most important—what those entities signify in the minds of people. The international system of security and defence, for example, consists of territories, populations, weapons, and other physical assets. But it is the ideas and understandings according to which those assets are conceived, organized, and used—e.g., in alliances, armed forces, and so on— that is most important. The physical element is there. But that element is secondary to the intellectual element which infuses it with meaning, plans it, organizes it, and guides it. The thought that is involved in international security is more important, far more important, than the physical assets that are involved, because those assets have no meaning without the intellectual component; they are mere things in themselves.

Wendt illustrates the constructivist view with the following statement: '500 British nuclear weapons are less threatening to the United States than 5 North Korean nuclear weapons' because 'the British are friends and the North Koreans are not' (Wendt 1995: 73). Therefore, it is less the material fact of numbers of nuclear warheads that matter; what matters is how the actors think about each other; i.e., their ideas and beliefs. Material facts enter the picture but are secondary to ideas.

Therefore, it is helpful to emphasize the contrast between a **materialist view** held by neorealists (and neoliberals) and the **ideational view** held by constructivists. According to the

---

BOX 8.1	**Wendt's constructivist conception of social structures**

Social structures have three elements: shared knowledge, material resources, and practices. First, social structures are defined, in part, by shared understandings, expectations, or knowledge. These constitute the actors in a situation and the nature of their relationships, whether cooperative or conflictual. A security dilemma, for example, is a social structure composed of intersubjective understandings in which states are so distrustful that they make worst-case assumptions about each other's intentions, and as a result define their interests in self-help terms. A security community is a different social structure, one composed of shared knowledge in which states trust one another to resolve disputes without war. This dependence of social structure on ideas is the sense in which constructivism has an idealist (or 'idea-ist') view of structure.

Wendt (1992: 73)

materialist view, power and national interest are the driving forces in international politics. Power is ultimately military capability, supported by economic and other resources. National interest is the self-regarding desire by states for power, security, or wealth (Wendt 1999: 92). Power and interest are seen as 'material' factors; they are objective entities in the sense that because of anarchy states are compelled to be preoccupied with power and interest. In this view, ideas matter little; they can be used to rationalize actions dictated by material interest. In the ideational view held by social constructivists ideas always matter. 'The starting premise is that the material world is indeterminate and is interpreted within a larger context of meaning. Ideas thus define the meaning of material power' (Tannenwald 2005: 19). This constructivist view of ideas is emphasized by Wendt in Box 8.2.

The core ideational element upon which constructivists focus is intersubjective beliefs (and ideas, conceptions, and assumptions) that are widely shared among people. Ideas must be widely shared to matter; nonetheless, they can be held by different groups, such as organizations, policymakers, social groups, or society. 'Ideas are mental constructs held by individuals, sets of distinctive beliefs, principles and attitudes that provide broad orientations for behaviour and policy' (Tannenwald 2005: 15). There are many different kinds of ideas. Nina Tannenwald identifies four major types: 'ideologies or shared belief systems, normative beliefs, cause–effect beliefs and policy prescriptions' (Tannenwald 2005: 15); they are described in Box 8.3.

Constructivism is an empirical approach to the study of international relations—empirical in that it focuses on the intersubjective ideas that define international relations. The theory displays some distinctive research interests and approaches. If the social and political world consists, at base, of shared beliefs, how does that affect the way we should account for important international events and episodes? Constructivists, as a rule, cannot subscribe to mechanical positivist conceptions of causality. That is because the positivists do not probe the intersubjective content of events and episodes. For example, the well-known billiard ball image of international relations is rejected by constructivists

---

BOX 8.2   The social constructivist view of ideas

The claim is *not* that ideas are more important than power and interest, or that they are autonomous from power and interest. The claim is rather that power and interest have the effects they do in virtue of the ideas that make them up. Power and interest explanations *presuppose* ideas, and to that extent are not rivals to ideational explanations at all . . . Let me [propose] a rule of thumb for idealists: when confronted by ostensibly 'material' explanations, always inquire into the discursive conditions which make them work. When Neorealists offer multipolarity as an explanation for war, inquire into the discursive conditions that constitute the poles as enemies rather than friends. When Liberals offer economic interdependence as an explanation for peace, inquire into the discursive conditions that constitute states with identities that care about free trade and economic growth. When Marxists offer capitalism as an explanation for state forms, inquire into the discursive conditions that constitute capitalist relations of production. And so on.

Wendt (1999: 135–6)

BOX 8.3	**Four types of ideas**

Ideologies or shared belief systems are a systematic set of doctrines or beliefs that reflect the social needs and aspirations of a group, class, culture, or state. Examples include the Protestant ethic or political ideologies such as liberalism, Marxism, and fascism.

Normative (or principled) beliefs are beliefs about right and wrong. They consist of values and attitudes that specify criteria for distinguishing right from wrong or just from unjust and they imply associated standards of behaviour, [for example] the role of human rights norms at the end of the Cold War.

Causal beliefs are beliefs about cause-effect, or means-end relationships. They . . . provide guidelines or strategies for individuals on how to achieve their objectives . . . [for example,] Soviet leaders' changing beliefs about the efficacy (or more precisely non-efficacy) of the use of force influenced their decision in 1989 not to use force to keep Eastern Europe under Soviet control.

Finally, policy prescriptions are the specific programmatic ideas that facilitate policymaking by specifying how to solve particular policy problems. They are at the centre of policy debates and are associated with specific strategies and policy programs.

Tannenwald (2005: 15–16)

because it fails to reveal the thoughts, ideas, and beliefs of the actors involved in international conflicts. Constructivists want to probe the inside of the billiard balls to arrive at a deeper understanding of such conflicts (see web link 8.10).

The constructivist approach argues that a further development of basic concepts is needed in order to allow for the full analysis of ideas and meaning. A recent study of power in global governance provides an example of this. The authors note that their subject

requires a consideration of different forms of power in international politics. Power is the production, in and through social relations, of effects that shape the capacities of actors to determine their own circumstances and fate. But power does not have a single expression or form. It has several.

(Barnett and Duvall 2005: 3)

The authors go on to identify four different forms of power; they are presented in Box 8.4. The claim is that a full consideration of power in international relations needs to address all four dimensions.

Constructivists generally agree with Max Weber that they need to employ interpretive understanding (*verstehen*) in order to analyse social action (Ruggie 1998). But they are not in agreement about the extent to which it is possible to emulate the scientific ideas of the natural sciences and produce scientific explanations based on hypotheses, data collection, and generalization. On the one hand, constructivists reject the notion of objective truth; social scientists cannot discover a 'final truth' about the world which is true across time and place. On the other hand, constructivists do make 'truth claims about the subjects they have investigated . . . while admitting that their claims are always contingent and partial interpretations of a complex world' (Price and Reus-Smit 1998: 272).

BOX 8.4	The concept of power in constructivist analysis

Power does not have a single expression or form. It has several. In this volume we identify four. Compulsory power refers to relations of interaction that allow one actor to have direct control over another. It operates, for example, when one state threatens another and says, 'change your policies, or else'. Institutional power is in effect when actors exercise indirect control over others, such as when states design international institutions in ways that work to their long-term advantage and to the disadvantage of others. Structural power concerns the constitution of social capacities and interests of actors in direct relation to one another. One expression of this form of power is the workings of the capitalist world-economy in producing social positions of capital and labour with their respective differential abilities to alter their circumstances and fortunes. Productive power is the socially diffuse production of subjectivity in systems of meaning and signification. A particular meaning of development, for instance, orients social activity in particular directions, defines what constitutes legitimate knowledge, and shapes whose knowledge matters. These different conceptualizations, then, provide distinct answers to the fundamental question: in what respects are actors able to determine their own fate, and how is that ability limited or enhanced through social relations with others?

Quoted from Barnett and Duvall (2005: 3–4)

At the same time, it is fair to say that constructivists do not agree entirely on this issue (Fierke 2001). The view expressed here is closer to what has been called 'conventional' constructivism (Hopf 1998) represented by such scholars as Peter Katzenstein (1996b); Christian Reus-Smit (1997); Emanuel Adler and Michael Barnett (1998); John Ruggie (1998); Alexander Wendt (1999); Ted Hopf (2002); Martha Finnemore (2003); Alistair Johnston (2008); and Samuel Barkin (2010). 'Critical' or 'post-positivist' constructivists are much more sceptical about this position; they argue that 'truth claims' are not possible because there is no neutral ground where we can decide about what is true. What we call truth is always connected to different, more or less dominant, ways of thinking about the world. Truth and power cannot be separated; indeed, the main task of critical constructivism is to unmask that core relationship between truth and power, to criticize those dominant versions of thinking that claim to be true for all. Our presentation of constructivist scholarship focuses on 'conventional' constructivism because it is this strand of constructivism that has done most in terms of developing new theories of IR; 'critical' constructivism, which we label post-structuralism, is discussed in Chapter 9.

Constructivist Theories of International Relations

Constructivism was introduced to IR by Nicholas Onuf (1989), who coined the term. It gathered a larger following among scholars with a series of influential articles and a book by Alexander Wendt (1987, 1992, 1994, 1995, 1999). We begin this brief and selective overview of constructivist IR theory with Wendt's contribution.

Cultures of Anarchy

The core of Wendt's argument is the rejection of the neorealist position, according to which anarchy must necessarily lead to self-help. Whether it does or not cannot be decided a priori; it depends on the interaction between states. In these processes of interaction, the identities and interests of states are created. For neorealists, identities and interests are a given; states know who they are and what they want before they begin interaction with other states. For Wendt, it is the very interaction with others that 'create and instantiate one structure of identities and interests rather than another; structure has no existence or causal powers apart from process' (Wendt 1992: 394). States want to survive and be secure; neorealists and constructivists agree about that. But what kind of security policy follows from this? Do states seek to become as powerful as possible or are they content with what they have? Wendt argues that we can only find out by studying identities and interests as they are shaped in the interaction between states (Box 8.5).

In concrete terms,

if the United States and the Soviet Union decide that they are no longer enemies, 'the cold war is over'. It is collective meanings that constitute the structures which organize our actions. Actors acquire identities—relatively stable, role-specific understanding and expectations about self—by participating in such collective meaning.

(Wendt 1992: 397)

Western European states need not start power balancing against each other because the Cold War is over; four decades of cooperation may have led to a new 'European identity' of cooperation and friendship between them (Wendt 1992: 418) (see web link 8.12).

Wendt's 1999 book further develops the argument introduced in the earlier articles. His point of departure is the same as Waltz's: interaction between states in a system characterized by anarchy. However, anarchy need not lead to self-help; that calls for further study of the discursive interaction between states in order to discover what specific 'culture of anarchy' has developed between them. Wendt suggests three major ideal types of anarchy: Hobbesian, Lockean, and Kantian (1999: 257). In the Hobbesian culture, states view each other as enemies; the logic of Hobbesian anarchy is 'war of all against all'. States are adversaries and war is endemic because violent conflict is a way of survival. Hobbesian anarchy, according to Wendt, dominated the states system until the seventeenth century.

In the Lockean culture, states consider each other rivals, but there is also restraint; states do not seek to eliminate each other, they recognize the other states' right to exist. Lockean anarchy became a characteristic of the modern states system after the Peace of Westphalia in 1648. Finally, in a Kantian culture, states view each other as friends, settle disputes peacefully, and support each other in the case of threat by a third party (Wendt 1999: 299). A Kantian culture has emerged among consolidated liberal democracies since the Second World War (see web link 8.12).

The three different cultures of anarchy can be internalized in different degrees; that is to say, the way states view each other may be more or less deeply shared. Wendt makes a distinction between three degrees of 'cultural internalization' (Wendt 1999: 254): the first

BOX 8.5	Social constructivism: key terms and language

- Focus of constructivism: ideas and beliefs that inform the actors on the international scene.

- Material facts and ideas: material facts enter the picture but they are secondary to ideas. '500 British nuclear weapons are less threatening to the United States than 5 North Korean nuclear weapons' because 'the British are friends and the North Koreans are not' (Wendt 1995: 73). That is to say, it is less the material fact of numbers of nuclear warheads that matter; what matters is how the actors think about each other; i.e., their ideas and beliefs.

- Structures and actors: 'Structures are not reified objects that actors can do nothing about, but to which they must respond. Rather structures exist only through the reciprocal interaction of actors. The means that agents, through acts of social will, can change structures. They can thereby emancipate themselves from dysfunctional situations that are in turn replicating conflictual practices' (Copeland 2000: 190); because ideas can change, states do not have to be enemies: 'anarchy is what states make of it' (Wendt 1992).

- The emphasis is on meaning: is the patting of another person's face a punishment or a caress? We cannot know until we assign meaning to the act. Weber concluded that 'subjective understanding is the specific characteristic of sociological knowledge' (Weber 1977: 15). Constructivists rely on such insights to emphasize the importance of 'meaning' and 'understanding' (Fierke and Jørgensen 2001).

- Identity: for neorealists, identities and interests are a given; states know who they are and what they want before they begin interaction with other states. For constructivists, it is the very interactions with others that 'create and instantiate one structure of identities and interests rather than another' (Wendt 1992: 394). States want to survive and be secure; neorealists and constructivists agree about that. But what kind of security policy follows from this? Do states seek to become as powerful as possible or are they content with what they have? Constructivists argue that we can only find out by studying identities and interests as they are shaped in interactions between states.

- Knowledge about the world: one group of 'conventional' constructivists believe that we can explain the world in causal terms; that is, we can find out 'why one thing leads to another'; we can understand 'how things are put together to have the causal powers that they do' (Wendt 1999: 372). According to this view, constructivist analysis 'depends on publicly available evidence and the possibility that its conclusions might in some broad sense be falsified' (Wendt 1999: 373).

- Another group of 'critical' or 'post-positivist' constructivists argue that 'truth claims' are not possible and truth and power cannot be separated; therefore, the main task of critical constructivism is to unmask that core relationship between truth and power and to criticize those dominant versions of thinking that claim to be true for all.

degree is a relatively weak commitment to shared ideas; the third degree a strong commitment. We get a three-by-three table of 'degrees of cooperation' and 'degrees of internalization' respectively (see Figure 8.1).

Wendt drives home the point that constructivism is not merely about 'adding the role of ideas' to existing theories of IR. Material power and state interest are fundamentally formed

FIGURE 8.1   **Cultures of anarchy and degrees of internalization.**

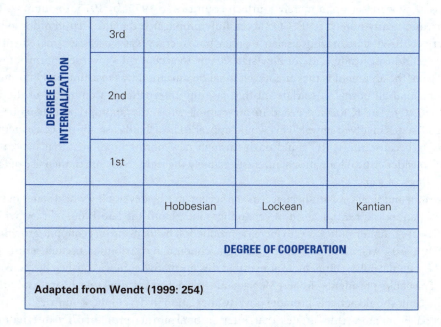

Adapted from Wendt (1999: 254)

by ideas and social interaction. Therefore, states in an anarchic system may each possess military and other capabilities which can be seen as potentially threatening by other states; but enmity and arms races are not inevitable outcomes. Social interaction between states can also lead to more benign and friendly cultures of anarchy.

Norms of International Society

Wendt's analysis is systemic; it focuses on interaction between states in the international system and disregards the role of domestic factors. Martha Finnemore has proposed another variant of constructivist, systemic analysis in her 1996 book, *National Interests in International Society*. Her starting point is the definition of states' identities and interests. Instead of looking at the social interaction between states, her focus is on the norms of international society and the way in which they affect state identities and interests. State behaviour is defined by identity and interest. Identity and interests are defined by international forces; that is, by the norms of behaviour embedded in international society. The norms of international society are transmitted to states through international organizations. They shape national policies by 'teaching' states what their interests should be (see web links 8.11 and 8.15).

Finnemore's analysis contains three case-studies: the adoption of science policy bureaucracies by states after 1955; states' acceptance of rule-governed norms of warfare; and states accepting limits to economic sovereignty by allowing redistribution to take priority over production values. The first case-study argues that the United Nations Educational, Scientific, and Cultural Organization (UNESCO) has taught states how to develop science bureaucracies. Science policy bureaucracies did not exist in many states prior to the mid-1950s. At that time, UNESCO began a drive to establish them, with considerable success: they were set up in merely fourteen countries in 1955; by 1975, the number had increased to nearly ninety. UNESCO successfully propagated the idea that in order to be a 'modern civilized' state, having a science policy bureaucracy was a necessary ingredient.

The second case-study is about how states came to accept rule-governed norms of warfare. Again, the argument is that an international organization was instrumental in promoting humanitarian norms in warfare; in this case the International Committee of the Red Cross (ICRC). The ICRC succeeded in prescribing what was 'appropriate behaviour' for 'civilized' states involved in war. This would appear to be a 'hard case' for the constructivist approach, because the ICRC could push through new norms in an area that neorealists would consider critical for national interests, namely the right to unconstrained use of force during times of war.

The third and final case-study concerns the acceptance by developing world states of poverty alleviation as a central norm of economic policy. Until the late 1960s, the overriding objective of economic policy was to increase production by focusing on economic growth. By the early 1970s, welfare improvement through economic redistribution became a principal goal of economic policy. Finnemore argues that this normative shift was pushed by the World Bank. The bank's president—Robert McNamara—played an essential role; he was convinced that the bank should actively promote poverty alleviation in developing countries.

Martha Finnemore thus argues that international norms promoted by international organizations can decisively influence national guidelines by pushing states to adopt these norms in their national policies. Against neorealism, she argues that the changes brought forward by the case-studies cannot be explained by pure national interests in power-maximation. They need to be explained by a constructivist analysis emphasizing the central role of norms in international society (Box 8.6).

In his book, Alistair Johnston (2008) seeks to demonstrate the processes by which norms in the international system change the behaviour of states. During the period 1980–2000, China was facing an increasingly unipolar system, dominated by the United States. At the same time, China was traditionally oriented towards Realpolitik. Still, the country opted to participate and cooperate in international organizations, protocols, and treaties. Johnston argues that this is due to a practice of socialization involving 'mimicking', 'social influence', and 'persuasion'. In other words, processes of social learning take place in the interaction of

---

BOX 8.6 Martha Finnemore on norms in international society

The fact that we live in an international society means that what we want and, in some ways, who we are, are shaped by the social norms, rules, understandings, and relationships we have with others. These social realities are as influential as material realities in determining behaviour. Indeed, they are what endow material realities with meaning and purpose.

In political terms, it is these social realities that provide us with ends to which power and wealth can be used.

Finnemore (1996: 128)

policymakers from different states. These processes are less connected to material power and have more to do with 'pro-social' or 'good' behaviour, where Chinese representatives adopt norms which help increase their image and standing in relation to the standards of international society pursued by the representatives of other countries.

The Power of International Organizations

The traditional realist view of international organizations (IOs) emphasizes that they exist to carry out important functions for states; they 'provide public goods, collect information, establish credible commitments, monitor agreements, and generally help states overcome problems associated with collective action and enhance individual and collective welfare' (Barnett and Finnemore 2005: 161). Barnett and Finnemore's analysis makes the argument that IOs are much more important and should not be reduced to handmaidens of states. On the one hand, they are autonomous actors who might exercise power in their own right; on the other hand, they 'construct the social world in which cooperation and choice takes place. They help define the interests that states and other actors come to hold' (Barnett and Finnemore 2005: 162). IOs are powerful because they are bureaucracies and because they pursue liberal social goals considered attractive by other major actors (see Box 8.7).

The power of IOs can be analysed on several of the dimensions of power introduced in Box 8.4. IOs have compulsory power in that they control material resources that can be used to influence others. For example, the World Bank has money and the UN peacekeepers have weapons; another form of compulsory power is made up of normative resources. The European Union, for example, 'is hard at work persuading members to reconfigure domestic institutions and practices in ways that harmonize with European and international standards' (Barnett and Finnemore 2005: 176).

Institutional power of IOs stems from their ability to guide behaviour in more indirect ways. One major example is the agenda-setting activities of IOs. The organizations are often able to determine the agenda of meetings and conferences held under their auspices.

BOX 8.7	Authority and autonomy of IOs

The reason IOs have authority, we argue, is that the rationalization processes of modernity and spreading global liberalism constitute them in particular kinds of relations to others. IOs are bureaucracies, and Weber recognized that bureaucracy is a uniquely authoritative (and powerful) social form in modern societies because of its rational-legal (i.e., impersonal, technocratic) character. But IOs are also conferred authority because they pursue liberal social goals that are widely viewed as desirable and legitimate. IOs are thus powerful both because of their form (as rational-legal bureaucracies) and because of their (liberal) goals. This authority gives them a sphere of autonomy and a resource they can use to shape the behaviour of others in both direct and indirect ways.

Quoted from Barnett and Finnemore (2005: 162)

BOX 8.8	IOs and productive power

Development agencies have a readymade solution to the problem of development—more market mechanisms. If development is not occurring, then it is because the economy and polity are not organized properly. So, the development agencies propose various policies that are designed to institutionalize market mechanisms but also to teach producers how to respond efficiently and properly to market signals. In this way, they view their goals as transforming self-sufficient 'peasants' into market-dependent 'farmers'. Although development officials see the introduction of the market as a technical solution to the problem of development, the consequence of this technical solution is deeply political because it completely upends social relations in the family, between producers and consumers, and between the village and the state apparatus.

Quoted from Barnett and Finnemore (2005: 180)

Therefore, they significantly influence what is discussed and what is eventually decided. For example,

the UN Secretary-General's decision to make humanitarian intervention a defining theme of his 1999 address to the General Assembly shaped subsequent discussions. EU officials are renowned for possessing this sort of influence . . . World Bank officials are directly involved in drawing up the agenda for meetings. In this significant way, IO staff can help to orient discussions and actions in some directions and away from others.

(Barnett and Finnemore 2005: 178)

Finally, productive power refers to the role of IOs in constituting the problems that need to be solved. In this respect, IOs act as authorities who formulate, define, and present certain problems to others; they also contribute to solving problems by offering solutions and convincing others to accept them. Box 8.8 presents an example of this process; it concerns organizations involved in economic development. By defining the solution to development problems as one of 'more market' they help define what counts as progress and they change social relations in the villages and the families.

In sum, IOs are not purely innocent servants of states; they are frequently powerful actors because they are bureaucracies that promise to deliver goals that others want. But being powerful, the IOs are not always necessarily a force for good; they may also follow narrow interests of their own and 'run roughshod over the interests of states and citizens that they are supposed to further' (Barnett and Finnemore 2005: 184).

A Constructivist Approach to European Cooperation

Various aspects of European cooperation have been a central theme in constructivist analyses. Constructivists argue that their approach is particularly relevant for the study of European cooperation. This is because Europe is a complex setting, with many issues on the table and a large number of informal linkages among the actors involved. Rather than pursuing fixed preferences, the actors mutually influence each other in their interactions. The study of these processes is very well suited for a constructivist approach (Saurugger 2013).

Kenneth Glarbo, for example, studied the common foreign and security policy (CFSP) of the European Union. According to realists, the history of European cooperation in this area is a dismal one. Due to diverging national interests—so runs the realist argument—integration and close cooperation in the high politics area of foreign and security policy will remain blocked, and occasional progress in the field is merely tactical manoeuvring. Taking a constructivist approach, Glarbo tells a different story. His argument is that foreign policy cooperation is not simply the product of national interests; it is due to processes of social interaction, 'the results of national diplomacies intentionally and unintentionally communicating to themselves and to each other their intents and perceptions of political co-operation' (Glarbo 1999: 635). Social interaction builds intersubjective structures that help further cooperation. In other words, EU Member States may not agree on important aspects of foreign policy; but in spite of this, day-to-day practices of political cooperation significantly promote a shaping of common perspectives and mutual coordination. In sum:

integration does prevail within European political co-operation, or at least within the CFSP of recent years, even if this does not totally refute the importance of national interest. Despite interest, however, constructivist theory argues that political co-operation leaves room for a social integration that stems from diplomatic communication processes set up through political co-operation history, and which is not easily discernible from the intergovernmentalist formal codes of CFSP.

(Glarbo 1999: 636)

Studies of this kind have led constructivists towards the analysis of socialization and learning; that is, the ways in which collective understandings are adopted and organized by groups of actors. In other words, how does a norm become a general reference and 'not just an idea or ideological position of one single individual?' (Saurugger 2013: 894). Empirical research on this mainly concentrates on specific professional groups active in the EU realm, such as European civil servants, the committee of permanent representatives (COREPER), or members of interest groups.

In a book on *European Identity*, edited by Jeff Checkel and Peter Katzenstein (2009), it is demonstrated that the 'single European identity' project pursued by European elites is up against serious obstacles. European publics are sceptic and a single European identity is not in the making. Rey Koslowski (1999) offers a constructivist approach to understanding the European Union as a federal polity. He attempts to move on from traditional debates on federalism and the EU, which tend either to advocate the transformation of the EU into a federal state, or anticipated a roll-back towards more conventional intergovernmental cooperation. His argument is that a constructivist approach better reveals European cooperation for what it is rather than the 'either or' perspectives of federalism or intergovernmentalism. Overall, there is now a large number of research projects concerning aspects of EU studies or Europe that take a constructivist starting point (for an overview, see *Journal of European*

Public Policy 2013). Constructivists claim that they can add nuances and insights to the analysis of European cooperation which are played down or overlooked in conventional analyses of that complex process.

Domestic Formation of Identity and Norms

Systemic constructivists such as Finnemore and Wendt stress the importance of the international environment in shaping state identities. Other constructivists put more emphasis on the domestic environment. One way of moving in this direction is to study how international norms have dissimilar effects in different states and then speculate about the domestic factors responsible for such variation. A volume edited by Thomas Risse et al. (1999) takes on this task in the area of international human rights norms. The authors demonstrate how regime type, the experience of civil war, and the presence of domestic human rights organizations impinge on the degree to which states are ready to comply with international human rights norms.

The book edited by Peter Katzenstein, *The Culture of National Security: Norms and Identity in World Politics* (1996a), aims to drive home the general constructivist claim that culture, norms, and identity matter, also in the core area of national security. In this context, many essays put special emphasis on domestic norms. Alastair Johnston, for example, takes up the case of Maoist China in order to see 'how far ideational arguments can go in accounting for realpolitik behaviour' (Johnston 1996: 217). He identifies a specific 'hard realpolitik' strategic culture in the Chinese tradition that informs and shapes Chinese security policies. The argument is that Chinese decision makers have 'internalized this strategic culture' and that it 'has persisted across vastly different interstate systems, regime types, levels of technology, and types of threat' (Johnston 1996: 217). In other words, neorealist accounts of Chinese behaviour are incomplete because they fail to include such a notion of an idea-based strategic culture; and precisely because its presence can be shown across different systems it is clear that 'anarchy' is not sufficient to account for the Chinese position. Peter Katzenstein has also written a book on Japan which further develops a constructivist argument about the role of domestic norms in the area of national security (Katzenstein 1996b). Systemic theorizing is inadequate, says Katzenstein, because it does not sufficiently appreciate how the internal make-up of states affects their behaviour in the international system. The emphasis in his analysis is on the domestic normative structure and how it influences state identity, interests, and policy. A major puzzle addressed is the shift from a militaristic foreign policy before 1945 to a pacifist foreign policy after the world war. The analysis explains why there was a broad consensus favouring a militaristic foreign policy before the war and how the norms on which that consensus was based became profoundly contested as a result of the war. The military's position within the government was severely weakened; furthermore, the new constitution committed Japan to a pacifist standing and put a low ceiling on defence expenditures (1 per cent of the national income). Again, the argument is constructivist, but a systemic analysis is rejected in favour of an analysis of the domestic environment (Box 8.9).

BOX 8.9	**Peter Katzenstein on the importance of culture and identity**

Today's problem is no longer that of E. H. Carr, one of avoiding the sterility of realism and the naïveté of liberalism. Our choice is more complex. We can remain intellectually riveted on a realist world of states balancing power in a multipolar system. We can focus analytically with liberal institutionalists on the efficiency effects that institutions may have on the prospects for policy coordination between states. Or, acknowledging the partial validity of these views, we can broaden our analytical perspective, as this book suggests, to include culture as well as identity as important causal factors that help define the interests and constitute the actors that shape national security policies and global insecurities.

Katzenstein (1996a: 537)

BOX 8.10	**Yücel Bozdaglioglu on the importance of domestic analysis**

Domestic political developments can transform identities in several ways. First, domestic developments independent of systemic interaction such as revolutions can change a state's identity and replace it with a new one. Second, through domestic institutional arrangements or elections, the role of domestic political groups/state institutions or individuals in the foreign policy making process can be altered. In this case, the foreign policy discourse can be dominated by entirely new organizations or individuals with different identity conceptions that may perceive the national interest in a different way . . . Considering domestic roots of that change would be a good starting point in the constructivist analysis.

Bozdaglioglu 2007: 141

Ted Hopf has made a study of Soviet and Russian foreign policy that also focuses on the domestic formation of identity in order to understand how national interests are defined and what foreign policies they lead to (Hopf 2002). He seeks to provide 'an account of how a state's own domestic identities constitute a social cognitive structure that makes threats and opportunities, enemies and allies, intelligible, thinkable, and possible' (Hopf 2002: 16).

State identity is expressed through key decision makers. The identity of key decision makers is uncovered through textual sources, including archives, journals, newspapers, memoirs, and textbooks. Two case-studies are undertaken: Moscow 1955 and Moscow 1999. The claim is that the reconstructed domestic identities go a long way in explaining Soviet/Russian foreign policy in 1955 and 1999 (Box 8.10; web link 8.22).

Even if constructivists have a debate about the relative importance of domestic versus international environments, the disagreement between them should not be exaggerated. Constructivists are united by much more than what divides them; especially, they all emphasize the importance of culture and identity, as expressed in social norms, rules, and understandings. The social and political world is made up of shared beliefs rather than physical entities. For constructivists, that must always be the starting point for analysis.

Constructivist IPE

Constructivism has also made its entry to the study of international political economy (IPE, see Chapters 6 and 7). Rawe Abdelal, Mark Blyth, and Craig Parsons' book, *Constructing the International Economy* (2010), provides a constructivist take on several IPE issues, including IMF policy and operations, liberalization of trade in services, the 'good governance' initiative of the World Bank, and the politics of agricultural trade.

The authors argue that there are four 'distinct paths to constructivism' which they label meaning, cognition, uncertainty, and subjectivity. 'Meaning' concerns issues related to identity; 'cognition' looks at practices of information selection and analysis; 'uncertainty' is about the formation of institutions and norms; and 'subjectivity' includes what we have labelled 'post-positivist' constructivism in the analysis of how power relations influence the subjective meanings held by actors. Power thereby helps define what is possible or 'thinkable'.

These distinctions help demonstrate how constructivism has developed in different directions that focus on various aspects of the chosen subject. One chapter by Jeffrey Chwieroth on neoliberal economics in Latin America, for example, demonstrates the significance of 'identity'. It focuses on the background of the finance ministers and the heads of the central bank in fourteen countries. If they were trained at Chicago, Stanford, or Columbia, reductions in social spending in order to confront public debt burdens would be higher than if neither had received such training. A chapter by Cornelia Woll takes up 'uncertainty' by looking at business lobbying in connection with liberalization of trade services in telecommunications and air transport. Surprisingly, lobbyists supported liberalization. Their position was connected to uncertainty: firms do not always know what they want, and they are influenced by policies and politics. Firms certainly influence policy outcomes, but they also adjust their demands to the agenda of regulators, both in the case of the US and of the EU.

Critiques of Constructivism

Since neorealism is the main theoretical opponent for most constructivists, let us begin with a neorealist critique of the constructivist approach. First of all, neorealists are sceptical about the importance that constructivists attach to norms, in particular international norms. Such norms surely exist, but they are routinely disregarded if that is in the interest of powerful states. Ever since the Peace of Westphalia in 1648, writes Stephen Krasner:

Powerful states have violated the autonomy and the integrity of weak ones. The Peace of Westphalia included elaborate provisions concerning religious practices within Germany . . . and specified electoral procedures for the selection of the Holy Roman Emperor. Hardly a testimony to respect for sovereign autonomy. Every other major postwar settlement since 1648 has attempted to restructure domestic political institutions in defeated states . . . If there is an international society out there it has not had much more impact on the behaviour of states than conventional norms about sex, family and marriage now have on the behaviour of individuals in North America and Europe.

(Krasner 1994: 16–17)

At the same time, neorealists are not ready to accept that states can easily become friends due to their social interaction. Such a goal may be

desirable in principle, but not realizable in practice, because the structure of the international system forces states to behave as egoists. Anarchy, offensive capabilities and uncertain intentions combine to leave states with little choice but to compete aggressively with each other. For realists, trying to infuse states with communitarian norms is a hopeless cause.

(Mearsheimer 1995b: 367)

The major problem that states face in anarchy, according to neorealists, is a problem that is not sufficiently analysed by constructivists; it is the problem of uncertainty (Copeland 2000). Uncertainty is about the present intentions of other states and it is about future intentions of other states. At any given moment, there may be peace and quiet in the international system. But in anarchy, states are always seeking security; moves in that direction can be misread by other states; that is what the security dilemma is all about. 'Realism only needs states to be uncertain about the present and future interests of the other, and in anarchies of great powers, such uncertainty may often be profound' (Copeland 2000: 200). According to Dale Copeland, Wendt's constructivist analysis overly downplays the fact that states have difficulties in obtaining trustworthy information about the motives and intentions of other states (see web links 8.29 and 8.30).

The problem of uncertainty is significantly increased by the fact of deception. Constructivists tend to assume that social interaction between states is always sincere and that states genuinely attempt to express and understand each other's motives and intentions. But there is a pervasive element of deception in the relations between many states. Deceptive actors 'will stage-manage the situation to create impressions that serve their narrow ends, and other actors, especially in world politics, will understand this' (Copeland 2000: 202). In other words, are states really peaceful or do they merely pretend to be peaceful? In the case of the Hitler–Stalin pact, it was probably clear to most that it was not based on good and sincere intentions about cooperation between the two states; but it is easy to find other examples where states say one thing and mean another. The analysis by Ted Hopf on Soviet and Russian foreign policy introduced earlier is a case in point. It

takes at face value comments made by Khrushchev to party gatherings praising China and advocating closer ties. In reality, that is only part of the story. That same year, 1955, Khrushchev warned West German Chancellor Konrad Adenauer in private conversations that China represented a real threat to the USSR and to the West . . . Which is the real Khrushchevian view of China? One cannot explain Soviet policy in 1955 without engaging in that discussion.

(Stent 2005: 185)

Against this critique, constructivists will maintain that anarchy is a more complex entity than posited by neorealists. It need not always lead to self-help, mutual aggression, and the risk of violent conflict. The claim by Mearsheimer, that 'realism was the dominant discourse from about the start of the late medieval period in 1300 to 1989, and that states and other political entities behaved according to realist dictates during these seven centuries' (Mearsheimer 1995b: 371), is not accurate, according to constructivists. Without incorporating a focus on ideas and social interaction, on the formation of interests and identities, it will not be possible, say constructivists, to produce a precise analysis about the nature of anarchy in particular historical periods. Furthermore, it may be true that shared ideas about friendship do not reflect a deep commitment between some states; but that point can be addressed by carefully analysing the 'degree of internalization' (see Figure 8.1 above) of shared ideas. Neorealists, in turn, can retort that Wendt's 'first degree of internalization' reflects a thin commitment to shared ideas among states; at the same time this 'first degree' level is commonplace in the real world. Wendt's 'first degree' is thus, in effect, another way of admitting the core relevance of the neorealist analysis of anarchy.

Another critique by neorealists concerns the constructivist view of change. Constructivists:

provide few insights on why discourses rise and fall . . . [therefore, they] say little about why realism has been the dominant discourse, and why its foundations are so shaky. They certainly do not offer a well–defined argument that deals with this important issue . . . Nevertheless, [constructivists] occasionally point to particular factors that might lead to changes in international relations discourse. In such cases, however, they usually end up arguing that changes in the material world drive changes in discourse.

(Mearsheimer 1995b: 369)

Robert Jervis contends that constructivists fail to explain:

how norms are formed, how identities are shaped, and how interests are defined as they do . . . [Constructivism] does not, by itself, tell us something about the processes at work in political life, it does not, by itself, tell us anything about the expected content of foreign policies or international relations.

(Jervis 1998: 976)

Constructivists claim that they do study change. It is rather neorealism that downplays change by claiming international relations to be 'the same damned things over and over again'; a constant logic of anarchy (Wendt 1999: 17). Constructivists, by contrast, claim that they most certainly study change through the analysis of social interaction. 'Regarding the mechanisms of change, some constructivists emphasize collective learning, cognitive evolution, epistemic change and the "life cycles of norms," all of which involve the institutionalization of people's knowledge, practices and discourses' (Adler 2001: 102).

The analysis of change points to areas where constructivists can cooperate with liberals and International Society theorists. Liberals (Chapter 4) focus on processes of democratization, interdependence, and international institutions. These processes can act as inspiration for a constructivist interpretation of why actors choose to cooperate, even to become friends. Liberal progress can help create norms and ideas of cooperation. As for International Society theorists (Chapter 5), they emphasize the existence of common interests and common values between states. That is precisely what makes relations between states into an international society instead of a mere 'system of states'. Constructivists can thus cooperate with liberals and International Society theorists. At the same time, International Society theorists may claim that constructivists add little new to the analysis of anarchy already produced by International Society scholars. Wendt readily admits that his identification of three cultures of anarchy is an argument that 'builds directly on Bull's' (Wendt 1999: 253). Yet, it would be unfair to say that constructivists bring nothing new. Their emphasis on the importance of social theory and the detailed analyses of social interaction in international relations breaks new ground. And as we have seen above, several constructivists emphasize the role of domestic norms, an area little studied by International Society theorists.

Some Marxists are critical of constructivism. Wallerstein's world system theory focuses on the material structure of global capitalism and its development since the sixteenth century (see Chapter 6). This analysis leaves little room for the social interaction analysed by constructivists. Robert Cox's neo-Marxist view of 'historical structures' (see Chapter 6) makes more room for 'ideas' and will thus be more sympathetic to a constructivist approach.

In sum, neorealism remains the main contender and intellectual opponent for constructivist theory. When it comes to liberal and International Society theory, and even to some versions of neo-Marxist theory, constructivists can find more room for intellectual cooperation.

The Constructivist Research Programme

One ongoing debate among constructivists concerns basic social theory. The outline made above recorded the controversy between 'conventional' and 'critical' constructivists. From the 'conventional' camp, Emanuel Adler argues that in order to make an impact in the discipline of IR, constructivists need to develop 'a coherent constructivist methodological base that suggests a practical alternative to imitating the physical sciences' (Adler 2001: 109). From the 'critical' side, Maja Zehfuss wants to move in a very different direction: 'the assertion of an independently existing reality, which in itself cannot be proved and seems to demand no proof, works to support particular political positions and to exclude others from consideration' (Zehfuss 2002: 245). In other words, clarification of basic social theory is important for the constructivist research programme.

The debate about basic theory is of course relevant for the constructivist ambition of demonstrating that 'ideas matter'. How exactly is it that ideas matter? Do changes in ideas always come before changes in material conditions? Do ideas guide policy or are they justifications for policy? Should ideas be seen as causes of behaviour in IR or should they rather be seen as constitutive elements that define what IR is all about? (See Tannenwald 2005 for an excellent discussion of these questions.) Further clarification in these areas is of vital importance for the constructivist research programme. The major challenge for constructivists is to demonstrate that ideas matter much more in IR than assumed by other theoretical perspectives (Moravcsik 1999a).

An additional vital element in the constructivist research programme concerns the direction scholars will take in building constructivist IR theory. Is emphasis going to be put on systemic or domestic aspects? If emphasis is on systemic aspects, should theorizing focus on interaction between states or should it focus on normative and ideational aspects of international society? If emphasis is on domestic aspects, which domestic norms should be given attention; what are the major domestic sources of state identity? Such questions need not be very problematic. The other major theoretical approaches to IR also have a continuing

> **BOX 8.11   Combining theories to explain ICC**
>
> The constructivists explain development of the consensus on which the Court is based; the realists explain states' compulsions to protect sovereignty and to seek relative advantage; the liberal institutionalists explore how the ICC embodies states' cooperative efforts to improve absolute welfare.
>
> Schiff (2008: 9)

discussion about the most relevant specific research focus. A comprehensive research programme will always be active in a variety of concrete areas.

Finally, it will be important for constructivists to further clarify the relationship to the approaches that have dominated IR so far: realism, liberalism, International Society, and IPE. To what extent are they compatible with constructivism and how far are they capable of fruitful cooperation? For example, early constructivist contributions indicated a deep gulf between materialist neorealism and a norms-idea-focused constructivism. The debate has demonstrated that the gulf is much smaller: neorealists do recognize the importance of ideas (Dessler 2000); constructivists do recognize the importance of material factors (Sørensen 2008b). Recent projects (Schiff 2008; Barkin 2010) draw on constructivist analysis in combination with other theoretical perspectives. Benjamin Schiff, for example, wants to explain the development of the International Criminal Court (ICC); his argument is that constructivism, realism, and liberal institutionalism are all relevant in this regard (Box 8.11).

In conclusion, a recent analysis of constructivist scholarship in relation to the EU identifies three challenges to constructivism (Box 8.12).

> **BOX 8.12   Challenges to constructivism**
>
> - Methodological challenges referring to the fact that research based on micro-sociological studies or even detailed case studies . . . do not seem entirely sufficient to understand the extent to which the embeddedness of actors explains their positions in policy negotiations, or the final policy outcome . . . Which macro-sociological world views (if there are any) influence the policy results?
>
> - The establishment of a correlation between ideas, norms or world views and policy outcomes is still not entirely convincing. The central criticism voiced by Andrew Moravcsik . . . that ideas constantly float around . . . and that it is therefore vain to try to understand these often contradictory variables . . . still echoes in constructivist research.
>
> - Finally, some constructivist public policy approaches are in danger of becoming so concentrated with small-scale case studies that they forget to be interested in the bigger picture of European integration . . . Widening the research scope of these approaches might lead to more general comments and less evidence-based research, as norms, ideas or world views can be catch-all terms if not precisely defined.
>
> Saurugger (2013: 901–2)

Constructivists have demonstrated that 'ideas matter' in international relations. They have shown that culture and identity help define the interests and constitute the actors in IR. Whether they agree with constructivists or not, students of IR should be familiar with the debates raised by the approach, about basic social theory, and about the different ways in which ideas can matter in international relations.

KEY POINTS

- The focus of social constructivism is on human awareness or consciousness and its place in world affairs. The international system is constituted by ideas, not by material forces.

- Social theory is the more general theory about the social world. In social theory, constructivists emphasize the social construction of reality. The social world is not a given. The social world is a world of human consciousness: of thoughts and beliefs, of ideas and concepts, of languages and discourses. Four major types of ideas are: ideologies; normative beliefs; cause–effect beliefs; and policy prescriptions.

- Constructivist Alexander Wendt rejects the neorealist position of anarchy necessarily leading to self-help. That cannot be decided a priori; it depends on the interaction between states. In these processes of interaction, the identities and interests of states are created.

- Martha Finnemore argues that identities and interests are defined by international forces; that is, by the norms of behaviour embedded in international society.

- Peter Katzenstein argues that the internal make-up of states affects their international behaviour. The approach is employed to explain the shift in Japanese foreign policy from militaristic to pacifist.

- Ted Hopf focuses on the domestic foundation of identity in a study of Soviet and Russian foreign policy. The claim is that the identities of key decision makers go a long way in explaining foreign policy.

- Constructivists have recently embarked on studies of IPE, demonstrating how attention to 'meaning' and 'cognition' can provide new insights into IPE-questions.

- Constructivists have brought home the point that 'ideas matter' in international relations. The critical debate is about how much they matter and what the exact relationship is to policy outcomes.

QUESTIONS

- Social constructivists argue in favour of an ideational view and against a materialist view of the world. They claim that the international system is constituted by ideas, not by material forces. Explain the distinction and discuss whether it is valid.

- Is social constructivism primarily a meta-theory about the nature of the social world or is it primarily a substantial set of theories about IR?

- Identify the four types of ideas discussed by Nina Tannenwald and think of ways in which each type can influence international relations.

- Alexander Wendt says that 'if the United States and the Soviet Union decide they are no longer enemies, "the Cold War is over"'. Do you agree? Why or why not?

- Significant global changes have occurred since the end of the Cold War. How can constructivism help us make sense of processes of global change? What does it bring to the table?

→ GUIDE TO FURTHER READING

Abdelal, R., Blyth, M., and Parsons, C. (2010). *Constructing the International Economy*. Ithaca, NY: Cornell University Press.

Adler, E. (2001). 'Constructivism and International Relations', in W. Carlsnaes, T. Risse, and B. A. Simmons (eds), *Handbook of International Relations*. London: Sage, 95–118.

Barkin, S. (2010). *Realist Constructivism: Rethinking International Relations Theory*. Cambridge: Cambridge University Press.

Fierke, K. M. and Jørgensen, K. E. (eds) (2001). *Constructing International Relations*. Armonk, NY: M. E. Sharpe.

Finnemore, M. (1996). *National Interests in International Society*. Ithaca, NY and London: Cornell University Press.

Guzzini, S. and Leander, A. (eds) (2006). *Constructivism and International Relations: Alexander Wendt and his Critics*. London: Routledge.

Hurd, I., Reus-Smit, C., and Snidal, D. (2008). 'Constructivism', in (eds), *The Oxford Handbook of International Relations*. Oxford: Oxford University Press, 298–317.

Katzenstein, P. (1996b). *Cultural Norms and National Security*. Ithaca, NY and London: Cornell University Press.

Risse, T., Wiener, A., and Diez, T. (2009). 'Social Constructivism and European Integration', in (eds), *European Integration Theory*. Oxford: Oxford University Press, 159–76.

Saurugger, S. (2013). 'Constructivism and Public Policy Approaches in the EU: From Ideas to Power Games', *Journal of European Public Policy*, 20/6: 888–906.

Wendt, A. (1999). *Social Theory of International Politics*. Cambridge: Cambridge University Press.

⊕ WEB LINKS

Web links mentioned in the chapter, together with additional material including a case-study on the United States–China relationship, can be found on the Online Resource Centre that accompanies this book.

www.oxfordtextbooks.co.uk/orc/jackson_sorensen6e/

Post-positivism in IR

▋ Summary

This chapter introduces **post-positivist approaches** in IR. Three different strands are discussed. **Post-structuralism** is focused on language and discourse; it adopts a critical attitude towards established approaches in that it highlights the ways in which these theories represent and discuss the world. It is particularly critical of neorealism because of its one-sided focus on (Northern) states. **Post-colonialism** adopts a post-structural attitude in order to understand the situation in areas that were conquered by Europe, in particular in Africa, Asia, and Latin America. **Feminism** underlines that women are a disadvantaged group in the world, in both material terms and in terms of a value system which favours men over women. A gender-sensitive perspective on IR investigates the inferior position of women in the international political and economic system and analyses how our current ways of thinking about IR tend to disguise as well as reproduce a gender hierarchy.

Introduction

Post-positivist approaches is an umbrella term for a variety of contemporary issues in the study of IR. What unites them is dissatisfaction with the established theoretical traditions in the discipline, in particular with neorealism, which is seen as the dominant conventional theory. In their critique of established traditions, post-positivist scholars raise both methodological issues and substantial issues. They argue against positivist methodology with its focus on observable facts and measurable data and its ambition to scientifically explain the world of international relations. Post-positivists emphasize that IR theorists (as are all theorists of human affairs) are an integrated part of the world they study.

In that sense, theorists are insiders, not outsiders. They make certain assumptions and create certain images of reality. Because other theorists make other assumptions and create other images, knowledge is not and cannot be neutral. Therefore, we always need to critically discuss the assumptions and claims made by any theory, because there is no single, final truth out there. There are competing claims about how the world hangs together and what makes it tick. Some scholars call this attitude postmodern; **postmodernism** has been defined as an 'incredulity towards metanarratives' (Lyotard 1984: xxiv); we shall stay with the label of '**post-positivism**'.

In sum, post-positivists are critical of any claim of an established truth valid for all. The task is rather to examine the world from a large variety of political, social, cultural, economic, ethnic, and gendered perspectives. That opens up a 'free space' for competing reflections and to arrive at that space is the best we can do as scholars of IR (web link 9.01).

Post-positivist approaches move in a number of different directions and take up a variety of substantial issues. We cannot present them all here, but three of the most important ones are discussed: post-structuralism, post-colonialism, and feminism. *Post-structuralism* is focused on language and discourse; it adopts a critical attitude towards established approaches in that it highlights the ways in which these theories represent and discuss the world. It is particularly critical of neorealism because of its one-sided focus on (Northern) states. Neorealism presents a world where a variety of actors (e.g., women, the poor, groups in the South, protest movements) and processes (e.g., exploitation, subordination, environmental degradation) are not identified and analysed. Neorealism, therefore, constructs a biased picture of the world that needs to be exposed and criticized.

Post-colonialism adopts a post-structural attitude in order to understand the situation in areas that were conquered by Europe, in particular in Africa, Asia, and Latin America. When Western scholars talk about 'traditional' and 'underdeveloped', 'Third World' countries, they are really constructing certain images of these areas that reflect how the powerful dominate and organize the ways in which states in the South are perceived and discussed. Any real liberation of the South thus needs to critically expose such images; only in that way can the road be paved for really democratic and egalitarian relationships.

Feminism underlines that women are a disadvantaged group in the world, in both material terms and in terms of a value system which favours men over women. A gender-sensitive perspective on IR investigates the inferior position of women in the international political and economic system and analyses how our current ways of thinking about IR tend to disguise as well as to reproduce a gender hierarchy.

This is, of course, not the first time that methodological issues are debated in IR (web link 9.05). The second debate, between traditionalists and behaviouralists, also raised the issues of theorists inside and outside the subject and of best ways of approaching the study of international relations. Social constructivism (Chapter 8) focuses on shared knowledge and understanding rather than on material structures and capabilities. The post-positivist approaches discussed here go a step further in their critique of the established traditions in the discipline.

The reader should be aware that this chapter grapples with a number of complex ontological and epistemological issues, and that the debate about them contains a large number of different views that seldom agree on everything, even if the authors belong to the same (positivist or post-positivist) camp. Max Weber once said that science (including social science) consists of 'a thoughtful ordering of empirical reality' (Weber, quoted from Jackson 2010: 193). It sounds simple, but it most certainly is not. That is because there is no agreement about the actual content of the 'empirical reality' that we study; nor is there any agreement about what it means to make a 'thoughtful' inquiry.

Several of these nuances will not be discussed here; we simplify in order to paint the larger picture (web link 9.02). For a detailed introduction to the philosophical debates connected with positivist and post-positivist approaches, see Jackson (2010), Lebow (2011), and Suganami (2013).

Post-structuralism in IR

Post-structuralists are first and foremost critical of the approaches to IR that are based on positivist methodology. What is the positivist persuasion in IR? Fundamentally, it is a scholarly conviction that there can be a cumulative science of IR of increasing sophistication, precision, parsimony, and predictive and explanatory power. Positivists believe in the unity of science: that social science is not fundamentally different from natural science; that the same analytical methods—including quantitative methods—can be applied in both areas.

The aim is to collect data that can lead to scientific explanation. That requires scientific methodology and a scientific attitude on the part of the researcher. Then it becomes possible to provide empirical explanations of political behaviour: to determine 'why people behave politically the way they do, and why, as a result, political processes and systems function as they do' (Eulau 1963: 25). Positivism views the social and political world, including the international world, as having regularities and patterns that can be explained if the correct methodology is properly applied. It argues that observation and experience are keys to constructing and judging scientific theories. It holds that there can be an objective knowledge of the world—or at least 'a great deal of intersubjective agreement' (Nicholson 1996a: 131). It emphasizes the centrality of empirical propositions; i.e., the reasons for accepting hypotheses are evident from careful observation of reality. 'We observe events and on the basis of these observations hope to predict the consequences of actions carried out now or in the future' (Nicholson 1996a: 132).

Post-structuralists are not at all happy about this way of approaching IR and social science in general. In particular, they reject its *empiricism*, the view that science is based merely on observation of facts. Most importantly, pure, 'objective' observation is not possible; it requires previous ideas about what to observe and how to go about it, as emphasized by Steve Smith in Box 9.1.

This critique rejects three basic postulates of positivism: an objective external reality; the subject/object distinction; and value-free social science. It follows that there are no world politics or global economics that operate in accordance with immutable social laws. The social world is a construction of time and place: the international system is a specific construction of the most powerful states. Everything that is social, including international relations, is changeable and thus historical. Since world politics is constructed rather than discovered, there is no fundamental distinction between subject (the analyst) and object (the focus of analysis) (web link 9.12).

The larger consequence of this critique is that knowledge is not and cannot be neutral, either morally or politically, or ideologically. There are a thousand ways of looking at the real world; which distinctions and concepts are the more important and which are the less important? Dominant theories underpin and inform practice; that makes them hugely powerful. 'Defining common sense is therefore the ultimate act of political power' (Smith 1996: 13).

All knowledge reflects the interests of the observer. Knowledge is always biased because it is produced from the social perspective of the analyst. Knowledge thus discloses an inclination—conscious or unconscious—towards certain interests, values, groups, parties, classes, nations, and so on. All IR theories are in this sense biased too; Robert Cox (1981) expressed that view in a frequently quoted remark: 'Theory is always for someone and for some purpose'.

Cox draws a distinction between positivist or 'problem-solving' knowledge and critical or 'emancipatory' knowledge. Problem-solving knowledge, such as, for example, neorealist theory, is conservative in that it seeks to know that which exists at present: it takes

---

BOX 9.1   Objective observation not possible

There can be no 'objective' observation, nor any 'brute experience'. Observation and perception are always affected by prior theoretical and conceptual commitments. Empiricism, in other words, underestimates the amount of theory involved in perception and observation. To describe what we experience we have to use concepts, and these are not dictated by what we observe; they are either a priori in the mind, or they are the result of a prior theoretical language . . . Our senses cannot give us access to 'the truth' since there is no way of describing experience independently of its interpretation. There are, therefore, no brute facts, no facts without interpretation, and interpretation always involves theory.

Smith (1996: 20)

the international system of sovereign states for granted. It is therefore biased towards an international status quo which is based on inequality of power and excludes many people. It cannot lead to knowledge of human progress and emancipation.

By contrast, the critical theory advocated by Cox is not confined to an examination of states and the state system but focuses more widely on power and domination in the world generally. Critical theorists seek knowledge for a larger purpose: to liberate humanity from the oppressive structures of world politics and world economics which are controlled by hegemonic powers, particularly the capitalist United States. They seek to unmask the global domination of the rich North over the poor South. Critical theorists are in this regard pursuing a neo-Marxist analysis. Cox's approach to IPE is presented in Chapter 7; here, we move to that part of post-structuralism that is focused on language and text.

The starting point for these theorists is that language is much more than a means of communication; it is 'a process intrinsic to human social activity . . . to engage in a speech act is to give meaning to the activities which make up social reality. Language thus no longer describes some essential hidden reality; it is inseparable from the necessarily social construction of that reality' (George and Campbell 1990: 273). Here, post-structuralists are inspired by French philosophers, including Foucault, Derrida, Lacan, Kristeva, Barthes, Bourdieu, and Baudrillard (web link 9.15, 9.16, and 9.17). In their view, texts are instruments of power. Therefore, theory is less a 'tool for analysis' than it is an 'object of analysis'; when we critically analyse the established theories of IR, we can learn how they 'privilege certain understandings of global politics and marginalize and exclude others' (George and Campbell 1990: 285).

Post-structuralists see empirical theory as a myth. Every theory, including neorealism and neoliberalism, decides for itself what counts as 'facts'. In other words, there is no objective reality; everything involving human beings is subjective. The dominant theories of IR can be seen as stories that have been told so often that they appear as 'reality per se' (Bleiker 2001: 38). But they are not; they are stories from a certain point of view which must be exposed as such and contrasted with other stories from different points of view (Valbjørn 2008a).

Knowledge and power are intimately related: knowledge is not at all 'immune from the workings of power' (Smith 1997: 181); see Box 9.2.

BOX 9.2   Knowledge and power

All power requires knowledge and all knowledge relies on and reinforces existing power relations. Thus there is no such thing as 'truth', existing outside of power. To paraphrase Foucault, how can history have a truth if truth has a history? Truth is not something external to social settings, but is instead part of them . . . Postmodern international theorists have used this insight to examine the 'truths' of international relations to see how the concepts and knowledge—claims that dominate the discipline in fact are highly contingent on specific power relations.

Smith (1997: 181)

Important post-structuralist theorists are Richard Ashley, David Campbell, James Der Derian, Jim George, Fritz Kratochwil, Michael Shapiro, and Rob Walker (web link 9.18). A seminal contribution was Ashley's 1984 (reprinted 1986) article on 'The Poverty of Neorealism' (Ashley 1984, 1986). Neorealism is a theory that claims that only a few elements of information about sovereign states in an anarchical international system can tell us most of the big and important things we need to know about international relations. And the theory even claims to validly explain international politics 'through all the centuries we can contemplate' (Waltz 1993: 75).

Post-structuralist critique of neorealism targets the ahistorical bias of the theory (Ashley 1986: 189; Walker 1993: 123). Because the theory is ahistorical it leads to a form of reification in which historically produced social structures are presented as unchangeable constraints given by nature. Emphasis is on 'continuity and repetition' (Walker 1995: 309). Individual actors are 'reduced in the last analysis to mere objects who must participate in reproducing the whole or fall by the wayside of history' (Ashley 1986: 291) (web link 9.14). It follows that neorealism has great difficulty in confronting change in international relations. Any thought about alternative futures remains frozen between the stark alternatives of either domestic sovereign statehood and international anarchy or the (unlikely) abolition of sovereign statehood and the creation of world government (see Box 9.3).

Rob Walker (1993, 2010; Ashley and Walker 1990) posits 'sovereignty' as another conceptual prison of modernity which forces us to think in binary terms of 'inside' and 'outside'. Within the state, we are part of a community of citizens with rights and aspirations to the good life of peace and progress. Outsiders are excluded; our obligations to the members of 'humanity' rest on a much more insecure basis. But the relevance of the inside/outside dichotomy is increasingly challenged by processes of globalization, of intensified relations across borders. Yet, both the discipline of IR and the practice of international relations continue to be constituted by the principle of state sovereignty. In his recent book, *After the Globe, Before the World* (2010), Walker continues to grapple with this problem without finding definite answers: 'I do not think anyone is able to offer more than very tentative and humble responses to the kinds of questions about political possibilities that might emerge out of various skepticisms about the claims of the modern sovereign state and states system' (Walker 2010: 71).

BOX 9.3   Ashley on neorealism

[N]eorealism is itself an 'orrery of errors', a self-enclosed, self-affirming joining of statist, utilitarian, positivist, and structuralist commitments . . . What emerges is a positivist theoretical perspective that treats the given order as the natural order, limits rather than expands political discourse, negates or trivializes the significance of variety across time and place, subordinates all practice to an interest in control, bows to the ideal of a social power beyond responsibility, and thereby deprives political interaction of those practical capacities which make social learning and creative change possible.

Ashley (1986: 258)

So for Ashley and Walker, current neorealist theory and its understanding of dominant concepts such as sovereignty is not really helpful if we are looking for a nuanced and many-faceted understanding of international relations that views the subject from a wide array of different social, political, and philosophical standpoints. That is because these theories and concepts close us off from alternative viewpoints; they do so by claiming that their way of looking at the world is universally true and valid. But that is not the case.

David Campbell, for example, argues that foreign policy is not a given activity concerning relations between states. It is an ongoing process of producing boundaries between 'us' and 'them'. That is to say, 'foreign policy' is a continuing power game on many different levels of society where the exact definition of the danger stemming from anarchy can take many different forms, be it international terrorism, illegal immigrants, or anything else. Our focus should then be on the discursive practice that establishes such boundaries because they also have consequences for identities (who 'we' are) and the domestic social order 'we' entertain (Campbell 1998).

Post-structuralists go on to argue that current neorealist theory is not at all representative of the rich philosophical tradition of realism. If one goes back to the original texts of such realist scholars as Hans Morgenthau or E. H. Carr, there are many more tensions and nuances pointing to a richer and more diversified understanding of international relations than is the case with present-day neorealism (Ashley 1981). That is to say, different readings of the realist tradition that move in directions other than the dominant views are highly possible and urgently required.

Further, this reductionism is an act of power: if there are no alternative understandings there can be no alternative futures. By questioning traditional theories and concepts, post-structuralism represents 'the great skepticism' (George and Campbell 1990: 280) of our time. By refusing to privilege any particular point of view, post-structuralism aims to keep the future open and undecided and that is the only possible road towards real freedom (see Box 9.4).

A major contribution of post-structuralism to IR is the critical examination of the discipline's dominant theories and concepts. Scholars have a tendency to claim too much for their theories. Neorealism is a good example: it does not really live up to its billing; it provides less knowledge of IR in the broadest sense than it claims to provide. Another benefit is the scepticism that post-structuralism attaches to the notion of universal truths that are said to be valid for all times and places. That is typical of realism and also of much liberalism.

BOX 9.4	The politics of post-structuralism

Poststructuralism, by definition, is an emphatically political perspective. But it is one which refuses to privilege any partisan political line, for it equates such privileging with the grand, universal claims for unity and truth in modern theory, and the dogma of the hermetically sealed tradition. It is in the act of not privileging that it offers emancipation and liberation.

George and Campbell (1990: 281)

It follows that all theories have a history: they can be located in terms of space, time, and cultural attachment. In that sense, theories are not separate from the world; they are part of it. Therefore, says Steve Smith, 'there can never be a "view from nowhere," and *all* theories make assumptions about the world, both ontological ones (what features need explaining) and epistemological ones (what counts as explanation)' (Smith 2010: 9). For that reason, a proliferation of different theories in IR is highly desirable; a larger number of competing views opens up and enhances our understanding of the subject.

Critics are not convinced. Their charge against post-structuralism is that it spends a lot of time criticizing others and very little time coming up with its own analysis of international relations. Post-structuralists are cannibalistic: they thrive on critique but come up with little in terms of their own view of the world. Post-structuralists need to convince us, says Robert Keohane, that they 'can illuminate important issues in world politics'; until that happens, 'they will remain on the margins of the field, largely invisible to the preponderance of empirical researchers, most of whom explicitly or implicitly accept one or another version of rationalistic premises' (Keohane 1989a: 173). Thomas Biersteker suspects that post-structuralist critique will lead us down blind alleys: 'How are we to ensure that post-positivist pluralism, in the absence of any alternative criteria, will avoid legitimizing ignorance, intolerance, or worse?' (Biersteker 1989).

Post-structuralists reject this critique because they see in it an act of power; those defending established theories in IR request of the marginalized critics to 'become like us'—adopt a certain viewpoint, accept conventional assumptions about how the world hangs together and from there, get on with your work. In Ashley and Walker's formulation, 'the choice is presented as one of disciplinary authority versus a gathering of marginal challengers of unproven legitimacy: the maturity and wisdom of elders versus the bravado of tawdry youth' (Ashley and Walker 1990: 373). But this is exactly what post-structuralists want to avoid; they refuse to be boxed into a certain standpoint 'a position, a subjective perspective that enables them to justify what they say and do' (Ashley 1996: 241). The intellectual posture of a post-structuralist is a different one from that of the agnostic critic, welcoming as many different viewpoints on international relations as possible from different locations in terms of cultural, political, ethnic, social, and other positions.

At the same time, over the last decade a new generation of post-structuralist scholars have taken up substantial issues of IR and analysed them with post-structuralist concepts and frameworks. This represents a new development of post-structuralism in IR; instead of critique of others, focus is on substantial analysis of international affairs. One major example in this regard is Lene Hansen's book on Western decision making in relation to the war in Bosnia (Hansen 2006). Hansen argues that post-structural discourse analysis is better suited to understand the Western debate on the war in Bosnia than is a positivist approach. The study sets forth a post-structuralist theory about the relationship between identity and foreign policy. In this view, the formulation of foreign policy is not merely about taking concrete measures; policy is 'performatively linked' to identity. Facts and events are constituted by the discourses through which they are presented. Hansen identifies a 'Balkans discourse' and a 'Genocide discourse' in the Western debate and traces the role of these discourses in an American and a British setting. In this way, the study throws new light on the ways in which discourse and the formation of national identity are linked.

The study by Hansen is an example of how discourse analysis can be used to further a post-structuralist study of the ways in which our perception and understanding of security developed in relation to the war in Bosnia. The employment of discourse analysis presents one possible way forward for post-structural analysis (Neumann 2008); but post-structuralists will remain careful not to favour one theory over another. A plurality of theories will always be necessary and it is always important to ask critical questions about the assumptions made by any theory.

Post-colonialism in IR

Post-colonialism is inspired by post-structuralism. We have noted the critical attitude of post-structuralism towards the ways in which established approaches represent and analyse the world. Post-colonialism adopts this critical attitude and turns it in a specific direction: focus is on the relationship between on the one hand, Western countries in Europe and North America, and on the other hand, the areas in Africa, Asia, Latin America, and elsewhere that were colonized or dominated by Western countries.

Since the end of the Second World War, a process of decolonization has taken place. Previous colonies are now sovereign states and members of the international society of states; they are formally equal with Western states. But post-colonialism argues that the logic and ideas underpinning the relationship between the West and these areas continues to be one of hierarchy, reflecting Western concepts and understandings. Therefore, intellectual strategies of 'decolonization' are needed in order to liberate our thinking from that Western dominance. Post-colonialism, then, is about different ways of critically undertaking this process of intellectual decolonization (web link 9.23).

Eurocentrism, according to John Hobson, is 'the assumption that the West lies at the centre of all things in the world and . . . [the West] is projecting its global will-to-power outwards through a one-way diffusionism so as to remake the world in its own image' (Hobson 2007: 93). The task for post-colonialism is to abandon this way of thinking and offer a different analysis which treats and respects the dominated areas on their own terms (see Box 9.5.)

BOX 9.5	The post-colonial position

IR is constructed around the exclusionary premise of an imagined *Western subject* of world politics. Decolonising strategies are those that problematise this claim and offer alternative accounts of subjecthood as the basis for inquiry. The recognition of possible alternative subjects of inquiry is the essential precondition for a *dialogic* mode of inquiry in IR . . . without challenging the implicit and assumed universality of a particular subject, the possibility for genuine dialogue—rather than simply conversation—in the discipline becomes remote.

Sabaratnam (2011: 785)

In making this argument, post-colonial IR theorists draw on studies from other disciplines including historical and literature studies. A major early contribution towards the post-colonial project was offered by Edward Said (professor of comparative literature) in his book on *Orientalism* (2003 [1978]) (web link 9.26). The intellectual dominance of the West and the corresponding suppression of the Orient are reflected in the ways in which the Orient is represented in Western thinking. Oriental societies are backward, traditional, and despotic. Western societies, by contrast, are advanced, modernized, and democratic. Western thinking is substantially uninterested in the Arab world. Instead of trying to understand the vast tapestry of different cultural, social, economic, and political traditions and practices, the Western view of the Orient is a dark counterpoint of irrationality in contrast to the Western light of civilization and rationality. The enlightened identity of the West is reinforced by contrast with the backward Orient.

Power and knowledge are intimately connected in this view. If the Orient is backward, traditional, and underdeveloped, it is only logical and rational that it is subjected to Western dominance in order to be able to progress towards modernity and civilization. It is a view that can legitimize various kinds of power politics, from intervention in Iraq and elsewhere, to the defence of Western borders from large groups of Arabian peoples.

Yves Winter (2011) reflects on the concept of 'asymmetric' war, a notion frequently used to characterize conflicts between states and non-state actors. He argues that the notion of asymmetry carries normative implications because powerful states are portrayed as vulnerable victims of 'uncivilized warfare'. In that way, the notion of asymmetry allows states to take extraordinary measures against civilians: 'to selectively rationalize brutal tactics against non-state actors . . . and to defend manoeuvres that cause high casualties among civilians' (Winter 2011: 490).

Roxanne Lynn Doty discusses the US colonization of the Philippines at the turn of the twentieth century. Her argument is that the process of colonization was enabled by a previous discourse which established a hierarchical relationship between the United States and the Philippines. The former are Western peoples representing civilization, liberty, enlightenment, and progress. The latter are uncivilized, primitive, backward, and in need of civilized leadership; they must be 'willingly or unwillingly brought into the light' as one American observer wrote in 1900 (quoted from Doty 1996: 340). The whole process of colonization is facilitated by this construction of different identities. By contrast, the US never considered colonizing Spain after the Spanish–American war, although it had the capabilities of doing so. The colonial discourse created a social context that was decisive in paving the way for actual colonization; 'if we want to understand possibilities for international relations more generally, it is important to examine the processes that construct the "reality" upon which such relations are based' (Doty 1996: 343).

Mark Laffey and Jutta Weldes (2008) adopt a 'decolonizing' strategy towards an analysis of the Cuban missile crisis. The vast majority of IR scholars look at the crisis as a major confrontation between two superpowers, involving decision making, deterrence, and nuclear proliferation. In this way, a 'heroic missile crisis myth' is created where the United States and the Soviet Union stood 'eyeball to eyeball'. Laffey and Weldes argue that the Cuban position on the crisis has been almost entirely ignored in this view. The marginalization of Cuba 'obscures the pre-1961 origins of the crisis in a persistent pattern of US aggression and subversion of the Cuban revolution' (Laffey and Weldes 2008: 564). A full understanding of the missile crisis is only possible when the Cuban position is considered, in particular as concerns its historically subordinate position to the United States (web link 9.27). The American interpretation emphasizes how 'Cuba had vacated its sovereignty by aligning itself with the Soviet Union'; in that sense, the United States 'constructed a Cuba whose concerns could be ignored' (Laffey and Weldes 2008: 562). In other words, taking the Cuban viewpoint seriously puts a larger responsibility on the US and throws light on Cuba's subordinate position in the hierarchy of states (see also Tickner 2003).

Another aspect of post-colonialism's critique of Eurocentrism involves turning a critical eye towards the West. One does not have to go too far back in history in order to discover that Europe was not a repository of potential modernity, enlightenment, and progressive development. European state-building history is one of massive violent conflict and extermination (Tilly 1992); a number of areas failed to develop for a considerable period of time and were 'peripheral' rather than 'core' economies (Senghaas 1982). The propagation of liberal values of freedom and equality was a rather late occurrence, taking place in hard struggles against elites that supported hierarchy and imperialism (Jahn 2005). Non-liberal ideologies, such as fascism and Nazism, played important roles in Europe in the twentieth century. In short, 'the West' needs to be deconstructed as 'the primary subject of world history' (Sabaratnam 2011: 787).

Overall, post-colonialism is critical of established, Western views, because where these views rule, supreme genuine dialogue is not possible. A new situation can only be created by making different voices heard in world politics, in particular the marginalized voices from the developing world who have not so far received any representation. At the same time, the call for dialogue also means that post-colonialism does not aim at entering a 'win-or-lose' battle with existing theories. Rather than 'ships passing in the night', the idea is that established IR-theories and post-colonialism can both benefit from engaging with each other (see Box 9.6).

BOX 9.6 **Post-colonialism and established IR theories**

[We contend] that there should be an engagement between postcolonialism and international relations; that each approach would benefit from being situated in relation to the other; that the opening up of differences would spark rethinking and perhaps suggest new avenues of inquiry . . . Dialogue should proceed on terms that acknowledge that the two have different strengths that are intrinsic to their intellectual formations. In the case of postcolonialism this would involve recognition that its imaginative and critical capacities are tied to its free-floating character . . . That is to say, postcolonialism cannot of itself be the principal repository of scholarly understanding of the North–South relationship and the architect of Third World futures.

Darby and Paolini (1994: 371)

Feminism in IR

Gender issues have received increasing attention in recent decades in many areas of the social sciences. IR feminists focus on basic inequalities between men and women and the consequences of such inequalities for world politics. Gender refers to 'socially learned behaviour and expectations that distinguish between masculinity and femininity' (Peterson and Runyan 2010: 5). We currently live in a gendered world in which qualities associated with 'masculinity' (e.g., rationality, ambition, strength) are assigned higher value and status than qualities associated with 'femininity' (e.g., emotionality, passivity, weakness). This amounts to a gender hierarchy: a system of power where maleness is privileged over femaleness (web link 9.28).

Many feminists are inspired by post-structuralism in that they are critical of the ways in which conventional IR scholars approach the study of world politics. Conventional approaches contain gendered thinking; the feminist critique points out that the realist idea of security, for example, is a masculinist way of looking at the world. Realist security is based on military defence of states in an international anarchy; but that conceals the continued existence of a gender hierarchy in world politics in the sense that protection from an outside threat is also protection of a domestic jurisdiction that underwrites a persisting subordination of women (Sylvester 1994). Laura Sjoberg has applied a gender perspective to the wars in Iraq (Sjoberg 2006). In this context, women formally enjoy a status as protected; they are uninvolved civilians. But instead of security, this situation leads to gendered violence because there is no concern for the real protection of women. Iraq is not a unique case; violent conflicts almost always contain a gender dimension that reveals the extraordinary hardships of the affected women and families (Chandler et al. 2010).

Feminist approaches emerged in the discipline in the late 1980s. The formal 'breakthrough' for feminist perspectives is sometimes connected with the establishment of a seminar course on 'gender and IR' at the London School of Economics in 1988. An important book from this period is Cynthia Enloe's *Bananas, Beaches and Bases: Making Feminist Sense of International Politics* (1989). Enloe argued that gender was of huge importance in the world but this remained undiscovered in IR. She went on to demonstrate the subordinate, yet vital, position of women in a number of areas, especially in the international economic order. Many low-paid, low-status, industrial jobs are now undertaken by women from developing countries. Women occupy the low-end jobs in the service sectors (cleaning, washing, cooking, and serving).

But it is not merely the international division of labour that subordinates women. International politics also depends on men's control of women, as (passive and serving) diplomatic wives, around foreign military bases (the sex industry), and so on. Her major point is that gender is crucial in international politics and economics ('gender makes the world go around') but remains invisible because the private relationships between men and women rely on conventional definitions of 'masculinity' and 'femininity', which subordinates women to men (web link 9.29).

Cynthia Weber criticizes the conventional approaches to US foreign policy in Latin America. She does so by presenting an alternative, radical gender perspective to those relations. The perspective is queer theory, and the argument is that US foreign policies in the Caribbean can be seen as an attempt to 'fake' phallic power. That is because US policy is animated by a masculine identity crisis. Castro has castrated the US body politic by denying 'him' the normal (or 'straight') exercise of hegemony in the Caribbean. In order to 'fake' phallic power the US must strap on a queer organ which serves to recover 'America's international phallic power' while at the same time 'throwing its normalized (or straight) masculine hegemonic identity into a crisis' (Weber 1999: 7).

Ronald Reagan attempted to 'remasculinize' America through the invasion of Grenada, but became trapped in the Iran-Contra scandal. The Bush Sr invasion of Panama rather avoids confrontation and uses feminine tactics of 'entrapment' and 'encirclement' instead. The analysis of course upsets and questions the accounts of US foreign policy that we consider 'normal'. In doing so, it critically sheds light on the United States' perception of itself and the ways in which it frames the use of hegemonic power.

Feminism is also inspired by post-colonialism. The latter wants to criticize and deconstruct the Eurocentrism that pervades IR because it marginalizes and subordinates the developing world; the former wants to engage critically with the masculine biases that inform IR, in order to develop gender-sensitive accounts that restore and highlight the position of women.

There can be little doubt that compared with men, women are a disadvantaged group in the world. Women own about 1 per cent of the world's property and make up fewer than 5 per cent of the heads of state and cabinet ministers. Women put in about 60 per cent of all working hours, yet take home 10 per cent of all income. They account for 60 per cent of all illiterates, and (together with their children) for about 80 per cent of all refugees (Peterson and Runyan 2010).

At the same time, statistical and other indicators of development conceal the position of women. Growth rates, the gross national product per capita, unemployment rates, etc., reveal little about the secondary position of women. A gender-sensitive focus on world politics seeks to bring gender inequalities into the open, to demonstrate empirically the subordinate positions of women, and to explain how the working of the international political and economic system reproduces an underprivileged position for women. For example, Peterson and Runyan point out that much work done by men is visible and paid, while much work done by women is invisible and unpaid (see Box 9.7). Gender inequality and discrimination can be found in all societies, even in the advanced industrialized countries where women have high rates of participation in the workforce.

BOX 9.7 **Women and unpaid work**

In spite of the changes that have occurred in women's participation in the labour market, women continue to bear most of the responsibilities for the home: caring for children and other dependent household members, preparing meals and doing other housework. In all regions, women spend at least twice as much time as men on unpaid domestic work. Women who are employed spend an inordinate amount of time on the double burden of paid work and family responsibilities. When unpaid work is taken into account, women's total work hours are longer than men's in all regions.

UNdata: The World's Women 2010, at http://unstats.un.org/unsd/demographic/products/ Worldswomen/Executive%20summary.htm

We have noted how feminist scholars are inspired by post-structuralists and post-colonialists. But feminist IR draws on other theoretical perspectives as well, including constructivism, liberalism, and Marxism. These different theoretical commitments must create tensions because they invigorate the general debate between positivist and post-positivist approaches. Many feminists reject the devotion to a positivist methodology and a single standard of methodological appropriateness. They suspect that claims about any universal truth are arguably based on a more narrow masculine perspective. Therefore, many feminist scholars are worried about an alliance with established approaches; they fear that it will involve the subordination of a gender approach to an established mainstream theory which seeks to mould the gender view according to its own priorities (Steans 2006).

What is the standing of feminism in IR? Most feminist scholars consider the 'infiltration' of feminism into IR a successfully completed operation. Already in the late 1990s, V. Spike Peterson was able to claim the 'remarkable success' of IR feminists (1998: 587); in 2007, Judith Squires and Jutta Weldes also pronounced feminist IR a success (see Box 9.8).

Gender studies in relation to IR now have a substantial presence at international IR conferences. The annual meetings of the International Studies Association (web link 9.39) are an example. A large number of papers invoke a gender perspective in relation to politics, economics, security, institutions, war and peace, transnational relations, terrorism, national identities, development, drug trade, and so on. In this new generation of research, there is more going on than the simple addition of a gender focus on areas of study that otherwise remain unchanged. The gender perspective helps to develop and reconceptualize these existing concerns in new ways (Squires and Weldes 2007: 189).

One example in this regard is the study by Lauren Wilcox 'Gendering the Cult of the Offensive' (Wilcox 2009). Existing studies have shown that states often perceive themselves to be in a much more insecure situation than they really are. In particular, they tend to exaggerate the dangers they face, which leads to overly belligerent responses. Feminism can be of great help in understanding the causes of this syndrome, according to Wilcox. Her study is

---

BOX 9.8   Feminism and IR

Gendered analyses of international relations have developed a confidence that enables them to move beyond the margins of the discipline of IR to make a distinctive contribution to the study of things international . . . young scholars trained within a British IR context, display the vibrancy and sophistication of contemporary gendered work and mark a distinctive coming of age of 'Gender and International Relations' (GIR) . . . GIR scholars are now actively reconstructing IR without reference to what the mainstream asserts rightly belongs inside the discipline. In so doing they show that it is more effective to refuse to engage in the disciplinary navel-gazing inspired by positivist epistemological angst . . . When I/international R/relations is coupled with gender, the resulting GIR quite dramatically expands the substantive concerns of IR, adding significant areas of inquiry to IR's traditional focus on co-operation and conflict under anarchy.

Squires and Weldes (2007: 185)

> ### BOX 9.9   Gender and belligerence
>
> Gendered perceptions of technology, gendered discourses of nationalism, and the protection racket are three related ways in which offensive wars may be legitimated and thus enabled . . . By explaining the impact gender has on issues related to the perception of offense–defense balance, feminist analysis shows how gender discourses and the production of gender identities are not confined to individuals and the private realm but rather are a pervasive fact of social life on an international scale. International relations theorists concerned with determining the causes of war would do well to consider the ways in which gender can shape the conditions under which wars occur.
>
> Wilcox (2009: 240)

not primarily concerned with the status of women; it rather employs the concept of gender 'to analyze the workings of power through gendered discourses and identities' (see Box 9.9).

However, the success of feminist scholarship also opens up to new tensions, for example in feminist security studies. It has been the prevailing procedure of a gender approach to associate women with peace and non-violence. But women are active 'in national militaries, in combat in Afghanistan and Iraq, in militant movements in Kashmir, urging genocidal acts in Rwanda and committing other war crimes' (Sylvester 2010: 609). A gender approach must be able to accommodate this reality, and that requires moving away from a stylized concept of 'peaceful' women; several recent studies are moving in that direction (Alison 2009; Parashar 2009).

This development can be seen as a fruitful move towards better integrating feminist IR in the larger debate of the discipline. Together with other post-positivist approaches, feminism is now less a marginal voice and more of a set of acknowledged approaches with a common starting point. But many post-positivists will argue that there is still a clear hierarchy in the discipline where such approaches, including feminism, are kept at the margins (see web links 9.35 and 9.35).

Critique of Post-positivist Approaches

A major critique of post-positivist approaches concerns methodology. Post-positivists are unhappy with positivist methodology; positivists maintain that the scientific method they employ is superior. Behind these views are different understandings of the nature of the social world (**ontology**) and of the relation of our knowledge to that world. The ontology issue is raised by the following question: is there an objective reality 'out there' or is the world one of experience only; i.e., a subjective creation of people (Oakeshott 1966)? The extreme objectivist position is purely naturalist and materialist; i.e., international relations are basically a thing, an object, out there. The extreme subjectivist position is purely idealist; i.e., international relations are basically an idea or concept that people share about how they should organize themselves and relate to each other politically—it is constituted exclusively by language, ideas, and concepts.

The **epistemology** issue is raised by the following question: in what way can we obtain knowledge about the world? At one extreme is the notion of scientifically explaining the world. The task is to build a valid social science on a foundation of verifiable empirical propositions. At the other extreme is the notion of understanding the world; that is, to comprehend and interpret the substantive topic under study. According to this view, historical, legal, or moral problems of world politics cannot be translated into terms of science without misunderstanding them.

Scholars of a positivist leaning criticize post-positivists for what they see as a lack of scientific method. For example, Robert Keohane (1998) suggests that feminists should pursue a research programme based on that method. This would involve formulating hypotheses and collecting the necessary data to test these hypotheses in order to falsify or validate them. That would be, according to Keohane, 'the best way to convince non-believers of the validity of the message that feminists are seeking to deliver' (Keohane 1998: 196).

Post-positivists mostly reject taking that course. In doing so, they make two arguments. First, social science, including IR, must necessarily work with a plurality of approaches that use different ways of obtaining knowledge about the world. There is no 'single standard of methodological correctness' (Tickner 2005: 3; see also Jackson 2010) that can be applied across the board. Second, post-positivist approaches to scholarship have already been able to question the established truths as they appear in mainstream theorizing and they have been able to formulate a larger number of new critiques and different insights. The whole purpose of post-positivist scholarship is to avoid being boxed in to a conventional approach.

In recent years, the discipline of IR has moved towards a less confrontationist view of methodology. Many scholars strive to avoid extreme positions in the debate. They seek out a middle ground which avoids a stark choice between 'positivist' and 'post-positivist' methodology. The option for the middle ground is contained already in Max Weber's (1964: 88) definition of 'sociology' as 'a science which attempts the interpretive understanding of social action in order thereby to arrive at a causal explanation of its course and effects' (see web link 9.11). Weber is saying that scholars must emphatically understand the world in order to carry out their research into social phenomena. He is also saying, however, that that does not prevent scholars from framing hypotheses in order to test empirical theories that seek to explain social phenomena. We need explaining as well as understanding because the world is made up of both material forces 'out there' and social understandings, ideas, and perceptions 'in here'. Both elements must be included in our analysis (Sørensen 2008b).

This is a road towards 'combining methods and critically reflecting on which of them are the most useful tools for designing and implementing research' (Tickner 2005: 19). Many scholars from both the 'positivist' and 'post-positivist' side of the fence support that eclectic position today; but not all. Steve Smith, for example, maintains that different theories see the world differently and tell dissimilar stories about it that cannot be freely combined because of the intimate connection between knowledge and power (Smith 2008; see Box 9.2). 'Eclecticists' will retort that even if this is the case, a large amount of theoretical cooperation in the 'middle ground' remains possible; many scholars have demonstrated the advantages of an 'eclecticist' approach to theorizing (Sil and Katzenstein 2010).

There is another potential problem connected with Steve Smith's view. It ultimately proposes that the value of any theory is based on political values ('no "truth" outside of power'). If IR theory is mainly politics in disguise, then any theory must be as good as any other theory because we are left with no neutral way of deciding which theory is best academically. Academic debates are really political debates in disguise. If theory is always an expression of political interest rather than academic curiosity, political science is neither science nor scholarship: it is politics; and in politics 'anything goes'.

Most scholars would not go that far. They accept the insight that no knowledge is completely value-free; but even if that is the case, there is a difference between pure politics and the academic undertaking of understanding and explaining international relations. That academic enterprise does not take place in complete isolation from or ignorance of politics, but it does attempt to come up with systematic and detached analysis. Academic knowledge is bound by common standards of clarity of exposition and documentation. Put differently, such knowledge is compelled to demonstrate that it is not the result of wishful thinking, guesswork, or fantasy; it must contain more than purely subjective evaluations (Brecht 1963: 113–16).

On that basis, some parts of academic work are better than other parts; it is not a case of 'anything goes'. Most post-positivists would agree to this but they would emphasize that one theory is not better than any other merely by virtue of being based, for example, on positivist assumptions about the world.

We have spent some time on methodology because that has been an important issue in the debate about post-positivist approaches. But there has also been critique of the substantial analyses made by these scholars. Take Said's analysis of the intellectual dominance of the West in the analysis of the Orient. He claims that the West is not really interested in the many rich nuances of the Arab world. However, his own analysis similarly reduces the West to a caricature that stands for imperialism and ethnocentrism and nothing else. Said is not himself interested in the rich nuances of the Western world and, ironically, he does not offer better analytical ways to bring forward the rich reality of the Orient (Valbjørn 2008b).

This can be seen as a more general critique of post-positivist approaches: they often tend to reduce their opponent's theory, and view of the world, to a straw man easy to destroy. In some post-colonial thinking this involves a tendency to see 'everything bad' as coming from the colonizing West. This corresponds with the view of radical dependency theory (see Chapter 7) when it criticizes Western modernization thinking for the opposite view: that 'everything good' comes from the West. Both views are wrong; the real world is more complex and differentiated than that. A one-way critique is always in danger of missing out on something important.

The Post-positivist Research Programme

It is not possible to succinctly outline a post-positivist research programme, because post-positivism comprises a large number of different theories and approaches that move in different directions. What can be said with some certainty is that post-positivism is coming of age in the sense that less time is spent on deconstructing and criticizing established IR

BOX 9.10	Fragmentation of IR

We are now an IR of camps that form around, and develop particularistic notions of, the international and its key relations. Camps follow particular personages and texts, often interact minimally with one another, and can be unfamiliar with texts and theories that do not concern them; increasingly, the camps even develop their own journals . . . In some ways, this means that IR is at an end: there is little agreement today on what the field is about.

Sylvester (2007: 551)

theories, and more time on substantial analyses of international relations from post-positivist perspectives.

A major item in coming years concerns the extent to which post-positivists will continue to cast themselves as outsiders on the margins of the discipline or whether they will more actively seek links and cooperate with other theories and approaches in the 'middle ground' we talked about in the previous section. In any case, post-positivism has contributed significantly towards making the discipline of IR more pluralistic, with a number of different theories to choose from that reflect dissimilar social, political, and cultural positions; it has certainly also helped shed a critical light on the assumptions and commitments of established theories. The 're-discovery' of IR theories and perspectives coming to field from non-Western countries and cultures (Tickner and Weaver 2009; Tickner and Blaney 2012) further adds to this pluralism.

Radically increasing pluralism also has a downside. IR is becoming less of a coherent discipline and more of a fragmented undertaking divided into different camps that do not always listen to each other (see Box 9.10 and Dunne, Hansen, and Wight 2013).

There are no longer theories in the discipline that are undisputedly hegemonic. When there are no leading theories, there can be no great debates. What we have instead is a significant amount of ongoing reflections emerging from a large number of different camps. In that way, the downside of pluralism is more confusion. The optimistic take on this is that confusion is the necessary by-product of a rich and nuanced analysis of international affairs.

KEY POINTS

- Post-positivist approaches is an umbrella term for a variety of contemporary issues in the study of IR. What unites them is dissatisfaction with the established theoretical traditions in the discipline, in particular with neorealism, which is seen as the dominant conventional theory. In their critique of established traditions, post-positivist scholars raise both methodological and substantial issues.

- Three of the most important post-positivist approaches are: post-structuralism, post-colonialism, and feminism.

- Post-structuralism is focused on language and discourse; it adopts a critical attitude towards established approaches in that it highlights the ways in which these theories represent and discuss the world. It is particularly critical of neorealism because of its one-sided focus on (Northern) states. Neorealism presents a world where a variety of actors (e.g., women, the poor, groups in the South, protest movements) and processes (e.g., exploitation, subordination, environmental degradation) are not identified and analysed. Neorealism, therefore, constructs a biased picture of the world that needs to be exposed and criticized.

- Post-colonialism adopts a post-structural attitude in order to understand the situation in areas that were conquered by Europe, in particular in Africa, Asia, and Latin America. When Western scholars talk about 'traditional' and 'underdeveloped', 'Third World' countries, they are really constructing certain images of these areas that reflect how the powerful dominate and organize the ways in which states in the South are perceived and discussed. Any real liberation of the South thus needs to critically expose such images; only in that way can the road be paved for really democratic and egalitarian relationships.

- Feminism underlines that women are a disadvantaged group in the world, in both material terms and in terms of a value system that favours men over women. A gender-sensitive perspective on IR investigates the inferior position of women in the international political and economic system and analyses how our current ways of thinking about IR tend to disguise as well as to reproduce a gender hierarchy.

- Post-positivism has contributed significantly towards making the discipline of IR more pluralistic with a number of different theories to choose from that reflect dissimilar social, political, and cultural positions; it has certainly also helped shed a critical light on the assumptions and commitments of established theories. Radically increasing pluralism also has a downside. IR is becoming less of a coherent discipline and more of a fragmented undertaking divided into different camps that do not always listen to each other.

? QUESTIONS

- Identify the major post-positivist approaches.
- Why are post-positivists dissatisfied with positivist methodology?
- Outline the substantial contributions that post-positivist analyses make to the study of IR.
- 'There can be no "objective" observation' says Steve Smith. Discuss.
- What is the relationship between knowledge and power, according to post-positivists?
- Is the discipline of IR dissolving into different camps that have little to say to each other?
- What is the dominant discourse on gender issues in your country? How does it influence political practice?

→ GUIDE TO FURTHER READING

Chowdhry, G. and Nair, S. (2013). *Power, Postcolonialism and International Relations: Reading Race, Gender, and Class*. London: Routledge.

Dunne, T., Hansen, L., and Wight, C. (2013). 'The End of International Relations Theory?' *European Journal of International Relations*, 19/3: 405–25.

Hansen, L. (2006). *Security as Practice: Discourse Analysis and the Bosnian War*. London: Routledge.

Jackson, P.T. (2010). *The Conduct of Inquiry in International Relations: Philosophy of Science and Its Implications for the Study of World Politics*. London: Routledge.

Peterson, V. S. and Runyan, A. S. (2010). *Global Gender Issues in the New Millennium*, 3rd edn. Boulder, CO: Westview Press.

Sabaratnam, M. (2011). 'IR in Dialogue . . . but Can We Change the Subjects? A Typology of Decolonising Strategies for the Study of World Politics', *Millennium Journal of International Studies*, 39/3: 781–3.

Sjoberg, L. (2006). *Gender, Justice and the Wars in Iraq*. Lanham, MD: Lexington Books.

Steans, J. (2013). *Gender and International Relations*, 3rd edn. Bognor Regis: Wiley.

Sylvester, C. (2007). 'Whither the International at the End of IR?', *Millennium Journal of International Studies*, 35/3: 551–873.

Tickner, A. B. and Blaney, D. L. (eds) (2012). *Thinking International Relations Differently (Worlding Beyond the West)*. London: Routledge.

WEB LINKS

Web links mentioned in the chapter, together with additional material including a case-study based on a post-colonial approach, can be found on the Online Resource Centre that accompanies this book.

www.oxfordtextbooks.co.uk/orc/jackson_sorensen6e/

PART 4

Policy and Issues

Foreign Policy

▍ Summary

This chapter addresses theories and approaches involved in **foreign policy analysis**. Foreign policy analysis is a study of the management of external relations and activities of nation-states, as distinguished from their domestic policies. The chapter unfolds as follows: first, the concept of **foreign policy** is outlined. Next, various approaches to foreign policy analysis are discussed. The arguments of major theories are introduced by using a **'level-of-analysis' approach** that addresses the international system level, the nation-state level, and the level of the individual decision maker. A case-study on the Gulf War demonstrates how insights from various approaches to foreign policy analysis can be brought together, and concludes with comments on the limits of such knowledge. Finally, a note on foreign policy experts and **'think tanks'** is included to indicate the extent of research on the subject which extends well beyond universities.

The Concept of Foreign Policy

Foreign policy analysis is a study of the management of external relations and activities of nation-states, as distinguished from their domestic policies. Foreign policy involves goals, strategies, measures, methods, guidelines, directives, understandings, agreements, and so on, by which national governments conduct international relations with each other and with international organizations and non-governmental actors. All national governments, by the very fact of their separate international existence, are obliged to engage in foreign policy directed at foreign governments and other international actors. Governments want to influence the goals and activities of other actors whom they cannot completely control because they exist and operate beyond their sovereignty (Carlsnaes 2013: 298–326).

Foreign policies consist of aims and measures that are intended to guide government decisions and actions with regard to external affairs, particularly relations with foreign countries. Managing foreign relations calls for carefully considered plans of action that are adapted to foreign interests and concerns—i.e., goals—of the government (see web link 10.01). Government officials in leading positions—presidents, prime ministers, foreign ministers, defence ministers, finance ministers, and so on—along with their closest advisers—are usually the key policymakers.

Policymaking involves a means–end way of thinking about goals and actions of government. It is an instrumental concept: what is the problem or goal and what solutions or approaches are available to address it? Instrumental analysis involves thinking of the best available decision or course of action—e.g., giving correct advice—to make things happen according to one's requirements or interests. The analyst seeks to provide knowledge that is of some relevance to the policymaker. It involves calculating the measures and methods that will most likely enable him or her to reach a goal, and the costs and benefits of different available policy options. It may extend to recommending the best course to enable a government to solve its foreign policy problems or achieve its foreign policy goals. At that point policy analysis becomes not only instrumental but also prescriptive: it advocates what ought to be done.

Foreign Policy Analysis

Foreign policy analysis ordinarily involves scrutinizing the external policies of states and placing them in a broader context of academic knowledge. That academic context is usually defined by theories and approaches—such as the ones discussed in previous chapters (see web link 10.09). The relationship between theory and policy does not necessarily lead to any one clear policy option; in most cases there will be several different options. Even so, the choice of theory—how policymakers view the world—is likely to affect the choice of policy.

That is partly because different theories emphasize different social values. Realists underline the value of national security: enhancing national military power and balancing that of other states is the correct way of achieving national security. International Society scholars emphasize the values of order and justice: a rule-based and well-ordered international society is a major goal. Freedom and democracy are the core values for liberals: they are convinced that liberal democracies will support peaceful international cooperation based on international institutions. Finally, scholars who emphasize the importance of socioeconomic wealth and welfare as a central goal of foreign policy are likely to take an IPE approach. For them, the promotion of a stable international economic system that can support economic growth and welfare progress is a major goal. It should be noted, however, that some of these theories are more policy-oriented than others. That is clearly the case with Realism and Liberalism.

Foreign policy theorists who are concerned with defence or security issues are likely to take a realist approach, emphasizing the inevitable clash of interests between state actors, the outcomes of which are seen to be determined by relative state power (see web links 10.16 and 10.17). On the other hand, those concerned with multilateral questions are likely to take a **liberal approach**, emphasizing international institutions—such as the United Nations or the World Trade Organization (WTO)—as means of reducing international conflict and promoting mutual understanding and common interests.

In addition to the general IR theories discussed in previous chapters, there are various approaches that are specific to foreign policy analysis. Some approaches are derived from IR theories. Some are adapted from other disciplines, such as economics or social psychology. Policy analysis approaches are evident not only in academic scholarship but also in advocacy think tanks and the analyses of experts associated with them (see section on think tanks). Box 10.1 presents major approaches to foreign policy analysis; they are explained in what follows.

1. A **traditional approach to foreign policy** analysis involves being informed about a government's external policies: knowing their history or at least their background; comprehending the interests and concerns that drive the policies; and thinking through the various ways of addressing and defending those interests and concerns. That includes knowing the outcomes and consequences of past foreign policy decisions and actions. It also involves an ability to recognize the circumstances under which a government must operate in carrying out its foreign policy. In addition, the traditional approach involves the exercise of judgement and common sense in assessing the best practical means and courses of action available for carrying out foreign policies.

BOX 10.1   **Approaches to foreign policy analysis**

1. traditional approach: focus on the decision maker
2. comparative foreign policy: behaviouralism and 'pre-theory'
3. bureaucratic structures and processes; decision making during crisis
4. cognitive processes and psychology
5. 'multilevel, multidimensional'; the general theories
6. the constructivist turn: identities before interests.

That 'feel' for what is possible under the circumstances is usually derived from experience. It could be said that a satisfactory grasp of a country's foreign policy is best achieved by direct knowledge of its government's foreign affairs; e.g., by serving in a foreign ministry or similar government agency. The next best thing would involve trying to put oneself into the mindset of such an official: attempting to grasp the circumstances of such a person; endeavouring to understand the reasons such an official arrived at a decision; and trying to ascertain its consequences, both good and bad. In short, traditional foreign policy study is a matter of gaining insight into the activity of foreign policymakers, either from experience or by careful scrutiny of past and present foreign policies.

Foreign policy analysis was traditionally the domain of diplomatic historians and public commentators. The subject still exists, although it now has many rivals. It was rooted in the state system and statecraft of modern Europe as that emerged and acquired its classical characteristics, between the late seventeenth and early twentieth centuries. There were several distinctive features of traditional foreign policy analysis (Carlsnaes 2013). It was seen as a virtually separate sphere from domestic policies and activities of sovereign states. It was the realm of 'high politics' defined and guided by reason of state, now more commonly labelled 'national interests'. It was directed and managed by the leading state officials (emperors, kings, presidents, prime ministers, chancellors, secretaries of state, foreign ministers, defence secretaries, etc., and their closest advisers). It was not subject to popular scrutiny or democratic control. It was an exclusive and often secretive sphere of statecraft.

Traditional foreign policy analysis, accordingly, was a body of wisdom and insights which could only be acquired by lengthy study and reflection. The main writers on the subject were historians, jurists, and philosophers. Some were practitioners as well, such as Machiavelli and Grotius at an early period in modern history (see web links 10.10 and 10.11), and George Kennan and Henry Kissinger at a later period (see web links 10.12, 10.13, 10.14, and 10.15). Their commentaries on foreign policy attempted to distil that wisdom and those insights. The approach continues to appeal to historically minded International Society scholars and classical realists, because it gets into the detailed substance of foreign policy. It is cautious of allowing theory to get ahead of practice and experience.

2. The **comparative approach to foreign policy** was inspired by the behaviouralist turn (see Chapter 2) in political science. The ambition was to build systematic theories and explanations of the foreign policy process in general. This was to be achieved by gathering and amalgamating large bodies of data, and by describing the content and context of the foreign policy of a large number of countries. It was theoretically informed by James Rosenau's (1966) 'pre-theory' of foreign policy. Rosenau identified numerous possibly relevant sources of foreign policy decisions and grouped them into five categories, which he called: idiosyncratic, role, governmental, societal, and systemic variables. He then proposed a ranking of the relative importance of these variables, depending on the issue at hand and on the attributes of the state (e.g., size, political accountability/level of democracy, level of development). A large number of empirical studies of foreign policy employed Rosenau's scheme, but the 'pre-theory' never emerged as a clear explanation of foreign policy; it remained a classification scheme.

3. The **bureaucratic structures and processes approach to foreign policy** focuses on the organizational context of decision making, which is seen to be conditioned by the dictates and demands of the bureaucratic settings in which decisions are made. Analysing processes and channels whereby organizations arrive at their policies is seen to be a superior way of obtaining empirical knowledge of foreign policy. The strength of the bureaucratic politics approach is its empiricism: its detailed attention to the concrete way policies are carried out in the bureaucratic milieus within which policymakers work. The approach seeks to find out not only what happened but also why it happened the way it did.

The best-known study of this kind is Graham Allison's book on the 1962 Cuban missile crisis, *Essence of Decision* (Allison 1971; Allison and Zelikow 1999). The analysis suggests three different and complementary ways of understanding American decision making during that crisis: (1) a 'rational actor approach' that provides models for answering the question: with that information what would be the best decision for reaching one's goal? The assumption is that governments are unified and rational; they want to achieve well-defined foreign policy goals. (2) An 'organizational processes' model, according to which a concrete foreign policy emerges from clusters of governmental organizations that look after their own best interests and follow 'standard operating procedures'. (3) A 'bureaucratic politics model' which portrays individual decision makers (as bargaining and competing for influence, each with their own particular goals in mind). Despite criticism (Bendor and Hammond 1992), Allison's three models have informed much research on foreign policy.

4. The **cognitive processes and psychology approach** also focused on the individual decision maker, this time with particular attention to the psychological aspects of decision making, such as perceptions of actors. Robert Jervis (1968, 1976) studied misperception: why do actors mistake or misunderstand the intentions and actions of others? Jervis gives several reasons: actors see what they want to see instead of what is really going on; they are guided by ingrained, pre-existing beliefs (e.g., the tendency to perceive other states as more hostile than they really are); and they engage in 'wishful thinking'. Another example in this category is the work of Margaret Herman (1984). She studied the personality characteristics of fifty-four heads of government, making the claim that such factors as the leaders' experience in foreign affairs, their political styles, their political socialization, and their broader views of the world should all be taken into account to understand their foreign policy behaviour.

5. The '**multilevel and multidimensional approach**' was developed over the last several decades, as it became increasingly clear that there would never be one all-encompassing theory of foreign policy, just as there is not one consolidated theory of IR. Many scholars now study particular aspects of foreign policymaking by using the various major theories presented in Parts 2 and 3 of this book. Studies of balance of power behaviour and of deterrence and security dilemmas—both Realist approaches—are examples of that. Thomas Schelling's strategic realism, which was derived from game theory (see Chapter 3), focuses directly on foreign policy decision making. It was applied most successfully in strategic studies during the Cold War, when the United States and the Soviet Union were locked in a struggle involving nuclear weapons (Schelling 1980 [1960]) (see web links 10.38 and

10.40). Schelling won the 2005 Nobel Prize for economics for his groundbreaking application of game theory to foreign policy.

As indicated in Chapter 4, liberals study complex interdependence, the role of international institutions, processes of integration, and paths of democratization. In the liberal view, all of these elements contribute in their separate ways to foreign policies that are more orientated towards peaceful cooperation for mutual benefit. International Society scholars (Chapter 5) trace the three traditions (realism, rationalism, and revolutionism) in the thought and behaviour of statespeople and ponder their consequences for foreign policy. In IPE (see Chapter 6), neo-Marxists focus on the relationship between core and periphery, and they identify the vulnerable position of underdeveloped, peripheral states in relation to developed core states as the basic explanation of their lack of room for manoeuvre in foreign policy.

6. A focus on the role of ideas, discourse, and identity is characteristic of a **social constructivist approach** to foreign policy analysis (see Chapter 8). Constructivists see foreign policymaking as an intersubjective world, whose ideas and discourse can be scrutinized in order to arrive at a better theoretical understanding of that process. They trace the influence of ideas and the discourse of policymakers on the processes and outcomes in foreign policy—since many actions are conveyed by speech and writing (Goldstein and Keohane 1993). 'Strategic culture' is an example of the influence of ideas. Over time, countries tend to develop a more lasting set of ideas about how they want to go about using military force in conducting foreign affairs; this set of ideas is the strategic culture (Johnston 1995). A study by Henrik Lindbo Larsen has shown how the difficulties of formulating a common European Security and Defence Policy can be explained by the incompatibilities of strategic cultures in France, Britain, and Germany (Lindbo Larsen 2008) (see web link 10.22).

A more ambitious version of constructivism is not satisfied with the notion of ideas as one among several factors influencing foreign policy. These constructivists claim that identity, rooted in ideas and discourse, is the basis for a definition of interests and thus lies behind any foreign policy (see web links 10.23, 10.24, and 10.25). Some constructivists focus on domestic sources of ideas and identities (Hopf 2002); others concentrate on the dialogue and discourse of states (Wendt 1999).

How to Study Foreign Policy: A Level-of-Analysis Approach

The different theories and approaches briefly identified in the previous section can all be of some assistance in the analysis of foreign policy. It will not be possible to present all of them in detail here; simplification is necessary. We propose to demonstrate the arguments of major theories by using a **level-of-analysis approach**. The level-of-analysis approach was introduced by Kenneth Waltz in his study of the causes of war (Waltz 1959; see also Singer 1961). Waltz searched for the causes of war at three different levels of analysis: the level of the individual (are human beings aggressive by nature?); the level of the state (are some states more prone to conflict than others?); and the level of the system (are there conditions in the international system that lead states towards war?). We can study foreign policy at these same three levels of analysis:

- the systemic level (e.g., the distribution of power among states; their political and economic interdependence);
- the nation-state level (e.g., type of government, democratic or authoritarian; relations between the state apparatus and groups in society; the bureaucratic make-up of the state apparatus);
- the level of the individual decision maker (his/her way of thinking, basic beliefs, personal priorities).

The Systemic Level

Theories at the systemic level explain foreign policy by pointing to conditions in the international system that compel or pressure states towards acting in certain ways; that is, to follow a certain foreign policy. Therefore, systemic theories first need to say something about the conditions that prevail in the international system; they then need to create a plausible connection between those conditions and the actual foreign policy behaviour of states. As we have seen in previous chapters, the various theories of the international system are not in full agreement about the conditions that primarily characterize the system. Realists focus on anarchy and the competition between states for power and security; liberals find more room for cooperation because of international institutions and a common desire by states for progress and prosperity. For many social constructivists, the goals of states are not decided beforehand; they are shaped by the ideas and values that come forward in the process of discourse and interaction between states. For present purposes, these different views of the international system can be summarized as shown in Table 10.1.

TABLE 10.1   Three conceptions of the international system

	REALISM	LIBERALISM	CONSTRUCTIVISM
Main theoretical proposition	Anarchy. States compete for power and security	States want progress and prosperity; commitment to liberal values	Collective norms and social identities shape behaviour
Main instruments of policy	Military and economic power	Institutions, liberal values, networks of interdependence	Ideas and discourse
Post-Cold War prediction	Resurgence of great-power competition	Increased cooperation as liberal values spread	Agnostic: depends on content of ideas

Significantly modified version of Walt (1998: 174)

So different images of the international system lead to different ideas about how states will behave. However, even if we agree on one of these theories, it remains complicated to get from the general description of the system to specific foreign policies by states. Let us focus on realism; it proclaims a post-Cold War resurgence of great-power competition in an anarchic world where states compete for power and security. This would appear to be accurate in the broad sense, for example, that US foreign policy 'is generally consistent with realist principles, insofar as its actions are still designed to preserve US predominance and to shape a post-war order that advances American interests' (Walt 1998: 37).

How exactly does anarchy and self-help in the system lead to a certain aspect of US foreign policy? For neorealists such as Kenneth Waltz or Stephen Krasner, the basic factor explaining state behaviour is the distribution of power among states. With a bipolar distribution of power, the two competing states are compelled to 'balance against' each other and thus to become rivals:

Britain was bound to balance against Germany in the First and Second World Wars because Germany was the one state that had the potential to dominate the continent and thereby pose a threat to the British Isles . . . Realism is less analytically precise when the international system is not tightly constraining. A hegemonic state, for instance, does not have to be concerned with its territorial and political integrity, because there is no other state . . . that can threaten it.

(Krasner 1992: 39–40)

In the absence of constraints, the balance of power will be less helpful in understanding the leading state's foreign policy. According to Stephen Krasner, 'it may be necessary to introduce other arguments, such as domestic social purpose or bureaucratic interests. A realist explanation always starts with the international distribution of power but it may not be able to end there' (Krasner 1992: 41). In the post-Cold War world, the United States is by far the predominant power. Therefore, the US is not particularly constrained by other states or groups of states in the system.

Even in cases where the balance of power is tightly constraining, however, assumptions need to be made about what it is that states want when they compete with other states. An important distinction here is between defensive and offensive realists (Brooks and Wohlforth 2008; Glaser 2010). Defensive realists take a benign view of anarchy; states seek security more than power. Offensive realists, such as John Mearsheimer, believe that states 'look for opportunities to gain power at the expense of rivals, and to take advantage of those situations when the anticipated benefits outweigh the costs. A state's ultimate goal is to be the hegemon in the system' (Mearsheimer 2001: 21). For defensive realists, states are generally satisfied with the prevailing balance of power when it safeguards their security; for offensive realists, states are always apprehensively looking to increase their relative power position in the system. It is clear that different foreign policies can follow from adopting either the defensive or the offensive assumption.

For realists, the systemic distribution of power among states is the most important level for analysing and explaining foreign policy. According to Kenneth Waltz:

The third image [the systemic level] describes the framework of world politics, but without the first and second images there can be no knowledge of the forces that determine policy; the first and second images [the level of the individual and the level of the nation-state] describe the forces in world politics, but without the third image it is impossible to assess their importance or predict their results.

(Waltz 1959: 238)

The Level of the Nation-state

A comprehensive explanation of foreign policy would have to include the level of the nation-state as well as the level of the individual decision maker. One approach is to examine the relationship between a country's state apparatus and domestic society. For some realists, this relationship is important because it assesses the ability of a government to mobilize and manage the country's power resources.

Foreign policy is made not by the nation as a whole but by its government. Consequently, what matters is state power, not national power. State power is that portion of national power the government can extract for its purposes and reflects the ease with which central decision makers can achieve their ends.

(Zakaria 1998: 9)

According to this argument, the United States may be a very powerful nation, but national power may not be at the ready disposal of the government. For long historical periods, the US was a 'weak state' facing a 'strong society'. Consequently, the government was unable to conduct an expansive and more assertive foreign policy that matched the actual power resources of the country (see Box 10.2).

This realist analysis indicates that it is not sufficient to examine the overall or systemic distribution of power. It is also necessary to examine the connection between a country's

---

BOX 10.2	Fareed Zakaria on the US as a 'weak state'

The decades after the Civil War saw the beginning of a long period of growth in America's material resources. But this national power lay dormant beneath a weak state, one that was decentralized, diffuse, and divided. The presidents and their secretaries of state tried repeatedly to convert the nation's rising power into influence abroad, but they presided over a federal state structure and a tiny central bureaucracy that could not get men or money from the state governments or from society at large . . . The 1880s and 1890s mark the beginnings of the modern American state, which emerged primarily to cope with the domestic pressures generated by industrialization . . . This transformation of state structure complemented the continuing growth of national power, and by the mid-1890s the executive branch was able to bypass Congress or coerce it into expanding American interests abroad. America's resounding victory in the Spanish–American War crystallized the perception of increasing American power . . . America expanded dramatically in the years that followed.

Zakaria (1998: 10–11)

government and its society in order to properly assess the government's ability to mobilize and extract resources from society for foreign policy purposes (e.g., military expenditures, foreign aid) (see McCormick (ed.) 2012). Unlike realists, liberals believe that individuals, groups, and organizations in society play an important role in foreign policy (see Chapter 4). They not only influence or frustrate the government; they also conduct international relations (or 'foreign policies') in their own right by creating transnational relations that are an important element in international interactions between countries. Sociological liberals argue that international relations conducted by governments have been 'supplemented by relations among private individuals, groups, and societies that can and do have important consequences for the course of events' (Rosenau 1980: 1). Interdependence liberals note that international relations are becoming more like domestic politics, where 'different issues generate different coalitions, both within governments and across them, and involve different degrees of conflict. Politics does not stop at the water's edge' (Keohane and Nye Jr 1977: 25; see also Chapter 4). According to these liberals, then, it is too narrow to consider foreign policy as exchanges between state elites from different countries; the complex networks of relations between societies must enter the picture as well.

Another important liberal theory of foreign policy stems from republican liberalism. As explained in Chapter 4, the claim is that foreign policies conducted between liberal democracies are more peaceful and law-abiding than are foreign policies involving countries that are not liberal democracies. This can be seen as a liberal theory of foreign policy: liberal democracies are based on political cultures that stem from peaceful conflict resolution. That leads to pacific relations with other democracies because democratic governments are controlled by citizens who will not advocate or support wars with other democracies. The processes of democratization that took place in many countries at the end of the Cold War renewed the intense debate about the liberal theory of democratic peace. Some critics claim that on the one hand, early processes of democratization may lead to more, rather than less, conflict in the country (Vorrath and Krebs 2009); other critics argue that there are serious flaws in the theoretical logic, according to which liberal democracy leads to more peaceful behaviour in foreign policy (Hegre 2014).

We should thus take note of a general difference in the approach of realists and liberals when it comes to foreign policy analysis focusing on the nation-state level. Realists most often see the state (i.e., the government) as a robust, autonomous unit, capable—at least most of the time—of extracting resources from society and imposing its will on society. Therefore, the analysis of foreign policy should first and foremost focus on government of the state. Liberals, by contrast, most often see the state as a relatively weak entity which follows the bidding of strong groups in society. As noted by Andrew Moravcsik, foreign policy reflects and follows the preferences of different combinations of groups and individuals in domestic society (see Chapter 4). Foreign policy analysis should therefore concentrate on how different groups in society not only influence, but also even preside over, the formulation of foreign policy. In both cases, the relationship between state and society plays a role in the analysis of foreign policy; but the realist approach is state-centred whereas the liberal approach is society-centred (see web links 10.20 and 10.21).

One major example of corporations influencing government is what President Eisenhower called 'the military industrial complex' in his farewell speech in 1961. Eisenhower said:

In the councils of government we must guard against the acquisition of unwarranted influence, whether sought or unsought, by the military industrial complex. The potential for the disastrous rise of misplaced power exists and will persist. We must never let the weight of this combination endanger our liberties or democratic processes.

(Quoted from Eisenhower's farewell address at: www.pbs.org/wgbh/americanexperience/features/primary-resources/eisenhower-farewell accessed 20 March 2015)

In 2002, James Fallows claimed that 'the military–industrial complex has returned to the situation that worried Eisenhower: it doesn't matter whether weapons are used (or usable) as long as they are bought. The military budget is, of course growing rapidly' (Fallows 2002: 47).

The foregoing approaches at the nation-state level of analysis focus on different types of relationships between the state (government) and society. The approaches to which we now turn focus on the decision-making process within the state apparatus. They call into question whether decisions made by states are really based on 'rational choice'. According to rational choice, states are able to correctly identify foreign policy challenges and to make the best possible decisions in terms of benefits and costs, taking into account the goals and values of the state. This is the **Rational Actor Model (RAM)** of decision making in foreign policy (Allison and Zelikow 1999). Is this really the way states make decisions or is it more complicated than that?

The 'bureaucratic politics' approach rejects the idea of bureaucratic decision making as a rational process. Decision making in bureaucracies is much more a process in which individuals compete for personal position and power: 'the name of the game is politics: bargaining along regularized circuits among players positioned hierarchically within the government. Government behaviour can thus be understood . . . not as organizational outputs, but as results of these bargaining games' (Allison 1971: 144). A study by David Kozak and James Keagle (1988) has identified the core characteristics of the bureaucratic politics model (see Box 10.3).

Critics of the bureaucratic politics model claim that it goes too far in its non-rational view of bureaucratic decision making. Some scholars argue that decision making during crisis is less prone to bureaucratic politics because such decisions would be made at the top level by a few key decision makers with access to the best available information (see web link 10.39). The model also downplays the role of president in the American system. He/she is 'not just another player in a complex bureaucratic game. Not only must he ultimately decide but he also selects who the other players will be, a process that may be critical in shaping the ultimate decisions' (Holsti 2004: 24).

That brings us to the 'groupthink' approach. The term was coined by psychologist Irving Janis to describe a process by which a group arrives at faulty or irrational decisions. Janis defined groupthink as follows: 'a mode of thinking that people engage in when they

| BOX 10.3 | The bureaucratic politics model |

- Bureaucrats and bureaucracy are driven by agency interests in order to ensure their survival.
- Agencies are involved in a constant competition for various stakes and prizes. The net effect is a policy process whereby struggles for organizational survival, expansion and growth, and imperialism are inevitable.
- Competition produces an intra-agency bureaucratic culture and behaviour pattern. The axiom 'where you stand depends on where you sit' accurately describes this condition.
- Bureaucracies have a number of advantages over elected officials in the realm of policymaking. They include expertise, continuity, responsibility for implementation, and longevity. These characteristics create an asymmetrical power and dependence relationship between the professional bureaucrats and the elected officials.
- Policy made in the arena of bureaucratic politics is characterized by bargaining, accommodation, and compromise.
- In the bureaucratic politics system, proposals for change are driven by political considerations. Bureaucracies have a deep-seated interest in self-preservation.
- By its nature, bureaucratic politics raises questions concerning control, accountability, responsiveness, and responsibility in a democratic society.

Modified from a longer list in Kozak and Keagle (1988: 3–15)

are deeply involved in a cohesive in-group, when the members' strivings for unanimity override their motivation to realistically appraise alternative courses of action' (Janis 1982: 9). When groupthink occurs, the group fails to consider alternative ways to arrive at the best possible decision. When decisions are affected by groupthink, the following shortcomings occur: the objectives are not precisely defined; alternative courses of action are not fully explored; risks involved in the preferred choice are not scrutinized; the search for information is poor; the information is processed in a biased way; and there is a failure to work out contingency plans (Janis 1982). Janis identified eight primary characteristics of groupthink (Box 10.4).

Several major instances of groupthink involving United States foreign policy are identified by Janis: Pearl Harbor (the US naval commanding group believed that the Japanese would never risk attacking the US; the admiral in charge joked about the idea just before it happened); the Bay of Pigs invasion (the President Kennedy group convinced itself that Castro's army was weak and its popular support shallow; objections were suppressed or overruled); the Vietnam War (the President Johnson group focused more on justifying the war than on rethinking past decisions; dissenters were ridiculed). According to Janis, it is possible to devise a number of remedies that will avoid the negative consequences of groupthink and enhance the capabilities of groups for making better decisions (Janis 1982; see also Hart et al. 1997). The usefulness of knowing about groupthink is not only to better explain misguided foreign policies; it is to know how to avoid them next time.

BOX 10.4	**Characteristics of groupthink**

- Illusion of invulnerability: the group believes that its decision making is beyond question, which creates excessive optimism and extreme risk taking.
- Belief in the inherent morality of the group: members ignore the moral or ethical consequences of their decisions.
- Collective rationalization: the group discounts warnings that might have otherwise led them to reconsider their assumptions before they recommit to past policy decisions.
- Out-group stereotypes: others are framed as too evil or stupid to warrant consideration of their strategies or attempts to negotiate with them.
- Self-censorship: members feel inclined to avoid deviation from consensus, and minimize the significance of their doubts and counter-arguments.
- Illusion of unanimity: partly from the silence or self-censorship, members share the belief that they are unanimous in their judgements; silence means consensus.
- Direct pressure on dissenters: challenges or sanctioning comments are made to those who express strong arguments against the group's stereotypes, illusions, or commitments; loyal members do not bring up questions.
- Self-appointed 'mindguards': these members protect the group from adverse information that might threaten the shared illusions regarding the effectiveness or morality of the group's decisions.

Based on Janis (1982: 244)

The Level of the Individual Decision Maker

Just as bureaucracies or small groups may not always make decisions based on the RAM of decision making, this applies to the level of the individual decision maker as well. Human beings have limited capacities—cognitive constraints—for conducting rational and objective decision making. According to Ole Holsti,

the cognitive constraints on rationality include limits on the individual's capacity to receive, process, and assimilate information about the situation; an inability to identify the entire set of policy alternatives; fragmentary knowledge about the consequences of each option; and an inability to order preferences on a single utility scale.

(Holsti 2004: 27; see also Rosati 2000)

These limitations are connected to the way in which individuals perceive and process information. In Alexander George's summation:

every individual acquires during the course of development a set of beliefs and personal constructs about the physical and social environment. These beliefs provide him with a relatively coherent way of organizing and making sense of what would otherwise be a confusing and overwhelming array of signals and cues picked up from the environment . . . These beliefs and constructs necessarily simplify and structure the external world.

(George 1980: 57)

A recent analysis by Jerel Rosati suggests several ways in which human cognition (i.e., the process of acquiring knowledge by the use of reasoning, intuition, or perception) and policymaker beliefs matter (Box 10.5).

These effects can be expanded as follows (based on Rosati 2000):

1. The content of policymaker beliefs; an early study by Nathan Leite (1951) characterized the belief system of the Soviet Communist elite as an 'operational code' consisting of 'philosophical beliefs' steering the diagnosis of the situation, and 'instrumental beliefs' framing the search for courses of action. Stephen Twing (1998) has explained how American cultural myths and traditions helped structure the world views and decision-making styles of John Foster Dulles, Averell Harriman, and Robert McNamara during the Cold War. Robert Axelrod and others studied the 'cognitive complexity' of international decision making by tracing the influence of foreign policy beliefs in relation to specific issues (Eagly and Chaiken 1993).

2. Organization and structure of policymaker beliefs: the belief systems of policymakers can vary; some are coherent and comprehensive while others are fragmented and sketchy. The latter type is prone to 'uncommitted thinking': decision makers who are 'beset with uncertainty and sitting at the intersection of a number of information channels, will tend at different times to adopt *different* belief patterns for the same decision problem' (Steinbrunner 1974: 136). Jimmy Carter, for example, was prone to 'uncommitted thinking', while experienced American foreign policy advisers such as Zbigniew Brzezinski and Cyrus Vance displayed coherent belief systems (Rosati 2000: 58).

3. Common patterns of perception (and misperception): there are several ways in which perception patterns can lead to biased views; one is the creation of a stereotype image of the opponent. Ole Holsti (1967) showed how John Foster Dulles held a hostile image of the Soviet Union during the Cold War, 'regardless of changes in Soviet

---

BOX 10.5	The effects of human cognition and policymaker beliefs on foreign policy

1. through the content of policymaker beliefs
2. through the organization and structure of policymaker beliefs
3. through common patterns of perception (and misperception)
4. through cognitive rigidity (and flexibility) for change and learning.

Quoted from Rosati (2000: 53)

behaviour. Dulles rejected information that was inconsistent with his "inherent bad faith image" of Moscow' (Rosati 2000: 60). Engaging in wishful thinking is another source of bias. During the Vietnam War, American policymakers were convinced that the US could not lose the war; that overconfidence led them down the path of increased entanglement and difficulty in South East Asia.

4. Cognitive rigidity (and inflexibility) for change and learning: deeply held images and beliefs tend to be resistant to change. In a review of Henry Kissinger's foreign policy beliefs, Harvey Starr demonstrated very considerable stability in their content over a lengthy period. When core convictions do change, they are most likely to do so following big shocks and setbacks. Mikhail Gorbachev's 'new thinking' emerged in a period of severe Soviet political and economic crisis. American leaders' image of Japan changed dramatically after the attack on Pearl Harbor. American elite views of the United States' role in world affairs were strongly affected by the Vietnam War (Holsti and Rosenau 1984).

When we study the general effects of systemic structures or domestic pressures on decision makers, the usual assumption we make is that of rationality, as emphasized by Robert Keohane: 'The link between system structure and actor behaviour is forged by the rationality assumption, which enables theorists to predict that leaders will respond to the incentives and constraints imposed by their environments' (Keohane 1986: 167). The literature on human cognition and belief systems raises important questions which should increase our scepticism about the rationality premise in foreign policy analysis:

Because the existence of threats depends on the perceptions of individuals and societies, we need to incorporate the psychological dimension of threat perception and identity formation into our more structural analyses . . . The growing attention given by neorealists to perceptual variables, the examination by neoliberals of the role of ideas, and the social constructivist focus on identity, all suggest that models operating at other levels of analysis could be strengthened by incorporating work operating at the psychological level.

(Goldgeier 1997: 164–5)

At the same time, taking the road of 'cognition' instead of that of 'rationality' also has a potential downside. Even a somewhat comprehensive study of human cognition in world politics raises an extremely large and complex research agenda that will be very time-consuming both in terms of collecting information and in terms of analysis. Furthermore,

there is a danger that adding levels of analysis may result in an undisciplined proliferation of categories and variables. It may then become increasingly difficult to determine which are more or less important, and ad hoc explanations for individual cases erode the possibilities for broader generalization across cases.

(Holsti 2004: 31–2)

However, many scholars are confident about the possibility of combining different theories and modes of analysis in an attempt to bring together insights from competing approaches. The following section introduces a study that attempts to do just that.

Going to War in the Persian Gulf: A Case-study

On 2 August 1990, Iraq invaded the small neighbouring state of Kuwait; four days later, the country was annexed as Iraq's nineteenth province. The United States and many other states feared that Iraq would next invade oil-rich Saudi Arabia. UN resolutions condemned the invasion and demanded Iraq's unconditional withdrawal from Kuwait. Five months of negotiations led nowhere. The only option remaining was war. A US-led military campaign to expel Iraq from Kuwait was launched in mid-January 1991. By the end of February, Iraq had been forced to withdraw from Kuwait.

Why did the United States decide to go to war in the Persian Gulf? (See web links 10.55, 10.56, and 10.66.) In an attempt to address that question, Steve A. Yetiv (2004) demonstrates how a combination of three different theoretical perspectives is necessary to arrive at a more comprehensive answer: the RAM; the groupthink model; and the cognitive model. They parallel the three different levels of analysis introduced above. The baseline model in Yetiv's analysis is the RAM, which views the United States as a unitary actor driven by its national interests; it also assumes that the decisions made by the US are based on rational choice. The explanation of how and why the United States went to war from an RAM perspective is summarized in Box 10.6.

The RAM model highlights the strategic interaction between the US and Iraq and plausibly explains why going to war was ultimately unavoidable. But there are also elements that leave us in the dark, and assumptions that are not questioned. RAM is clearly premised on a realist model of the international system; it is characterized by anarchy and self-help; therefore, war is always a possibility. This would appear entirely plausible in the present case; but, as noted in Table 10.1, there are different conceptions of the international system that can lead to different ideas about the systemic pressures on states. We cannot fully know

---

BOX 10.6	Applying the RAM perspective

The argument is that the United States perceived itself as having vital national interests in the Persian Gulf. In order to protect them, it tried to consider and exhaust diplomatic and economic alternatives to war. It faced an intransigent Iraqi regime, and over time believed that the costs of waiting for sanctions to work increasingly exceeded the benefits. Therefore, taking into consideration Iraq's behaviour in the crisis, and its continuing threat even if it had withdrawn from Kuwait, Washington came to see war as necessary. While Iraq may or may not have reached a similar conclusion, it was also the case that the two sides could not locate or agree upon a negotiated settlement, because their bargaining positions did not overlap very much, if at all. This further inclined the United States towards war. Furthermore, the structural condition of anarchy in international relations enforced this logic. In their strategic interaction, the United States could not trust Iraq to withdraw from Kuwait and not to invade it at a later time, and Iraq could not trust the United States not to attack or harass it, if it agreed to withdraw.

Quoted from Yetiv (2004: 32–3)

whether the decision makers were driven by a realist understanding of the international system until we open up the 'black box' of 'The United States' and further scrutinize their reflections. Nor can we know whether the process of decision making was fully rational, as the RAM model assumes. Were all possible alternative options to the war decision carefully identified and meticulously examined before the decision was taken? In order to know about this, other theoretical perspectives that further investigate the process of decision making are necessary.

The *cognitive model* focuses on the individual key decision maker, in this case President George Herbert Walker Bush. Why did he frequently employ emotional rhetoric against Saddam Hussein? What made him emphatically reject any compromise with Saddam? Why did he tend to prefer the war option ahead of his advisers? Yetiv's application of the cognitive approach focuses on the importance of historical analogies: 'how decision makers create their own images of reality and simplify decision making through the use of analogies' (Yetiv 2004: 99). In the Gulf War case, the most important historical analogy for President Bush was that of Munich, as explained in Box 10.7.

The cognitive model highlights aspects of the US war decision that are not accounted for in the RAM perspective. The notion of historical analogy helps explain why President Bush strongly preferred the war option and rejected compromise with Saddam. Did the strong reliance on historical analogy lead Bush towards acting in a non-rational way? That need not be the case; analogical thinking can help identify the nature of the problem at hand and inform the search for possible courses of action. However, such thinking can also 'undermine rational processes if it introduces significant biases, excludes or restricts the search for novel information, or pushes actors to ignore the facts and options that clash with the message encoded in the analogy' (Yetiv 2004: 61). Did that happen in the Gulf War case? Yetiv's analysis leaves the question open; on the one hand, the analogy supported the efforts of rational thinking; on the other hand, Bush also used the analogy 'to construct the crisis, so

---

BOX 10.7   Applying the cognitive perspective

For Bush, compromising with Saddam, as many wanted at home and abroad, would have made him a modern-day Neville Chamberlain. As Britain's Prime Minister, Chamberlain yielded to Germany the Sudetenland of Czechoslovakia at the 1938 Munich conference, a borderland area of German speakers that Hitler wanted to reintegrate into Germany. Chamberlain, duped by Hitler, believed that his action at Munich, which followed repeated efforts by Britain to appease Nazi Germany, would bring what he called 'peace in our time'. In fact, Hitler proceeded to seize Czechoslovakia and to invade Poland, forcing a change in British policy and creating the Munich analogy, which referred to the failure of appeasement in the face of brutal aggression. Through the Munich lens, Bush tended to see Saddam as a Hitler-like dictator who could not be accommodated or even offered a minor, veiled carrot . . . The analogy made Bush more likely to personalize the conflict with Saddam, to undermine others' efforts at compromise with Saddam, and to prefer war to the continued use of economic sanctions.

Quoted from Yetiv (2004: 61)

that we could say that the analogy was both heartfelt by a president who experienced World War II and used to advance the war option' (Yetiv 2004: 158).

The groupthink model emphasizes critical elements of small-group behaviour that can lead to defective decision making. Two overlapping groups are of interest in the Gulf War case: an inner group of four that consisted of President George Bush, Vice President Dan Quayle, National Security Adviser Brent Scowcroft, and Chief-of-Staff John Sununu. An outer group of eight comprised the group of four plus Secretary of State James Baker, Secretary of Defence Richard Cheney, Chairman of the Joint Chiefs-of-Staff Colin Powell, and Deputy National Security Adviser Robert Gates. Yetiv's analysis seeks to demonstrate that the conditions promoting groupthink were present and they did lead to defective decision making in the sense that alternative courses to the war option were not given greater consideration. The elements of groupthink in the Gulf War case are set forth in Box 10.8.

This section has briefly demonstrated how different analytical perspectives can be brought together and yield insights into a case-study of why the United States chose to go to war in the Persian Gulf in 1991. The RAM is the most general and comprehensive approach. It takes in the challenges to US national interests raised by the Iraqi invasion of Kuwait; it posits how the strategic interaction between Iraq and the US inclined the United States towards going to war. Other approaches are less comprehensive; even so, each of them contributes significantly towards understanding why the war option was preferred over other options. Additional perspectives that will yield other insights can be applied; they will generate further information about the case. Scholars will not agree on any 'best combination' of approaches; some will find that the RAM really tells us enough about the case because it examines the challenge to the US presented by Saddam and accounts for why the war option was the response to that challenge. Others might argue that we must include the nation-state level and the level of the individual decision maker to achieve a full analysis.

By way of conclusion: it may be worth remembering that many foreign policy decisions and actions are taken in circumstances of uncertainty and with imperfect knowledge. Foreign policy is more prone to uncertainty and more exposed to instability and conflict

---

BOX 10.8   Applying the groupthink approach

The exclusive nature of the group of eight and the rejection of methodical decision-making procedures both contributed to groupthink and made it easier for Bush and Scowcroft to advance the war option without carefully considering the costs and benefits of other alternatives. The group of eight had slowly coalesced, behind its strong and partial group leader, around the notion that economic sanctions would fail . . . Bush insisted on that decision ahead of most of his advisers, and it was adopted without consulting the most senior US generals and admirals, including Powell, who was disturbed by it, and Schwarzkopf, who was furious about it. [Chas W.] Freeman [US ambassador to Saudi Arabia], who played a fundamental role with Schwarzkopf in the field and was in communication with Washington, asserted his view that 'the record will show that a lot of issues were not fully discussed'.

Quoted from Yetiv (2004: 118)

than is domestic policy, which is carried out under the jurisdiction of a sovereign government that possesses the legal authority to preside over domestic society. Not only that: many of the issues and problems that foreign policymakers have to come to grips with are in motion, in flux, and that too will introduce uncertainties and difficulties. Rarely, if ever, can there be 'correct' or 'incorrect' foreign policies known to the policymakers at the time. Usually, that knowledge only becomes evident in retrospect. The foregoing difficulties of the subject should perhaps make us sceptical of analytical models that claim to provide definitive accounts of foreign policy decision making.

A Note on Experts and 'Think Tanks'

Foreign policy has prompted a great deal of interest and research, much of it directed at influencing and possibly improving the foreign policy process and goals of countries. Over the past century many so-called think tanks have been established with that aim in mind (see web links 10.58 and 10.59). These are organizations that disseminate useful information and provide expert advice on international issues and problems. It is important to know about them because they have entered into the foreign policy process in many countries, especially the United States, where their influence is widely registered. They supplement conventional policymaking organizations, such as foreign ministries, departments of defence, ministries of foreign trade and commerce, and so forth. Some think tanks have the status and standing of annexes to government ministries and departments. The Rand Corporation, a well-known American think tank, is a highly trusted policy unit of the United States Department of Defense.

Some of the most important think tanks are private organizations engaged in developing and marketing foreign policy ideas and strategies with a view to shaping public opinion and influencing government policy. Many of the leading experts on foreign policy are members of these organizations rather than regular university departments of international relations. In the United States, such experts have a prominent role as public intellectuals. Included among them at the present time would be Ivo Daalder, Robert Kaplan, Thomas Friedman, Michael Hirsh, Samantha Power, Jonathan Schell, Benjamin Barber, and Fareed Zakaria (see web links 10.60–10.66). It is possible to build a successful career in foreign policy analysis entirely in the private sector outside of both government bureaus and university departments.

The first foreign policy think tanks emerged in the early part of the twentieth century in the United States. They reflected the desire of the leading American philanthropists and public intellectuals of that time to create institutions where scholars and leaders could meet to discuss and debate international issues with a view to solving them or at least addressing them more effectively than in the past. Three institutions from that period are particularly significant: the Carnegie Endowment for International Peace (1910) which was established by steel tycoon Andrew Carnegie; the Hoover Institution on War, Revolution and Peace (1919) founded by Herbert Hoover, later US president; and the Council on Foreign Relations

(1921) which evolved into one of the most respected foreign policy institutes in the world (see web link 10.67). There are approximately 2,000 think tanks in the United States alone. Most are affiliated with universities, but perhaps as many as 500 are private organizations. Major American think tanks such as the American Enterprise Institute, the Brookings Institute, the Rand Corporation, and the Council on Foreign Relations, among others, have substantial numbers of staff, sometimes running into hundreds, and budgets running into many millions of dollars (Box 10.9).

The United States is home to some of the most distinguished foreign policy institutes. But over the past century, think tanks have also been established in many other countries. Of these, the best known is Britain's Royal Institute of International Affairs (Chatham House) which was founded around the same time as its US counterparts (1920). Foreign policy organizations of similar vintage are the Canadian Institute of International Affairs (1928) and the Australian Institute of International Affairs (1933). These organizations were supposed to generate and disseminate practical knowledge of how to bring an end to the problems of war and how to institute peace on a more permanent foundation. The historical context of their formation was the misery and destruction caused by the First World War.

More foreign policy think tanks were established after the Second World War in Europe and beyond. A few of the more noteworthy include the German Institute for International and Security Affairs (1962), the Stockholm International Peace Research Institute (1966), the French Institute of International Relations (1979), the Japanese Institute for International Policy Studies (1988), the Netherlands Cicero Foundation on European Integration (1992), the Danish Institute for International Studies (1995), and the Indian Institute of Peace and Conflict Studies (1996). Such organizations deal with a remarkable diversity of foreign policy issues, including: defence and strategy; terrorism; human rights; global poverty; European integration; peace research; regional conflicts; international trade, energy, science, and technology; social policy; and much else besides.

What differentiates leading American think tanks from their counterparts in other parts of the world is the readiness of government policymakers to turn to them for policy advice and often to follow that advice. Foreign policy expertise has high visibility and prestige. It is the opportunity and ability to participate in policymaking that leads some scholars to conclude that US think tanks have greater impact on public policy than those of most other countries. Immediately following the terrorist attacks on New York and Washington, policy experts from some of America's leading foreign policy institutes appeared prominently in the mass media to offer their thoughts and advice. Some think tanks used the event as an opportunity to market ideas to policymakers and the public (see web links 10.41 and 10.42). That is only one example of the expertise that exists in the United States for dealing with foreign policy issues and problems.

After the Second World War, and faced with responsibilities of being the pre-eminent world power, decision makers in Washington sought the advice of experts who could help them to create a new security strategy that could come to terms with the emerging threat from the Soviet Union. They turned to think tanks for expertise, and they particularly found what they were looking for in the new Rand Corporation. It was formed in 1948, by means of government funds, to develop US security policies at the dawn of the nuclear age. It took

BOX 10.9   Foreign policy think tanks

THE CARNEGIE ENDOWMENT—UNITED STATES

The Carnegie Endowment for International Peace was established in 1910 in Washington, DC, with a gift from Andrew Carnegie. As a tax-exempt operating (not grant-making) foundation, the endowment conducts programmes of research, discussion, publication, and education in international affairs and US foreign policy. The endowment also publishes the quarterly magazine *Foreign Policy*.

COUNCIL ON FOREIGN RELATIONS—UNITED STATES

The Council on Foreign Relations, established in 1921, is a non-profit, non-partisan membership organization that takes no position on issues but is dedicated to improving the understanding of international affairs and American foreign policy through the free exchange of ideas.

FOREIGN POLICY INSTITUTE—TURKEY

FPI was founded in 1974 as an independent research organization to study issues related to Turkish foreign policy. Since its establishment, it has enlarged its activities to cover strategic and regional studies and international affairs.

FRENCH INSTITUTE OF INTERNATIONAL RELATIONS

Founded in 1979 by Thierry de Montbrial, the French Institute of International Relations—Institut français des relations internationals, or Ifri—is France's leading independent international relations centre dedicated to policy-oriented research and analysis of global political affairs.

GEORGE C. MARSHALL EUROPEAN CENTER FOR SECURITY STUDIES—UNITED STATES

Founded on 5 June 1993, the George C. Marshall European Center for Security Studies is dedicated to stabilizing and thereby strengthening post-Cold War Europe. Specifically, it aids defence and foreign ministries in Europe's aspiring democracies to develop national security organizations and systems that reflect democratic principles.

GERMAN COUNCIL ON FOREIGN RELATIONS

The German Council on Foreign Relations (DGAP) is Germany's national foreign policy network. As an independent, private, non-partisan, and non-profit organization, the council actively takes part in political decision making and promotes the understanding of German foreign policy and international relations.

INTERNATIONAL INSTITUTE FOR STRATEGIC STUDIES—UNITED KINGDOM

The International Institute for Strategic Studies (IISS), founded in 1958, is an independent centre for research, information, and debate on the problems of conflict, however caused, that have, or potentially have, an important military content. Its work is grounded in an appreciation of the various political, economic, and social problems that can lead to instability, as well as in factors that can lead to international cooperation.

NETHERLANDS INSTITUTE FOR INTERNATIONAL RELATIONS ('CLINGENDAEL')

This is the leading Dutch international affairs research organization. 'Special attention is devoted to European integration, transatlantic relations, international security, conflict studies, policymaking on national and international energy markets, negotiations and diplomacy, and to the United Nations and other international organizations.'

STOCKHOLM INTERNATIONAL PEACE RESEARCH INSTITUTE

The task of the Institute is to conduct research on questions of conflict and cooperation of importance for international peace and security, with the aim of contributing to an understanding of the conditions for peaceful solutions of international conflicts and for a stable peace.

a technical–scientific approach, was staffed by scientists and economists, and became famous for providing cost–benefit and rational choice analyses of foreign policy problems. Unlike earlier think tanks, which sought to influence and advise governments from outside, Rand was involved in the development of foreign policy on the inside of government. Rand ushered in a new generation of policy research institutions funded by government departments and agencies whose research was intended to address specific concerns of policymakers.

More recently a new kind of advocacy think tank began to appear in the United States as well as other countries. Unlike policy organizations of an earlier period, such as the Council on Foreign Relations—which was concerned to keep some distance from government—and unlike policy organizations such as Rand—which were directly involved with government in the making of policy—these later organizations were not concerned only to give policy advice or provide expertise. They were concerned with advocating policy doctrines and prescribing policy values which they were established to promote. Many human rights organizations are advocacy think tanks: Amnesty International is the most famous of them. Many environmental organizations are advocacy think tanks, Greenpeace being perhaps the most famous.

Some of the most noteworthy American advocacy think tanks on foreign policy are the Center for Strategic and International Studies (1962), the Heritage Foundation (1973), and the CATO Institute (1977). These organizations, and others like them, have given foreign policy studies a doctrinal and combative tone, especially evident in the mass media, which frequently invites opposing positions in op-ed newspaper articles or in live television interviews on current questions of US foreign policy.

 KEY POINTS

- Foreign policy analysis is a study of the management of external relations and activities of nation-states, as distinguished from their domestic policies. Foreign policy involves goals, strategies, measures, methods, guidelines, directives, understandings, agreements, and so on, by which national governments conduct international relations with each other and with international organizations and non-governmental actors.

- The relationship between theory and policy is complex, because any one theory does not necessarily lead to one clear policy option; in most cases there will be several different options. Even so, the choice of theory affects the choice of policy. That is partly because different theories emphasize different social values, as explained in Chapter 1.

- 'Multilevel, multidimensional'. Over the last two or three decades, it has become increasingly clear that there will never be one all-encompassing theory of foreign policy, just as there will never be one exclusive theory of IR. Many scholars now use the various major theories presented in Parts 2 and 3 of this book as approaches to study particular aspects of foreign policymaking. These major theories often contain implications for foreign policy or elements that are directly relevant for foreign policy.

- Bureaucratic structures and processes. This approach focuses on the organizational context of decision making, which is seen to be conditioned by the dictates and demands of the bureaucratic settings in which decisions are made. Analysing processes and channels whereby organizations arrive at their policies is seen to be a superior way to acquire empirical knowledge of foreign policy.

- Cognitive processes and psychology. This approach focuses on individual decision maker, paying particular attention to the psychological aspects of decision making.

- Social constructivists focus on the role of ideas and discourse, as recorded in Chapter 8. For constructivists, foreign policymaking is an intersubjective world, whose ideas and discourse can be scrutinized in order to arrive at a better theoretical understanding of the process.

- The usual situation facing foreign policymakers is one of having to choose between different possible courses of action. That raises two fundamental questions: what policy choices, if any, are available? Of those, what is the best course to follow? Responding to such questions takes us to the heart of foreign policymaking.

- The RAM approach indicates the challenges to US national interest raised by the Iraqi invasion of Kuwait; it posits how strategic interaction between Iraq and the US inclined the United States towards going to war against Iraq as leader of a military coalition.

- Despite the many approaches to foreign policy and levels of analysis outlined in this chapter, it remains an imperfect and controversial body of knowledge, where even the most knowledgeable experts are likely to disagree on vital issues.

? QUESTIONS

- What is foreign policy analysis fundamentally concerned with?

- Which is the best approach to foreign policy analysis, and why?

- Which level of foreign policy analysis makes most sense, and why?

- Should foreign policy be confined to foreign ministries or state departments (as realists and International Society scholars argue), or should it extend also to groups in society (as liberals argue)?

- How useful is the RAM approach for explaining why the United States chose to go to war in the Persian Gulf in 1991?

- Can theories or models of foreign policymaking be applied in making foreign policy decisions or can they only be used to explain those decisions after they have been made?

- Do the pressures and uncertainties of making foreign policy in reality and on the go require experienced policymakers, if they are to be successful?

- Several commentators complain that the West is doing 'too little' against the self-proclaimed Islamic State in Syria and Iraq in 2014. Is this true? Use some of the foreign policy theories from this chapter to explain Western motivations or hesitations.

→ GUIDE TO FURTHER READING

Alden, C. and Amnon, A. (2011). *Foreign Policy Analysis: New Approaches*. London: Routledge.

Beach, D. (2012). *Analyzing Foreign Policy*. Basingstoke: Palgrave Macmillan.

Carlsnaes, W. W. Carlsnaes, T. Risse, and B. Simmons (2013). 'Foreign Policy', in (eds), *Handbook of International Relations*, 2nd edn. London: Sage, 298–326.

Hill, C. (2003). *The Changing Politics of Foreign Policy*. Basingstoke: Palgrave Macmillan.

Ikenberry, G. J. (ed.) (2011). *American Foreign Policy: Theoretical Essays*, 6th edn. Boston, MA: Houghton Mifflin Harcourt.

McCormick, J. M. (ed.) (2012). *The Domestic Sources of American Foreign Policy: Insights and Evidence*. Lanham, MD: Rowman and Littlefield.

⊕ WEB LINKS

Web links mentioned in the chapter, together with additional material including a case-study on foreign policy in practice, can be found on the Online Resource Centre that accompanies this book.

www.oxfordtextbooks.co.uk/orc/jackson_sorensen6e/

Key Issues in Contemporary IR

▮ Summary

This chapter discusses four of the most important contemporary issues in IR: international terrorism; religion; the environment; and new patterns of war and peace. Some of these issues were evident earlier; but for several reasons they stand higher on the agenda today. The chapter further discusses the different ways in which these issues are analysed by the various theories presented in this book.

Introduction

This chapter discusses four of the most important issues raised by current events; we could have chosen other issues, but these are sufficient to illustrate how different issues can enter the discipline and challenge its theoretical focus. An issue in IR is a topic which is considered to be important in terms of both values and theory. Values come into the picture because the decision on what is important and what is not is always based on certain values. Theory comes in because arguing in favour of an issue must derive from some theoretical idea that this issue is important for the study of IR. For these reasons, raising new issues often involves new approaches to IR.

The discussion of issues will proceed in the following way. First, we shall examine what the issue is about in empirical terms. What are the problems raised and why are they claimed to be important? Second, we shall consider the relative significance of the issue on the agenda of IR. Finally, we shall discuss the nature of the theoretical challenge that the issues present to IR and the different ways in which classical and contemporary theories handle the analysis of these issues (Box 11.1).

We shall start with international terrorism, proceed to religion, the environment, and then new patterns of war and peace. The order of presentation is not an indication that one issue is more important than another. The introduction to concrete issues will necessarily have to be brief; the reader is urged to consult the guide to further reading at the end of the chapter for references to in-depth treatment of a particular issue.

International Terrorism

Terrorism is the unlawful use or threatened use of violence against civilians, often to achieve political, religious, or similar objectives. International terrorism involves the territory or the citizens of more than one country. Terrorism is nothing new; it has probably existed ever since human societies began to regulate the use of violence. It is the unusual scale and intensity of the 11 September 2001 attacks in New York and Washington, and later attacks in Ankara, Madrid, London, and elsewhere that has put the issue of international terrorism high on the agenda. It is an issue that concerns IR for obvious reasons; IR is not least about

BOX 11.1	Current issues in IR: international terrorism, religion, the environment, new patterns of war and peace

1. Concrete content of the issue: what is it we should study and why?

2. Relative significance of the issue: how important is it?

3. Nature of theoretical challenge: how is the issue handled by classical and contemporary approaches?

national and international security. When the only superpower in the international system, the United States, defined international terrorism as the first-rank threat to US security (National Security Strategy (NSS) 2002) and went on to launch a 'war on terror', the issue must rank high on the political and scholarly agenda.

The precise definition of terrorism raises several problems (Box 11.2); when two scholars asked a hundred individuals working in the field to define terrorism, the questionnaires yielded 109 definitions (Weinberg and Eubank 2008: 186) (see also web link 11.01). One controversy concerns the relationship between terrorism and other forms of political violence. Some think that there are legitimate forms of political violence which are not then terrorism. For example, one of the leaders of the Palestinian Fatah movement declared in 1973 that he was 'firmly opposed . . . to terrorism'; but he went on to add that 'I do not confuse revolutionary violence with terrorism, or operations that constitute political acts with others that do not' (Iyad 1983: 146).

Another controversy concerns the inclusion or not of state-sponsored terrorism in the definition. It is clear that states (for example, Saudi Arabia and the Soviet Union) have sponsored terrorism in a number of cases (Sluka 2000; Menjivar and Rodriguez 2005) (see web link 11.04). At the same time, the mass-murder terrorist attacks of recent years appear not to be directly supported by states, but that is of course not a strong argument for excluding states from the definition altogether. A final controversy concerns the term 'civilians'. Some find the term misleading because attacks on military personnel who are not on active duty should also be considered terrorism. For that reason, some prefer to use the term 'non-combatants' instead of 'civilians'.

Most terrorism is national; it is related to political struggles, most often in weak states where democratic politics is fragile or absent and incumbent leaders are considered illegitimate, such as in Colombia, Nepal, Sri Lanka, or Indonesia. In the weakest states, most of which are in sub-Saharan Africa, terrorism takes place in a context of more or less permanent civil war. However, more consolidated states have also had severe problems with terrorism, including Britain, France, India, Spain, Norway, and Argentina. Such terrorism is national because the enemy is national and often groups can fight as guerrillas, getting support from local sympathizers.

An upsurge in international terrorism, in the form of aircraft hijackings, took place from the late 1960s. Air travel had expanded significantly since the 1950s; there were no

---

BOX 11.2   UN Security Council definition of terrorism (2004)

Criminal acts, including those against civilians, committed with the intent to cause death or serious bodily injury, or taking of hostages, with the purpose to provoke a state of terror in the general public . . . intimidate a population or compel a government or an international organization to do or abstain from doing any act, which constitute offences within the scope of and as defined in the international protocols relating to terrorism, are under no circumstances justifiable by considerations of a political, philosophical, ideological, racial, ethnic, religious or other similar nature.

Quoted from Weinberg and Eubank (2008: 186)

effective security systems in airports; and the international media—in particular, television—provided extensive coverage that appealed to groups eager to send their messages to the world. The hijacking of airliners increased from five incidents in 1966 to ninety-four in 1969 (Kiras 2005: 483). Improved security measures helped in reducing hijacking, but international terrorism did not disappear. During the 1980s, there was an increased incidence of radical Muslim groups attacking American targets in Lebanon, Iran, Somalia, and elsewhere.

Such attacks continued after the end of the Cold War. International terrorism has become a phenomenon primarily connected with radical Muslim groups (see web links 11.03, 11.04, and 11.06). The best known of these groups or networks is al-Qaeda (The Base).

International terrorism has revived the spectre of physical security threat to states and civil societies in the OECD world. With the end of the Cold War, there was hope that this event would signal the end of war and large-scale violence altogether in these countries. Colin Powell made the point in 1991: 'I'm running out of demons. I'm running out of enemies. I'm down to Castro and Kim Il Sung'. The al-Qaeda attacks put national security in the sense of ordinary people's safety back on the agenda. The attacks of 9/11 helped create a great expansion of terrorism studies; a recent overview lists no less than one hundred journals relevant for terrorism research (Tinnes 2013). While it is true that most acts of terrorism take place in weak states in the global South, there are also weak states in the North with serious terrorism problems, as demonstrated in the dissolution of Yugoslavia and in the violent conflicts in Ukraine. In order to address the second question in Box 11.1, we need to evaluate the extent and gravity of the terrorist threat. The question is controversial; some think the threat is of no great concern; others argue that it is highly significant. Those who argue the former view claim that, in general terms, the scale of terrorist operations make them more like crime than like organized warfare. And just as crime has existed in most or all types of societies, terrorism 'has been around forever and will presumably continue to exist' (Mueller 2004: 199) without presenting existential threats to society.

At the same time, just as there can be organized crime, there can be organized terrorism. The al-Qaeda network is a case in point and the 11 September 2001 attacks were of unusual magnitude; during the entire twentieth century, 'fewer than twenty terrorist attacks managed to kill as many as 100 people, and none caused more than 400 deaths. Until [11 September], far fewer Americans were killed in any grouping of years by all forms of international terrorism than were killed by lightning' (Mueller 2004: 110).

From this view, it appears highly unlikely that terrorism as represented by al-Qaeda will grow into a large-scale threat to Western societies. While there are a great number of terrorist groups scattered around the world, especially in weak states, their ambitions remain national, not international; only very few move to become international terrorists. Second, al-Qaeda's kind of international terrorism is specifically connected to a radical, fundamentalist version of Islam which is not representative of Islam as such. Finally, those who think the terrorist threat is not so serious emphasize how the al-Qaeda network is specifically connected to marginalized Muslim groups of *Mujahedin* (fighters for Allah's cause) who joined together to fight against the Soviet occupation of Afghanistan and were able to use that country as a safe haven. These groups are not very large and they no longer have easy access to countries where they can set up bases.

However, it can also be argued that the threat of international terrorism is very serious. First of all, open, complex societies are necessarily vulnerable: there are limited possibilities for surveillance and control; suicide terrorists carrying forceful, low-tech bombs cannot easily be stopped. The London bomb attacks of 2005 demonstrated that Muslims with a relatively 'normal' background as citizens of the UK had been recruited for the assaults. This could be taken to mean that the potential recruiting base for terrorist actions is very large indeed; it is not merely confined to ex-Afghani *Mujahedins*; it also comprises self-selected members of local Muslim societies in the UK and other Western countries. The conflict in Syria and Iraq has involved some substantial recruitment of Muslim militants from Western countries. Furthermore, some commentators argue that the US–Western involvement in the war in Iraq leads to 'blowback terrorism', meaning that the war tends to increase, rather than decrease, the recruitment potential to international terrorism (Mann 2003: 159–93) (see web links 11.06 and 11.11).

Finally, there is the danger of international terrorists gaining access to and using weapons of mass destruction (WMD); that is, chemical, biological, and nuclear weapons. It is clear that terrorist groups have incentives to use WMD; they would be able to create massive destruction and fear, and that would possibly elevate the groups to a new power position vis-à-vis their adversaries (Schmid 2005). A 2004 study by Graham Allison argued that a nuclear attack by terrorists on America was more likely than not in the decade ahead (Allison 2004). If policymakers take immediate countermeasures, such an attack is 'preventable'. If they do not, says Allison, the attack is 'inevitable' (Box 11.3). Meanwhile, other commentators consider it less likely that terrorists can gain access to and will use WMD (Pearlstein 2004); the barriers to entry in terms of getting hold of materials and the competence required to use them remain significant (see web link 11.19).

What can we conclude about the terrorist threat? The question is not easy; no doubt people in Western metropolitan areas such as London, New York, or Madrid will be more worried about the threat than many others, and understandably so. On the one hand, the threat is not an overriding, existential menace to the states and civil societies of the world;

BOX 11.3	**Graham Allison on nuclear terrorism**

First, thefts of weapons-usable material and attempts to steal nuclear weapons are not a hypothetical possibility, but a proven and recurring fact.

Second, . . . the only high hurdle to creating a nuclear bomb is access to fissionable material . . . as John Foster, a leading American bomb maker . . . wrote a quarter century ago, 'if the essential nuclear materials are at hand, it is possible to make an atomic bomb using information that is available in the open literature'.

Third, terrorists would not find it difficult to smuggle such a nuclear device into the United States. The nuclear material in question is smaller than a football.

Allison (2004: 9–11)

on the other hand, the threat is real and must be taken seriously. The International Institute of Strategic Studies (IISS) said that

> groups and others inspired by bin Laden still pose a clear threat to public security and a challenge to law enforcement and intelligence agencies. Al-Qaeda may be increasingly dependent on local groups and subject to dispersing impulses, but it remains a viable transnational terrorist organization.

IISS (2004: 1)

The death of Osama bin Laden was a blow against al-Qaeda, but some observers argue that the immediate effect is an increased terrorist threat (see web link 11.18).

Let us turn to the third question in Box 11.1: the theoretical challenge posed by the issue of international terrorism. On first impression, existing theories of IR would appear to be well suited to deal with international terrorism. It is a security threat, and security problems are at the heart of the realist approach. Liberals identify terrorist groups as a set of non-state actors that substantially influence the international agenda. IPE theorists study the political economy of international terror (Porpora 2011). In short, existing approaches would appear to be able to handle the issue very well.

However, a closer look reveals a different picture. Realism is focused on security threats *between states*. Non-state actors, such as international terrorist groups, often tend to be ignored by realists, because compared with states, they are considered insignificant. One outspoken realist, Colin Gray, simply says that transnational terrorism is 'pretty small beer' (see Box 11.4). Assessment of terrorist threats clearly depends on one's perspective. Another well-known realist, John Mearsheimer, admitted that realism does not have 'much to say about the causes of terrorism' (Mearsheimer 2002); furthermore, terrorists are non-state actors and realists do not have much to say about them either. That said, Mearsheimer also maintained that because terrorism plays out in the state arena, realism and terrorism are 'inextricably linked' (Mearsheimer 2002).

According to one commentator, this realist view explains why the Bush administration was slow to react in spite of warnings before 11 September 2001. Condoleezza Rice and other top members of the George W. Bush administration were realists. Rice's understanding of international relations was 'state-centric'. 'Her policy ends [were] filtered through

---

BOX 11.4	**International terrorism: a realist view**

[I]t seems improbable that transnational actors such as al-Qaeda will shape the (in)security environment for decades to come. Compared with the unpleasantness in Indo-Pakistani relations, the ambition of China to be sovereign throughout maritime east Asia, and the determination of Russia to regain positions of authority by the imperial marches lost in 1991, transnational terrorism is pretty small beer. Geopolitics, not transnationalisms (including 'civilizations'), shapes the mainstream of historical events.

Gray (2002: 231)

national self-interests. Her privileged means [were] military. And her self-understanding of world events was demarcated by a clear division between international and domestic realms' (Klarevas 2004: 21). Furthermore, when realists react to the terrorist threat, they have a tendency to *territorialize* it. That is, given their focus on interstate relations, realists are compelled to believe that international terrorist groups 'can flourish only with some significant measure of official state acquiescence, if not necessarily state sponsorship' (Gray 2002: 231).

In other words, realists tend to translate the terrorist threat into a threat from another state; and some of them tend to think that the response to such threat must be by way of military force. However, there is no necessary link between a realist view of the world and a commitment to the 'war on terror'. John Mearsheimer argues that:

what the United States wants to do is not rely too heavily on military force—in part, because the target doesn't lend itself to military attack, but more importantly, because using military force in the Arab and Islamic world is just going to generate more resentment against us and cause the rise of more terrorists and give people cause to support these terrorists. So I'd privilege diplomacy much more than military force in this war, and I think the Bush administration would be wise if it moved more towards diplomacy and less towards force.

(Mearsheimer interview 2002: http://globetrotter.berkeley.edu/people2/Mearsheimer)

Liberals, by contrast, appreciate non-state actors. Therefore, they are more ready to accept that international terrorist groups claim priority on the international agenda. At the same time, liberals are more ready to emphasize the need for international cooperation in facing the terrorist threat. Joseph Nye says that 'the best response to transnational terrorist networks is networks of cooperating government agencies' (Nye Jr 2003: 65). He may certainly be right; yet the remark also discloses a liberal leaning towards problem solving via cooperation.

World systems analysis inspired by Immanuel Wallerstein (Chapter 6) has another take on international terrorism. The idea is that this kind of terrorism is connected to systemic factors, in particular to the rise and decline of leading states in the world system. The leading state, the United States, is currently under pressure and that opens it to more activity by terrorist actors: 'if terrorist activity is aided by breakdowns in the system's normative and political order structure, then some forms of terrorism may be more likely when the system is undergoing transition or the system leader is in a state of decline' (Lizardo 2008: 109). Globalization, involving closer integration among states and technological advances in communication and transportation, has also pushed the expansion of international terrorism.

Poststructuralist analysis has noted the different perceptions of terrorism in the realist and the liberal discourse on the subject. The claim is that an analysis of the discourse on terrorism is an important element in understanding the way Western societies approach the terrorist threat (see Box 11.5.)

Scholars sceptic of the mainstream approaches to the analysis of terrorism call for the strengthening of 'critical terrorism studies' (Gunning 2007; Jackson 2007). They charge that mainstream analyses are too closely tied in with government agencies and that puts

BOX 11.5	Post-structuralist analysis: the discourse on terror

. . . terrorism is a social construction. The terrorist actor is a product of discourse, and hence dis-course is the logical starting point for terrorism research . . . Hence [we] suggest a shift of per-spective in terrorism studies—from an actor-centred to a discourse-centred perspective. [We] develop a discourse approach that emphasizes the crucial role of metaphors in the making of reality . . . Terrorism was first constituted as war, but from 2004 onwards the principal metaphor shifted from war to crime, constructing Al-Qaeda as a criminal rather than a military organization. This shift has transformed Al-Qaeda from an external to an internal threat, which has entailed a shift in counter-terrorism practices from a military to a judicial response.

Hülsse and Spencer (2008: 571)

limitations on their work. Other scholars are not convinced (Weinberg and Eubank 2008). These debates indicate that terrorism studies are coming of age as a field in their own right with discussions between different approaches. This can be considered 'a perfectly normal process of evolution' (Weinberg and Eubank 2008: 188) of a new field of study.

In sum, several approaches can provide important insights in the analysis of international terrorism. Each perspective also tends to 'shape' the issue so it fits into the particular theo-retical point of view. As IR analysts, we need to evaluate the relative merits of each approach. As indicated, this evaluation is only possible if we also assess the larger question of the character and magnitude of the terrorist threat.

Religion in IR: A Clash of Civilizations?

Many scholars argue that the events of 11 September 2001 signal a 'resurgence of religion' in international affairs. In other words, the claim is that there is an 'increasing importance of religious beliefs, practices, and discourses in personal and public life' (Thomas 2005: 26) and this has significant implications for international relations (see web links 11.41 and 11.45).

Religion and politics were deeply integrated in earlier days, as explained in Chapter 1. Medieval authority was dispersed among a hierarchy of religious rulers on the one hand, and political rulers on the other; they often competed for power and influence. The Pope not merely ruled the Church through a hierarchy of bishops and other clergy, but he also oversaw political disputes between kings and other semi-independent rulers. Members of the clergy were often advisers to kings and other secular rulers. The Thirty Years War in Europe (1618–48) pitted Protestant against Catholic across the continent; when it ended with the Peace of Westphalia, a new, modern era heralded the liberation of European rulers from the religious–political authority of Christendom. Power and authority were concentrated at one point: the King and his government; in most countries, the Christian churches fell under state control. Religion did not disappear, of course; but religious beliefs were dispelled from public, political life. Religion became a private matter, separate from politics. Political rulers, on their part, agreed not to interfere in matters of religion in other countries.

The expulsion of religion from politics in the context of the modern sovereign state came to be a model for other parts of the world. Westerners tend to think of modernization as simultaneously involving secularization; that is to say, when new areas of the world embarked on the Western path of modernization, they would more or less automatically also become secular and proceed to separate religion from politics. According to sociologist José Casanova, the theory of secularization is so strong that it 'may be the only theory which was able to attain a truly paradigmatic status within the modern social sciences' (Casanova 1994: 17).

It is this claim of secularization that is being increasingly called into question. Religion never completely left the stage, not even in the Western world; it influences the political agenda in many countries, most notably the United States. Only a few years after Casanova's statement, another leading sociologist, Peter Berger, wrote (see web link 11.42) that:

the assumption that we live in a secularized world is false. The world today, with some exceptions to which I will come presently, is as furiously religious as it ever was, and in some places more so than ever. This means that a whole body of literature by historians and social scientists loosely labelled 'secularization theory' is essentially mistaken.

Berger (1999: 17)

Perhaps the most influential and well-known analysis emphasizing the continued importance and, indeed, resurgence of religion in politics is the 'Clash of Civilizations' thesis by Samuel Huntington (1993, 1996) (see web links 11.36 and 11.37). His central claim is summarized in Box 11.6.

Huntington speaks of 'civilizations', but at the core of a civilization is religion: 'To a very large degree, the major civilizations in human history have been closely identified with the world's great religions' (Huntington 1996: 42). Therefore, Huntington's statement is a

---

BOX 11.6   The 'clash of civilizations'

The fundamental source of conflict . . . will not be primarily ideological or primarily economic. The great divisions among humankind and the dominating source of conflict will be cultural. Nation states will remain the most powerful actors in world affairs, but the principal conflicts of global politics will occur between nations and groups of different civilizations. The clash of civilizations will dominate global politics. The fault lines between civilizations will be the battle lines of the future (Huntington 1993: 22).

The most important countries in the world come overwhelmingly from different civilizations. The local conflicts most likely to escalate into broader wars are those between groups and states from different civilizations . . . The key issues on the international agenda involve differences among civilizations (Huntington 1996: 29).

Quoted from Huntington (1993, 1996)

powerful assertion about the significant role of culture, meaning first and foremost religion, in international politics.

There are several ways of questioning Huntington's analysis. First, there is the idea of civilizations; is it possible to draw together a common religious–cultural pattern across a wide range of societies and thus identify them as 'civilizations'? Huntington is himself in doubt as to whether there is an African civilization, perhaps because he considers religion a central defining characteristic of civilizations and there is not a religion shared by all Africans. Confucianism is seen to lie at the heart of the Sinic civilization and that is not a religion in the ordinary meaning of the term. So, one major objection to the analysis is that the complex pattern of religions, cultures, and civilizations is not spelled out with great clarity; and if they were, it would not be possible to summarize those patterns in terms of general civilizational identities. Identities are much more diverse and religion is not necessarily the primary core, be it in Europe or China. Paul Berman argues that cultural boundaries are not sufficiently distinct to permit the designation of civilizations; he therefore rejects that there is an 'Islamic Civilization' or a 'Western Civilization' (Berger 2003).

Furthermore, Huntington identifies these civilizational qualities at the macro-level across larger periods of time. But in order to do that, it is necessary to ascribe primordial qualities to religious–cultural identifications. That is to say, what it means to be 'Islamic', 'Orthodox', or 'Hindu' is highly consistent over time; empires may 'rise and fall, governments come and go, civilizations remain' (Huntington 1996: 43). Such a claim of consistency over time does not fit the historical pattern; the exact qualities connected with religious–cultural labels are dynamic and not static. They have developed and changed dramatically over time; religious–cultural identities are always contested. What it means to be 'Islamic' or 'Hindu' or even 'Western' today is not the same as it was several decades ago and there continues to be intense debate within civilizations about basic values (see Box 11.7). In order to set civilizations in opposition to each other, they have to be attributed certain consistent qualities and that is not possible because there is too much diversity and dynamic change *within* civilizations.

These objections question the claim made by Huntington, that 'conflict between groups in different civilizations will be more frequent, more sustained and more violent than conflicts between groups in the same civilization' (Huntington 1993: 48). A systematic empirical analysis of militarized interstate disputes between 1950 and 1992 indicates that:

pairs of states split across civilizational boundaries are no more likely to become engaged in disputes than are other states *ceteris paribus* . . . Contrary to the thesis that the clash of civilizations will replace the Cold War rivalries as the greatest source of conflict, militarized interstate disputes across civilizational borders became less common, not more so, as the Cold War waned.

Russett et al. (2000: 583)

If the 'clash of civilizations' can be called off as the defining feature of post-Cold War world order, it raises the issue of valid insights in the analysis. Huntington would appear to be right in claiming that 'in the coming decades, questions of identity, meaning cultural heritage, language and religion, will play a central role in politics' (Huntington 2007).

BOX 11.7	The 'West' against 'Islam'? Not exactly

'Western' values are described as individualist, 'Asian' and 'Islamic' ones as collectivist. The Universal Human Rights Declarations and Covenants are . . . considered to be the paragon of an individualist [Western] culture . . . Here it is worthwhile reminding of several precursors of this debate. Before 1933 in Germany, 'Western *civilizational* values' that were regarded as 'superficial' had been contrasted with substantially different, profound *cultural* 'German values' . . . there was a similar discussion in Czarist Russia whose spokesmen could count on Germany's intellectual support.

The . . . assumption in declarations of fundamental rights that all men are born free and equal in dignity and rights was considered in the old Europe . . . a strangely deviant and absurd idea.

Advocates of Asian and Islamic values emphasize the rootedness of such values in centuries-old cultural traditions. But neither at the official nor at the unofficial level do Asians all along stand up for 'Asian' values. Not even in East and Southeast Asia where this debate started from do they agree . . . As far as 'Islamic' values are concerned, it is striking that they are maintained in the Arab–Iranian region especially. Here, prominent fundamentalist authors are at home . . . In contrast, a debate on reform-oriented Islam takes place mainly in Southeast Asia. This different emphasis in the discourses on Islam reflects the chronic crisis of development in North Africa and the Middle East on the one hand, and the relatively . . . successful development of Southeast Asia on the other.

Quoted from Senghaas (2007: 199, 2008: 8–9)

However, this is of course a much broader set of issues than the 'clash' which is focused narrowly on certain conflicts seen to involve civilizations. This broader religion and identity issue was also raised by Benjamin Barber; he used the label of 'jihad', but extended it to include all kinds of ethnic, religious, or tribal conflict (Barber 1995). Box 11.8 presents a summary of the ways in which religion influences politics (see web link 11.40).

Ethno-religious identities are often significant elements in violent conflict. After the end of the Cold War, the vast majority of armed conflicts have taken place *within* states rather than between states (see the section below on current patterns of conflict) (Themnér and Wallensteen 2013). If issues of religion, together with broader identity issues, play a more important role in IR, is the discipline theoretically equipped to handle the challenge? Some think not; Vendulka Kubálková proposes the foundation of a new paradigm, called International Political Theology (IPT); the aim of which is to analytically confront the resurgence of religion in IR (Kubálková 2003: 79–107, 2013). Others find that this is going much too far. The major theories in IR may not have focused specifically on religion, but that does not necessarily mean they have nothing to say about it.

Realism, for example, does not deny a role for religious beliefs or other ideological convictions in international affairs; classical realism focuses on human nature and the ways in which interests are defined. It is clear that religion can play an important role in this context, be it in Iran, India, or the United States. A classical realist such as Morgenthau (Chapter 3) emphasizes that politics is governed by laws which are rooted in human nature. Human nature provides an entry to the inclusion of religion in the analysis of international politics.

> ### BOX 11.8   A rise in the influence of religion on politics
>
> First, religious organizations are growing in their power to shape public debate and the policies of governments. The Hindu nationalist parties in India, Muslim movements in Turkey, Orthodox Christians in Russia, conservative Christians in America, ultra-Orthodox Jews and Orthodox Jewish nationalists in Israel, and evangelicals in Latin America have all come to exercise increasing influence over laws governing marriage, education, foreign policy toward favored groups and states, religious minorities, and the relationship between religion and the institutions of the state. Second, religious organizations exercise a transnational influence upon the politics of outside states . . . Jews in America provide strong direct support to Israel. Worldwide Islamic organizations like the Muslim Brotherhood provide social services in many nations, building loyal followings who then articulate Islamic politics, sometimes through violence. Third, even more powerfully, religion shapes not only the policies of states but also their very constitutions, thus becoming 'the law of the land'. This is most dramatic in the Muslim world, where, in an 'Islamic resurgence' over the past couple of decades, *sharia* has become public law in Iran, Sudan, Saudi Arabia, Pakistan, Malaysia, and twelve of Nigeria's thirty-six states . . . Most radical of all, religiously motivated groups are questioning the very legitimacy of the international order, the Westphalian synthesis, in all of its strands. The most influential of these are networks of Muslims who act on behalf of the unity of the *umma*, the people of Islam. Like al-Qaeda.
>
> Quoted from Philpott (2002: 86)

That is because religious convictions are part of human nature and thus influences the actors that pursue power and interest on behalf of states, sometimes in decisive ways. Morgenthau himself was a deeply religious person, and the renewed interest in religion in international affairs has sparked another round of reflection on the writings of Morgenthau and other classical realists in order to reassess their views on the role of religion (Sandal and James 2011) (see box 11.9)

As regards neorealism, the accommodation of religion is less easy. Neorealists would argue that in an anarchical world security concerns come first: 'states have a hierarchy of interests: security at the top, but then economic welfare, ideological and humanitarian

> ### BOX 11.9   Classical realism and religion
>
> In short, Morgenthau's and Niebuhr's broad interpretations of power and interest . . . is good news for scholars who are interested in using cultural variables in the framework of realism . . . Morgenthau's understanding of politics as captured in classical realism is a 'moral and political' project in addition to an analytic device. Niebuhr's linkage of human nature to state of conflict via will-to-power and the tendency of society to ignore moral considerations also allows classical realist investigations of behavior as well as issues of interpretation of the divine. Therefore, religion can be easily integrated into this strand of realism both as an independent and as an intervening variable.
>
> Quoted from Sandal and James (2011: 11–12)

concerns in descending order' (Desch 1998: 160). In other words, when survival is at stake, religious convictions cannot be the top concern; yet, in many situations, survival is not at stake, and that leaves more room for religious matters (Barnett 1996; Bellin 2008). When the Cold War ended, for example, and the Soviet Union folded, the United States became a power strong enough not to be constrained by the international system: no other state, or combination of states, could mount a serious threat against the survival and autonomy of the United States; that is to say, survival was not at stake. States in that situation 'may follow a wide range of policies. The most likely explanation for the policies followed by a particular state would be the values embodied in the domestic political order . . .' (Krasner 1992: 41). In other words, religious issues can enter the equation, even in a neorealist analysis, in situations where the anarchic pressure does not put survival on top of the agenda. A case in point might be the significant role that the Tea Party movement has in American politics. Several commentators argue that the Tea Party is at base a religious movement; Sarah Posner makes the point: '. . . to understand why the Tea Party resonates with the religious right and vice versa, one must understand how the anti-government rhetoric of the Tea Party movement is driven by a fundamental tenet of Christian reconstructionism: that there are certain God-ordained spheres—family, church and government—and that government has exceeded the authority God gave it, to the detriment of church, family and the individual, whose rights, both Tea Partiers and religious right-ists maintain, are granted by God, not the government' (Posner 2010).

Religion is, of course, virulent in many other contexts. For example, is Iran primarily a conventional regional power or is it a promoter of Islamic faith? Are Indian Hindu nationalists trying to increase the power of India in the world or are they primarily guardians of Hindi convictions? In most cases, realists would stress the pursuit of power over the pursuit of religious principles. Yet, even here it is the case that rivalry between Iran and Saudi Arabia, for example, is connected to a larger Sunni-Shi'a rivalry in the Middle East (Sandal and James 2011).

Liberals and International Society theorists focus on international norms and institutions. They are well equipped to study the emergence and significance of religious norms and institutions in the international arena (Sandal and James 2011). The liberal focus on individuals and groups from civil society as important actors in international relations also widens to the study of religious groups. At the same time, liberal theorizing assumes that actors are rational, seeking to maximize their interests and that limits the role of religion because it is considered an 'idiosyncratic exercise which feeds on man's irrational impulse with limited material implications for the conduct of global relations' (Mgba and Ukpere 2013: 539). On this view, the influence of religious ideas on international norms is presently more indirect: ideas about international justice, humanitarian intervention, and justifications for going to war are indebted to theological debates about moral values and appropriate behaviour (Haynes 2006; Sandal and Fox 2013).

Constructivists are very well placed to study the role of religion in international affairs; according to one analysis, 'bringing culture and religion back into international relations is part of a wider effort to bring ideas, values, more broadly, ideational factors back into the study of international relations' (Thomas 2005: 69). But Thomas also complains that constructivists have not 'adequately considered the role of culture and religion' (Thomas 2005: 93). In his view, there is something more fundamental about religion in the sense that it is more deeply embedded in actors' identities and thus less open to change. In any case, constructivism is a useful perspective through which to examine the discourses and narratives influenced by religion and to assess how religious elements play a role in shaping the identities and interests of political actors (Sandal and Fox 2013).

This connects to the larger debate about the actual importance of religion in today's international politics. Is it really relevant to talk about a 'resurgence of religion' or is it merely 'a growing awareness of global manifestations of political religion by the Western world, and the perception that they are often intimately connected to core Western security interests?' (Haynes 2006: 539). There is no general agreement on the appropriate view of religion; what seems certain, however, is that a plurality of different approaches—existing and perhaps to some extent new ones—will be needed in order to provide a full analysis of religion in IR.

The Environment

Environmental topics have appeared more and more frequently on the international agenda over the past three decades. An increasing number of people, at least in Western countries, believe that human economic and social activity is taking place in a way that threatens the environment. In the past fifty years, more people have been added to the world's population than in all previous millennia of human existence. A vastly increasing global population pursuing higher standards of living is a potential threat to the environment.

Food production is an example of that. World food supply has grown faster than the global population over the past forty years. But the supply is unevenly distributed; there is a huge food surplus in the developed countries in the West and substantial shortages in many poor countries. Where food is scarce, people will often over-exploit the land in order to squeeze out of it what they can; that can lead to deforestation and desertification. Where food is abundant, there may still be environmental problems due to the use of pesticides, the depletion of scarce water resources, and the energy input required for high productivity agriculture.

Industrial mass production threatens the depletion of scarce resources of raw materials and energy. Local problems of environmental degradation have international ramifications. Air pollution does not stop at borders; acid rain from France, for example, threatens people, groundwater, fish in lakes, and forests, not only in France but also in neighbouring European countries. The production of CFC (chlorofluorocarbon) gases, used for refrigeration, air conditioning, solvents, and other industrial products, is a major threat to the ozone layer, the gaseous mantle that protects the earth from the ultraviolet rays of the sun. CFC interacts chemically with the ozone layer so as to deplete it. Carbon dioxide and other chemical compounds lock in heat close to the surface of the earth and thereby produce global warming, the so-called greenhouse effect. Global warming means severe air pollution and rising sea levels, a potential threat to perhaps half of the world's population that lives in coastal areas.

If international security and global economics are the two major traditional issue areas in world politics, some scholars now claim that the environment has emerged as the third major issue area (O'Neill 2009; Chasek et al. 2010: 1). International attention to the environment issue began in earnest in 1972, when the first United Nations conference on the environment convened in Stockholm. That same year, the Club of Rome think tank published what became the best-selling environmental book in history, *Limits to Growth*. It argued that the earth has a limited carrying capacity; that is, there are limits as to how much the global environment can support in terms of population growth if serious problems of degradation are to be avoided. This led to ideas about **sustainable development**, defined as 'development that meets the needs of the present without compromising the ability of future generations to meet their own needs' (World Commission on Environment and Development (WCED) 1987: 43). The WCED is also known as the Brundtland Commission. Its report from 1987, *Our Common Future*, sparked a new round of debate. The Commission argued that economic growth and poverty eradication were fully compatible with a healthy environment provided that it took place in an appropriate context of sustainable development, in contrast to the unconstrained growth of the 1960s and 1970s.

The UN Conference on Environment and Development, which took place in Rio in 1992, was the first global environmental summit in world history (see web link 11.27). The meeting marked the beginning of a process in which most countries started to think about ways of integrating sustainable development goals into their economic policies. However, behind this process, there is massive disagreement about the extent to which growth and environmental concerns can really go together. Many developing countries are not necessarily interested in prioritising environmental matters at the expense of other development goals. In several cases, this has led to lofty international declarations about the environment in theory and little concrete action in practice.

A major element of these disagreements concerns the gravity of the environment problem. We do not know precisely how serious it is, because any assessment will have to rest on uncertain estimates and a number of disputable assumptions about future developments. One side in this debate is taken up by '**modernists**' who believe that continued improvement in scientific knowledge and in our technological competence will enhance our capability to protect the environment. In other words, we shall continue to improve our skills and techniques of producing and consuming in environment-friendly ways. For example, emissions of CFC gases are being cut down; industrial production requires less input of scarce raw materials than before; more food is grown in ecologically sustainable ways (see, for example, Lomborg 2001, 2007; see also Mol et al. 2009).

The other side in the debate is taken up by '**ecoradicals**' who think that the ecosystem has a limited carrying capacity. Such a limit 'defines how large a species population can become before it overuses the resources available in the ecosystem' (Hughes 1991: 410). Ecoradicals believe that human societies on earth are moving dangerously closer to the limits of the planet's carrying capacity; they also think that there are no simple technological fixes that can take care of the problem. Therefore, many ecoradicals call for strict population control and dramatic changes in modern lifestyles towards a more environment-friendly, less consumption-oriented and waste-producing way of life (Hughes 1991: 409; Eckersley 2004; see web links 11.28 and 11.33; Box 11.10 and table 11.1).

Let us turn to the second question mentioned in Box 11.1; the relative significance of the environment issue for the core problems in IR. In which ways can environment problems increase international conflict? A current example is the dispute over water resources in the Middle East. Water conflicts in the Middle East are not a new issue at all; they have been present in the area for a long time. The region is extremely arid and conflicts over water date back to the seventh century BCE. Today, this issue is part of the Arab–Israeli conflict. The relatively small Jordan River basin is shared by Syria, Lebanon, Israel, and Jordan; there are not many other sources of water. The Arab League attempted to divert the river Jordan away from Israel in the early 1960s; this was one of the major factors in the war between Israel and the Arabs in 1967, which Israel won. More than a third of Israel's current water supplies come from territories occupied since the 1967 war. If a permanent peace in the area is going to be built, it will have to be based, at least in part, on a resolution of the conflict over water (Wolf 2006; Rahaman 2012). Water in the Middle East is a clear example of how environmental scarcity can exacerbate interstate conflict.

As some of the previous chapters indicate, the classical focus of IR is on international conflict, and particularly war between states. Some scholars argue that the typical violent

---

BOX 11.10 Opposing views on the environment issue

The human predicament is driven by overpopulation, overconsumption of natural resources, and the use of unnecessarily environmentally damaging technologies and socio-economic-political arrangements to service *Homo sapiens'* aggregate consumption. How far the human population size now is above the planet's long-term carrying capacity is suggested (conservatively) by ecological footprint analysis. It shows that to support *today's* population of seven billion sustainably (i.e. with business as usual, including current technologies and standards of living) would require roughly half an additional planet; to do so, if all citizens of Earth consumed resources at the US level would take four to five more Earths. . . . Overall, careful analysis of the prospects does not provide much confidence that technology will save us or that gross domestic product can be disengaged from resource use.

Paul Ehrlich and Anne Ehrlich (2013: 1–2)

It took thousands of years to increase life expectancy at birth from just over 20 years to the high 20s. Then in just the past two centuries, then length of life one could expect for a newborn in the advanced countries jumped from less than 30 to perhaps 75 years . . . Since antiquity, people have worried about running out of natural resources. Yet, amazingly, all the historical evidence shows that raw materials—all of them, even oil—have become more abundant rather than less. And there is no reason why that trend should not continue forever. The evidence is particularly strong that the trends in food production and nutrition are benign despite rising population. The long-run price of food is down sharply, even relative to consumer products, as a result of increased productivity. And per person food consumption has risen during the last 30 years.

Julian Simon and Sheldon Richman (1996)

TABLE 11.1 **The environment issue: main positions in the debate**

MODERNISTS	ECORADICALS
Environment not a serious problem. Progress in knowledge and technology will enable us to protect the environment.	Environment a very serious problem. Drastic change of lifestyles plus population control to promote sustainable development is necessary.
A modernist statement:	An ecoradical statement:
'More people and increased income produce problems in the short run. These problems present opportunity, and prompt the search for solutions. In a free society, solutions are eventually found, though many people fail along the way at cost to themselves. In the long run the new developments leave us better off than if the problems had not arisen.'	'[O]nly a thoroughgoing ecocentric Green political theory is capable of providing the kind of comprehensive framework we need to usher in a lasting resolution to the ecological crisis . . . an ecocentric polity would be one in which there is a democratic state legislature (which is part of a multileveled decision-making structure that makes it less powerful than the existing nation state and more responsive to the political determinations of local, regional, and international democratic decision-making bodies); a greater dispersal of political and economic power both within and between communities; a far more extensive range of macro-controls on market activity; and the flowering of an ecocentric emancipatory culture.'
Myers and Simon (1994: 65)	Eckersley (1992: 179, 185)

conflict stemming from environment problems is not interstate but intrastate—i.e., within countries. A research project led by Thomas Homer-Dixon argues that environmental scarcity involves persistent, low-intensity conflict that may not lead to dramatic confrontations, but can wear down governments (Homer-Dixon 1995: 178, 1999). For example, it can cause urban migration and unrest, decreased economic productivity, ethnic conflicts, and so on. Homer-Dixon argues, in a more speculative vein, that 'countries experiencing chronic internal conflict because of environmental stress will probably either fragment or become more authoritarian . . . Authoritarian regimes may be inclined to launch attacks against other countries to divert popular attention from internal stresses' (1995: 179). However, more recent research has not been able to demonstrate a clear connection between climate change and conflict. It is rather the case that the connection is 'contingent on a number of political and social variables' (Salehyan 2008; Bernauer et al. 2011). That is to say, climate change may or may not lead to conflict depending of a number of political and social factors.

Environmental problems can also put pressures on states to engage in greater international cooperation. The reason is that environmental degradation can be said to make up a special kind of 'threat' which is a threat not to states but to humanity itself. It is a threat to the 'global commons'—i.e., the oceans, the seas, the ozone layer, and the climate system, which are a life support system for humankind as a whole (UNDP 2007). Environmental problems have, in fact, encouraged international cooperation in recent years. International regimes (see Chapter 4) have been set up in a number of specific areas to address various environment issues, including acid rain, ozone depletion, whaling, the toxic waste trade, the Antarctic environment, global warming, and biodiversity loss (see web link 11.35) (Deere-Birkbeck 2009; Chasek et al. 2010). The ozone regime is one of the more prominent examples of international cooperation on the environment. It contains an international agreement to cut back and eventually phase out the production of CFCs and thus aims to reverse the damage to the ozone layer that has occurred in recent decades. Several other regimes, by contrast, have been less promising because of the lack of sufficient commitment and tangible cooperation from participating countries (UNEP 2006). In sum, the environment issue can involve international conflict over scarce resources, such as water, as well as international cooperation to preserve the global commons, such as the ozone regime. It is not possible to predict whether collaboration or discord will prevail because that depends on a number of different, unforeseen circumstances (Box 11.11).

It remains to address the third item in Box 11.1: the nature of the theoretical challenge posed by the environment issue. Many of the questions raised by the environment issue can be comfortably tackled by traditional approaches. For realists, the environment issue is merely one more explainable source of conflict between states which can be added to an already long list. For liberals, the environment adds one more issue, albeit a very important one, to the agenda of international cooperation and regime formation. For IPE scholars, the environment can be accounted for as an aspect of the global economy. In short, the traditional approaches take us a long way in dealing with the environment issue (O'Neil 2009).

However, some aspects of that issue sit uncomfortably with the traditional approaches. Domestic social and political conflict is one such aspect; the environment cuts across the dividing line between domestic politics and international politics in ways not taken sufficiently into account by the traditional approaches' focus on international relations. IR environmentalist scholars argue that it is necessary to get beyond the traditional focus on states, because so many other actors are important when it comes to the environment: e.g., transnational corporations, NGOs, consumers, and so on. Yet, it is possible to argue, in reply, that liberals and IPE theorists are used to dealing with domestic conflict and with many different types of actors (Tanner and Allouche 2011).

We made a distinction earlier between 'modernists' and 'ecoradicals'. It is the ecoradical position that especially challenges traditional IR approaches. Ecoradicals call for dramatic changes in lifestyles, including very significant changes in economic and political

---

BOX 11.11   Environment, cooperation, and conflict

1. Environment as a source of *interstate* conflict: e.g., water in the Middle East.
2. Environment as a source of *intra-state* conflict: e.g., soil erosion, population growth, migration.
3. Environmental pollution and degradation as a *special hazard* requiring international cooperation: e.g., regimes to preserve the global commons.

BOX 11.12   A Judeo-Christian view

Then God said, 'Let us make man in our image, after our likeness; and let them have dominion over the fish of the sea, and over the birds of the air, and over the cattle, and over all the earth, and over every creeping thing that creeps upon the earth.'

Genesis, 1, 26; extract from *Oxford Annotated Bible* (1962)

---

organization. They criticize arguments, such as the Brundtland Report, which call for environment protection within a framework of sustainable growth. Ecoradicals find that this is not at all sufficient. For some, real sustainability means abandoning industrial mass production and reverting to some form of deindustrialized society (Lee 1993). Behind such radical ideas lies a world view profoundly different from the 'modernist', anthropocentric view that is dominant in Western secular thinking—i.e., that 'man is above nature'. This point is also dominant in Judaeo-Christian thinking; i.e., in Genesis (see Box 11.12), man is commanded to master the natural environment. The corollary of this view is that man is allowed to exploit nature in pursuit of human destiny and development. The ecoradical world view is very different; it puts equal value on humans and nature as part of one single biosystem. In this view, man has no right to exploit nature. Humans have a duty to live in harmony with nature and to respect and sustain the overall ecological balance (Eckersley 1992; Goodin 1992).

Ecoradicals call for profound changes not only in economic but also in political organization. They argue that the state is more of a problem than a solution for environmental issues. The state is part of modern society, and modern society is the cause of the environmental crisis (Carter 1993). However, there is no agreement among ecoradicals about the role of the state or what to put in place of the state. The current debate, then, concerns scope and depth of necessary reforms for facing the environmental challenge. Many argue that modernists are too optimistic and do not go nearly far enough in suggesting major reforms of the current model of capitalist development. But many also argue that the more extreme proposals from some ecoradicals go too far and are unrealistic. In the space between these extremes, there is a debate about what would be the concrete content of a 'green state' (Eckersley 2004) and what a transition to more sustainable development could look like, given the experience of the earlier great transition from pre-modern to modern industrial society (Grin et al. 2011).

New Patterns of War and Peace: Changes in Statehood

Armed conflict today increasingly takes place *within* states that are weak in the sense that they are unable or unwilling to provide security and order, not to mention freedom, justice, and welfare for the population. At the same time, among advanced states, especially among the liberal democracies, there is peace, cooperation, and no risk of interstate war.

These developments are connected to changes in statehood. The old distinction between a First, a Second, and a Third world is being replaced by a new typology of states: the *advanced capitalist state* is today postmodern rather than modern; a group of *weak* states in the South are increasingly marginalized, fragile, and unable to stand on their own feet. Between these two groups are a number of *modernizing* states in Asia, Eastern Europe, Latin America, and elsewhere. These changes are critical for the study of IR because they profoundly affect the prospects for violent conflict, for war and peace (Sørensen 2004).

In order to trace how states have changed it is necessary to identify the basic features of the concept of the modern state as it existed in the mid-twentieth century. That creates a 'baseline model' against which recent developments can be characterized. What is the substance of the modern state—i.e., what is the content of actual, empirical statehood? We can think of it in terms of three different dimensions: the government; the nation; and the economy. The core characteristics of the modern state are set forth in Table 11.2.

The concept of the modern state corresponds to the picture of the state in conventional theories of IR. The modern state is understood to be a valuable place that provides for the good life of its citizens, including their security, their freedom, and their welfare; safeguarding the defence of the realm from external threat and the upholding of domestic order and security via police and courts. Freedom is achieved through democratic institutions and a political order based on civil and political rights and liberties. Welfare can be provided by the resources produced in the national economy.

To the extent that this is an accurate picture of current statehood, the conventional theories have no problems. They can proceed to focus on the international relations of states on the assumption that all is well on the domestic front; the modern state actually provides for the good life for its citizens (see Chapter 1). But states are historical institutions; they are open to change. The modern state emerged from a very long process of development that took place between the seventeenth and twentieth centuries. It came to full maturity in the developed world around the mid-twentieth century. Since then, of course, it has not stood still. Changes in statehood continue to take place. Nobody can know where they will eventually lead. But it is possible to theorize about those changes. In this section we shall review the main elements of the theory that statehood is undergoing important change.

TABLE 11.2 The modern state

Government	A centralized system of democratic rule, based on administrative, policing, and military organizations, sanctioned by a legal order, claiming a monopoly of the legitimate use of force, within a defined territory.
Nationhood	A people within a territory making up a community of citizens (with political, social, and economic rights) and a community of sentiment (based on linguistic, cultural, and historical bonds). Nationhood involves a high level of cohesion that binds nation and state together.
Economy	A segregated and self-sustained national economy that comprises the necessary sectors for its reproduction and growth. The major part of economic activity takes place within independent countries.

We begin with the emergence of weak or fragile states (Jackson 1990; Sørensen 2001; Brock et al. 2011). Colonialism was given up after the Second World War. Many of the newly independent states, especially in sub-Saharan Africa, became weak states. What is a weak state? Three major characteristics must be mentioned: first, the economy is defective; there is a lack of a coherent national economy capable of sustaining a basic level of welfare for the population and of providing the resources for running an effective state. Defective econo-mies often depend crucially on the world market, because they are mono-economies based on the export of one or a few primary goods. In sub-Saharan Africa, primary products account for 80 to 90 per cent of total exports. Furthermore, the economy is highly hetero-geneous with elements of a modern sector, but also feudal or semi-feudal structures in agriculture. In both urban and rural areas, large parts of the population are outside of the formal sector, living in localized subsistence economies at very low standards.

The second major characteristic of weak states concerns relations between people in soci-ety; they do not make up a coherent national community. A national 'community of citizens' was created at independence, but only in the formal sense of providing people with identity cards and passports. This was combined with some scattered attempts to launch nation-building projects that would develop a common idea of the state. But the real substance of citizenship—legal, political, and social rights—was not provided on a major scale by the new states. When the state does not deliver, people turn elsewhere for the satisfaction of material and non-material needs. In sub-Saharan Africa, they have primarily turned to the local communities that are the focal points for a 'moral economy': the moral economy enables individuals 'to rely on nonbureaucratic mutual aid networks and to reciprocate toward those who belong to a common society' (Ndegwa 1997: 601).

The lack of community is connected to the third characteristic of weak states: the absence of effective and responsive state institutions. In most cases, the new post-independence leaders were not actively interested in the creation of strong states; they feared it would be a potential threat to their firm grip on state power. But in contrast to the colonial elite, the new rulers were not insulated from society; they were closely connected to it via ties of clan, kin-ship, and ethnic affiliation. The network of clients had great expectations of benefits from the power over the state apparatus. This opened the way to clientelism, patronage, and nepotism. According to Jackson and Rosberg, the Africanization of the state took place in context of a political culture that:

conceived of government offices and resources in terms of possession and consumption; mul-tiethnic societies that wanted at least their equitable share of the governmental cake, if they could not have it all; politicians who recognized that granting or denying access to government offices and resources was a crucial modus operandi for expanding and retaining power, and, of course, the absence of, or at most the scarcity of, alternative sources of power, status, and wealth.

Jackson and Rosberg (1994: 302)

State elites in weak states are strong in the sense that they do not face serious domestic or external threat. In the domestic realm, civil society is divided among many different groups and it is unorganized with few possibilities of earnestly challenging the holders of state power. In the external realm, the weak entities that were the newly independent, post-colonial states were left alone because borders were now considered sacrosanct. The UN, backed by the superpowers, provided these countries with a certified life insurance: no matter how bad things might go, no matter how little development they might be capable of, the international community would continue to respect their newly won sovereignty and their right to formal independence (Jackson 1992) (Table 11.3).

Some intervention by the superpowers did take place during the Cold War, but the East–West confrontation also helped strengthen the new norms of the right of former colonies to sovereign statehood. The new states could play on the fact that the global contenders were looking for allies around the world and they were anxious not to see too many countries line up on the side of the opponent. In this regard, state elites in weak states are powerful and unconstrained. At the same time, however, they remain vulnerable and easily exposed to rival groups, often including parts of the military that want to establish their own hold on state power (Goldsmith 2004). State elites often do not have the resources or the political will to accommodate rival groups; challenges are rather met by increasing repression. In sum, basing themselves on patron–client relationships, self-seeking state elites lacked legitimacy from the beginning and they were facing populations divided along ethnic, religious, and social lines. They created 'captured states' which benefitted the leading strongman and his select groups of clients. The majority of the population was excluded from the system and they faced a state which is rather an enemy and a mortal threat than a protector and a champion of development (Brock et al. 2011).

This, then, is the general background for the insecurity dilemma in weak states. It emerges from the paradoxical situation that weak states are relatively free from serious external threat, while simultaneously the weak state itself poses a serious security threat to major parts of its own population. In a basic sense, anarchy is domesticized: there is an international system or relative order with fairly secure protection of the borders and territories of weak states; and there is a domestic realm with a high degree of insecurity and conflict. As seen from the perspective of the populations of weak states, this is an insecurity dilemma, because they cannot know what to expect from the state; furthermore, strategies of resistance and support may be counterproductive in terms of achieving security.

TABLE 11.3 **The weak post-colonial state**

Government	Inefficient and corrupt administrative and institutional structures. Rule based on coercion rather than the rule of law. Monopoly on the legitimate use of violence not established.
Nationhood	Predominance of local/ethnic community. Neither the 'community of citizens' nor the 'community of sentiment' has developed to become the primary bond between people. Low level of state legitimacy.
Economy	Incoherent amalgamations of traditional agriculture, an informal petty urban sector, and some fragments of modern industry. Significant dependence on world market and on external economic interests.

The government's primary task should ideally be to provide security for its population, but instead it makes up the greatest potential threat to people within its boundaries. For this reason:

groups may fear that others control the government and may use its resources (the army, the secret police, the courts, economic influence) against them. Thus the search for security motivates groups in divided societies to seek to control the state or secede if the state's neutrality cannot be assured. Obviously, these efforts exacerbate the situation, because one group's attempts to control the state will reinforce the fears of others, so they respond by competing to influence and even control the government.

Saideman et al. (2002: 106–7)

An early analysis of the insecurity dilemma in weak states was provided in a volume edited by Brian Job (1992); the term itself was suggested in that volume. Job notes four ways in which the insecurity dilemma differs from the traditional security dilemma: (1) the sense of threat that dominates is domestic threat to and from the regime that holds power; (2) the state lacks effective capacities for providing internal peace and order; (3) popular support for the regime is missing; the existence and security interests of the regime are not considered legitimate; and (4) primary identification is with communal groups contending for their own security (Job 1992: 17–18).

Weak statehood is a matter of degree meaning that the insecurity dilemma can be more or less pressing. That is no different from the security dilemma which can also be more or less pressing. The characteristics of weak statehood identified above may be present in varying combinations; hence, there are various attempts to measure the degree of weakness and sensitivity to complete breakdown or state failure (see, for example, Fund for Peace 2014). Weak statehood is also present outside of the global South; Ukraine is a case in point. A divided population cannot agree on the political rules of the game in the country, in particular how much autonomy should be granted to the areas dominated by a Russia-oriented sector of the population. External involvement in this conflict, in particular from Russia, has made it a complex issue which threatens new tensions between Russia and the Western countries.

The human cost of weak and failed statehood has been extremely high. Three conflicts in Sudan, Ethiopia, and Mozambique each demanded the lives of somewhere between 500,000 and one million people; casualties in Angola, Rwanda, Sierra Leone, Liberia, and Uganda have also been very high. In sum, violent conflict in the world today is no longer mainly interstate war; it is primarily intra-state conflict (or intra-state conflict with external participation) (Themnér and Wallensteen 2013).

So, violent conflict today is connected to fragile states. Advanced states, by contrast, have often chosen to cooperate to an extent that has created a very high level of integration among them: economic integration, political integration, and social integration. Modern liberal states have become so densely integrated that both territorial integrity and the autonomy of their domestic political orders are no longer upheld. In that specific sense, state survival is not the primary goal.

In context of the EU, the development of supranational authority and free movement across borders sets a new context where countries may continue to be formally independent, but at the same time deeply integrated in a cross-border community. In some areas, the EU can now make binding rules for its members. Such forms of supranational cooperation are beginning to emerge in other contexts as well; for example, in the WTO. Increasingly, governance is changing away from its confinement to the context of national governments towards multilevel governance in several interlocked arenas overlapping each other. Some of that multilevel governance reflects a more intense conventional cooperation between independent states; and some of it reflects a more profound transformation towards supranational governance. To the degree that the latter is happening, modern statehood will be significantly changed.

What about nationhood, the national community? According to the theory of changing statehood, important changes are taking place here also. *Citizen* rights used to be exclusively granted by the state, but other organizations are now active in this area. In the UN system, a set of universal *human* rights has been legally instituted. In some world regions, notably Europe, close cooperation has led to *common* rights for citizens of different countries. Citizens of the EU enjoy some common rights in all member states, including right of employment and residence and political rights of voting in local and European elections. In Scotland, Northern Italy, Quebec, Spain, and elsewhere, movements for greater autonomy have emerged; some even seek secession from their respective states.

According to the theory of changing statehood, the community of sentiment also appears to be undergoing transformation. There appear to be two major developments in different directions. One trend is towards a common civic identity for the Western political order, the core of which is political democracy, individual rights, and an economy based on the market and private property (Deudney and Ikenberry 1999). The other trend is towards fragmentation along ethnic, national, and religious fault lines which disclose a more narrow and exclusive conception of community (Castells 1998) (see web links 11.52 and 11.62). These changes together would appear to indicate a significant transformation of the modern state. However, the changes are still underway and nobody can be sure where the present process of change is taking us. That is the reason for suggesting the label of 'the postmodern state'. As an ideal type, the postmodern state contains the features shown in Table 11.4.

TABLE 11.4 The postmodern state

Government	Multilevel governance in several interlocked arenas overlapping each other. Governance in context of supranational, international, transgovernmental, and transnational relations.
Nationhood	Supranational elements in nationhood, both with respect to the 'community of citizens' (rights and obligations between citizens and the state) and the 'community of sentiment' (cultural–historical relations between citizens as a group). Collective loyalties increasingly projected away from the state.
Economy	'Deep integration': major part of economic activity is embedded in cross-border networks. The 'national' economy is much less self-sustained than it used to be.

That cross-border community among **postmodern states** cannot begin to be grasped with a notion of 'anarchy', because the community is densely framed by legitimate international and supranational authority. In such a framework, the use of organized violence to solve conflicts is no longer an option. The countries have become a security community (Deutsch 1957; Adler and Barnett 1998; Sørensen 2001) where states no longer resort to force as a means of conflict resolution. The adoption of non-violent conflict resolution means that the security dilemma is eliminated; states do not fear each other in the classical sense of fear of attack, and war between them is not a possibility. In other words, the liberal view that the security dilemma can be transcended has been validated when it comes to the relations between the consolidated liberal democracies depicted as 'postmodern' states in Table 11.4.

The idea of a security community is not merely relevant for the EU. It is true that in terms of the development of supranational authority, the EU stands out; but the general level of integration is also high across the Atlantic, in the triad relation between Europe, North America, and Japan (East Asia); and even in the OECD area. At the same time, the security community defined by postmodern statehood has developed in different degrees among different countries. Relations between North America and Europe are more institutionalized than relations between these areas and Japan; some countries are part of the institutional and economic networks without being fully democratic (e.g., Turkey); some countries are fully democratic without being deeply integrated in the institutional networks (e.g., Switzerland). The inner circle of the security community is EU–Europe, followed by Western Europe and Western Europe/North America, Western Europe/North America/Japan, and the members of the OECD.

The emergence of a security community does not remove all threats in relation to postmodern states. A very significant and shocking instance of postmodern insecurity was the terrorist attack on New York and Washington on 11 September 2001. It clearly revealed the extreme vulnerability of open societies. There is a peculiar security dilemma here: how to create sufficient protection of open societies without shutting down or even reducing their openness. Openness requires freedom of movement, speech, organization, and behaviour in general, within constitutional limits. Sufficient protection, however, requires surveillance, undercover intelligence, and control of the behaviour and movements of civilians—the citizens. This dilemma is not entirely new, of course; it was also present during the Cold War. But it has become much more pertinent since 11 September 2001.

Meanwhile, the forces of political and economic integration are relevant elsewhere and that further reduces the relevance of the security dilemma. Two basic factors are in play; first, a general process of democratization and liberalization. Second, modernizing states—such as China—know that the road to greatness involves focus on manufacture upgrading and deep involvement in economic globalization; by no means does it involve territorial conquest and militarization. In this sense, China is following the 'trading state' path set by Japan and Germany after the Second World War (Rosecrance 1986, 1999). (Modernizing states combine features of the three ideal types of state presented above: the modern, the postmodern, and the weak state. Brazil, China, and India are major examples of modernizing states.)

These normative and substantial developments have all but eradicated the occurrence of interstate war (defined as armed conflict between governments in which at least 1,000 people are killed, or killed yearly as a direct (or fairly direct) consequence of the fighting). Few such wars have taken place since the end of the Second World War; fewer still since the end of the Cold War (Themnér and Wallensteen 2013).

In short, the classical security dilemma is either irrelevant (among postmodern states) or in decline (among modernizing and democratizing states). Setbacks are possible in the latter group of countries. During 2014, the relationship between Russia and the West, for example, underwent a cooling process due to the conflict in Ukraine. At the same time, other emerging powers, including China and India, appear less keen on reverting to policies of militarization and confrontation.

Weak and postmodern states disclose security dilemmas that are markedly different from the classical security dilemma of modern statehood. So, in order to understand the most important security challenges facing states, analysis of their external relations is not enough. It is also necessary to look inside states, at their domestic developments. 'Domestic' and 'international' are tied closely together and each significantly affects the other. In order to understand the most important security challenges in the present international system, the transformation of statehood will have to be incorporated in the analysis.

Let us recall the third question in Box 11.1: in what way do these insights challenge conventional IR theories (for a comprehensive discussion, see Sørensen 2001)?

Realists will be sceptical towards this analysis of weak and postmodern states. Neorealists, especially, maintain a systemic focus: it is not necessary to look inside states in order to understand international relations and patterns of war and peace. But weak states and postmodern states are distinct entities with peculiar security dilemmas. New research questions concerning war and peace and international security emerge from the development of new types of state. The standard realist answer to all this is that these developments do not really pertain to the great powers and, therefore, they are less interesting for what goes on in the international system. The big and important things in IR concern great power relations and here realist assumptions continue to be valid.

Is this a satisfactory answer? Perhaps not: first, the development of postmodern statehood does involve several of the major states in the system; second, the exceptional problems of weak statehood concern such large groups of people that they qualify as 'big and important things' (Sørensen 2009).

Liberals can better accommodate the transformation from modern towards postmodern statehood because it is in major ways a further development of the liberal democratic peace based on liberal democracy, common international institutions, and economic interdependence. Weak states can be seen through a liberal lens as pre-modern entities which have yet to progress towards modernity.

Yet, given the belief in progress, liberal thinking has not been very clear in explaining why development does not seem to arrive in weak states. The problem for liberals is that some of the core elements of liberal advancement to which they point (i.e., democratization and economic modernization) do not work very well in weak states. If the last five decades are anything to go by, this is not merely a temporary problem. More generally, the processes of democratization and liberalization mentioned above may not be as secure as many liberals indicate; there can be setbacks, and great powers such as China and Russia would not appear to be on a firm path towards democracy anytime soon (Sørensen 2011).

BOX 11.13	A post-colonial view

[T]here are no modern solutions to many of today's problems. This is clearly the case, for instance, with massive displacement and ecological destruction, but also with development's inability to fulfil its promise of a minimum of well-being for the world's people.

Escobar (2004: 209)

The development of postmodern statehood, furthermore, has produced new problems upon which liberals need to reflect. First, intense cooperation undermines the national framework for a democratic polity; many commentators speak of a 'democratic deficit' problem in the EU (i.e., too bureaucratic; too closed; too far away from citizens). Second, intense cooperation across borders produces not only transnational 'goods' but also transnational 'bads': disease, pollution, terror, ecological imbalances, crime, drugs, illegal migration, and economic crisis are examples of that. In sum, liberals need to come to terms with the fact that change will not always be for the better; what is considered liberal progress can also be the source of new problems.

Post-colonial theorists (see Chapter 9) will be critical of this analysis of changes in statehood. Their major argument is that such an assessment is based on Western concepts about development, modernity, and weak statehood. In other words, weak states are not discussed on their own terms, in ways that reflect their distinctive realities. Instead, they are seen through Western lenses as traditional, primitive, and backward, in need of a process of modernization in order to catch up with the West (Escobar 1995). From this perspective, modernity today is primarily made up of a global capitalist hegemony which does not point forward (see Box 11.13). Therefore, there is a need to think about alternative models of development, as expressed by some of the anti-globalization and global justice movements (Escobar 2004).

Conclusion

We have looked at four contemporary issues in IR and discussed the ways in which they are handled by IR theory. The nature of the theoretical challenge to IR posed by these issues depends on one's valuation of what is actually at stake. Radical views demand radical solutions. A radical view of the environment issue, for example, demands that we reconsider our whole way of thinking about IR. These radical interpretations point away from traditional IR approaches, but the conceptual and theoretical directions taken are not at all the same. This brings us back to a point made in Chapter 2 about the three main factors that influence IR thinking. The first is changes in the real world which keep throwing up new issues, such as those taken up in this chapter. The second is debates between IR scholars both within and between different traditions. Such debates help us come to a decision about the challenge posed by different issues and what the consequences will be for the discipline. The third element is the influence of other areas of scholarship, especially debates about methodology in a broad sense.

The joint shaping of IR thinking by these three main factors is an ongoing process. There is no end station where scholars can sit back and proclaim that IR thinking is finally developed to perfection. History does not stand still. Intellectual inquiry does not stop. There are always new issues to confront, new methods to apply, and new insights to discover. There are always new generations of scholars inquiring into them. Scholars are not architects working on buildings that will one day be finished. There is no one blueprint. There are several: some plans are abandoned, others are adopted; scholars are more like travellers with different maps and open-ended tickets. A textbook such as this one is a sort of unfinished travelogue of IR. We know where the journey began and we know about the main stations visited so far. But we are less certain about where IR will go from here because old and new travellers will continue the debate about the best direction to take and the proper places to visit on the way. Some readers of this book might eventually take IR to destinations that we have never heard of.

 KEY POINTS

- International terrorism has revived the spectre of physical security threats to states and societies in the OECD world. It is not an overriding, existential menace, but it is a clear threat to public security that must be taken seriously.

- The 'clash of civilizations' is not a defining feature of post-Cold War world order; but it is true that questions of identity and religion play an important role in contemporary IR.

- There is some debate as to the severity of the problem of environmental degradation. 'Modernists' believe that continued improvement in human knowledge will enhance our ability to protect and safeguard the environment for future generations. 'Ecoradicals' think that there are no simple technological fixes that can take care of the problem. They want revolutionary changes towards environment-friendly lifestyles.

- Armed conflict today increasingly takes place *within* states that are weak in the sense that they are unable or unwilling to provide security and order, not to mention freedom, justice, and welfare for the population. At the same time, among advanced states, especially among the liberal democracies, there is peace, cooperation, and no risk of interstate war. These developments are connected to changes in statehood.

- The nature of the challenge to IR posed by these issues depends on one's valuation of what is at stake. A radical view of the environment issue demands that we reconsider our whole way of thinking about IR, for example. Many scholars who study the non-traditional issues are less radical and more prone to operate within existing traditions in IR.

? QUESTIONS

- Should international terrorism be the top issue on the international agenda? Why or why not?

- How serious is the problem of environmental degradation? What are the consequences for IR?

- Is religion a relevant new issue in IR? Why or why not?

- Outline the characteristics of the postmodern state. How does it challenge traditional thinking about IR?

- As an advisor to the UN, how would you recommend confronting the problems connected with weak states?

- Does the arrival of 'new issues' in IR mean that the discipline will have to be fundamentally changed and some or all of the established ways of thinking will have to be discarded? Why or why not?

→ GUIDE TO FURTHER READING

Chasek, P. S. Downie, D. L. , and Brown, J. W. (2010). *Global Environmental Politics*, 5th edn. Boulder, CO: Westview.

Desch, M. and Philpott, D. (eds) (2014). *Religion and International Relations: A Primer for Research*. University of Notre Dame, at: http://rmellon.nd.edu/assets/101872/religion_and_international_relations_report.pdf

Eckersly, R. (2004). *The Green State: Rethinking Democracy and Sovereignty*. Cambridge, MA: Massachusetts Institute of Technology Press.

Jackson, R. H. (1990). *Quasi-States: Sovereignty, International Relations and the Third World*. Cambridge: Cambridge University Press.

Lomborg, B. (2001). *The Sceptical Environmentalist*. Cambridge: Cambridge University Press.

O'Neil, K. (2009). *The Environment and International Relations*. Cambridge: Cambridge University Press.

Pearlstein, R. M. (2004). *Fatal Future? Transnational Terrorism and the New Global Disorder*. Austin, TX: University of Texas Press.

Sandal, N. and Fox, J. (2013). *Religion in International Relations Theory: Interactions and Possibilities*. Abingdon: Routledge.

Sandal, N. and James, P. (2011). 'Religion and International Relations Theory: Towards a Mutual Understanding', *European Journal of International Relations*, 17/1: 3–25.

Snyder, J. (ed.) (2011). *Religion and International Relations Theory*. New York: Columbia University Press.

Sørensen, G. (2004). *The Transformation of the State: Beyond the Myth of Retreat*. Basingstoke: Palgrave Macmillan.

Thomas, S. (2005). *The Global Resurgence of Religion and the Transformation of International Relations*. Basingstoke: Palgrave Macmillan.

Tinnes, J. (2013). '100 Core and Periphery Journals for Terrorism Research', *Perspectives on Terrorism*, 7/2, at: http://www.terrorismanalysts.com/pt/index.php/pot/article/view/258/html

Weinberg, L. and Eubank, W. (2008). 'Problems with the Critical Studies Approach to the Study of Terrorism', *Critical Studies on Terrorism*, 1/2: 185–95.

WEB LINKS

Web links mentioned in the chapter, together with additional material including a case-study on fragile states, can be found on the Online Resource Centre that accompanies this book.

www.oxfordtextbooks.co.uk/orc/jackson_sorensen6e/

▍GLOSSARY

anarchical society A term used by Hedley Bull to describe the worldwide order of independent states who share common interests and values, and subject themselves to a common set of rules and institutions in dealing with each other. The concept of 'anarchical society' combines the realist claim that no world 'government' rules over sovereign states, with idealism's emphasis on the common concerns, values, rules, institutions, and organizations of the international system.

behaviouralism An approach that seeks increasing precision, parsimony, and the predictive and explanatory power of IR theory. Behaviouralists believe in the unity of science: that social science is not fundamentally different from natural science; that the same analytical methods—including quantitative methods—can be applied in both areas. Behaviouralists also believe in interdisciplinary studies among the social sciences.

Bretton Woods The system of international economic management, setting the rules for commercial exchange between the world's major industrial states. Allied states set up the system in the New Hampshire resort town of Bretton Woods in July 1944.

bureaucratic structures and processes approach to foreign policy A strongly empirical (evidence-based) sociological approach to foreign policy that focuses primarily on the organizational (or bureaucratic) context in which decision making takes place. The 'bureaucratic' approach is seen by supporters to be superior to other approaches by virtue of its empirical analysis of the relationship between decision making and organizational structure. This approach, therefore, emphasizes specific context over the inherent rationality of any foreign policy decision; it seeks to clarify the context-based reasons for individual foreign policies, but does not have a strong normative, prescriptive component.

classical realism A theory of IR associated with thinkers such as Thucydides, Niccolò Machiavelli, and Thomas Hobbes. They believe that the goal, the means, and the uses of power are central preoccupations of international relations, which is an arena of continuous rivalry and potential or actual conflict between states that are obliged to pursue the goals of security and survival. In comparison with neorealism, which largely ignores moral and ethical considerations in IR, classical realism has a strong normative doctrine.

cognitive processes and psychology approach Unlike the bureaucratic and other sociological approaches, this approach focuses on the individual decision maker, with particular attention to the psychological aspects of decision making. Robert Jervis has studied misperception, and the construction of erroneous 'images' of others, as it pertains to these state leaders. Margaret Herman studied the personalities of dozens of government leaders, arguing that such factors as experience, political style, and world view affect the ways leaders conduct their foreign policies.

communitarianism A normative doctrine that focuses on political communities, especially nation-states, which are seen as fundamental agents and referents in world politics. According to this position, states' interests come before those of individuals or that of humanity in general.

comparative approach to foreign policy A form of policy analysis inspired by the behaviouralist movement in political science. Unlike the traditional approach to foreign policy analysis, in which information is sought about one single country's policy, the comparative approach amasses substantial data about the content and context of many countries' foreign policies. Rather than merely prescribe action for a specific country in a specific context, the goal of the comparative approach is to develop systematic theories and explanations of the foreign policy process in general.

cosmopolitanism A normative doctrine that focuses on individual human beings and the whole of humanity, seen as fundamental agents and referents in world politics, whose needs should come before the interests of states.

critical theory A post-positivist approach to IR influenced by Marxist thought advanced by the Frankfurt School. Critical theory rejects three basic postulates of positivism: an objective external reality, the subject/object distinction, and value-free social science. Critical theorists emphasize the fundamentally political nature of knowledge. They seek to liberate humanity from the conservative forces and 'oppressive' structures of hegemonic (US-dominated) world politics and global economics. Critical theorists are similar to idealists in their support for progressive change and their employment of theory to help bring about that change.

defensive realism According to Kenneth Waltz's theory, a 'defensive realist' recognizes that states seek power for security and survival, but striving for excessive power is counterproductive because it provokes hostile alliances by other states.

dependency theory Draws on classical Marxist analysis, but is different from classical Marxism in one basic respect. Unlike Marx, dependency theorists do not expect capitalist development to take root and unfold in the developing world in the same way that capitalism first took place in Western Europe and North America. The main aim of dependency theory is to critique the dependency form that capitalist development is seen to take in developing countries. In short, dependency theory is an attack on late capitalism. It is an effort to provide the theoretical tools by which developing countries can defend themselves against globalizing capitalism.

economic liberalism Adam Smith (1723–90), the father of economic liberalism, believed that markets tend to expand spontaneously for the satisfaction of human needs—provided that governments do not interfere. He builds on the body of liberal ideas that are summarized in Chapter 4. These core ideas include the rational individual actor, a belief in progress and an assumption of mutual gain from free exchange. But Smith also adds to liberal thinking some elements of his own, including the key notion that the economic marketplace is the main source of progress, cooperation, and prosperity. Political interference and state regulation, by contrast, is uneconomical, retrogressive, and can lead to conflict.

ecoradicals Believe that environmental problems are highly serious. Dramatic changes of lifestyles plus population control are necessary in order to promote sustainable development.

emancipatory theory Seeking to counter realism, emancipatory theorists, such as Ken Booth and Andrew Linklater, argue that IR should seek to understand how men and women are prisoners of the existing state system, and how they can be liberated from the state and from the other oppressive structures of contemporary world politics, which can be reconstructed along universal, solidarist lines.

empirical statehood Part of the external basis of a state's sovereignty is the extent to which a state fulfils its role as a substantial political–economic organization. A successful state in terms of empirical statehood has developed efficient political institutions, a solid economic basis, and a substantial degree of national unity (internal popular support for the state).

epistemology The philosophical study of how one comes to 'know' something, and what is ultimately 'knowable'. One position is that the world can be 'explained', from outside, by a social-scientific test of empirical propositions. That view is particularly widespread among American IR scholars. The opposite position holds that the world can only be 'discerned', 'comprehended', and 'interpreted', from inside, by historical, legal, and philosophical analysis. While this view is gaining ground in the United States, it remains more likely to be found among British and continental European IR scholars.

ethics of statecraft Ensuring national security and state survival is the fundamental responsibility of statecraft and the core normative doctrine of classical realism. The state is considered to be essential for the good life of its citizens. The state is thus seen as a protector of its territory, of the population, and of their distinctive and valued way of life. The national interest is the final arbiter in judging foreign policy.

failed states Weak states incapable of creating domestic order. State failure is a case of extreme weakness involving a more or less complete breakdown of domestic order. Examples are Somalia, Rwanda, Liberia, and Sudan.

feminism Emphasizes that women are a disadvantaged group in the world, in both material terms and in terms of a value system that favours men over women. A gender-sensitive perspective on IR investigates the inferior position of women in the international political and economic system, and analyses how our current ways of thinking about IR tend to disguise as well as reproduce a gender hierarchy.

foreign policy The manner in which states interact with other states, international organizations, and foreign non-governmental actors (such as NGOs, corporations, and terrorist organizations). Foreign policy thus includes all competitive and cooperative strategies, measures, goals, guidelines, directives, understandings, agreements, etc., through which a state conducts its international relations. By virtue of their separate international existence, all states are obliged to develop and execute foreign policy towards these other states and international organizations. Normally, key policymakers are leading government officials, namely presidents, prime ministers, foreign ministers, defence ministers, etc. Dealing with everything from the conduct of war to the regulation of imported goods, policymaking tends to involve means–end and cost–benefit analyses of realistic goals and available means to achieve them.

foreign policy analysis Involves scrutinizing foreign policies and placing them in a broader context of academic knowledge. There are many approaches to the analysis of foreign policy, with each having different descriptive and prescriptive goals and paying attention to various dimensions (sociological, psychological, historical context, etc.) of the decision-making process. Foreign policy analysis often involves instrumental analysis, studying the best means for reaching an advisable goal; it may also include a prescriptive component; that is, making recommendations for the best course to follow.

functionalist theory of integration A theory coined by David Mitrany. He argued that greater interdependence in the form of transnational ties between countries could lead to peace. Mitrany believed, perhaps somewhat naively, that cooperation should be arranged by technical experts, not by politicians. The experts would devise solutions to common problems in various functional areas: transport, communication, finance, etc. Technical and economic collaboration would expand when participants discovered the mutual benefits to be obtained from it. When citizens saw the welfare improvements resulting from efficient collaboration in international organizations, they would transfer their loyalty from the state to international organizations.

gender issues The starting point for introducing gender to IR is often the debate about basic inequalities between men and women, and the consequences of such inequalities for world politics. Compared with men, women are a disadvantaged group in the world. Women own about 1 per cent of the world's property and make up fewer than 5 per cent of heads of state and cabinet ministers. Women put in about 60 per cent of all working hours, but they take home only 10 per cent of all income. Women also account for 60 per cent of all illiterates and, together with their children, about 80 per cent of all refugees.

globalization Is the spread and intensification of economic, social, and cultural relations across international borders.

hegemonic stability theory A hegemon—a dominant military and economic power—is necessary for the creation and full development of a liberal world market economy, because in the absence of such a power, liberal rules cannot be enforced around the world. That, in its simplest form, is the theory of hegemonic stability, which is indebted to mercantilist thinking about politics being in charge of economics.

hegemony In IR, a concept referring to a state's power relative to that of other states. A state may be considered a hegemon if it is so powerful economically and militarily that it is a dominant influence on the domestic and foreign policies of other states. Depending on its level of power, a state may be a regional hegemon (e.g., Germany immediately prior to and during the Second World War) or a global hegemon (e.g., many agree, the United States in the late twentieth and early twenty-first centuries).

ideational view In the ideational view held by social constructivists, ideas always matter. The material world is indeterminate; it needs to be interpreted.

Without ideas there can be no larger context of meaning. Ideas define the meaning of material power.

imperialism The projection of power by a political entity for the purpose of territorial expansion and political and economic influence beyond its formal borders. Much of history has been marked by the expansion and demise of empires; the Roman Empire, the Mongol Empire, the British Empire, and the Ottoman Empire, to name but a few. After the Second World War, the last of the great empires (with the possible exception of the Chinese) were dissolved.

institutional liberalism This strand of liberalism picks up on earlier liberal thought about the beneficial effects of international institutions. The earlier liberal vision was one of transforming international relations from a 'jungle' of chaotic power politics to a 'zoo' of regulated and peaceful intercourse. This transformation was to be achieved through the building of international organizations, most importantly the League of Nations. Present-day institutional liberals are less optimistic than their more idealist predecessors. They do agree that international institutions can make cooperation easier and far more likely, but they do not claim that such institutions can by themselves guarantee a qualitative transformation of international relations, from a 'jungle' to a 'zoo'. Powerful states will not easily be completely constrained. However, institutional liberals do not agree with the realist view that international institutions are mere 'scraps of paper', that they are at the complete mercy of powerful states. They are of independent importance, and they can promote cooperation between states.

interdependence liberalism A branch of liberal thinking which argues that a high division of labour in the international economy increases interdependence between states, and discourages and reduces violent conflict between states. There still remains a risk that modern states will slide back to the military option and once again enter into arms races and violent confrontations. But that is not a likely prospect. It is in the less developed countries that war now occurs, because at lower levels of economic development land continues to be the dominant factor of production; modernization and interdependence are far weaker.

international justice Is, along with international order, a fundamental normative value of the International Society tradition. This approach discerns tendencies towards both communicative justice (as in diplomatic practices) and distributive justice (as in the provision of development aid) in international relations.

international order An order between states in a system or society of states. Along with international justice, international order is a fundamental normative value of the International Society tradition. Hedley Bull identifies four goals necessary for international order: preserving international society; upholding the independence of member states; maintaining peace; and adhering to norms governing war, diplomacy, and sovereignty. Responsibility for the pursuit and preservation of international order lies with the great powers, whose fundamental duty, according to Bull, is to maintain the 'balance of power'.

International Political Economy (IPE) IPE is about international wealth and international poverty; about who gets what in the international system. If economics is about the pursuit of wealth, and politics about the pursuit of power, the two interact in puzzling and complicated ways. It is this complex interplay in the international context between politics and economics, between states and markets, which is at the core of IPE.

International Relations (IR) IR is the shorthand name for the subject of international relations. The traditional core of IR concerns the development and change of sovereign statehood in the context of the larger system or society of states. Contemporary IR not only concerns political relations between states but also a host of other subjects: economic interdependence, human rights, transnational corporations, international organizations, the environment, gender, inequalities, development, terrorism, and so forth.

International Society/International Society School This approach to IR emphasizes the simultaneous presence in international society of both realist and liberal elements. There is conflict and there is cooperation; there are states and there are individuals. These different elements cannot be simplified and abstracted into a single theory that emphasizes only one aspect—e.g., power. International Society theorists argue for an approach that recognizes the simultaneous presence of all these elements.

international state of nature This is a permanent condition of actual or potential war between sovereign states. War is necessary, as a last resort, for resolving disputes between states that cannot agree and will not acquiesce. Human society and morality is confined to the state and does not extend into international relations, which is a political arena of considerable turmoil, discord, and conflict between states in which the great powers dominate everybody else.

international system According to Hedley Bull, an international system is formed when states have sufficient contact between them, and sufficient impact on one another's decisions, to make the behaviour of each a necessary element in the calculations of the other.

Islamic State of Iraq and the Levant (ISIL or ISIS) An acutely violent and barbaric form of terrorism in the Middle East, but also a better organized, more capable and more determined form, that aspires to be an Islamic State or Caliphate, and that seeks to destroy and displace Syria, Iraq, Jordan, and other existing states in that region by using the most shocking methods and tactics imaginable.

juridical statehood Part of the external basis of a state's sovereignty. A state must be viewed as a formal or legal institution by other states—hence the fact that, for example, Quebec will never be a sovereign state unless Canada, the United States, and others recognize it as such. In addition to sovereignty itself, this dimension of statehood includes the right to membership in international organizations and the possession of various international rights and responsibilities.

laissez-faire Is the idea of freedom of the market from all kinds of political restriction and regulation, supported by early economic liberals. Yet, even these liberals were aware of the need for a politically constructed legal framework as a basis for the market. Laissez-faire does not mean the absence of any political regulation whatsoever; it means that the state shall only set up those minimal underpinnings that are necessary for the market to function properly. This is the classical version of economic liberalism. At the present time this view is also put forward under labels such as 'conservatism' or 'neoliberalism'; the content is, however, basically the same. The 'conservative/neoliberal' economic policies of Margaret Thatcher in Britain and of Ronald

Reagan in the Unites States were both based on classical laissez-faire doctrines.

level-of-analysis approach Foreign policy theories analysed at three different levels initially conceptualized by Kenneth Waltz: the systemic level involving the distribution of power among states; the nation-state level involving the type of government, the relations between the state and groups in society, and the bureaucratic make-up of the state apparatus; and the level of the individual decision maker, involving his or her way of thinking, basic beliefs, personal priorities, and so forth.

liberal approach Foreign policy theorists concerned with multilateral questions are likely to take a liberal approach, emphasizing international institutions—such as the United Nations or the World Trade Organization (WTO)—as a means of reducing international conflict and promoting mutual understanding and common interests.

liberalism The liberal tradition in IR emphasizes the great potential for human progress in modern civil society and the capitalist economy, both of which can flourish in states which guarantee individual liberty. The modern liberal state invokes a political and economic system that will bring peace and prosperity. Relations between liberal states will be collaborative and cooperative.

Marxism The political economy of the nineteenth-century German philosopher and economist Karl Marx in many ways represents a fundamental critique of economic liberalism. Economic liberals view the economy as a positive-sum game with benefits for all. Marx rejected that view. Instead, he saw the economy as a site of human exploitation and class inequality. Marx thus takes the zero-sum argument of mercantilism and applies it to relations of classes instead of relations of states. Marxists agree with mercantilists that politics and economics are closely intertwined; both reject the liberal view of an economic sphere operating under its own laws. But where mercantilists see economics as a tool of politics, Marxists put economics first and politics second. For Marxists, the capitalist economy is based on two antagonistic social classes: one class, the bourgeoisie, owns the means of production; the other class, the proletariat, owns only its labour power which it must sell to the bourgeoisie. But labour puts in more work than it gets back in pay; there is a surplus value appropriated by the bourgeoisie. That is capitalist profit and it is derived from labour exploitation.

materialist view According to the materialist view, power and national interest are the driving forces in international politics. Power is ultimately military capability, supported by economic and other resources. National interest is the self-regarding desire by states for power, security, or wealth. Power and interest are seen as 'material' factors; they are objective entities in the sense that because of anarchy, states are compelled to be preoccupied with power and interest. In this view, ideas matter little; they can be used to rationalize actions dictated by material interest.

mercantilism The world view of political elites that were at the forefront of building the modern state. They took the approach that economic activity is and should be subordinated to the primary goal of building a strong state. In other words, economics is a tool of politics, a basis for political power. That is a defining feature of mercantilist thinking. Mercantilists see the international economy as an arena of conflict between opposing national interests, rather than an area of cooperation and mutual gain. In brief, economic competition between states is a 'zero-sum game' where one state's gain is another state's loss.

modernists Those who believe that environmental challenges are not a serious challenge to advanced societies. Progress in knowledge and technology will enable us to protect the environment.

modernization theory A liberal theory of development; the basic idea is that developing countries should be expected to follow the same developmental path taken earlier by the developed countries in the West: a progressive journey from a traditional, pre-industrial, agrarian society towards a modern, industrial, mass-consumption society. Development means overcoming barriers of pre-industrial production, backward institutions, and parochial value systems which impede the process of growth and modernization.

national security The policies employed and the actions undertaken by a state to counter real or potential internal and external threats and to ensure the safety of its citizens. This is one of the fundamental responsibilities of the state to its people, and *the* fundamental state responsibility according to the realist view of IR. Before the advent of the state and the state system, security was provided by family, clan, warlord, or another locally based entity; this responsibility, among others, was gradually transferred to the state.

neoclassical realism Seeks to improve upon neorealism by introducing elements that neorealists have left out of their analysis. Neoclassical realists clearly want to retain the structural argument of neorealism. But they also want to add to it the instrumental (policy or strategy) argument of the role of stateleaders on which classical realism places its emphasis. Anarchy and the relative power of states do not dictate the foreign policies of stateleaders. That is to say, international structure (anarchy and the balance of power) constrains states but it does not ultimately dictate to leadership policies and actions. Internal characteristics of states also affect the policy choices made by stateleaders.

neoliberalism A renewed liberal approach which seeks to avoid the utopianism of earlier liberalist theory. Neoliberals share classical liberal ideas about the possibility of progress and change, but they repudiate idealism. They also strive to formulate theories and apply new methods which are scientific.

neorealism This theory developed by Kenneth Waltz analyses how the decentralized and anarchical structure of the state system, in particular the relative distribution of power of states, is the central focus. Structures more or less determine actions. International change occurs when great powers rise and fall and the balance of power shifts accordingly. A typical means of such change is great-power war. Actors are less important because structures compel them to act in certain ways. An ethics of statecraft is thus unnecessary.

normative theory Can be viewed as the political theory or moral philosophy that underlies IR. Normative theory is primarily concerned to understand fundamental values of international life, the moral dimensions of international relations, and the place of ethics in statecraft. Although it focuses on values, rules, practices, and the like, normative theory is not necessarily a prescriptive approach to IR.

North Atlantic Treaty Organization (NATO) An international defence organization established in 1949 to provide the assured concerted defence of each of its member states. NATO (whose primary member was and is the United States), and the signatories of the Warsaw Pact (whose primary member was the Soviet Union) were the two rivals (though fundamentally the United States and the Soviet Union) in the Cold War and the bipolar world order. NATO outlived the Warsaw Pact and in 2004 accepted seven new members, including six former Warsaw Pact countries.

offensive realism A theory developed by John Mearsheimer, in contrast to 'defensive realism'. Great powers, according to this theory, are perpetually seeking ways to gain power over their rivals, towards the ultimate goal of hegemony.

ontology The philosophical study of the nature (or reality) of the world and its components. Methodological divisions and debates in IR often reflect differing and even contradictory ontologies; e.g., whether an 'objective' world exists outside human experience, or only a 'subjective' world constructed by human experience. The claim that international relations is an external 'thing' or 'object' or 'reality' is associated with behaviouralist and positivist approaches, such as neorealism. The alternative claim that international relations consists of shared human understandings expressed via language, ideas, and concepts is associated with International Society, normative theory, constructivism, and postmodernism.

pluralism Along with solidarism, one of two International Society approaches to the potential conflict between state sovereignty and respect for human rights. A pluralist view of the state system emphasizes the primacy of state sovereignty: a policy of non-intervention must be maintained even when another state is experiencing (or complicit in) a humanitarian crisis within its borders. Civil rights (within states) take precedence over human rights (between states).

positivism A methodology in IR that employs most of the attitudes and assumptions of behaviouralism but does so in a more sophisticated way. Positivism is a fundamentally scientific approach. Its advocates and adherents believe that there can be objective knowledge of the social and political dimensions of the world, and that this knowledge is obtainable through the careful development and testing of empirical propositions. The social scientist is no different from any other scientist in this regard.

post-colonialism Adopts a post-structural attitude in order to understand the situation in areas that were conquered by Europe; in particular, in Africa, Asia, and Latin America. When Western scholars talk about 'traditional' and 'underdeveloped' 'Third World' countries, they are really constructing certain images of these areas which reflect how the powerful dominate and organize the ways in which states in the South are perceived and discussed. Any real liberation of the South thus needs to critically expose such images; only in that way can the road be paved for really democratic and egalitarian relationships.

postmodern states Are states with high levels of cross-border integration. The economy is globalized rather than 'national'. The polity is characterized by multi-level governance at the supranational, national, and sub-national level. Collective loyalties are increasingly projected away from the state.

postmodernism A post-positivist approach to IR that rejects the modern, enlightenment idea that ever-expanding human knowledge will lead to an improved understanding and mastery of the international system. A distinctive feature of postmodernist discourse in IR is an inclination toward scepticism, debunking, and deconstruction of 'universal truths'—such as those advanced by Kant or Marx or Waltz—that are supposed to be valid for all times and places.

post-positivism A methodology developed largely in reaction to positivist claims. Post-positivism presupposes methods that acknowledge the distinctiveness of human beings as such; i.e., creatures that must live with and among each other in order to lead a human life. Post-positivist methodology rests on the proposition that people conceive, construct, and constitute the worlds in which they live, including the international world, which is an entirely human arrangement and nothing else. Social science is a different methodology from that of natural science.

post-positivist approaches Are united by a dissatisfaction with the established theoretical traditions in the discipline, in particular with neorealism.

They argue against positivist methodology with its focus on observable facts and measurable data. Post-positivists emphasize that IR theorists (as are all theorists of human affairs) are an integrated part of the world they study. In that sense, theorists are insiders, not outsiders. They make certain assumptions and create certain images of reality; knowledge is not and cannot be neutral. There is no single, final truth out there; there are competing claims about how the world hangs together and what makes it tick. Three of the most important ones are post-structuralism, post-colonialism, and feminism.

post-structuralism Is focused on language and discourse; it adopts a critical attitude towards established approaches in that it highlights the ways in which these theories represent and discuss the world. It is particularly critical of neorealism because of its one-sided focus on (Northern) states. Neorealism presents a world where a variety of actors (e.g., women, the poor, groups in the South, protest movements) and processes (e.g., exploitation, subordination, environmental degradation) are not identified and analysed. Neorealism, therefore, constructs a biased picture of the world that needs to be exposed and criticized.

public goods Such goods are characterized by non-excludability; others cannot be denied access to them. The air that we breathe is an example of such a good. A lighthouse is another example of a public good; so is a road or a pavement. The elements of a liberal world economy, such as a currency system for international payments, or the possibility to trade in a free market, are other examples of public goods. Once created, they are there for the benefit of all.

quasi-state A state that possesses juridical statehood but is severely deficient in empirical statehood. A large number of states in the developing world can be defined in this way: they are recognized as states and participate in the state system, but they have weak or corrupt political institutions, underdeveloped economies, and little or no national unity.

Rational Actor Model (RAM) An approach to foreign policy analysis at the systemic level that views the sovereign state as a unitary actor driven by a motivation to advance its national interests, and which assumes that decisions made by the state are based on rational choice.

rational choice theory Neoclassical economics present a simple model of individuals and their basic behaviour. That model—called rational choice theory—is relevant, so the economists claim, not merely for economics, but for every other sphere of human behaviour. Rational choice begins with individuals. Whatever happens in the social world, including in international relations, can be explained by individual choices. What a state or any other organization does can be explained by choices also made by individuals. This view is called methodological individualism. Furthermore, individual actors are rational and self-interested. They want to make themselves better off. This is true for everybody; not merely for sellers and buyers in economic markets, but also for bureaucrats and politicians. Finally, when individuals act in a rational and self-interested way, the overall result or outcome for states or systems will be the best possible. Just as 'the invisible hand' in liberal economics leads from individual greed to the best possible economic result for all, so individual actions by bureaucrats and politicians lead to the best possible outcomes. So if we want to understand what governments do, our first priority must be to understand the preferences; that is, the goals, of public officials. They will be looking for private benefits: re-election, promotion, prestige, and so on. Once we understand how these preferences condition their behaviour, we are in a position to understand how state policies are affected. That is a basic claim of rational choice theory.

rationalism Is one of three interacting philosophies (along with realism and revolutionism) whose dialogue, according to Martin Wight, is essential to an adequate understanding of IR. Rationalists, such as Hugo Grotius, are more optimistic in their view of human nature than are realists. Rationalism conceives of states as legal organizations that operate in accordance with international law and diplomatic practice; international relations are, therefore, norm-governed policies and activities based on the mutually recognized authority of sovereign states.

realism The realist tradition in IR is based on: (1) a pessimistic view of human nature—humans are self-interested and egoistic; (2) a conviction that international relations are conflictual and may always lead to war; (3) a high regard for the values of national security and state survival; and (4) a basic scepticism that there can be progress in international politics.

republican liberalism This strand of liberalism is built on the claim that liberal democracies are more peaceful and law-abiding than are other political systems. The argument is not that democracies never go to war; democracies have gone to war as often as have non-democracies; but the argument is that democracies do not fight each other. This observation was first articulated by Immanuel Kant in the late eighteenth century in reference to republican states rather than democracies. It was resurrected by Dean Babst in 1964 and it has been advanced in numerous studies since then.

responsibility to protect (R2P) An international norm according to which a state has a responsibility to protect its population from mass atrocities. If it fails to do so, the international community has a responsibility to intervene.

revolutionism One of three interacting philosophies (along with realism and rationalism) whose dialogue, according to Wight, is essential to an adequate understanding of IR. Revolutionists, such as Kant and Marx, are solidarists who believe in the 'moral unity' of humankind beyond the state. They hold in common a progressive aim of changing (even eliminating) the international state system in the expectation of creating a better world. Revolutionists are more optimistic than rationalists and realists about human nature: they believe in the achievability of human perfection.

security dilemma An important paradox inherent in the state system. A fundamental reason for the existence of states is to provide their citizens with security from internal and external threats; however, the existence of these armed states threatens the very security they are expected to maintain.

social constructivism Constructivists argue that the most important aspect of international relations is social, not material. Furthermore, they argue that this social reality is not objective, or external, to the observer of international affairs. The social and political world, including the world of international relations, is not a physical entity or material object that is outside human consciousness. Consequently, the study of international relations must focus on the ideas and beliefs that inform the actors on the international scene as well as the shared understandings between them.

social constructivist approach A theory of foreign policymaking as an intersubjective world, whose ideas and discourse can be scrutinized in order to arrive at a better understanding of the process. The discourse of actors is seen to shape policymaking, since policies are conveyed by speech and writing. Some constructivists claim that identity, rooted in ideas and discourse, is the basis for a definition of interests and thus lies behind any foreign policy.

social science realism An American theory that international relations are determined by the national interests of states, especially the great powers, who compete for domination especially in military and economic affairs. Their great contest ultimately shapes the relations of all other states.

society of states According to Hedley Bull, a society of states exists when a group of states conceive themselves to be bound by a common set of rules in their relations with one another, and they share in the working of common institutions.

sociological liberalism A branch of liberal thinking which stresses that IR is not only about state–state relations; it is also about transnational relations; i.e., relations between people, groups, and organizations belonging to different countries. The emphasis on society as well as the state, on many different types of actor and not just national governments, has led some to identify liberal thought by the term 'pluralism'.

soft power Also termed 'co-optive power', soft power is, according to Joseph Nye, the ability to structure a situation so that other nations develop preferences or define their interests in ways consistent with their own nation.

solidarism Along with pluralism, one of two International Society approaches to the potential conflict between recognition of state sovereignty and respect for human rights. A solidarist view stresses individuals, not states, as the ultimate members of international society; there exist both the right and the duty of states to intervene in foreign countries for humanitarian reasons.

sovereignty/sovereign state As applied to a state, sovereignty includes both ultimate internal authority and external recognition. Internally, a state is sovereign when it exercises supreme authority over the affairs and people within its territory; externally, a state is sovereign when it is recognized as such by the international community; i.e., its territorial integrity and *internal* sovereignty are respected and upheld. Currently, the greatest threat to sovereignty is the rise in prominence of IGOs, NGOs, and the global economy (and globalization in general), all of which increase state interdependence and accountability.

state The main actor in IR, sometimes referred to as a 'country' or a 'nation-state'. The term is used in reference to both the populated territory of the state and the political body that governs that territory. The state is a territory-based socio-political organization entrusted with the responsibility of defending basic social conditions and values, including security, freedom, order, justice, and welfare. Because of their role as protectors of security, states have a monopoly on the authority and power to engage in war. Though states differ in their level of success in defending the aforementioned values, the state is understood to have legal jurisdiction (sovereignty) over its own affairs and population. In popular view, the Peace of Westphalia (1648), following the Thirty Years War, marked the formal beginning of the modern sovereign state and modern international relations.

'state of nature' Thomas Hobbes's famous description of the original, pre-civil existence of humankind, a state in which life is 'solitary, poor, nasty, brutish, and short'. In their natural condition, all people are endangered by everyone else, and nobody is able to ensure his or her security or survival. This mutual fear and insecurity is, according to Hobbes, the driving force behind the creation of the sovereign state.

state system An organization of independent states wherein mutual sovereignty is recognized; relations are subject to international law and diplomatic practices; and a balance of power exists among states. Historically, the geopolitical outcome of the Peace of Westphalia was the first (albeit only European) state system in the modern sense. We now speak of a global state system, as the world's inhabitable land is covered entirely by states and their territories. With the dissolution of the Soviet Union, the break-up of both Czechoslovakia and Yugoslavia, and the end of the Cold War, there are now nearly 200 states in the state system.

strategic realism This theory developed by Thomas Schelling analyses how a state can employ power to persuade a rival to do what the state desires; i.e., through coercion instead of brute force, which is always dangerous and inefficient. Unlike classical and neoclassical realism, strategic realism does not make normative claims; values are taken as given and not weighed during analysis. Rather, the theory seeks to provide analytical tools for diplomacy and foreign policy, which are seen to be instrumental activities that can best be understood via game-theoretical analysis.

strong liberals Are liberal theorists who maintain that qualitative change has taken place. Today's economic interdependence ties countries much closer together; economies are globalized; production and consumption take place in a worldwide marketplace. It would be extremely costly in welfare terms for countries to opt out of that system. Today, there is also a group of consolidated liberal democracies for whom reversion to authoritarianism is next to unthinkable, because all major groups in society support democracy. These countries conduct their mutual international relations in new and more cooperative ways.

structural violence The oppression and hardship that people suffer from political and economic structures that subject them to unequal positions. Johan Galtung invented the concept in order to differentiate other types of violence from direct violence.

structuration A concept suggested by Anthony Giddens as a way of analysing the relationship between structures and actors. Structures (i.e., the rules and conditions that guide social action) do not determine what actors do in any mechanical way—an impression one might get from the neorealist view of how the structure of anarchy constrains state actors. The relationship between structures and actors involves intersubjective understanding and meaning. Structures do constrain actors, but actors can also transform structures by thinking about them and acting on them in new ways. The notion of structuration, therefore, leads to a less rigid and more dynamic view of the relationship between structure and actors. IR constructivists use this as a starting point for suggesting a less rigid view of anarchy.

sustainable development Development that meets the needs of the present without compromising the ability of future generations to meet their own needs (definition by World Commision On Environment and Development 1987).

terrorism The unlawful use or threatened use of violence against civilians, often to achieve political, religious, or similar objectives. International terrorism involves the territory or the citizens of more than one country. Terrorism is nothing new; it has probably existed ever since human societies began to regulate the use of violence. It is the unusual scale and intensity of the 11 September 2001 attacks in New York and Washington, DC, and later attacks in Ankara, Madrid, London, and elsewhere that has put the issue of international terrorism high on the agenda.

think tanks Are private research organizations that disseminate useful information and provide expert advice with the aim of influencing government policies. They were initially developed in the United States by philanthropists and public intellectuals who recognized the importance of addressing, debating, and (hopefully) solving troublesome issues of American foreign policy, particularly war. They have subsequently been developed in many other countries. American 'think tanks' are differentiated from their foreign counterparts by the degree to which politicians in the United States actively seek advice from these organizations.

traditional approach to foreign policy Proponents include Niccolò Machiavelli, Hugo Grotius, and Henry Kissinger. The traditional approach, with its attention to the specific historical foreign policies of a particular country, analyses the substance of foreign policy as practised, as opposed to the systematic theories and explanations advanced by more analytical and scientific approaches to foreign policy.

verstehen Max Weber emphasized that the social world (i.e., the world of human interaction) is fundamentally different from the natural world of physical phenomena. Human beings rely on 'understanding' of each other's actions and assigning 'meaning' to them. In order to comprehend human interaction, we cannot merely describe it in the way we describe physical phenomena, such as a boulder falling off a cliff; we need a different kind of interpretive understanding, or *verstehen*. Is patting another person's face a punishment or a caress? We cannot know until we assign meaning to the act. Weber concluded that 'subjective understanding is the specific characteristic of sociological knowledge'. Constructivists rely on such insights to emphasize the importance of 'meaning' and 'understanding'.

weak liberals Liberal theorists who accept a great deal of the realist critique of liberal theory, especially that anarchy persists and there is no escape from self-help and the security dilemma.

world system analysis An approach developed by Immanuel Wallerstein. A world system is characterized by a certain economic and a certain political structure with the one depending on the other. In human history, there have been two basic varieties of world systems: world empires and world economies. In world empires, such as the Roman Empire, political and economic control is concentrated in a unified centre. World economies, in contrast, are tied together economically in a single division of labour; but politically, authority is decentralized, residing in multiple polities, in a system of states. Wallerstein's key focus is the analysis of the modern world economy, characterized by capitalism.

BIBLIOGRAPHY

Abdelal, R., Blyth, M., and Parsons, C. (2010). *Constructing the International Economy*. Ithaca, NY: Cornell University Press.

Acharya, A. and Johnston, A. I. (eds) (2007). *Crafting Cooperation: Regional International Institutions in Comparative Perspective*. Cambridge: Cambridge University Press.

Adler, E. (2001). 'Constructivism and International Relations', in W. Carlsnaes, T. Risse, and B. A. Simmons (eds), *Handbook of International Relations*. London: Sage, 95–118.

Adler, E. and Barnett, M. N. (1996). 'Governing Anarchy: A Research Agenda for the Study of Security Communities', *Ethics and International Affairs*, 10/1: 63–98.

Adler, E. and Barnett, M. N. (eds) (1998). *Security Communities*. Cambridge: Cambridge University Press.

Alden, C., and Amnon, A. (2011). *Foreign Policy Analysis: New Approaches*. London: Routledge.

Alison, M. (2009). *Women and Political Violence: Female Combatants in Ethno-National Conflict*. London: Routledge.

Allison, G. (1971). *Essence of Decision: Explaining the Cuban Missile Crisis*. New York: HarperCollins.

Allison, G. (2004). *Nuclear Terrorism: The Ultimate Preventable Catastrophe*. New York: Times Books.

Allison, G. and Zelikow, P. (1999). *Essence of Decision: Explaining the Cuban Missile Crisis*, 2nd edn. New York: Longman.

Amin, S. (1976). *Unequal Development*. Hassocks, Sussex: Harvester Press.

Amin, S. (1990). *Delinking: Towards a Polycentric World*. London: Zed.

Andrews, N. and Bawa, S. (2014). 'A Post-Development Hoax? (Re-)Examining the Past, Present, and Future of Development Studies', *Third World Quarterly*, 35/6: 922–38.

Angell, N. (1909). *The Great Illusion*. London: Weidenfeld & Nicolson.

Archer, K., Bosman, M., Amen, M. M., and Schmidt, E. (2007). 'Locating Globalizations and Cultures', *Globalizations*, 4/1: 1–14.

Armstrong, D. (1999). 'Law, Justice and the Idea of World Society', *International Affairs*, 75/3: 547–61.

Ashley, R. K. (1981). 'Political Realism and Human Interests', *International Studies Quarterly*, 25/2: 204–36.

Ashley, R. K. (1984). 'The Poverty of Neorealism', *International Organization*, 38 (2): 225–86.

Ashley, R. K. (1986). 'The Poverty of Neorealism', in R. O. Keohane (ed.), *Neo-Realism and its Critics*. New York: Columbia University Press, 255–301.

Ashley, R. K. (1996). 'The Achievements of Post-Structuralism', in S. Smith, K. Booth, and M. Zalewski (eds), *International Theory: Positivism and Beyond*. Cambridge: Cambridge University Press, 240–53.

Ashley, R. K. and Walker, R. B. J. (1990). 'Conclusion: Reading Dissidence/Writing the Discipline: Crisis and the Question of Sovereignty in International Studies', *International Studies Quarterly*, 34/3: 367–416.

Balaam, D. N. and Dillman, B. (2014). *Introduction to International Political Economy*, 6th edn. London: Pearson Education.

Baldwin, D. A. (ed.) (1993). *Neorealism and Neoliberalism: The Contemporary Debate*. New York: Columbia University Press.

Barber, B. R. (1995). *Jihad vs McWorld*. New York: Times Books.

Barber, P. (1979). *Diplomacy: The World of the Honest Spy*. London: The British Library.

Barkin, S. (2010). *Realist Constructivism: Rethinking International Relations Theory*. Cambridge: Cambridge University Press.

Barnett, M. (1996). 'Identity and Alliances in the Middle East', in P. Katzenstein (ed.), *The Culture of National Security: Norms and Identity in World Politics*. New York: Columbia University Press, 400–47.

Barnett, M. and Duvall, R. (2005). 'Power in Global Governance', in M. Barnett and R. Duvall (eds), *Power in Global Governance*. Cambridge: Cambridge University Press, 1–33.

Barnett, M. and Finnemore, M. (2005). 'The Power of Liberal International Organizations', in M. Barnett and R. Duvall (eds), *Power in Global Governance*. Cambridge: Cambridge University Press, 161–85.

Beach, D. (2010). 'Leadership and Intergovernmental Negotiations in the EU', in W. E. Paterson, N. Nugent, and M. P. Egan (eds), *Research Agendas in EU Studies: Stalking the Elephant*. Basingstoke: Palgrave Macmillan.

Bellin, E. (2008). 'New Trends in the Study of Religion and Politics', *World Politics*, 60/2: 315–47.

Bendor, J. and Hammond, T. H. (1992). 'Rethinking Allison's Models', *American Political Science Review*, 86 (June): 301–22.

Berger, P. (1999). *The Desecularization of the World*. Grand Rapids, MI: William B. Eerdmann's Publishing.

Berger, P. (2003). *Terror and Liberalism*. New York: W. W. Norton.

Berlin, I. (1969). *Four Essays on Liberty*. Oxford: Oxford University Press.

Bernauer, T., Böhmelt, T., Buhaug, H., et al. (2011). 'Intrastate Water-Related Conflict and Cooperation: A new Event Dataset', paper for 52nd Annual Convention of the International Studies Association, Montreal, 16–19 March.

Biersteker, T. J. (1989). 'Critical Reflections on Post-Positivism in International Relations', *International Studies Quarterly*, 33: 263–67.

Birnie, P. (1992). 'International Environmental Law: Its Adequacy for Present and Future Needs', in A. Hurrell and B. Kingsbury (eds), *The International Politics of the Environment*. Oxford: Clarendon Press, 51–84.

Bleiker, R. (2001). 'Forget IR Theory', in S. Chan, P. Mandaville, and R. Bleiker (eds), *The Zen of International Relations. IR Theory from East to West*. New York: Palgrave, 37–66.

Blumenthal, M. W. (CEO, Unisys Company) (1988). 'The World Economy and Technological Change', *Foreign Affairs*, 66: 537–8.

Boggs, C. (2005). *Imperial Delusions: American Militarism and Endless War*. Lanham, MD: Rowman & Littlefield.

Booth, K. (1991). 'Security and Emancipation', *Review of International Studies*, 17 (Oct): 313–26.

Booth, K. (1995). 'Human Wrongs and International Relations', *International Affairs*, 71: 103–26.

Boulding, K. (1979). *Stable Peace*. Austin, TX: University of Texas Press.

Bozdaglioglou, Y. (2007). 'Constructivism and Identity Formation: An Interactive Approach', *Review of International Law and Politics*, 3/11: 121–44.

Brecht, A. (1963). *Man and his Government*. New York: Harcourt, Brace.

Bremmer, I. (2012). *Every Nation for Itself. Winners and Losers in a G-Zero World*. London: Penguin.

Bridges, R., Dukes, P. C., Hargreaves, J. D., and Scott, W. (eds) (1969). *Nations and Empires*. London: Macmillan.

Brock, L., Holm, H-H., Stohl, M., and Sørensen, G. (2011). *Fragile States*. Cambridge: Polity Press.

Brooks, S. G. and Wohlforth, W. C. (2008). *World Out of Balance: International Relations and the Challenge of American Supremacy*. Princeton: Princeton University Press.

Brown, C. and Ainley, K. (2009). *Understanding International Relations*, 4th edn. Basingstoke: Palgrave Macmillan.

Brown, S. (1994). *The Causes and Prevention of War*, 2nd edn. New York: St Martin's Press.

Brown, S. (2013). *The Future of US Global Power*. Basingstoke: Palgrave Macmillan.

Bull, H. (1969). 'International Theory: The Case for a Classical Approach', in K. Knorr and J. N. Rosenau (eds), *Contending Approaches to International Politics*. Princeton, NJ: Princeton University Press, 20–38.

Bull, H. (1979). 'Recapturing the Just War for Political Theory', *World Politics*, 32: 590–9.

Bull, H. (1980). 'The Great Irresponsibles', *International Journal*, 35.

Bull, H. (1995). *The Anarchical Society: A Study of Order in World Politics*, 2nd edn. London: Macmillan.

Bull, H. and Watson, A. (eds) (1984). *The Expansion of International Society*. Oxford: Clarendon Press.

Burton, J. (1972). *World Society*. Cambridge: Cambridge University Press.

Buzan, B. (2004). *From International to World Society?* Cambridge: Cambridge University Press.

Buzan, B. (2011). 'A World Without Superpowers: Decentred Globalism', *International Relations*, 25/1: 3–25.

Buzan, B. (2014). *An Introduction to the English School of International Relations*. Cambridge: Polity Press.

Buzan, B. and Lawson, G. (2014). 'Capitalism and the Emergent World Order', *International Affairs*, 90/1: 71–91.

Buzan, B., Jones, C., and Little, R. (1993). *The Logic of Anarchy: Neorealism to Structural Realism*. New York: Columbia University Press.

Campbell, D. (1998). *Writing Security—United States' Foreign Policy and the Politics of Identity*. Minneapolis, MN: University of Minnesota Press.

Campbell, I. (2004). 'Retreat from Globalization', *The National Interest*, 75: 111–17.

Cardoso, F. H. and Faletto, E. (1979). *Dependency and Development in Latin America*. Berkeley, CA: University of California Press.

Carlsnaes, W. (2013). 'Foreign Policy', in W. Carlsnaes, T. Risse, and B. Simmons (eds), *Handbook of International Relations*, 2nd edn. London: Sage, 298–326.

Carnoy, M. (1984). *The State and Political Theory*. Princeton, NJ: Princeton University Press.

Carr, E. H. (1964 [1939]). *The Twenty Years' Crisis*. New York: Harper & Row.

Carter, A. (1993). 'Towards a Green Political Theory', in A. Dobson and P. Lucardie (eds), *The Politics of Nature: Explorations in Green Political Theory*. London: Routledge, 39–62.

Casanova, J. (1994). *Public Religions in the Modern World*. Chicago, IL: University of Chicago Press.

Cerny, P. G. (2010). *Rethinking World Politics: A Theory of Transnational Neopluralism*. Oxford: Oxford University Press.

Chandler, R. M., Wang, L., and Fuller, L. K. (eds) (2010). *Women, War and Violence. Personal Perspectives and Global Activism*. Basingstoke: Palgrave Macmillan.

Chang, H. J. (2002). *Kicking away the Ladder*. London: Anthem Books.

Chasek, P. S., Downie, D. L., and Brown, J. W. (2010). *Global Environmental Politics*, 5th edn. Boulder: Westview.

Checkel, J., and Katzenstein, P. J. (eds) (2009). *European Identity*. New York: Cambridge University Press.

Chowdhry, G. and Nair, S. (2013). *Power, Postcolonialism and International Relations: Reading Race, Gender, and Class*. London: Routledge.

Cipolla, C. M. (1977). 'Introduction', in C. M. Cipolla (ed.), *The Fontana Economic History of Europe*. Glasgow: Fontana/Collins, 7–8.

Clark, I. (2011). *Hegemony in International Society*. Oxford: Oxford University Press.

Claude, I. (1971). *Swords into Ploughshares*, 4th edn. New York: Random House.

Cobden, R. (1903). *Political Writings*, 2 vols. London: Fisher Unwin.

Cohen, B. J. (2014). *Advanced Introduction to International Political Economy*. Cheltenham, UK: Edward Elgar.

Copeland, D. (2000). 'The Constructivist Challenge to Structural Realism', *International Security*, 25/2, 187–212.

Cox, R. W. (1981). 'Social Forces, States and World Orders', *Millennium*, 10: 126–55.

Cox, R. W. (1987). *Production, Power and World Order: Social Forces in the Making of History*. New York: Columbia University Press.

Cox, R. W. (1992). 'Towards a Post-Hegemonic Conceptualization of World Order: Reflections on the Relevancy of Ibn Khaldun', in J. N. Rosenau and E.-O. Czempiel (eds), *Governance without Government: Order and Change in World Politics*. Cambridge: Cambridge University Press, 132–59.

Cox, R. W. (2002). 'Reflections and Transitions', in R. W. Cox with M. G. Schechter, *The Political Economy of a Plural World: Critical Reflections on Power, Morals, and Civilization*. London: Routledge, 26–44.

Cox, R. W. with Schechter, M. G. (2002). *The Political Economy of a Plural World: Critical Reflections on Power, Morals, and Civilization*. London: Routledge.

Crotty, J. (2009). 'Structural Causes of the Global Financial Crisis: A Critical Assessment of the "New Financial Architecture"', *Cambridge Journal of Economics*, 33: 563–80.

Darby, P. and Paolini, A. J. (1994). 'Bridging International Relations and Postcolonialism', *Alternatives*, 19/3: 371–97.

Darwin, J. (2007). *After Tamerlane: The Global History of Empire*. London: Allen Lane.

Deere-Birkbeck, C. (2009). 'Global Governance in the Context of Climate Change: The Challenges of Increasingly Complex Risk Parameters', *International Affairs*, 85/6: 1173–94.

Desch, M. (1998). 'Culture Clash: Assessing the Importance of Ideas in Security Studies', *International Security*, 23/1: 141–70.

Desch, M. and Philpott, D. (eds) (2014). *Religion and International Relations: A Primer for Research*. University of Notre Dame, at: http://rmellon.nd.edu/assets/101872/religion_and_international_relations_report.pdf

Dessler, D. (2000). 'Review of Alexander Wendt: Social Theory of International Politics', *American Political Science Review*, 94/4: 1002–3.

Deudney, D. and Ikenberry, G. J. (1999). 'The Nature and Sources of Liberal International Order', *Review of International Studies*, 25/2: 179–96.

Deutsch, K. W., Kann, R. A., Lichterman, M., et al. (1957). *Political Community and the North Atlantic Area*. Princeton, NJ: Princeton University Press.

Dicken, P. (2011). *Global Shift: Mapping the Changing Contours of the World Economy*, 6th edn. New York: The Guilford Press.

Doty, R. L. (1996). *Imperial Encounters: The Politics of Representation in North—South Relations*. Minneapolis, MN: University of Minnesota Press.

Dougherty, J. E. and Pfaltzgraff, R. L. (1971). *Contending Theories of International Relations*. New York: Lippincott.

Doyle, M. W. (1983). 'Kant, Liberal Legacies and Foreign Affairs', pts 1 and 2, *Philosophy and Public Affairs*, 12/3: 205–35 and 12/4: 323–54.

Doyle, M. W. (1986). 'Liberalism and World Politics'. *American Political Science Review*, 80/4: 1151–69.

Doyle, M. W. (2012). *Liberal Peace: Selected Essays*. Abingdon: Routledge.

Drezner, D. W. (2012). 'The Irony of Global Governance. The System Worked', Washington, DC: Council on Foreign Relations, Working Paper.

Dunne, T. and Flockhart, T. (eds) (2013). *Liberal World Orders*. Oxford: Oxford University Press.

Dunne, T. and Wheeler, N. (1999). *Human Rights in Global Politics*. Cambridge: Cambridge University Press.

Dunne, T., Hansen, L., and Wight, C. (2013). 'The End of International Relations Theory?', *European Journal of International Relations*, 19/3: 405–25.

Dunne, T., Kurki, M., and Smith, S. (eds) (2010). *International Relations Theories: Discipline and Diversity*, 2nd edn. Oxford: Oxford University Press.

Eagly, A. H. and Chaiken, S. (1993). *The Psychology of Attitudes*. Dallas, TX: Harcourt Brace.

Ebenstein, W. (1951). *Great Political Thinkers: Plato to the Present*. New York: Holt, Rinehart, Winston.

Eckersley, R. (1992). *Environmentalism and Political Theory: Towards an Ecocentric Approach*. London: University College London Press.

Eckersley, R. (2004). *The Green State: Rethinking Democracy and Sovereignty*. Cambridge, MA: Massachusetts Institute of Technology Press.

Ehrlich, P. R. and Ehrlich, A. H. (2013). 'Can a Collapse of Global Civilization Be Avoided?', *Proceedings of the Royal Society*, at: http://rspb.royalsocietypublishing.org/content/280/1754/20122845.full.pdf

Elman, C. and Elman, M. F. (2008). 'The Role of History in International Relations', *Millennium*, 37/2: 357–64.

Enloe, C. (1989). *Bananas, Beaches & Bases: Making Feminist Sense of International Politics*. Berkeley, CA: University of California Press.

Eriksen, E. O. (2009). *The Unfinished Democratization of Europe*. Oxford: Oxford University Press.

Escobar, A. (1995). *Encountering Development: The Making and Unmaking of the Third World*. Princeton, NJ: Princeton University Press.

Escobar, A. (2004). 'Beyond the Third World: Imperial Globality, Global Coloniality and Anti-Globalisation Social Movements', *Third World Quarterly*, 25/1: 207–30.

Eulau, H. (1963). *The Behavioral Persuasion in Politics*. New York: Random House.

Evans, G. (2008). *The Responsibility to Protect*. Washington, DC: Brookings Institution.

Evans, G. and Newnham, J. (1992). *The Dictionary of World Politics*. London: Harvester Wheatsheaf.

Evers, T. and **Wogau, P. von** (1973). '"Dependencia". Lateinamerikanische Beiträge zur Theorie der Unterentwicklung', *Das Argument*, 79/4–6: 414–48.

Fallows, J. (1994). *Looking at the Sun*. New York: Pantheon.

Fallows, J. (2002). 'The Dustbin of History: The Military-Industrial Complex', *Foreign Policy*, 133: 46–9.

Falk, R. (1985). 'A New Paradigm for International Legal Studies', in **R. Falk**, **F. Kratochwil**, and **S. H. Mendlovitz** (eds), *International Law: A Contemporary Perspective*. Boulder, CA: Westview Press.

FAO (2012). 'New Hunger Report', at: http://www.fao.org/news/story/en/item/161819/icode/

Fettweis, C. J. (2004). 'Evaluating IR's Crystal Balls: How Predictions of the Future have Withstood Fourteen Years of Unipolarity', *International Studies Review*, 6/1: 79–105.

Fierke, K. M. (2001). 'Critical Methodology and Constructivism', in **K. M. Fierke** and **K. E. Jørgensen** (eds), *Constructing International Relations: The Next Generation*. London: M. E. Sharpe, 115–35.

Fierke, K. and **Jørgensen, K. E.** (eds) (2001). *Constructing International Relations: The Next Generation*. London: M. E. Sharpe.

Finnegan, R. B. (1972). 'International Relations: The Disputed Search for Method', *Review of Politics*, 34: 40–66.

Finnemore, M. (1996). *National Interests in International Society*. Ithaca, NY, and London: Cornell University Press.

Finnemore, M. (2003). *The Purpose of Intervention: Changing Beliefs about the Use of Force*. Ithaca, NY, and London: Cornell University Press.

Forde, S. (1992). 'Classical Realism', in **T. Nardin** and **D. Mapel** (eds), *Traditions of International Ethics*. Cambridge: Cambridge University Press, 62–84.

Frank, A. G. (1967). *Capitalism and Underdevelopment in Latin America*. New York: Monthly Review Press.

Frank, A. G. (1969). *Latin America: Underdevelopment or Revolution?* New York: Monthly Review Press.

Frank, A. G. (1971). 'On the Mechanisms of Imperialism: The Case of Brazil', in **K. Fann** and **D. Hodges** (eds), *Readings in US Imperialism*. Boston, MA: Porter Sargent, 237–8.

Frank, A. G. (1977). 'Dependence is Dead, Long Live Dependence and the Class Struggle: An Answer to Critics', *World Development*, 5/4: 355–70.

Friedman, M. (1962). *Capitalism and Freedom*. Chicago, IL: University of Chicago Press.

Friedman, M. (1993). 'Cooperation, Competition Go Hand in Hand', *Nikkei Weekly*, 15 November: 1–23.

Friedman, T. (2005). *The World Is Flat*. New York: Farrar, Straus, and Giroux.

Fukuyama, F. (1989). 'The End of History?', *National Interest*, 16: 3–18.

Fukuyama, F. (1992). *The End of History and the Last Man*. New York: Avon.

Fukuyama, F. (2012). 'The Future of History: Can Liberal Democracy Survive the Decline of the Middle Class?', *Foreign Affairs*, 53, at: http://www.foreignaffairs.com/articles/136782/francis-fukuyama/the-future-of-history

Fukuyama, F. (2014). *Political Order and Political Decay: From the Industrial Revolution to the Globalization of Democracy*. London: Profile Books.

Fund for Peace (2014). *Fragile States Index 2014*, at: http://ffp.statesindex.org/rankings-2014

Gaddis, J. (1987). *The Long Peace: Inquiries into the History of the Cold War*. New York: Oxford University Press.

Gallie, W. B. (1978). *Philosophers of Peace and War: Kant, Clausewitz, Marx, Engels and Tolstoy*. Cambridge: Cambridge University Press.

George, A. (1980). *Presidential Decisionmaking in Foreign Policy: The Effective Use of Information and Advice*. Boulder, CO: Westview Press.

George, J. and **Campbell, D.** (1990). 'Patterns of Dissent and the Celebration of Difference: Critical Social Theory and International Relations', *International Studies Quarterly*, 34/3: 269–93.

Giddens, A. (1984). *The Constitution of Society*. Berkeley, CA: University of California Press.

Gilbert, M. (1995). *The First World War*. London: HarperCollins.

Gilpin, R. (1987). *The Political Economy of International Relations*. Princeton, NJ: Princeton University Press.

Gilpin, R. (2001). *Global Political Economy: Understanding the International Economic Order*. Princeton, NJ: Princeton University Press.

Glarbo, K. (1999). 'Wide-awake Diplomacy: Reconstructing the Common Foreign and Security Policy of the European Union', *Journal of European Public Policy*, 6/4: 634–52.

Glaser, C. L. (2010). *Rational Theory of International Politics: The Logic of Competition and Cooperation*. Princeton: Princeton University Press.

Goldgeier, J. (1997). 'Psychology and Security', *Security Studies*, 6: 137–66.

Goldhagen, D. J. (1996). *Hitler's Willing Executioners: Ordinary Germans and the Holocaust*. New York: Knopf.

Goldsmith, A. A. (2004). 'Predatory versus Developmental Rule in Africa', *Democratization*, 11/3: 88–110.

Goldstein, J. and Keohane, R. O. (eds) (1993). *Ideas and Foreign Policy: Beliefs, Institutional and Political Change*. Ithaca, NY: Cornell University Press.

Goodin, R. (1990). 'International Ethics and the Environment Crisis', *Ethics and International Affairs*, 4: 93–110.

Goodin, R. (1992). *Green Political Theory*. Cambridge: Polity.

Gowa, J. (1999). *Ballots and Bullets: The Elusive Democratic Peace*. Princeton, NY: Princeton University Press.

Gray, C. (2002). CT 'World Politics as Usual after September 11: Realism Vindicated', in K. Booth and T. Dunne (eds), *Worlds in Collision: Terror and the Future of Global Order*. London: Palgrave Macmillan, 235–45.

Grieco, J. M. (1993). 'Anarchy and the Limits of Cooperation: A Realist Critique of the Newest Liberal Institutionalism', in D. A. Baldwin (ed.), *Neorealism and Neoliberalism: The Contemporary Debate*. New York: Columbia University Press, 116–43.

Grieco, J. M. (1997). 'Realist International Theory and the Study of World Politics', in M. W. Doyle and G. J. Ikenberry (eds), *New Thinking in International Relations*. Boulder, CO: Westview Press, 163–202.

Griffiths, M. (2011). *Rethinking International Relations Theory*. Basingstoke: Palgrave Macmillan.

Grin, J., Rothmans, J., and Schot, J. (2011). *Transitions to Sustainable Development*. London: Routledge.

Gross, M. L. (2010). *Moral Dilemmas of Modern War: Torture, Assassination and Blackmail in an Age of Asymmetric Conflict*. Cambridge: Cambridge University Press.

Gunning, J. (2007). 'A Case for Critical Terrorism Studies?', *Government and Opposition*, 17/37: 363–93.

Guzzini, S. and Leander, A. (eds) (2006). *Constructivism and International Relations: Alexander Wendt and his Critics*. London: Routledge.

Haas, E. B. (1953). 'The Balance of Power: Prescription, Concept, or Propaganda', *World Politics*, 5/4: 442–77.

Haas, E. B. (1958). *The Uniting of Europe: Political, Social and Economic Forces 1950–1957*. Stanford, CA: Stanford University Press.

Haas, E. B. (1976). 'Turbulent Fields and the Theory of Regional Integration', *International Organization*, 30/2: 173–212.

Hacking, I. (1999). *The Social Construction of What?* Cambridge, MA: Harvard University Press.

Hall, P. A. and Soskice, D. (2001). *Varieties of Capitalism: The Institutional Foundations of Comparative Advantage*. Oxford: Oxford University Press.

Hansen, L. (2006). *Security as Practice: Discourse Analysis and the Bosnian War*. London: Routledge.

Hardin, D. (1982). *Collective Action*. Baltimore, MD: Johns Hopkins University Press.

Hardt, M. and Negri, A. (2000). *Empire*. Cambridge, MA: Harvard University Press.

Harrison, E. (2010). 'The Democratic Peace Research Program and System Level Analysis', *Journal of Peace Research*, 47/2: 155–65.

Hart, P., Stern, E. K., and Sundelius, B. (eds) (1997). *Beyond Groupthink: Political Dynamics and Foreign Policy-making*. Ann Arbor, MI: University of Michigan Press.

Haynes, J. (2006). *The Politics of Religion: A Survey*. London: Routledge.

Hegre, H. (2014). 'Democracy and Armed Conflict', *Journal of Peace Research*, 51/2: 159–72.

Herman, M. (1984). 'Personality and Foreign Policy Decision Making: A Study of 54 Heads of Government', in S. Chan and D. Sylvan (eds), *Foreign Policy Decision Making*. New York: Praeger, 53–80.

Hettne, B. (1995). *Development Theory and the Three Worlds*. Harlow: Longman.

Hettne, B. (1996). *Internationella relationer*. Lund: Studentlitteratur.

Hill, C. (2003). *The Changing Politics of Foreign Policy*. Basingstoke: Palgrave Macmillan.

Hirst, P. and Thompson, G. (1992). 'The Problem of "Globalization": International Economic Relations, National Economic Management and the Formation of Trading Blocs', *Economy and Society*, 21/4: 357–94.

Hix, S. (2005). *The Political System of the European Union*, 2nd edn. Basingstoke: Palgrave Macmillan.

Hobbes, T. (1946). *Leviathan*. Oxford: Blackwell.

Hobson, C., Smith, S., Owen, J. M. et al. (2011). 'Roundtable. Between the Theory and Practice of Democratic Peace', *International Relations*, 25/2: 147–85.

Hobson, J. (2007). 'Is Critical Theory Always for the White West and for Western Imperialism? Beyond Westphilian Towards a Post-Racist Critical IR', *Review of International Studies*, 33: 91–116.

Hoffmann, S. (1977). 'An American Social Science: International Relations', *Daedalus*, 106: 41–61.

Hoffmann, S. (1990). 'International Society', in J. D. B. Miller and R. J. Vincent (eds), *Order and Violence: Hedley Bull and International Relations*. Oxford: Clarendon Press, 13–17.

Hoffmann, S. (1991). 'Ethics and Rules of the Game between the Superpowers', in L. Henkin (ed.), *Right v. Might: International Law and the Use of Force*. New York: Council on Foreign Relations Press, 71–93.

Hollis, M. and Smith, S. (1990). *Explaining and Understanding International Relations*. Oxford: Clarendon Press.

Holm, H.-H., and Sørensen, G. (eds) (1995). *Whose World Order? Uneven Globalization and the End of the Cold War*. Boulder, CO: Westview Press.

Holsti, K. J. (1988). *International Politics: A Framework for Analysis*. Englewood Cliffs, NJ: Prentice Hall.

Holsti, K. J. (1991). *Peace and War: Armed Conflicts and International Order 1648–1989*. Cambridge: Cambridge University Press.

Holsti, K. J. (1996). *The State, War, and the State of War*. Cambridge: Cambridge University Press.

Holsti, O. (1967). 'Cognitive Dynamics and Images of the Enemy: Dulles and Russia', in J. C. Farrell and A. P. Smith (eds), *Image and Reality in World Politics*. New York: Columbia University Press, 16–39.

Holsti, O. (2004). 'Theories of International Relations', at: www.duke.edu/-p.feaver/holsti

Holsti, O. and Rosenau, J. N. (1984). *American Leadership in World Affairs: Vietnam and the Breakdown of Consensus*. Boston, MA: Allen Unwin.

Homer-Dixon, T. F. (1995). 'Environmental Scarcities and Violent Conflict', in S. M. Lynn-Jones and S. Miller (eds), *Global Dangers: Changing Dimensions of International Security*. Cambridge, MA: Massachusetts Institute of Technology Press, 144–79.

Homer-Dixon, T. F. (1999). *Environment, Scarcity and Violence*. Princeton: Princeton University Press.

Hook, S. W. (ed.) (2006). *Liberal Order and Liberal Ambition: Essays on American Power and World Politics*. Cambridge: Polity Press.

Hook, S. W. (2010). *Democratic Peace in Theory and Practice*. Kent, OH: Kent State University Press.

Hopf, T. (1998). 'The Promise of Constructivism in International Relations Theory', *International Security*, 23/1: 171–200.

Hopf, T. (2002). *Social Construction of International Politics*. Ithaca, NY, and London: Cornell University Press.

Howard, M. (1976). *War in European History*. Oxford: Oxford University Press.

Howard, P. (2010). 'Triangulating Debates Within the Field: Teaching International Relations Research Methodology', *International Studies Perspectives*, 11/4: 393–408.

Hughes, B. B. (1991). *Continuity and Change in World Politics: The Clash of Perspectives*. Englewood Cliffs, NJ: Prentice Hall.

Hulsemeyer, A. (2010). *International Political Economy: A Reader*. Oxford: Oxford University Press.

Hülsse, R. and Spencer, A. (2008). 'The Metaphor of Terror: Terrorism Studies and the Constructivist Turn', *Security Dialogue*, 39/6: 571–92.

Huntington, S. (1993). 'The Clash of Civilizations?' *Foreign Affairs*, 72/3: 22–49.

Huntington, S. (1996). *The Clash of Civilizations and the Remaking of World Order*. London: Simon and Schuster.

Huntington, S. (2007). 'Interview', *New Perspectives Quarterly*, 24/1: 5–8.

Hurd, I. (2008). 'Constructivism', in **C. Reus-Smit** and **D. Snidal** (eds), *The Oxford Handbook of International Relations*. Oxford: Oxford University Press, 298–317.

Hurrell, A. (2007). *On Global Order: Power, Values and the Constitution of International Society*. Oxford: Oxford University Press.

Hurrell, A. and **Kingsbury, B.** (eds) (1992). *The International Politics of the Environment*. Oxford: Clarendon Press.

Ikenberry, G. J. (2002). 'America's Imperial Ambition', *Foreign Affairs*, 81/5: 49–60.

Ikenberry, G. J. (2009). 'Liberal Internationalism 3.0: America and the Dilemmas of Liberal World Order', *Perspectives on Politics*, 7/1: 71–87.

Ikenberry, G. J. (ed.) (2011). *American Foreign Policy: Theoretical Essays*, 6th edn. Boston, MA: Houghton Mifflin Harcourt.

International Institute of Strategic Studies (IISS) (2004). 'Combating Transnational Terrorism', *IISS Strategic Comments*, 10: 10.

Iyad, A. (1983). *Without a Homeland*. Tel Aviv: Mifras.

Jackson, P. T. (2010). *The Conduct of Inquiry in International Relations: Philosophy of Science and its Implications for the Study of World Politics*. London: Routledge.

Jackson, R. (2007). 'The Core Commitments of Critical Terrorism Studies', *European Political Science*, 6/3: 244–51.

Jackson, R. H. (1990). *Quasi-States: Sovereignty, International Relations and the Third World*. Cambridge: Cambridge University Press.

Jackson, R. H. (1992). 'Dialectical Justice in the Gulf War', *Review of International Studies*, 18: 335–54.

Jackson, R. H. (2000). *The Global Covenant: Human Conduct in a World of States*. Oxford: Oxford University Press.

Jackson, R. H. (2005). *Classical and Modern Thought on International Relations: From Anarchy to Cosmopolis*. New York: Palgrave Macmillan.

Jackson, R. H. (2006). 'Human Rights Protection in a World of Sovereign States', in **R. Tinnevelt** and **G.**

Verschraegen (eds), *Between Cosmopolitan Ideals and State Sovereignty*. New York: Palgrave Macmillan, 134–46.

Jackson, R. H. and **Rosberg, C. G.** (1994). 'The Political Economy of African Personal Rule', in **D. E. Apter** and **C. G. Rosberg** (eds), *Political Development and the New Realism in Sub-Saharan Africa*. Charlottesville, VA: University Press of Virginia, 278–319.

Jahn, B. (2005). 'Kant, Mill and Illiberal Legacies in International Affairs', *International Organization*, 59/1: 177–207.

Janis, I. L. (1982). *Groupthink: Psychological Studies of Policy Decisions and Fiascos*, 2nd edn. Boston, MA: Houghton Mifflin.

Jervis, R. (1968). 'Hypotheses on Misperception', *World Politics*, 20: 454–79.

Jervis, R. (1976). *Perception and Misperception in International Politics*. Princeton, NJ: Princeton University Press.

Jervis, R. (1998). 'Realism in the Study of World Politics', *International Organization*, 52/4: 971–91.

Job, B. (ed.) (1992). *The Insecurity Dilemma: National Security of Third World States*. Boulder, CO: Lynne Rienner.

Johnston, A. (2008). *Social States: China in International Institutions, 1980–2000*. Princeton, NJ: Princeton University Press.

Johnston, A. I. (1995). 'Thinking about Strategic Culture', *International Security*, 19/4: 32–64.

Johnston, A. I. (1996). 'Cultural Realism and Strategy in Maoist China', in **P. Katzenstein** (ed.), *The Culture of National Security: Norms and Identity in World Politics*. New York: Columbia University Press, 216–51.

Jones, E. L. (1981). *The European Miracle: Environments, Economies and Geopolitics in the History of Europe and Asia*. Cambridge: Cambridge University Press.

Jönsson, C. and **Tallberg, J.** (2008). 'Institutional Theory in International Relations', in **J. Pierre, B. G. Peters,** and **G. Stoker** (eds), *Debating Institutionalism*. New York: Manchester University Press, 86–115.

Journal of European Public Policy (2013). 'Special Issue: Building better theoretical frameworks of the European Union's policy process', Nicolas Zahariadis (ed), 20/6.

Kagan, R. (2003). *Paradise and Power: America and Europe in the New World Order*. New York: Atlantic Books.

Kant, I. (1992 [1795]). 'Perpetual Peace', repr. in H. Reiss (ed.), *Kant's Political Writing*. Cambridge: Cambridge University Press, 93–131.

Kapstein, E. B. (1993). 'Territoriality and who Is "US"?', *International Organization*, 47/3: 501–3.

Katzenstein, P. (ed.) (1996a). *The Culture of National Security: Norms and Identity in World Politics*. New York: Columbia University Press.

Katzenstein, P. (1996b). *Cultural Norms and National Security*. Ithaca, NY, and London: Cornell University Press.

Kaufman, S., Little, R., and Wohlforth, W. (eds). (2007). *The Balance of Power in World History*. London: Palgrave Macmillan.

Kay, C. (1989). *Latin American Theories of Development and Underdevelopment*. London: Routledge.

Keene, E. (2002). *Beyond the Anarchical Society*. Cambridge: Cambridge University Press.

Kennan, G. (1954). *Realities of American Foreign Policy*. Princeton, NJ: Princeton University Press.

Keohane, R. O. (1984). *After Hegemony: Cooperation and Discord in the World Political Economy*. Princeton, NJ: Princeton University Press.

Keohane, R. O. (ed.) (1986). *Neo-Realism and its Critics*. New York: Columbia University Press.

Keohane, R. O. (1989). *International Institutions and State Power: Essays in International Relations Theory*. Boulder, CO: Westview Press.

Keohane, R. O. (1993). 'Institutional Theory and the Realist Challenge after the Cold War', in D. A. Baldwin (ed.), *Neorealism and Neoliberalism: The Contemporary Debate*. New York: Columbia University Press, 269–301.

Keohane, R. O. (1998). 'Beyond Dichotomy. Conversations Between International Relations and Feminist Theory', *International Studies Quarterly*, 42/1: 193–7.

Keohane, R. O. (2002). 'Institutional Theory in International Relations', in Michael Brecher and Frank P. Harvey (eds), *Realism and Institutionalism in International Studies*. Ann Arbor, MI: University of Michigan Press.

Keohane, R. O. (2009). 'The Old IPE and the New', *Review of International Political Economy* 16/1: 34–46.

Keohane, R. O. and Martin, L. L. (1995). 'The Promise of Institutionalist Theory', *International Security*, 20/1: 39–51.

Keohane, R. O. and Nye, J. S., Jr (eds) (1971). *Transnational Relations and World Politics*. Cambridge, MA: Harvard University Press.

Keohane, R. O. and Nye, J. S., Jr (eds) (1975). 'International Interdependence and Integration', in F. Greenstein and N. Polsby (eds), *Handbook of Political Science, viii: International Politics*. Reading, MA: Addison-Wesley, 363–414.

Keohane, R. O. and Nye, J. S., Jr (eds) (1977). *Power and Interdependence: World Politics in Transition*. Boston, MA: Little, Brown.

Keohane, R. O. and Nye, J. S., Jr (eds) (1987). 'Power and Interdependence Revisited', *International Organization* 41/4: 725–53.

Keohane, R. O. and Nye, J. S., Jr (eds) (1993). 'Introduction: The End of the Cold War in Europe', in R. O. Keohane, J. S. Nye, Jr, and S. Hoffmann (eds), *After the Cold War: International Institutions and State Strategies in Europe 1989–1991*. Cambridge, MA: Harvard University Press, 1–23.

Keohane, R. O. and Nye, J. S., Jr (eds) (2001). *Power and Interdependence*, 3rd edn. New York: Longman.

Keohane, R. O., Nye, J. S., Jr, and Hoffmann, S. (eds) (1993). *After the Cold War: International Institutions and State Strategies in Europe, 1989–1991*. Cambridge, MA: Harvard University Press.

Keynes, J. M. (1963). *Essays in Persuasion*. New York: Norton.

Kindleberger, C. (1973). *The World in Depression, 1929–1939*. Berkeley, CA: University of California Press.

Kiras, J. D. (2005). 'Terrorism and Globalization', in J. Bayliss and S. Smith (eds), *The Globalization of World Politics*. Oxford and New York: Oxford University Press, 480–97.

Kissinger, H. (1994). *Diplomacy*. New York: Simon & Schuster.

Kissinger, H. (2014). *World Order. Reflections on the Character of Nations and the Course of History*. London: Penguin.

Klarevas, L. (2004). 'Political Realism: A Culprit for the 9/11 Attacks', *Harvard International Review*, Fall: 18–22.

Knutsen, T. L. (1997). *A History of International Relations Theory*. Manchester: Manchester University Press.

Koslowski, R. (1999). 'A Constructivist Approach to Understanding the European Union as a Federal Polity', *Journal of European Public Policy*, 6/4, 561–79.

Kozak, D. C. and Keagle, J. (eds) (1988). *Bureaucratic Politics and National Security: Theory and Practice*. Boulder, CA: Lynne Rienner.

Krasner, S. D. (1992). 'Realism, Imperialism, and Democracy: A Response to Gilbert', *Political Theory*, 20/1: 38–52.

Krasner, S. D. (1994). 'International Political Economy: Abiding Discord', *Review of International Political Economy*, 1/1: 13–19.

Krauthammer, C. (2004). 'Democratic Realism: An American Foreign Policy for a Unipolar World'. Irving Kristol Lecture, Washington, DC.

Kubálková, V. (2003). 'Toward an International Political Theology', in P. Hatzopoulos and F. Petito (eds), *Religion in International Relations*. Basingstoke: Palgrave Macmillan, 79–107.

Kubálková, V. (2013). 'The "Turn to Religion" in International Relations Theory', at: http://www.e-ir.info/2013/12/03/the-turn-to-religion-in-international-relations-theory/

Kupchan, C. A. (2012). *No One's World. The West, the Rising Rest, and the Coming Global Turn*. Oxford: Oxford University Press.

Kutting, G. (2010). *Global Environmental Politics: Concepts, Theories and Case Studies*. London: Routledge.

Laffey, M. and Weldes, J. (2008). 'Decolonizing the Cuban Missile Crisis', *International Studies Quarterly*, 52/3: 555–77.

Lal, D. (1983). *The Poverty of 'Development Economics'*. London: Institute of Economic Affairs.

Larsen, H. (1997). *Foreign Policy and Discourse Analysis: France, Britain, and Europe*. London: Routledge.

Lawson, G. (2012). 'The Eternal Divide? History and International Relations', *European Journal of International Relations*, 18/2: 203–26.

Layne, C. (1993). 'The Unipolar Illusion: Why New Great Powers Will Rise', *International Security*, 17: 5–51.

Layne, C. (1994). 'Kant or Cant: The Myth of the Democratic Peace', *International Security*, 19/2: 5–49.

Layne, C. (2006). 'The Unipolar Illusion Revisited: The Coming End of the United States' Unipolar Moment', *International Security*, 31/2: 7–41.

Lebow, R. N. (2011). 'Philosophy and International Relations', *International Affairs*, 87/5: 1219–28.

Lee, K. (1993). 'To De-Industrialize: Is it so Irrational?' in A. Dobson and P. Lucardie (eds), *The Politics of Nature: Explorations in Green Political Theory*. London: Routledge, 105–18.

Leite, N. (1951). *The Operational Code of the Politburo*. New York: McGraw Hill.

Lenin, V. I. (1999) [1917]. *Imperialism: The Highest Stage of Capitalism*. London: Resistance Books.

Lewis, J. (2008). 'Strategic Bargaining, Norms and Deliberation: Modes of Action in the Council of the European Union', in D. N. Baurin and H. Wallace (eds), *Unveiling the Council: Games Governments Play in Brussels*. Basingstoke: Palgrave Macmillan, 165–84.

Lewis, W. A. (1970). *Theory of Economic Growth*. New York: Harper & Row.

Liberal International (1997). 'The Liberal Agenda for the 21st Century: The Quality of Liberty in Open Civic Societies'. Oxford: Congress of Liberal International.

Lindberg, T. (2005). 'The Atlanticist Community', in T. Lindberg (ed.), *Beyond Paradise and Power*. Abingdon: Routledge, 215–35.

Lindbo Larsen, H. (2008). *Strategic Culture in ESDP*. Aarhus: Department of Political Science.

Linklater, A. (1989). *Beyond Realism and Marxism*. New York: St Martin's Press.

Lipson, C. (2003). *Reliable Partners: How Democracies Have Made a Separate Peace*. Princeton, NJ: Princeton University Press.

List, F. (1966). *The National System of Political Economy*. New York: Kelley.

Little, R. (1996). 'The Growing Relevance of Pluralism?' in S. Smith et al. (eds), *International Theory: Positivism and Beyond*. Cambridge: Cambridge University Press, 66–86.

Lizardo, O. (2008). 'Defining and Theorizing Terrorism: A Global Actor-Centered Approach', *Journal of World-Systems Research*, XIV/2: 91–118.

Lobell, S., Ripsman, N., and Taliaferro J. (eds) (2009). *Neoclassical Realism, the State, and Foreign Policy*. Cambridge: Cambridge University Press.

Lomborg, B. (2001). *The Sceptical Environmentalist*. Cambridge: Cambridge University Press.

Lomborg, B. (2007). *Cool It: The Skeptical Environmentalist's Guide to Global Warming*. New York: Knopf.

Long, D. and Schmidt, B. C. (eds) (2005). *Imperialism and Internationalism in the Discipline of International Relations*. New York: SUNY Press.

Lyotard, J.-F. (1984). *The Postmodern Condition: A Report on Knowledge*. Manchester: Manchester University Press.

Machiavelli, N. (1984). *The Prince*, trans. P. Bondanella and M. Musa. New York: Oxford University Press.

Mann, M. (2003). *Incoherent Empire*. London: Verso.

Mansfield, E. D. and Pollins, B. M. (eds) (2003). *Economic Interdependence and International Conflict*. Ann Arbor: University of Michigan Press.

Marx, K. and Engels, F. (1955). The Communist Manifesto, ed. S. Beer. New York: Appleton-Century-Crofts.

Mayall, J. (1982). 'The Liberal Economy', in J. Mayall (ed.), *The Community of States: A Study in International Political Theory*. London: Allen and Unwin.

McCormick, J. M. (ed) (2012). *The Domestic Sources of American Foreign Policy: Insights and Evidence*. Lanham, MD: Rowman and Littlefield.

Mearsheimer, J. (1993). 'Back to the Future: Instability in Europe after the Cold War', in S. Lynn-Jones (ed.), *The Cold War and After: Prospects for Peace*. Cambridge, MA: Massachusetts Institute of Technology Press, 141–92.

Mearsheimer, J. (1995a). 'A Realist Reply', *International Security*, 20/1: 82–93.

Mearsheimer, J. (1995b). 'The False Promise of International Institutions', in M. E. Brown, S. M. Lynn-Jones, and S. E. Miller (eds), *The Perils of Anarchy: Contemporary Realism and International Security*. Cambridge, MA: Massachusetts Institute of Technology Press, 332–77.

Mearsheimer, J. (2001). *The Tragedy of Great Power Politics*, New York: W. W. Norton.

Mearsheimer, J. (2002). 'The Problem of Terrorism', at: http://rmellon.nd.edu/assets/101872/religion_and_international_relations_report.pdf

Menjivar, C. and Rodriguez, N. (eds) (2005). *When States Kill: Latin America, the US and Technologies of Terror*. Austin, TX: University of Texas Press.

Mgba, C. and Ukpere, W. I. (2013). 'Religious Resurgence and IR Mainstream Theories: The Imperative for Theoretical Rethink and Expansion', *Mediterranean Journal of Social Sciences*, 4/14: 535–42.

Mill, J. S. (1963). 'A Few Words on Non-Intervention', in G. Himmelfarb (ed.), *Essays on Politics and Culture: John Stuart Mill*. New York: Anchor, 68–84.

Mitchell, S. (2006). 'Cooperation in World Politics: The Constraining and Constitutive Effect of International Organizations', at: http://ir.uiowa.edu/cgi/viewcontent.cgi?article=1004&context=polisci_pubs

Mitrany, D. (1966). *A Working Peace System*, repr. with introd. by H. J. Morgenthau. Chicago, IL: Quadrangle.

Mol, A. P. J., Sonnenfeld, D. A., and Spaargaren, G. (eds) (2009). *The Ecological Modernization Reader: Environmental Reform in Theory and Practice*. London: Routledge.

Moravcsik, A. (1997). 'Taking Preferences Seriously: A Liberal Theory of International Politics', *International Organization*, 51/4: 513–53.

Moravcsik, A. (1999a). 'Is Something Rotten in the State of Denmark? Constructivism and European Integration', *Journal of European Public Policy*, 6/4: 669–82.

Moravcsik, A. (1999b). *The Choice for Europe. Social Purpose and State Power from Messina to Maastricht*. London: Cornell University Press.

Moravcsik, A. (2008). 'The New Liberalism', in C. Reus-Smit and D. Snidal (eds), *The Oxford Handbook of International Relations*. Oxford: Oxford University Press, 235–54.

Morgenthau, H. J. (1960). *Politics among Nations: The Struggle for Power and Peace*, 3rd edn. New York: Knopf.

Morgenthau, H. J. (1965). *Scientific Man versus Power Politics*. Chicago, IL: Phoenix Books.

Morgenthau, H. J. (1985). *Politics among Nations: The Struggle for Power and Peace*, 6th edn. New York: Knopf.

Morrison, K. (1995). *Marx, Durkheim, Weber*. London: Sage.

Mueller, J. (1990). *Retreat from Doomsday: The Obsolescence of Major War*. New York: Basic Books.

Mueller, J. (1995). *Quiet Cataclysm: Reflections on the Recent Transformation of World Politics*. New York: HarperCollins.

Mueller, J. (2004). *The Remnants of War*. Ithaca, NY: Cornell University Press.

Mueller, J. (2009). *Atomic Obsession: Nuclear Alarmism from Hiroshima to Al-Qaeda*. Oxford: Oxford University Press.

Münkler, H. (2005). *Imperien*. Berlin: Rohwolt.

Myers, N. and Simon, J. L. (1994). *Scarcity or Abundance? A Debate on the Environment*. New York: Norton.

Myrdal, G. (1957). *Economic Theory and Underdeveloped Regions*. London: Duckworth.

Naím, M. (2013a). *The End of Power: From Boardrooms to Battlefields and Churches to States, Why Being in Charge Isn't What it Used to Be*. New York: Basic Books.

Naím, M. (2013b). 'The End of Power', at: http://reason.com/archives/2013/04/14/the-end-of-power

Naisbitt, J. (1994). *Global Paradox*. New York: Avon.

National Security Strategy (NSS) (2002). *The National Security Strategy of the United States of America*. Washington, DC: Office of the President.

Navari, C. (1989). 'The Great Illusion Revisited: The International Theory of Norman Angell', *Review of International Studies*, 15: 341–58.

Ndegwa, S. N. (1997). 'Citizenship and Ethnicity: An Examination of Two Transition Moments in Kenyan Politics', *American Political Science Review*, 91/3: 599–617.

Neumann, I. B. (2008). 'Discourse Analysis', in A. Klotz and D. Prakesh (eds), *Qualitative Methods in International Relations. A Pluralist Guide*. Basingstoke: Palgrave Macmillan, 61–77.

Nexon, D. (2009). 'The Balance of Power in the Balance', *World Politics*, 61/2: 330–59.

Nicholls, D. (1974). *Three Varieties of Pluralism*. London: Macmillan.

Niemann, A. (2006). *Explaining Decisions in the European Union*. Cambridge: Cambridge University Press.

Nixson, F. (1988). 'The Political Economy of Bargaining with Transnational Corporations: Some Preliminary Observations', *Manchester Papers on Development*, 4/3: 377–90.

Nye, J. S., Jr (1988). 'Neorealism and Neoliberalism', *World Politics*, 40/2: 235–51.

Nye, J. S., Jr (1990). *Bound to Lead: The Changing Nature of American Power*. New York: Basic.

Nye, J. S., Jr (1993). *Understanding International Conflicts*. New York: HarperCollins.

Nye, J. S., Jr (2002). *The Paradox of American Power*. New York: Oxford University Press.

Nye, J. S., Jr (2003). 'US Power and Strategy after Iraq', *Foreign Affairs*, 82/4: 60–73.

Nye, J. S., Jr (2011). *The Future of Power*. New York: Public Affairs.

Oakeshott, M. (1966). *Experience and its Modes*. Cambridge: Cambridge University Press.

Oakeshott, M. (1975). *Hobbes on Civil Association*. Oxford: Blackwell.

O'Brien, R. and Williams, M. (2013). *Global Political Economy*, 4th edn. Basingstoke: Palgrave.

O'Neil, K. (2009). *The Environment and International Relations*. Cambridge: Cambridge University Press.

Onuf, N. (1989). *A World of Our Making*. Columbia, SC: University of South Carolina Press.

Osiander, A. (1994). *The States System of Europe, 1640–1990*. Oxford: Clarendon Press.

Osland, J. (2003). 'Broadening the Debate. The Pros and Cons of Globalization', *Journal of Management Inquiry*, 12/2: 137–54.

Parashar, S. (2009). 'Feminist International Relations and Women Militants: Case Studies from Sri Lanka and Kashmir', *Cambridge Journal of International Affairs*, 22/2: 235–56.

Paterson, W. E., Nugent, N., and Egan, M. P. (2010). *Research Agendas in EU Studies: Stalking the Elephant*. Basingstoke: Palgrave Macmillan.

Paul, T. V., Wirtz, J., and Fortmann, M. (eds) (2004). *Balance of Power Theory and Practice in the 21st Century*. Stanford, CA: Stanford University Press.

Payne, A. (2005). *The Global Politics of Unequal Development*. Basingstoke: Palgrave Macmillan.

Pearlstein, R. M. (2004). *Fatal Future? Transnational Terrorism and the New Global Disorder*. Austin, TX: University of Texas Press.

Peters, B. G. (2011). *Institutional Theory in Political Science*, 3rd edn. London: Continuum.

Peterson, M. J. (1992). 'Transnational Activity, International Society and World Politics', *Millennium*, 21: 371–88.

Peterson, V. S. (1998). 'Feminism and International Relations', *Gender & History*, 10/3: 581–9.

Peterson, V. S. and Runyan, A. S. (2010). *Global Gender Issues in the New Millennium*, 3rd edn. Boulder: Westview Press.

Philpott, D. (2002). 'The Challenge of September 11 to Secularism in International Relations', *World Politics*, 55/1: 66–95.

Pikkety, T. (2014). *Capital in the Twenty-First Century*. Harvard, MA: Belknap Press.

Plato (1974). *The Republic*. Indianapolis, IN: Hackett.

Polanyi, K. (1957). *The Great Transformation: The Political and Economic Origins of Our Time*. New York: Farrar Rinehart.

Pollack, M. A. (2005). 'Theorizing the European Union: International Organization, Domestic Polity, or Experiment in New Governance?', *Annual Review of Political Science*, 357–98.

Pompa, L. (1982). *Vico: Selected Writings*. Cambridge: Cambridge University Press.

Porpora, D. V. (2011). 'Critical Terrorism Studies: A Political Economic Approach Grounded in Critical Realism', *Critical Studies on Terrorism*, 4/1: 39–55.

Posner, S. (2010). 'The Tea Party's Religious Roots Exposed', at: http://www.theguardian.com/commentisfree/belief/2010/oct/12/tea-party-religious-right

Prebisch, R. (1950). *The Economic Development of Latin America and Its Principal Problems*. New York: United Nations.

Price, R. and Reus-Smit, C. (1998). 'Dangerous Liaisons? Critical International Theory and Constructivism', *European Journal of International Relations*, 4/3: 259–94.

Quandl (2014). Economic Growth Data, at: https://www.quandl.com/search/us%2C%20china%12C%20growth?page=1

Rahaman, M. M. (2012). 'Water Wars in the 21st Century: Speculation or Reality', *International Journal of Sustainable Society*, 4/1–2: 3–10.

Ravenhill, J. (2008). 'In Search of the Missing Middle', *Review of International Political Economy*, 15/1: 18–29.

Ravenhill, J. (ed.) (2011). *Global Political Economy*, 3rd edn. Oxford: Oxford University Press.

Ravenhill, J. (ed.) (2014). *Global Political Economy*. Oxford: Oxford University Press.

Rengger, N. (2006). 'Theorizing World Politics for a New Century', *International Affairs*, 82/3: 427–30.

Ricardo, D. (1973). *The Principles of Political Economy and Taxation*. London: Dent.

Risse, T. (2009). 'Social Constructivism and European Integration', in A. Wiener and T. Diez (eds), *European Integration Theory*. Oxford: Oxford University Press, 159–76.

Risse, T., Ropp, S. C., and Sikkink, K. (eds) (1999). *The Power of Human Rights: International Norms and Domestic Change*. Cambridge: Cambridge University Press.

Rodrik, D. (2011). *The Globalization Paradox. Why Global Markets, States, and Democracy Can't Coexist*. Oxford: Oxford University Press.

Rosati, J. A. (2000). 'The Power of Human Cognition in the Study of World Politics', *International Studies Review*, 2/3: 45–79.

Rose, G. (1998). 'Neoclassical Realism and Theories of Foreign Policy', *World Politics*, 15/1: 144–72.

Rosecrance, R. (1986). *The Rise of the Trading State: Commerce and Conquest in the Modern World*. New York: Basic Books.

Rosecrance, R. (1995). 'The Obsolescence of Territory', *New Perspectives Quarterly*, 12/1: 44–50.

Rosecrance, R. (1999). *The Rise of the Virtual State*. New York: Basic Books.

Rosenau, J. N. (1966). 'Pre-theories and Theories and Foreign Policy', in R. B. Farrell (ed.), *Approaches to Comparative and International Politics*. Evanston, IL: Northwestern University Press.

Rosenau, J. N. (1967). 'Games International Relations Scholars Play', *Journal of International Affairs*, 21: 293–303.

Rosenau, J. N. (1980). *The Study of Global Interdependence: Essays on the Transnationalisation of World Affairs*. New York: Nichols.

Rosenau, J. N. (1990). *Turbulence in World Politics: A Theory of Change and Continuity*. Princeton, NJ: Princeton University Press.

Rosenau, J. N. (1992). 'Citizenship in a Changing Global Order', in J. N. Rosenau and O. Czempiel (eds), *Governance Without Government: Order and Change in World Politics*. Cambridge: Cambridge University Press, 272–94.

Rosenau, J. N. (2003). *Distant Proximities: Dynamics Beyond Globalization*. Princeton, NJ: Princeton University Press.

Rosenberg, J. (2005). 'Globalization Theory: A Post Mortem', *International Politics*, 42/1: 2–74.

Rosenblum, N. L. (1978). *Bentham's Theory of the Modern State*. Cambridge, MA: Harvard University Press.

Rostow, W. W. (1960). *The Stages of Economic Growth: A Non-Communist Manifesto*. Cambridge: Cambridge University Press.

Rostow, W. W. (1978). *The World Economy: History and Prospect*. Austin, TX: University of Texas Press.

Ruggie, J. G. (1998). *Constructing the World Polity: Essays on International Institutionalization*. London: Routledge.

Rugman, A. M. and Doh, P. (2008). *Multinationals and Development*. New Haven, CT: Yale University Press.

Russett, B. M. (1989). 'Democracy and Peace', in B. Russett, H. Starr, and R. J. Stoll (eds), *Choices in World Politics: Sovereignty and Interdependence*. New York: Freeman, 245–61.

Russett, B. M. (1993). *Grasping the Democratic Peace: Principles for a Post-Cold War World*. Princeton, NJ: Princeton University Press.

Russett, B. M., Oneal, J. R., and Cox, M. (2000). 'Clash of Civilizations, or Realism and Liberalism déjà vu? Some Evidence', *Journal of Peace Research*, 37/5: 583–608.

Sabaratnam, M. (2011). 'IR in Dialogue … but Can We Change the Subjects? A Typology of Decolonising Strategies for the Study of World Politics', *Millennium: Journal of International Studies*, 39/3: 781–803.

Said, E. (2003 [1978]). *Orientalism*. New York: Vintage Books.

Saideman, S. M., Lanoue, D. J., and Campenni, M. (2002). 'Democratization, Political Institutions, and Ethnic Conflict: A Pooled Time-series Analysis, 1985–1998', *Comparative Political Studies*, 35/1: 103–29.

Salehyan, I. (2008) 'From Climate Change to Conflict? No Consensus Yet', *Journal of Peace Research*, 45/3: 315–26.

Samuelson, P. A. (1967). *Economics: An Introductory Analysis*, 7th edn. New York: McGraw Hill.

Sandal, N. and Fox, J. (2013). *Religion in International Relations Theory: Interactions and Possibilities*. Abingdon: Routledge.

Sandal, N. and James, P. (2011). 'Religion and International Relations Theory: Towards a Mutual Understanding', *European Journal of International Relations*, 17/1: 3–25.

Sartori, G. (ed.) (1984). *Social Science Concepts: A Systematic Analysis*. New York: Sage.

Saurugger, S. (2013). 'Constructivism and Public Policy Approaches in the EU: From Ideas to Power Games', *Journal of European Public Policy*, 20/6: 888–906.

Schelling, T. (1980 [1960]). *The Strategy of Conflict*. Cambridge, MA: Harvard University Press.

Schelling, T. (1996). 'The Diplomacy of Violence', in R. Art and R. Jervis (eds), *International Politics*, 4th edn. New York: HarperCollins, 168–82.

Schiff, B. N. (2008). *Building the International Criminal Court*. Cambridge: Cambridge University Press.

Schmid, A. P. (2005). 'Terrorism and Human Rights: A Perspective from the United Nations', *Terrorism and Political Violence*, 17: 25–35.

Schmidt, B. C. (1998). *The Political Discourse of Anarchy: A Disciplinary History of International Relations*. Albany, NY: SUNY Press.

Scholte, J. A. (2005). *Globalization: A Critical Introduction*, 2nd edn. London: Macmillan.

Schwartz, H. (2009). *States versus Markets: The Emergence of a Global Economy*, 3rd edn. London: Macmillan.

Schweller, R. L. (2006). *'Unanswered Threats': Political Constraints on the Balance of Power*. Princeton, NJ: Princeton University Press.

Sempa, F. (2009). *America's Global Role*. New York: University Press of America.

Senghaas, D. (1982). *Von Europa Lernen. Entwicklungsgeschichtliche Betrachtungen*. Frankfurt am Main: Suhrkamp.

Senghaas, D. (2007). *On Perpetual Peace: A Timely Assessment*. New York: Berghahn Books.

Senghaas, D. (2008). 'Liberalism Challenged: Is the World Sinking into Cultural Conflicts?', symposium paper, University of Aarhus, 24 October.

Shaw, M. (1992). 'Global Society and Global Responsibility', *Millennium*, 21: 421–34.

Sil, R. and Katzenstein, P. J. (eds) (2010). *Beyond Paradigms: Analytic Eclecticism in the Study of World Politics*. Basingstoke: Palgrave Macmillan.

Simon, J. L. and Richman, S. L. (1996). 'The State of Humanity: Good and Getting Better', at: http://www.cato.org/publications/commentary/state-humanity-good-getting-better

Singer, H. and Wildavsky, A. (1993). *The Real World Order: Zones of Peace, Zones of Turmoil*. Chatham, NJ: Chatham House.

Singer, J. D. (1961). 'The Level-of-Analysis Problem in International Relations', *World Politics*, 145/1: 77–92.

Sjoberg, L. (2006). *Gender, Justice and the Wars in Iraq*. Lanham, MD: Lexington Books.

Skowronek, S. (2006). 'The Reassociation of Ideas and Purposes: Racism, Liberalism, and the American Political Tradition', *American Political Science Review*, 100/3: 183–98.

Slaughter. A.-M. (2004). *A New World Order*. Princeton, NJ: Princeton University Press.

Sluka, J. A. (2000). *Death Squad: The Anthropology of State Terror*. Philadelphia, PA: University of Pennsylvania Press.

Smith, M. J. (1992). 'Liberalism and International Reform', in T. Nardin and D. Mapel (eds), *Traditions of International Ethics*. Cambridge: Cambridge University Press, 201–24.

Smith, S. (1996). 'Positivism and Beyond', in S. Smith, K. Booth, and M. Zalewski (eds), *International Theory: Positivism and Beyond*. New York: Cambridge University Press, 11–47.

Smith, S. (1997). 'New Approaches to International Theory', in J. Baylis and S. Smith (eds), *The Globalization of World Politics*. Oxford: Oxford University Press, 165–90.

Smith, S. (2008). 'Debating Schmidt: Theoretical Pluralism in IR', *Millennium: Journal of International Studies*, 36/2: 305–10.

Smith, S. (2010). 'Diversity and Disciplinarity in International Relations Theory', in T. Dunne, M. Kurki, and S. Smith (eds), *International Relations Theories*. Oxford: Oxford University Press, 1–14.

Smith, S., Booth, K., and Zalewski, M. (eds) (1996). *International Theory: Positivism and Beyond*. Cambridge: Cambridge University Press.

Snyder, J. (ed.) (2011). *Religion and International Relations Theory*. New York: Columbia University Press.

Sørensen, G. (2001). *Changes in Statehood: The Transformation of International Relations*. London and New York: Palgrave.

Sørensen, G. (2004). *The Transformation of the State: Beyond the Myth of Retreat*. Basingstoke: Palgrave Macmillan.

Sørensen, G. (2006). 'Liberalism of Restraint and Liberalism of Imposition: Liberal Values and World Order in the New Millennium', *International Relations*, 20/3: 251–72.

Sørensen, G. (2008a). *Democracy and Democratization. Processes and Prospects in a Changing World*, 3rd edn. Boulder, CO: Westview.

Sørensen, G. (2008b). 'The Case for Combining Material Forces and Ideas in the Study of IR', *European Journal of International Relations*, 14/1: 5–32.

Sørensen, G. (2009). '"Big and Important Things" in IR: Structural Realism and the Neglect of Changes in Statehood', *International Relations*, 23/2: 223–39.

Sørensen, G. (2011). *A Liberal World Order in Crisis: Choosing Between Imposition and Restraint*. Ithaca, NY: Cornell University Press.

Soros, G. (2014). *The Tragedy of the European Union: Disintegration or Revival?* New York: Public Affairs.

Souva, M. and Prins, B. (2006). 'The Liberal Peace Revisited: The Role of Democracy, Dependence, and Development in Militarized Interstate Dispute Initiation, 1950–1999', *International Interactions*, 32/2: 183–200.

Spero, J. E. (1985). *The Politics of International Economic Relations*. London: Allen & Unwin.

Squires, J. and Weldes, J. (2007). 'Beyond Being Marginal: Gender and International Relations in Britain', *The British Journal of Politics & International Relations*, 9/2: 185–203.

Steans, J. (2013). *Gender and International Relations*, 3rd edn. Bognor Regis: Wiley.

Steinbrunner, J. (1974). *The Cybernetic Theory of Decision*. Princeton, NJ: Princeton University Press.

Stent, A. E. (2005). 'Review of Ted Hopf: Social Construction of International Politics', *Journal of Cold War Studies*, 7/1: 184–86.

Stoessinger, J. G. (2010). *Why Nations Go to War*. Boston: Wadsworth Cengage Learning.

Strange, S. (1970). 'International Economics and International Relations: A Case of Mutual Neglect', *International Affairs*, 46/2: 304–15.

Strange, S. (1995). 'Theoretical Underpinnings: Conflicts Between International Relations and International Political Economy', paper for the British International Studies Association Annual Meeting, Southampton, December.

Streeten, P. P. (1979). 'Multinationals Revisited', *Finance and Development*, 16/2: 39–43.

Suganami, H. (2013). 'Meta-Jackson: Rethinking Patrick Thaddeus Jackson's *Conduct of Inquiry*', *Millennium*, 41/2: 248–69.

Sylvester, C. (1994). *Feminist Theory and International Relations in a Postmodern Era*. Cambridge: Cambridge University Press.

Sylvester, C. (2007). 'Whither the International at the End of IR?', *Millennium Journal of International Studies*, 35/3: 551–73.

Sylvester, C. (2010). 'Tensions in Feminist Security Studies', *Security Dialogue*, 41/6: 607–14.

Tannenwald, N. (2005). 'Ideas and Explanation: Advancing the Theoretical Agenda', *Journal of Cold War Studies*, 7/2: 13–42.

Tanner, T. and **Allouche, J.** (eds) (2011). 'Political Economy of Climate Change', *IDS Bulletin, Special Issue*, 42/3.

Tausch, A. and **Köhler, G.** (2002). *Global Keynesianism: Unequal Exchange and Global Exploitation*. Huntington, NY: Nova Science Publishers.

Taylor, A. J. P. (1957). *The Trouble Makers: Dissent over Foreign Policy 1792–1939*. London: Panther.

Teló, M. (2007). *The EU and New Regionalism*. London: Ashgate.

Themnér, L. and **Wallensteen, P.** (2013). 'Armed Conflicts 1946–2012', *Journal of Peace Research*, 50/4: 509–21.

Thomas, S. (2005). *The Global Resurgence of Religion and the Transformation of International Relations*. Basingstoke: Palgrave Macmillan.

Thompson, J. E. and **Krasner, S. D.** (1989). 'Global Transactions and the Consolidation of Sovereignty', in **E.-O. Czempiel** and **J. N. Rosenau** (eds), *Global Changes and Theoretical Challenges: Approaches to World Politics for the 1990s*. Lexington, MA: Lexington Books, 195–221.

Thucydides (1972). *History of the Peloponnesian War*, trans. **R. Warner**. London: Penguin.

Tickner, A. B. (2003). 'Seeing IR Differently: Notes from the Third World', *Millennium: Journal of International Studies*, 32/2: 295–324.

Tickner, A. B. and **Blaney, D. L.** (eds) (2012). *Thinking International Relations Differently (Worlding Beyond the West)*. London: Routledge.

Tickner, A. and **Weaver, O.** (eds) (2009). *International Relations Scholarship Around the World*. London and New York: Routledge.

Tickner, J. A. (2005). 'What Is Your Research Program? Some Feminist Answers to International Relations Methodological Questions', *International Studies Quarterly*, 49: 1–21.

Tilly, C. (1992). *Coercion, Capital and European States*. Oxford: Blackwell.

Tinnes, J. (2013). '100 Core and Periphery Journals for Terrorism Research', *Perspectives on Terrorism*, 7/2, at: http://www.terrorismanalysts.com/pt/index.php/pot/article/view/258/html

Toye, J. (1987). *Dilemmas of Development: Reflections on the Counterrevolution in Development Theory*. Oxford: Blackwell.

Tucker, R. W. (1977). *The Inequality of Nations*. New York: Basic Books.

Twing, S. (1998). *Myths, Models, and US Foreign Policy: The Cultural Shaping of Three Cold Warriors*. Boulder, CO: Lynne Rienner.

Underhill, G. R. D. (2015). *Political Economy and Global Governance: Theories, Issues, and Dynamics*. Basingstoke: Palgrave Macmillan.

United Nations Development Programme (UNDP) (annual edns). *Human Development Report*. New York: Oxford University Press.

United Nations Development Programme (UNDP) (2007). *Making Globalization Work for All*. New York: UNDP.

United Nations Environment Programme (UNEP) (2006). *Handbook for the Montreal Protocol on Substances that Deplete the Ozone Layer*. Nairobi: Ozone Secretariat.

Valbjørn, M. (2008a). 'Film(s) om international relationer', in **M. Østergaard** and **S. M. Thordsen** (eds), *Æstetik og politisk magt—8 analyser af aktuelle forhold mellem politik og æstetik*. Aarhus: Aarhus University Press, 180–225.

Valbjørn, M. (2008b). 'Before, During and After the Cultural Turn. A "Baedeker" to IR's Cultural Journey', *International Review of Sociology*, 18/1: 55–82.

Vasquez, J. (1996). *Classics of International Relations*, 3rd edn. Upper Saddle River, NJ: Prentice-Hall.

Vincent, R. J. (1986). *Human Rights and International Relations*. Cambridge: Cambridge University Press.

Vincent, R. J. (1990). 'Grotius, Human Rights, and Intervention', in **H. Bull** et al. (eds), *Hugo Grotius and International Relations*. Oxford: Clarendon Press, 241–56.

Vincent, R. J. and **Wilson, P.** (1993). 'Beyond Non-Intervention', in **I. Forbes** and **M. Hoffmann** (eds), *Political Theory, International Relations, and the Ethics of Intervention*. London: Macmillan.

Vorrath, J. and **Krebs, L. F.** (2009). 'Democratization and Conflict in Ethnically Divided Societies', *Living Reviews in Democracy*, 1, at: http://democracy.livingreviews.org/index.php/lrd/article/viewarticle/lrd-2009-1/7

Wade, R. (2008). 'Financial Regime Change?' *New Left Review*, 53 (September–October): 5–21.

Wade, R. H. (2013). 'Protecting Power: Western States in Global Organizations', in **D. Held** and **C. Roger** (eds), *Global Governance at Risk*. Cambridge: Polity, 77–111.

Waldron, J. (2003). 'Security and Liberty: The Image of Balance', *Journal of Political Philosophy*, 11/2: 191–210.

Walker, R. B. J. (1993). *Inside/Outside: International Relations as Political Theory*. Cambridge: Cambridge University Press.

Walker, R. B. J. (1995). 'International Relations and the Concept of the Political', in **K. Booth** and **S. Smith** (eds), *International Relations Theory Today*. University Park, PA: Pennsylvania State University Press, 306–28.

Walker, R. B. J. (2010). *After the Globe, Before the World*. London and New York: Routledge.

Wallerstein, I. (1974). *The Modern World System, 1*. New York: Academic Press.

Wallerstein, I. (1979). *The Capitalist World-Economy: Essays*. Cambridge: Cambridge University Press.

Wallerstein, I. (1983). *Historical Capitalism*. London: Verso.

Wallerstein, I. (2004). *World-Systems Analysis: An Introduction*. Durham, NC: Duke University Press.

Wallerstein, I., Collins, R., Mann, M., Derluguian, G., and **Calhoun, C.** (2013). *Does Capitalism Have a Future?* Oxford: Oxford University Press.

Walt, S. M. (1998). 'International Relations: One World, Many Theories', *Foreign Policy* (Spring): 29–46.

Waltz, K. N. (1959). *Man, the State and War: A Theoretical Analysis*. New York: Columbia University Press.

Waltz, K. N. (1979). *Theory of International Politics*. New York: McGraw-Hill; Reading: Addison-Wesley.

Waltz, K. N. (1986). 'Reflections on "Theory of International Politics": A Response to My Critics', in **R. O. Keohane** (ed.), *Neorealism and its Critics*. New York: Columbia University Press, 322–47.

Waltz, K. N. (1993). 'The Emerging Structure of International Politics', *International Security*, 18/2: 44–79.

Waltz, K. N. (2002). 'Structural Realism after the Cold War', in **G. J. Ikenberry** (ed.), *America Unrivaled: The Future of the Balance of Power*. Ithaca, NY, and London: Cornell University Press, 29–68.

Watson, A. (1992). *The Evolution of International Society*. London: Routledge.

Watson, M. (2014). 'The Historical Roots of Theoretical Traditions in Global Political Economy', in **J. Ravenhill** (ed.), *Global Political Economy*, 4th edn. Oxford: Oxford University Press, 25–50.

WCED (1987). *Our Common Future* (Brundtland Report), New York: United Nations, at: http://conspect.nl/pdf/Our_Common_Future-Brundtland_Report_1987.pdf

Webber, D. (2014). 'How Likely Is it that the European Union Will Disintegrate? A Critical Analysis of Competing Theoretical Perspectives', *European Journal of International Relations*, 20/2: 341–65.

Weber, C. (1999). *Faking it: US Hegemony in a 'Post-Phallic' Era*. Minneapolis, MN: University of Minnesota Press.

Weber, M. (1964). *The Theory of Social and Economic Organization*. New York: Free Press.

Weber, M. (1977). *Critique of Stammler*, trans. **Guy Oakes**. New York: Free Press.

Weinberg, L. and Eubank, W. (2008). 'Problems with the Critical Studies Approach to the Study of Terrorism', *Critical Studies on Terrorism*, 1/2: 185–95.

Weiss, J. (1988). *Industry in Developing Countries: Theory, Policy and Evidence*. London: Croom Helm.

Weissmann, J. (2013). 'How Wall Street Devoured Corporate America', *The Atlantic*, 5 March, at: http://www.theatlantic.com/business/archive/2013/03/how-wall-street-devoured-corporate-america/273732/

Weller, M. (ed.) (1993). *Iraq and Kuwait: The Hostilities and their Aftermath*. Cambridge: Grotius Publications.

Wendt, A. (1987). 'The Agent-Structure Problem in International Relations Theory', *International Organization*, 41: 335–70.

Wendt, A. (1992). 'Anarchy Is what States Make of it', *International Organization*, 46: 394–419.

Wendt, A. (1994). 'Collective Identity Formation and the International State', *American Political Science Review*, 88: 384–96.

Wendt, A. (1995). 'Constructing International Politics', *International Security*, 20/1: 71–81.

Wendt, A. (1999). *Social Theory of International Politics*. Cambridge: Cambridge University Press.

Wheeler, N. (1996). 'Guardian Angel or Global Gangster: A Review of the Ethical Claims of International Society', *Political Studies*, 44: 123–35.

White, G. (1984). 'Developmental States and Socialist Industrialisation in the Third World', *Journal of Development Studies*, 21/1: 97–120.

Wiener, A. and Dietz, T. (2004). *European Integration Theory*. Oxford: Oxford University Press.

Wight, M. (1952). *British Colonial Institutions 1947*. Oxford: Clarendon.

Wight, M. (1966). 'Why Is There No International Theory?' in H. Butterfield and M. Wight (eds), *Diplomatic Investigations*. London: Allen & Unwin, 12–33.

Wight, M. (1977). *Systems of States*. Leicester: Leicester University Press.

Wight, M. (1991). *International Theory: The Three Traditions*, ed. G. Wight and B. Porter. Leicester: Leicester University Press.

Wilcox, L. (2009). 'Gendering the Cult of the Offensive', *Security Studies*, 18/2: 214–40.

Williams, J. and Little, R. (2006). *Anarchical Society in a Globalized World*. New York: Palgrave Macmillan.

Williams, M. C. (2007). *Realism Reconsidered: The Legacy of Hans Morgenthau in International Relations*. Oxford: Oxford University Press.

Willis, K. (2011). *Theories and Practices of Development*, 2nd edn. London: Routledge.

Winter, Y. (2011). 'The Asymmetric War Discourse and its Moral Economies: A Critique', *International Theory*, 3/3: 488–514.

Wolf, A. T. (2006). *A Long-Term View of Water and Security—International Waters, National Issues, and Regional Tensions*. Berlin: German Advisory Council on Global Change.

World Bank (2014). 'Poverty Overview', at: http://www.worldbank.org/en/topic/poverty/overview

Yetiv, S. A. (2004). *Explaining Foreign Policy: US Decision Making and the Persian Gulf War*. Baltimore, MD: Johns Hopkins University Press.

Young, O. R. (1986). 'International Regimes: Toward a New Theory of Institutions', *World Politics*, 39/1: 104–22.

Zacher, M. W. and Matthew, R. A. (1995). 'Liberal International Theory: Common Threads, Divergent Strands', in C. W. Kegley, Jr (ed.), *Controversies in International Relations: Realism and the Neo-liberal Challenge*. New York: St Martin's Press, 107–50.

Zakaria, F. (1998). *From Wealth to Power: The Unusual Origins of America's World Role*. Princeton, NJ: Princeton University Press.

Zehfuss, M. (2002). *Constructivism in International Relations: The Politics of Reality*. Cambridge: Cambridge University Press.

Zürn, M. (2011). *Transnational Conflicts and International Institutions. A research program*. Berlin: WZB, at: http://www.wzb.eu/en/research/civil-society-conflicts-and-democracy/international-institutions accessed 30 November 2011.

■ INDEX